YOUR

ASTROLOGY

GUIDE

2013

♊ ♉ ♈

♋

♌

♍

♎

♏

♐ ♑

♒ ♓

YOUR
ASTROLOGY
GUIDE
2013

RICK LEVINE & **JEFF** JAWER

STERLING ETHOS
New York

STERLING ETHOS
New York

An Imprint of Sterling Publishing
387 Park Avenue South
New York, NY 10016

ISBN 978-1-4027-7940-4

Distributed in Canada by Sterling Publishing
c/o Canadian Manda Group, 165 Dufferin Street
Toronto, Ontario, Canada M6K 3H6
Distributed in the United Kingdom by GMC Distribution Services
Castle Place, 166 High Street, Lewes, East Sussex, England BN7 1XU
Distributed in Australia by Capricorn Link (Australia) Pty. Ltd.
P.O. Box 704, Windsor, NSW 2756, Australia

For information about custom editions, special sales, and premium
and corporate purchases, please contact Sterling Special Sales at
800-805-5489 or specialsales@sterlingpublishing.com.

Manufactured in the United States of America

2 4 6 8 10 9 7 5 3 1

www.sterlingpublishing.com

TABLE OF CONTENTS

Acknowledgments   7

Introduction   8

PART 1: ASTROLOGY & YOU   17
How to Use This Book—Astrology Basics   19
The Planets, the Houses, and Aspects   27
Astrology World Report 2013   41

PART 2: AUGUST-DECEMBER 2012 OVERVIEW/   63
    2013 ASTROLOGICAL FORECASTS

Aries   (March 21–April 19)   65
Taurus   (April 20–May 20)   97
Gemini   (May 21–June 20)   129
Cancer   (June 21–July 22)   161
Leo   (July 23–August 22)   193
Virgo   (August 23–September 22)   225
Libra   (September 23–October 22)   257
Scorpio   (October 23–November 21)   289
Sagittarius   (November 22–December 21)   321
Capricorn   (December 22–January 19)   353
Aquarius   (January 20–February 18)   385
Pisces   (February 19–March 20)   417

ACKNOWLEDGMENTS

Many people continue to contribute to this annual book, both in conception and in production. Some have been with us from the start; some have only recently joined the team. First of all, our heartfelt thanks to Paul O'Brien, whose creative genius behind Tarot.com led us to this project. Paul is our agent and our friend, and his vision opened the doors to make this book possible. On the production side, we are grateful for our editor, Gail Goldberg. Her ability to clarify concepts, untangle sentences, and sharpen our words is matched by her commitment to presenting astrology in an intelligent light. We appreciate her energetic Mars in efficient Virgo; her persistent attention to detail continues to challenge us to write better books. Of course we are very grateful to Michael Fragnito, Editorial Director at Sterling Publishing, for his initial vision of what this book could be, his tireless support for the project, and his trust in our work. Barbara Berger, Sterling's supervising editor on this book, has shepherded the project with Taurean persistence and good humor under the ongoing pressures of very tight deadlines. We thank Laura Jorstad for her refinement of the text and project editor Mary Hern for her careful guidance. We are thankful to Marcus Leaver, Jason Prince, Elizabeth Mihaltse, Rodman Neumann, and Sasha Tropp at Sterling and designer Abrah Griggs. Thanks go to Bob Wietrak and Jules Herbert at Barnes & Noble, and whoever said yes in the beginning. We appreciate 3+Co and Asami Matsushima for the original design; and thanks for the art and ideas from Jessica Abel and the rest of the Tarot.com team. Thanks, as well, to Tara Gimmer and company for the author photo.

Rick: I am indebted to a truly great writing partner. Thank you, Jeff, for showing up with a combination of unwavering reliability, solid astrology, and the willingness to keep pushing the envelope of creativity. My deep appreciation also goes to Gail Goldberg, editor extraordinaire, who doesn't ever let us take the easy way out. Her steadfast commitment to making a difference through what we say in these annuals has made each of them better. And, of course, we are blessed with readers who are hungry for valid astrology information that is based on hope rather than fear. We are here because of you.

Jeff: Thanks, Rick, for the consistently high quality of your astrology, your writing, and the great gift of your friendship. I have special thanks for Gail Goldberg, who served this book and its readers with uncommon dedication and skill. Thanks, too, to my live-in inspirations: my wife, Danick, whose music fills our home with creativity, and my daughters, Laura and Lyana, whose joyous discoveries of life fill me with hope for the future.

INTRODUCTION

YOU ARE THE STAR OF YOUR LIFE

The more you learn about yourself, the better able you are to wisely use the energies in your life. For more than three thousand years, astrology has been the sharpest tool in the box for describing the human condition. Used by virtually every culture on the planet, astrology continues to illuminate the link between individual lives and planetary energies and cycles.

The purpose of this book is to help you take a more active role in creating your present and, by extension, your future by showing you how to apply astrology's ancient wisdom to today's world. Our aim is to facilitate your day-to-day journey by revealing the turns in the road of life and describing the best ways for you to navigate them.

Astrology's highest use is to enable you to gain knowledge of yourself and perspective of your surroundings. It is common to go through life feeling blown about by forces beyond your control. Astrology can help you see the changing tides within and outside you. By allowing you to recognize the shifting patterns of mood and circumstance at work in your life, it helps you to stay centered and empowered. As you follow along in this book, you will grow to better understand your own needs as well as the challenges and opportunities you encounter.

In *Your Astrology Guide 2013*, we describe the patterns of your life as they are reflected in the great cycles of the sky above. We do not simply predict events, although we give examples of them throughout the book. Rather, we are reporting the planetary energies—the cosmic weather in which you are living—so that you understand these conditions and know how to use them effectively. The power, though, is not in the stars, of course, but in your mind, your heart, and the choices that you make every day. Regardless of how strongly you are buffeted by the winds of change or bored by stagnation, your mind has many ways to see any situation. Learning about the energies of the Sun, Moon, and planets will both sharpen and widen your perspective. Thousands of years of human experience have proven astrology's value; our purpose is to show you how to enrich your life with it.

The language of astrology gives the gift of awareness, not a rigid set of rules. It works best when blended with common sense, intuition, and self-trust. This is your life, and no one knows how to live it as well as you. Take what you need from this book and leave the rest. Think of the planets as setting the stage for the year ahead, but it is you who are the writer, director, and star of your life.

ABOUT US

We were practicing astrology independently when we joined forces in 1999 to launch StarIQ.com. Our shared interest in making intelligent astrology available to as wide an audience as possible led to StarIQ, as well as a relationship with Tarot.com and the creation of this book. While we have continued to work independently as well, our collaboration has been a success and a joy as we've made our shared goals a reality, and we plan for it to continue long into the future.

RICK LEVINE

I've always wanted to know the answers to unanswerable questions. As a youth, I studied science and mathematics because I believed that they offered concrete answers to complex questions. I learned about the amazing conceptual breakthroughs made by modern man due to the developing technologies that allowed us to peer into the deep reaches of outer space and also into the tiniest subatomic realms. But as I encountered imaginary numbers in higher mathematics, along with the uncertainty of quantum physics, I began to realize that our modern sciences, as advanced as they are, would never satisfy my longing to understand my own individual life or the world around me. I learned that our basic assumptions of time and space fall apart at both ends of the spectrum—the very big and the very small. I became obsessed with solving the puzzle of the cosmos and discovering its hidden secrets.

As a college student at the State University of New York at Stony Brook in the late sixties, I studied psychology and philosophy, and participated in those times as a student of the universe. I read voraciously and found myself more interested in the unexplainable than in what was already known. As a psychology student, I was less concerned with running rats through mazes than with understanding how the human mind worked. I naturally gravitated to the depth psychologies of Sigmund Freud and Carl Jung. Additionally, the life-altering information coming from the humanistic psychology movement presented me with an academic framework with which to better understand how human potential could be further developed. I knew then and there that human consciousness was expanding and that I wanted to be a part of this evolutionary process. In this environment, I first encountered the writings of R. Buckminster Fuller. He appealed to my scientific mind-set, but blessed me with new ways to view my world. In the early twentieth century, Albert Einstein had clearly demonstrated that energy is simply the transformation of light into mass and mass into light—but that was just an intellectual concept to me.

Bucky Fuller, however, went on to establish a scientific language to describe the relationships between mass and light, particles and waves. His incredible geodesic domes are merely representations of what he discovered. I began to understand that what we can see is but a faint shadow of the knowable universe. I learned that everything vibrates. There are no things out there, just different frequencies of vibration—many of which are so fast that they give us the illusion of a solid world. Even something as basic as the colors green or red are merely labels for certain frequencies of light vibration.

This was my world when I first discovered that astrology was more than just a parlor game. Already acquainted with the signs of the zodiac, I knew that I was an impulsive Aries, a pioneer, and an independent thinker. I noticed how my friends and professors fit their sun signs. Then, I was astounded to learn that Jung's Analytical Psychology of Four Types was based upon the astrological elements of fire, earth, air, and water. And I was amazed to discover that a great scientist, such as Johannes Kepler—the Father of Modern Astronomy—was himself a renowned astrologer. The more I read, the more I realized that I had to become an astrologer myself. I needed to know more about astrology and how it works. Now, nearly forty years later, I know more about astrology—a lot more—with still so much to learn.

Astronomers have their telescopes, enabling them to see things *tele*, or far away. Biologists have microscopes to see what is *micro*, or small. We astrologers have the horoscope, extending our view of the *horo*, or hour. For more than three decades, I have calculated horoscopes—first by hand, later with computer—and have observed the movement of time in its relationship to the heavenly bodies. I have watched the timing of the transitions in my own life and in the lives of my family, friends, and clients. I have been privileged to see, again and again, the unquestionable harmony between the planetary cycles and our individual lives. I am proud to be a part of an astrological renaissance. Astrology has become increasingly popular because it fulfills our need to know that we are a part of the cosmos, even though modern culture has separated us from nature. It is not man versus nature. We are nature— and our survival as a species may depend on humanity relearning this concept. I take my role as an astrologer very seriously as I use what I have learned to help people expand their awareness, offer them choices, and educate them on how to cooperate with the cosmos instead of fight against them. I contributed to reestablishing astrology in academia as a founding trustee of the Kepler College of Astrological Arts and Science (Lynnwood, Washington). I maintain an active role in the international community of astrologers as a member of the International Society for Astrological Research (ISAR), the National Council for Geocosmic Research (NCGR), the Association for Astrological Networking (AFAN), and the Organization for Professional Astrology (OPA).

In 1999, I partnered with Jeff Jawer to create StarIQ.com, an innovative astrology website. Since then Jeff and I have been working together to raise the quality of astrology available to the public, first through StarIQ.com and, later, through our partnership with Tarot.com. It continues to be a real privilege and thrill to work with Jeff and to now offer the fruits of our labors to you.

JEFF JAWER

I've been a professional astrologer for more than thirty years. Astrology is my career, my art, and my passion. The excitement that I felt when I first began is still with me today. My first encounter with real astrology was in 1973 when I was going through a painful marriage breakup. All I knew about astrology at the time was that I was a Taurus, which didn't sound very exciting to me. "The reliable Bull is steadfast and consistent," I read. "Not given to risk taking or dramatic self-expression, Taurus prefers peace and comfort above all." Boring. Fortunately, I quickly discovered that there was more to astrology—much more.

An amateur astrologer read my chart for me on my twenty-seventh birthday, and I was hooked. I bought the biggest astrology book I could find, began intensive study, found a teacher, and started reading charts for people. Within a few months, I changed my major at the University of Massachusetts at Amherst from communications to astrology under the Bachelor's Degree with Individual Concentration program. There were no astrology classes at the university, but I was able to combine courses in astronomy, mythology, and psychology, with two special seminars on the history of astrology, to graduate in 1975 with a B.A. in the history and science of astrology. In 1976, I moved to Atlanta, Georgia, the only city in the United States with a mandatory examination for professional astrologers. I passed it, as well as the American Federation of Astrologers' professional exam, and served twice as president of the Metro Atlanta Astrological Society and as chairman of the City of Atlanta Board of Astrology Examiners.

For several years, I was the corporate astrologer for International Horizons, Inc., a company that sold courses on English as a second language in Japan. The owner had me research the founding dates of banks he was interested in acquiring so that I could advise him based on their charts. Later, he and I created Astro, the world's first electronic astrology calculator. In 1982, I was one of the founding members of the Association for Astrological Networking (AFAN), an organization that plays a major role in defending the legal rights of astrologers. AFAN joined with two other organizations, the International Society for Astrological Research (ISAR) and the National Council for Geocosmic Research (NCGR), to present the first United Astrology Congress (UAC) in 1986. UAC conferences were the largest astrology events in North America for more than a decade. I served on the UAC board for four years.

I began teaching at astrology conferences in the late 1970s, and there I met many of the world's leading astrologers, many of whom are my friends to this day. I have taught at dozens of conferences and local astrology groups around the United States. I have lectured at the World Astrology Congress in Switzerland four times, as well as in Holland, France, England, Belgium, Spain, Germany, Canada, Brazil, and Australia. However, the most important time for me personally was the two years I spent teaching for the Network of Humanistic Astrologers based in France. There I met my wife, Danick, in 1988. Her double-Pisces sensitivity has added to my work and my life immeasurably.

Counseling individual clients is the core of my professional life, as it is for most astrologers, but writing about astrology has always been important to me. I've written hundreds of articles for journals, magazines, books, websites, and newspapers, ranging from the monthly calendar for *The Mountain Astrologer* to sun-sign forecasts for *CosmoGIRL!* magazine. Currently, I write "LoveScopes" (a weekly sun-sign romance horoscope), the "New Moon Report," and other specialized material for Tarot.com, AOL, and StarIQ.com. I've also been employed in the astrology industry as director of public relations for Matrix Software and vice president of Astro Communication Services, two of the field's oldest companies. Rick and I founded StarIQ in 1999, the beginning of our professional collaboration. We produce a daily audio forecast called *Planet Pulse*, and *StarTalkers*, a weekly radio broadcast. Early in my career, I contributed to pioneering the field of experiential astrology, also called astrodrama. It's been a great adventure to combine theater games, psychodrama, Gestalt techniques, visualization, movement, art, and sound to bring astrology to life in workshops around the world. To experience astrology through emotions and in the body, rather than by the intellect alone, can ground one's understanding of the planets and signs in a very useful way.

Think about Venus, for example. She's the goddess of love, the planet of beauty and attraction. What if you need more sweetness in your life? Imagine how Venus walks. Now, get up and do your own Venus walk to the kitchen. Feel in balance and graceful as your feet embrace the floor and as your hips sway. Be Venus; invite her presence to you. Glide, slide, and be suave; you're so beautiful. Remember this walk if you're feeling unloved and, the next thing you know, Venus will arrive. Each planet is different, of course, according to its unique character. You'll learn another dance from responsible Saturn—a slower march across the floor, head upright, shoulders back—steady and straight, but not too stiff. Try that one for self-discipline.

Astrology describes the energy of time, how the quality of Tuesday afternoon is different from Wednesday morning. Seeing when and where patterns arise in your life gives you clearer vision and a better understanding of the choices that are open to you. The rich language of astrology makes a cosmic connection that empowers you and rewards the rest of us as you fulfill more and more of your potential.

AUTHOR'S NOTE

Your Astrology Guide uses the Tropical zodiac based on the seasons, not the constellations. This method of determining signs has been and continues to be the practice of Western astrologers for more than two thousand years. Aries, the beginning of the Tropical zodiac, starts on the first day of spring every year. Contrary to what you may have heard, no one's sign has changed, regardless of when you were born and the addition of a thirteenth sign is not relevant to Western astrology.

Measuring and recording the apparent movement of the Sun, the Moon, and the planets against the backdrop of the heavens is a complex task because nothing is stationary. Even the location of the constellations with respect to the seasons gradually changes from year to year. Since astrologers are concerned with human behavior here on Earth, they created a twelve-fold zodiac that is anchored to four seasons as their primary frame of reference. Obviously, astrologers fully understand that there are eighty-eight official constellations and that the moving planets travel through many of them (including Ophiuchus and Orion), but these are not—and never have been— part of the Tropical zodiac created by astrologers.

ASTROLOGY'S ORIGINS

Astrology is as old as time. It began when events in the sky were first observed to affect events here on Earth. The turning of day into night, the rising and falling of the tides with the Moon's cycles, and the changing seasons were watched by humanity long before written history, even at the very dawn of human civilization. Ancient Egyptians tracked the star Sirius to predict the flooding of the Nile River, which was essential to their agriculture. Babylonians, Mayans, Hindus, Chinese, and virtually every other group of people on the planet have practiced a form of astrology. Part science, part religion, calendar, mythology, and almanac, astrology remains the most comprehensive and coherent system for understanding life on this planet.

In the second century AD, Claudius Ptolemy codified astrology, based on its origins in Mesopotamia and development in classical Greece. Astrology was an essential part of the scientific and philosophical evolution that gave birth to Western civilization. Another major path of development occurred in India, where Vedic astrology remains an integral part of the culture. Astrology was originally used to address collective concerns such as climate and warfare. It was rarely applied to the lives of individuals, except for rulers whose fates were considered tied to those of the nation. Astrology is still applied to public concerns, especially in the burgeoning field of financial astrology, which is used for stock-market forecasting. Today, however, the vast majority of astrology is applied to the lives of individuals through personal consultations, computer-generated reports, horoscope columns, books, and the Internet.

The importance of astrology has risen, fallen, and risen again in the Western world. Through the Renaissance and the Elizabethan period, astrology was part and parcel of daily life. Shakespeare's numerous references to it are just one indicator of its wide acceptance and popularity in his time. However, the rationalism of René Descartes and his followers took hold in philosophical circles and demanded that modern science exclude anything that could not be proven according to its methods. Astrology was banished from academia in 1666, and it remained outside the intellectual mainstream for almost three hundred years. Modern astrology began its rebirth in the early part of the twentieth century largely due to the work of Alan Leo, the father of sun-sign astrology. A second, and larger, wave of interest grew out of the counterculture movement of the 1960s when interest in metaphysics and Eastern religions also gained momentum. The brilliant works of the Swiss psychologist Carl Jung and French-American astrologer Dane Rudhyar inspired a new generation of astrologers, including the authors of this book.

ASTROLOGY TODAY: EMPOWERMENT

Thanks to Jung, Rudhyar, and many other brilliant minds, modern astrology has largely separated itself from the fatalism of the past when, for example, the sighting of an approaching comet meant the king would die and nothing more. Today's astrology is, as Rudhyar wrote, "person-centered," with the focus on individual choice and personal growth rather than the simple prediction of events. In fact, while we do write about events in this book, we spend more time describing energy patterns and emotions for several reasons.

First, you're a unique individual. You may share characteristics and tendencies with fellow members of your sun sign, but you will experience them in your own way. In addition, you have a personal birth chart in which the positions of the Moon, planets, and other factors distinguish you from the other members of your sun-sign clan. Analyzing how all the planets and signs interact in a person's chart is the foundation of a personal consultation with a professional astrologer or a detailed custom report like those available at http://www.tarot.com/astrology/astroprofile.

ENERGY, EVENTS, AND EMOTION

At its essence, astrology describes energy. Energy can take many forms; it can be an event, emotion, or attitude. We suggest the possible outcomes of astrological events in this book, but they are examples or models of how the planetary energies might be expressed. Each person is going to experience these patterns in his or her own unique way. We have learned that it is more helpful to understand the underlying energy patterns of events than it is to describe them. You may not be able to change the world outside you, but you have an enormous range of choice when it comes to your thoughts and attitudes.

We are here to assist you with ideas and information rooted in history and woven into the cloth of our culture. We recognize and honor you as the center of your life. This book is not a collection of ideas that are foreign to your nature, but a recollection of human experiences that exist within all of us. Whether you know their meanings or not, all the signs and planets live within you. They are part of your human heritage, a gift of awareness, a language not meant to label you and stick you in a box, but a treasure map to yourself and the cosmos beyond. It is a glorious journey we all share. May your way be filled with light this year and in the years to come.

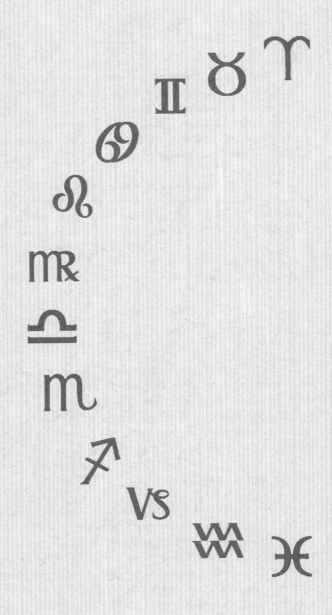

PART 1

2013

ASTROLOGY

& YOU

HOW TO USE THIS BOOK

ASTROLOGY BASICS

WHAT'S YOUR SIGN?

In this book, we present a view of the year ahead for each sun sign. Your sign is based on the Sun's position at the moment of your birth. As most people know, the Sun travels through the twelve signs of the zodiac over the course of a year. However, the Sun doesn't change signs at the exact moment on the same date every year. If you were born within two days of the cusp (the end or beginning) of a sign, a more exact calculation may be required to determine your sun sign. So, if you are uncertain about your sign, consult an astrologer or get a free copy of your birth chart from http://www.tarot.com/astrology/astroprofile to determine the correct one. In addition to giving you the exact position of the Sun at the moment of your birth, an individual birth or natal chart includes the positions of the Moon and planets as well, which provides a much more detailed astrological view of your life. This information is used in private consultations and computer-generated astrology reports. The sun sign does not tell your entire astrological story. But it is powerful enough to light up your consciousness with ideas that can change your life.

For those of you who have your astrology chart, in addition to reading the chapter in this book on your sun sign, you will also want to read about your moon and rising signs as well. Your intuition will guide you as you integrate the information.

TRANSITS

The information presented in this book is based on the relationship of the planets, including the Sun and the Moon, to the twelve signs of the zodiac in 2013. The movement of the planets in their cycles and their geometric relationship to one another as they interact are called **transits**; they are the primary forecasting tool for astrologers.

As planets enter into specific relationships with one another, astrologers consider the astrological events that occur. For example, when the Sun and the Moon align in a certain way, an event called an **eclipse** occurs. As you read this book, many of you will study more than one sign, whether you are checking up on someone you know or on your own moon or rising sign. You will notice that certain dates are often mentioned repeatedly from sign to sign. This is because major planetary events affect everyone, but some more than others, and in different ways.

For example, in 2013 there is a Full Moon Eclipse in Scorpio on April 25. Everyone will feel the power of the eclipse, but individual reactions will vary. Its effects are most obvious for Scorpio and its opposite sign, Taurus. Since this particular eclipse also opposes Mars, it will be challenging for Aries, the sign ruled by this planet. The cosmic weather rains on all of us and the water can be parted in twelve ways, each a door to a sign that will experience it differently.

RULING OR KEY PLANETS

Every sign is associated with a key or ruling planet. There is an affinity between signs and their planetary rulers—a common purpose that connects them, like lungs with breathing or feet with walking. In astrology's early days, the Sun (Leo) and the Moon (Cancer) ruled one sign each, and the rest of the known planets—Mercury, Venus, Mars, Jupiter, and Saturn—ruled two. However, in the modern era, new planets have been discovered and astrology has evolved to reflect this. The discovery of Uranus in the late eighteenth century coincided with revolutions in the United States and France, triggered a technological revolution that's still going on today, and transformed astrology's traditional rulership system. Radical Uranus was assigned to rule inventive Aquarius, while its old ruler, Saturn, took a step back. Neptune, discovered with photography sixty-five years later, became the ruler of Pisces, nudging Jupiter into the background. And if Pluto hasn't purged Mars from Scorpio, it's certainly taken the dominant role in expressing this sign's energy. We mention ruling planets quite a bit in the book as we track the cycles of a given sign. The sign Aries, named for the Greek god of war, is ruled by Mars, the Roman name for the same god. Transits of Mars, then, play a leading role in the forecasts for Aries. Venus is used in the same way in the forecasts for Taurus. For double-ruled Scorpio, Aquarius, and Pisces, we take the traditional and modern planetary rulers into account. The planets and the signs they rule are further discussed later in this section.

ELEMENTS

The four astrological elements are fire, earth, air, and water. The action-oriented fire signs—Aries, Leo, and Sagittarius—are warm and dynamic. The sense-oriented earth signs—Taurus, Virgo, and Capricorn—are practical and realistic. The thought-oriented air signs—Gemini, Libra, and Aquarius—are logical and sociable. The emotion-oriented water signs—Cancer, Scorpio, and Pisces—are intuitive and instinctual. Signs of the same element work harmoniously together. In addition, fire and air signs work well together, as do earth and water.

INGRESSES

An **ingress** is the entry of a planet into a new sign. The activities and concerns of the planet will be colored by that sign's energy. For example, when the communication planet Mercury enters Leo, the expressive qualities of that sign tend to make for more dramatic speech than in the previous sign, self-protective Cancer. When Mercury leaves Leo for detail-oriented Virgo, thoughts and words become more precise. Each planet has its own unique rhythm and cycle in terms of how long it takes that planet to move through all the signs. This determines how long it stays in one sign. The Moon, for example, flies through a sign in two and a half days, while Uranus takes seven years.

HOUSES

Your natal chart is divided into twelve astrological houses that correspond to different areas of your life. This book uses solar houses that place your sun sign in the 1st

House. In this system, when a planet enters a new sign, it also enters a new house. Thus, the effect of a planet's ingress into a particular sign also depends on which house of the sign in question it's entering. For example, for a Gemini sun sign, Gemini is its own 1st House, followed by Cancer for the 2nd, Leo for the 3rd House, and so on. If you are a Taurus, your 4th House is Leo. As a Scorpio, your 8th House is Gemini. If this is confusing, don't worry about counting houses; we do it for you. The influence of an astrological event differs considerably based on which house of a sign it falls in.

You'll notice that there are many different, but related, terms used to describe each house, sign, and planet. For example, Mars is called feisty, assertive, impatient, or aggressive at different times throughout the book. Also, we use different house names depending on the emphasis we perceive. You'll find the 4th House described as the 4th House of Home and Family, the 4th House of Security, and the 4th House of Roots—all are valid. We change the descriptions to broaden your understanding, rather than repeat the same limited interpretation over and over. Later in this section is a brief description of all the houses.

ASPECTS

Aspects are geometrically significant angles between planets and a key feature of any astrological forecast. A fast-moving body like the Moon will form every possible aspect to every degree of the zodiac during its monthly orbit around the Earth. The Sun will do the same in a year, Mars in two years, Jupiter in twelve. The slower a planet moves, the less common its aspects, which makes them more significant because their effect is longer. A lunar aspect lasts only a few hours, and one from Mercury a day or two, but a transit like the Jupiter-Neptune square that occurs three times this year can last for a week or two or more.

The qualities of the two planets involved in an aspect are important to its meaning, but so is the angle between them. Soft aspects like **sextiles** and **trines** grease the cosmic wheels, while hard ones like **squares** and **oppositions** often reflect bumps in the road. **Conjunctions**, when two planets are conjoined, are arguably the most powerful aspect and can be easy or difficult according to the nature of the planets involved. To learn more about the nature of the aspects, turn to the next chapter.

The effect of an aspect on each sun sign is modified according to the houses of that sign where the planets fall. A Venus-Mars trine from Cancer to Scorpio is the harmonious expression of Venus's desire for security with Mars's instinct to protect. They are both in water signs, thus compatible. And if you are a Pisces, Venus in Cancer is in your 5th House and Mars in Scorpio is in your 9th, stirring romance and adventure. Alternatively, if you are a Gemini, Venus in Cancer is in your 2nd House and Mars in Scorpio is in the 6th. Applying the cozy relationship of a trine to Gemini's chart gives the interpretation that there will be a comfortable flow in the practical realms of money and work.

RETROGRADES

All true planets (i.e., excluding the Sun and Moon) turn **retrograde** from time to time. This means that the planet appears to go backward in the zodiac, revisiting recently traveled territory. As with other planetary phenomena, astrologers have observed specific effects from retrogrades. The days when planets turn from direct, or forward, motion to retrograde and back again are called **stations** (because the planet appears to be stationary). These are significant periods that emphasize the energy of the stationing planet.

A retrograde station, when backward motion begins, indicates the beginning of a relatively introspective cycle for that planet's energy. At a direct station, the energy that has been turned inward during the retrograde period begins to express itself more overtly in the outer world once again. Retrogrades can cause certain aspects to occur three times—first forward, then retrograde, then forward again. These triple events can be like a play that unfolds in three acts. The first aspect often raises an issue that's reconsidered or adjusted during the second transit and completed during the third.

LUNATIONS AND ECLIPSES

New Moons, Full Moons, and eclipses are important astrological events. These aspects involving the Moon are called **lunations**. Every month the Sun and Moon join together at the New Moon, seeding a fresh lunar cycle that affects us each in a personal way. The New Moon in the partnership sign of Libra sparks relationships, while the New Moon in the resource sign of Taurus brings attention to money. Two weeks later, the Moon opposes the Sun at the Full Moon. This is often an intense time due to the pull of the Moon in one direction and the Sun in another. The Full Moon in Cancer, for example, pits the need (Moon) for inner security (Cancer) against the Sun in Capricorn's urge for worldly recognition. The Full Moon can be stressful, but it is also a time of illumination that can give rise to greater consciousness. At the Full Moon, instead of seeing yourself pulled apart by opposing forces, it helps to imagine that you're the meeting point where the opposition is resolved by a breakthrough in awareness.

Planets that form significant aspects with the New or Full Moon play a key role in shaping their character. A New Moon square to Jupiter is challenged by a tendency to be overexpansive, a negative quality of that planet. A Full Moon conjunct with Saturn is bound in seriousness, duty, or doubt symbolized by this planet of necessity.

Eclipses are a special class of New and Full Moons where the Sun and Moon are so close to their line of intersection with the Earth that the light of one of them is darkened. The shadow of the Moon on the Sun at a Solar Eclipse (New Moon) or of the Earth on the Moon at a Lunar Eclipse (Full Moon) makes them memorable. They work, in effect, like super New or Full Moons, extending the normal two- to four-week period of these lunations to an influence up to six months before or after the eclipse. An eclipse will affect each person differently, depending on where it falls in a chart. But they can be unsettling because they usually mark the ends of chapters in one's life.

HOW THIS BOOK IS ORGANIZED

In this book, we take a look at what 2013 holds in store for each of the twelve signs. We evaluate each sign according to the transits to it, its ruler, and its solar houses. The chapter on each sign begins with an overview of the year for the sign. Here we suggest some of the key themes that the sign will encounter in 2013 in general as well as in specific areas of life: love, career, money, health, home, travel, and spirituality. Each of these areas is identified with an icon, as shown at the top of the next page, for easy reference.

The overview is followed by a month-by-month analysis of all of the most important astrological events for that sign. This will enable you to look at where you are as well as what may be coming up for you, so that you can best make choices about how you'd like to deal with the planetary energies at work.

KEY TO ICONS IN OVERVIEW SECTIONS FOR EACH SIGN

 LOVE AND RELATIONSHIPS

 CAREER AND PUBLIC LIFE

 MONEY AND FINANCES

 HEALTH AND VITALITY

 HOME AND FAMILY

 TRAVEL AND HIGHER EDUCATION

 SPIRITUALITY AND PERSONAL GROWTH

TIMING, KEY DATES, AND SUPER NOVA DAYS

The monthly forecast for each sign includes a description of several Key Dates that month. (Eastern time is used throughout the book.) We provide some likely scenarios of what may happen or how someone born under the sign might experience the planetary effects at the time of the Key Dates. It is wise to pay closer attention to your own thoughts, feelings, and actions during these times. Certain Key Dates are called Super Nova Days because they are the most intense energetic periods, positive or negative, of the month.

Note that the exact timing of events, and your awareness of their effects, can vary from person to person, sometimes coming a day or two earlier or arriving a day or two later than the Key Dates given.

The period of influence of a transit from the Sun, Mercury, or Venus is a day before and a day after the exact aspect. A transit of Mars is in effect for about two days coming and going; Jupiter and Saturn lasts for a week or more; and Uranus, Neptune, and Pluto can be two weeks.

Although the Key Dates are the days when a particular alignment is exact, some people are so ready for an event that they'll act on a transit a day or two before. And some of us are so entrenched in the status quo or unwilling to change that it may take a day or two for the effect to manifest. Give yourself an extra day around each Key Date to utilize the energy, maximize the potential, and feel the impact of the event. If you find astrological events consistently unfold in your life earlier or later than predicted, adjust the dates accordingly.

Our goal is to help you understand what is operating within you, below the surface, rather than simply to tell you what's going to happen. This is where you have control so that, to a large degree, what happens is up to you. We describe which buttons are being pushed so that you can see your own patterns and have greater power to change them if you want. Every astrological event has a potential for gain or loss. Fat, juicy, easy ones can make us lazy, while tough ones can temper the will and make us stronger. It usually takes time and hindsight to measure the true value of an experience.

THE PLANETS, THE HOUSES,

AND ASPECTS

THE PLANETS

The planets are the basic building blocks of astrology. As our ancestors observed the cycles of these wandering stars, they attributed characteristics to them. Each of these richly symbolic archetypes represents a particular spectrum of meaning. Their intimate relationship to the Greek and Roman myths helps us tell stories about them that are still relevant to our lives today. No matter what your sun sign is, every planet impacts your life according to its symbolism and its placement.

THE SUN

Rules Leo
Keywords: *Consciousness, Will, Vitality*
The Sun is our home star, the glowing filament in the center of our local system, and is associated with the sign Leo. Our ancestors equated it with God, for it is the source of energy and is what animates us. In fact, we base our entire calendar system on the Earth's relationship to the Sun. It represents the core of individual identity and consciousness. The masculine Sun has dignity, courage, and willpower. We feel the Sun's role as our main purpose in life; it fuels our furnace to fulfill our mission. We recognize its brightness in anyone who has a "sunny" personality. It is charismatic, creative, and generous of heart. But it can also be proud, have too much pride, and turn arrogant or self-centered. When the Sun is shining, we can see the world around us; it gives us a world of "things" that we can name and describe. It could be said that the Sun symbolizes objective reality.

THE MOON

Rules Cancer

Keywords: *Subconscious, Emotions, Habits*

We've all seen how the Moon goes through its phases, reflecting the light of the Sun, and have felt the power of the Full Moon. Lunations are important astrological markers. The Moon changes signs every two and a half days and reflects the mood of the public in general. Although our year calendar is based upon the Sun, each month (comes from "moon"—moonth) closely approximates the cycle of the Moon. The Moon is closer to Earth than anything else in the heavens. Astrologically, it represents how we reflect the world around us through our feelings. The Moon symbolizes emotions, instincts, habits, and routine. It describes how we nurture others and need to be cared for ourselves. The feminine power of the Moon is also connected with the fertility cycle of women. Because it is the source of security and familial intimacy, our Moon sign is where we feel at home. The Moon is associated with the sign Cancer and with concerns about our home and family.

MERCURY

Rules Gemini and Virgo

Keywords: *Communication, Thoughts, Transportation*

Mercury, the Heavenly Messenger, races around the Sun four times each year. Its nearly ninety-day cycle corresponds with the seasons of the calendar. Mercury, our intellectual antenna, is the planet of perception, communication, rational thought, mobility, and commerce. It is the mental traveler, able to move effortlessly through the realms of thought and imagination. Mercury organizes language, allows us to grasp ideas, enables us to analyze and integrate data, and assists us in all forms of communication. Cars, bicycles, telephones, delivery services, paperwork, and the mind itself are all manifestations of quicksilver Mercury, the fastest of the true planets. However, Mercury also has a trickster side and can cleverly con us into believing something that just isn't true. Mercury is associated with curious Gemini in its information-gathering mode and with discerning Virgo when it is analytically sorting through the data.

VENUS

Rules Taurus and Libra

Keywords: *Desire, Love, Money, Values*

Venus is the goddess of love, our relationship antenna, associated with the spectrum of how we experience what is beautiful and pleasurable to us. With Venus, we attach desire to our perceptions. On one end, Venus can indicate romantic and sensual love. On the other end, Venus is about money and all things of value—financial and emotional. This manifests as our attraction to art, music, and even good food. Every beautiful flower and every act of love contains the essence of sweet Venus. We look to Venus to describe what we like—an important key to understanding partnerships, particularly personal ones. To a certain extent, our chemistry with other people is affected by Venus. Although Venus is traditionally associated with femininity, both women and men are impacted by its rhythms. A morning star, Venus rules Taurus and is associated with the simple and sensual side of physical reality. As an evening star, it rules Libra, where it represents the more intellectual side of love and harmony.

MARS

Rules Aries, co-rules Scorpio

Keywords: *Action, Physical Energy, Drive*

Mars, the god of war, is the planet of action, physical energy, initiative, and aggression. It is the first planet beyond Earth's orbit, and its role is to take what we have and extend it to the outer world. Mars represents the masculine force of individuality that helps define the ego and our sense of unique identity. It represents how we move forward in life and propels us toward new experiences and into the future. Mars drives us to assert ourselves in healthy ways, but the angry red planet can also be impatient and insensitive, engendering violence and destruction. When insecure, it turns offensive and can attack others. Mars can also express erotic passion, the male counterpart of the female Venus; together they are the cosmic lovers. As the pioneering risk taker, Mars rules fiery Aries. As a volcanic force of power, it is the traditional ruler of Scorpio.

♃ JUPITER

Rules Sagittarius, co-rules Pisces

Keywords: *Expansion, Growth, Optimism*

Jupiter is the largest of the true planets. It represents expansion, growth, and optimism. It was called the Greater Benefic by ancient astrologers due to its association with good fortune. Today, modern astrologers understand that too much of a good thing is not necessarily beneficial. Jupiter rules the excesses of life; undoubtedly, it's the planet of bigger, better, and more. Wherever there's too much, you're apt to find Jupiter. Often called the lucky planet, Jupiter symbolizes where opportunity knocks. Yet it is still up to us to open the door and walk through. Jupiterian people are jovial, but this gassy giant is also associated with humor, philosophy, enthusiasm, and enterprise. In its adventurous mode, Jupiter rules globetrotting Sagittarius, but as the planet of religion and belief systems, it has a traditional connection to Pisces.

♄ SATURN

Rules Capricorn, co-rules Aquarius

Keywords: *Contraction, Maturity, Responsibility*

Saturn is the outermost planet visible to the naked eye and as such represented the end of the road for our sky-watching ancestors. In premodern times, Saturn was the limit of our human awareness; beyond it were only the fixed stars. Now, even with our telescopic capability to peer farther into the vastness of space and time, Saturn still symbolizes the limits of perception. It is about structure, order, necessity, commitment, and hard-earned accomplishments. It's the stabilizing voice of reality and governs rules, regulations, discipline, and patience. Saturn is Father Time and represents the ultimate judgment that you get what you deserve. But Saturn isn't only stern or rigid; it is also the teacher and the wise old sage. When we embrace Saturn's discipline, we mature and learn from our experiences. As the serious taskmaster, Saturn is the ruler of ambitious Capricorn. As the co-ruler of Aquarius, Saturn reminds us that rigid rules may need to be broken in order to express our individuality.

CHIRON

(Does not rule a sign)
Keywords: *Healing, Pain, Subversion*

Chiron is the mythological Wounded Healer, and although not a true planet in the traditional sense, it has become a useful tool for modern astrologers. Chiron is a relative newcomer to the planetary lineup and was discovered in 1977 between the orbits of Saturn and Uranus. It describes where we can turn our wounds into wisdom to assist others. It is associated with the story of the wounded Fisher King, who, in medieval tales about the Holy Grail, fished (for souls) in order to salve his incurable suffering. Chiron not only symbolizes where and how we hurt, but also how our words and actions can soothe the pain of others. It doesn't, however, always play by the rules and can work against the status quo. Its rhythms can stir up old memories of emotional discomfort that can lead to increased understanding, vulnerability, and the transformation of heartache and grief into the gifts of love and forgiveness.

URANUS

Rules Aquarius
Keywords: *Awakening, Unpredictable, Inventive*

Uranus is the first planet discovered with technology (the telescope). Its discovery broke through the limitations imposed by our five senses. It symbolizes innovation, originality, revolution, and delighting in unexpected surprises. Uranus operates suddenly, often to release tensions, no matter how hidden. Its action is like lightning—instantaneous and exciting, upsetting and exhilarating. Uranus provokes and instigates change; its restless and rebellious energy hungers for freedom. Its high frequency and electrical nature stimulate the nervous system. This highly original planet abhors the status quo and is known to turn normal things upside down and inside out. As the patron planet of the strange and unusual, it is the ruler of eccentric Aquarius.

NEPTUNE

Rules Pisces

Keywords: *Imagination, Intuition, Spirituality*

Neptune is god of the seas, from which all life arises and is eventually returned. Imaginative Neptune lures us into the foggy mists where reality becomes so hazy that we can lose our way. It is the planet of dreams, illusions, and spirituality. It dissolves boundaries and barriers, leading us into higher awareness, compassion, confusion, or escapism. Grasping the meaning of Neptune is like trying to hold water in our hands. No matter how hard we try, it slips through our fingers—for Neptune is ultimately elusive and unknowable. It rules all things related to fantasy and delusion. A highly spiritual energy, the magic of Neptune encourages artistic vision, intuitive insight, compassion, and the tendency to idealize. Neptune governs the mystic's urge to merge with the divine and is associated with the spiritual sign Pisces.

♇ PLUTO

Rules Scorpio

Keywords: *Passion, Intensity, Regeneration*

Pluto, lord of the underworld, is the planet of death, rebirth, and transformation. As the most distant of the planets, Pluto moves us inexorably toward a deeper understanding of life's cycles. Under Pluto's influence, it often seems as though the apparently solid ground has disintegrated, forcing us to morph in ways we cannot intellectually understand. Pluto is the mythological phoenix, a magical bird that rises from the ashes of its own destruction by fire. It contains the shadow parts of ourselves that we would prefer to keep hidden, but healing and empowerment come from facing the unfathomable darkness and turning it into light. Manipulation and control are often issues with Pluto. A healthy relationship with Pluto adds psychological understanding and clarity about our motivations. As the ruler of magnetic Scorpio, it is associated with power and emotional intensity.

☊ ☋ NODES OF THE MOON

(Do not rule a sign)
Keywords: *Karma, Soul, Past Lives*
The Nodes of the Moon are opposing points where the Moon's orbit around the Earth intersects the Earth's orbit around the Sun. Although not real planets, these powerful points have an astrological influence in that they describe the ways we connect with others. They are useful in understanding the challenges and opportunities we face in our soul's journey through its lifetime here on Earth. For many astrologers, the Lunar Nodes are symbolic of past lives and future existences. The South Node, at one end of the nodal axis, represents the past—the unconscious patterns of our ancestral heritage or those brought into this life from previous incarnations. These are often talents that can easily be overused and become a no-growth path of least resistance. At the other end, the North Node represents the future—a new direction for growth, development, and integration.

THE HOUSES

Every astrology chart is divided into twelve houses, each ruling different areas of life and colored by a different sign. Just as planets move through the zodiac signs, they also move through the houses in an individual chart. The twelve houses correspond to the twelve signs, but in an individualized chart, the signs in each house will vary based on the sign on the cusp of the 1st House, called a rising sign or ascendant. The rising sign is determined by the exact time of your birth. We use solar houses, which place the sun sign as your 1st House, or rising sign.

1ST HOUSE

Corresponding Sign: Aries
Keywords: *Self, Appearance, Personality*
A primary point of self-identification: When planets move through this sector, the emphasis is on your individuality and surface appearances. It is often associated with how we interact with others when we first meet them. Planets here tend to take on great importance and become more integrated into your personality.

2ND HOUSE

Corresponding Sign: Taurus
Keywords: *Possessions, Values, Self-Worth*
Associated with values, resources, income, and self-esteem: When planets move
through the 2nd House, they can modify your attitudes about money and earning.
This is a concrete and practical area of the chart, and although it is linked to
possessions, the 2nd House typically does not include things you cannot easily
move, such as real estate or what you share with someone else.

3RD HOUSE

Corresponding Sign: Gemini
Keywords: *Communication, Siblings, Short Trips*
Relates to how you gather information from your immediate environment: It's
associated with the day-to-day comings and goings of your life. Siblings can be
found here, for this is where we first learn to build intimacy when we're young.
Planets moving through this house can affect the pace and quality of your day and
how you communicate with those around you.

4TH HOUSE

Corresponding Sign: Cancer
Keywords: *Home, Family, Roots*
Associated with the earliest imprints of childhood, your family roots, and how you're
connected to your own feelings: This is your emotional foundation and describes
what you need to feel at home. This is where you are nurtured, so when planets
travel through this sector, they stir up issues of security and safety. As the deepest
place in your chart, it is sometimes only you who knows about it.

5TH HOUSE

Corresponding Sign: Leo
Keywords: *Love, Romance, Children, Play*
Associated with fun, but also represents self-expression, creativity, love affairs, and
children: The 5th House is about the discovery of self through play, and includes
sports, games, and gambling. When planets move through your 5th House, they can
excite you to take risks and connect with the innocence of your inner child.

6TH HOUSE

Corresponding Sign: Virgo
Keywords: *Work, Health, Daily Routines*
Related to service and working conditions: Like the 3rd House, it describes your daily life, but the consistency of it rather than the noisy distractions—it's where you strive for efficiency and effectiveness. Planets here modify your habits, diet, and exercise. Although considered the house of health and hygiene, transits here don't always indicate illness; they can also increase our concern for healthier lifestyles.

7TH HOUSE

Corresponding Sign: Libra
Keywords: *Marriage, Relationships, Business Partners*
Encompasses one-to-one relationships: Its cusp is called the descendant and is the western end of the horizon. It's where and how we meet other people, both personally and professionally. In a larger sense, this is how you project who you are onto others. Planets moving through here can stimulate intimate relationships, but can also increase the intensity of all of your interactions with the outside world.

8TH HOUSE

Corresponding Sign: Scorpio
Keywords: *Intimacy, Transformation, Shared Resources*
A mysterious and powerful place, associated with shared experiences, including the most intimate: Traditionally the house of sex, death, and taxes, it's the place where you gain the deepest levels of relationships, personally and professionally. When planets move through your 8th House, perspectives can intensify, intimacy issues are stimulated, and compelling transformations are undertaken.

9TH HOUSE

Corresponding Sign: Sagittarius
Keywords: *Travel, Higher Education, Philosophy*
Associated with philosophy, religion, higher education of all kinds, and long-distance travel: It's where you seek knowledge and truth—both within and without. Planets moving through this house open portals to inner journeys and outer adventures, stretching your mind in ways that expand your perspectives about the world.

10TH HOUSE

Corresponding Sign: Capricorn
Keywords: *Career, Community, Ambition*
The most elevated sector of your chart; its cusp is called the midheaven: This is the career house, opposite to the home-based 4th House. When planets move through your 10th House, they activate your ambition, drive you to achieve professional excellence, and push you up the ladder of success. This is where your public reputation is important and hard work is acknowledged.

11TH HOUSE

Corresponding Sign: Aquarius
Keywords: *Friends, Groups, Associations, Social Ideals*
Traditionally called the house of friends, hopes, and wishes: It's where you go to be with like-minded people. The 11th House draws you out of your individual career aspirations and into the ideals of humanity. Planets traveling here can activate dreams of the future, so spending time with friends is a natural theme.

12TH HOUSE

Corresponding Sign: Pisces
Keywords: *Imagination, Spirituality, Secret Activities*
Complex, representing the ending of one cycle and the beginning of the next: It is connected with mysteries and places outside ordinary reality. When planets move through this house, they stimulate your deepest subconscious feelings and activate fantasies. It's a private space that can seem like a prison or a sanctuary.

ASPECTS

As the planets move through the sky in their various cycles, they form ever-changing angles with one another. Certain angles create significant geometric shapes. For example, when two planets are 90 degrees apart, they conform to a square. A sextile, or 60 degrees of separation, conforms to a six-pointed star. Planets create aspects to one another when they are at these special angles. All aspects are divisions of the 360-degree circle. Aspects explain how the individual symbolism of a pair of planets combines into an energetic pattern.

CONJUNCTION

0 degrees ★ **Keywords:** *Compression, Blending, Focus*
A conjunction is a blending of the separate planetary energies involved. When two planets conjoin, your job is to integrate the different influences—which in some cases is easier than others. For example, a conjunction of the Moon and Venus is likely to be a smooth blending of energy because of the similarity of the planets. But a conjunction between the Moon and Uranus is likely to be challenging because the Moon needs security, while Uranus prefers risk.

SEMISQUARE AND SESQUISQUARE

45 and 135 degrees ★ **Keywords:** *Annoyance, Mild Resistance*
Semisquares and sesquisquares are minor aspects that act like milder squares. They're one-eighth and three-eighths of a circle, respectively. Like the other hard aspects (conjunctions, oppositions, and squares) they can create dynamic situations that require immediate attention and resolution. Although they are not usually as severe as the other hard aspects, they remind us that healthy stress is important for the process of growth.

SEXTILE

60 degrees ★ **Keywords:** *Supportive, Intelligent, Activating*
Sextiles are supportive and intelligent, combining complementary signs—fire and air, earth and water. There's an even energetic distribution between the planets involved. Sextiles often indicate opportunities based on our willingness to take action in smart ways. Like trines, sextiles are considered easy: The good fortune they offer can pass unless you consciously take an active interest in making something positive happen.

QUINTILE

72 and 144 degrees ★ **Keywords:** *Creativity, Metaphysics, Magic*
Quintiles are powerful nontraditional aspects based on dividing the zodiac circle into five, resulting in a five-pointed star. Related to ancient goddess-based religious traditions, quintiles activate the imagination, intuition, and latent artistic talents. They're clever, intelligent, and even brilliant as they stimulate humor to relieve repressed tensions.

SQUARE

90 degrees ★ **Keywords:** *Resistance, Stress, Dynamic Conflict*
A square is an aspect of resistance, signifying energies at odds. Traditionally, they were considered negative, but their dynamic instability demands attention, so they're often catalysts for change. When differences in two planetary perspectives are integrated, squares can build enduring structures. Harnessing a square's power by managing contradictions creates opportunities for personal growth.

TRINE

120 degrees ★ **Keywords:** *Harmony, Free-Flowing, Ease*
A trine is the most harmonious of aspects because it connects signs of the same element. In the past, trines were considered positive, but modern astrologers realize they are so easy that they can create a rut that is difficult to break out of. When two planets are one-third of a circle apart, they won't necessarily stimulate change, but they can often help build on the status quo. With trines, you must stay alert, for complacency can weaken your chances for success.

QUINCUNX

150 degrees ★ **Keywords:** *Irritation, Adjustment*
A quincunx is almost like a nonaspect, for the two planets involved have a difficult time staying aware of each other. As such, this aspect often acts as an irritant, requiring that you make constant adjustments without actually resolving the underlying problem. This is a challenging aspect because it can be more annoying than a full-fledged crisis. Quincunxes are a bit like oil and water—the planets are not in direct conflict, but they have difficulty mixing with each other.

OPPOSITION

180 degrees ★ **Keywords:** *Tension, Awareness, Balance*
When two planets are in opposition, they are like two forces pulling at either end of a rope. The tension is irresolvable, unless you are willing to hold both divergent perspectives without suppressing one or the other. More often than not, we favor one side of the opposition over the other and, in doing so, project the unexpressed side onto others or situations. For this reason, oppositions usually manifest as relationship issues.

ASTROLOGY

WORLD REPORT 2013

ASTROLOGY WORLD REPORT 2013

Astrology works for individuals, groups, and humanity as a whole. You will have your own story in 2013, but it will unfold along with seven billion other tales of human experience. We are each unique, yet our lives touch one another; our destinies are woven together by weather and war, by the economy, science, music, politics, religion, and all the other threads of life on planet Earth. We make personal choices every day, yet great events usually appear to be beyond the control of any one of us. When a town is flooded, it affects everyone who lives there, yet individual astrology patterns describe the specific response of each person.

We are living in a time when sources of self-awareness fill books, TV and radio shows, websites, podcasts, newspapers, and DVDs, and we benefit greatly from them. Yet despite all this wisdom, conflicting ideas, desires, and values cause enormous suffering every day. Understanding personal issues is a powerful means for increasing happiness, but knowledge of our collective concerns is equally important for our safety, sanity, and well-being. This astrological look at the major trends and planetary patterns for 2013 provides a framework for comprehending the potentials and challenges we face together, so that we can move forward with tolerance and respect as a community as we also fulfill our potential as individuals.

The astrological events used in this World Report are the transits of the outer planets, Chiron, and the Moon's Nodes, as well as the retrograde cycles of Mercury and eclipses of the Sun and Moon.

MAJOR PLANETARY EVENTS

JUPITER IN GEMINI: LARGER THAN LIFE

June 11, 2012–June 25, 2013

Astrological tradition considers multifaceted Gemini an awkward place for truth-seeking Jupiter. We can be inundated with so much information that it's nearly impossible to see the forest for the trees. Jupiter's long-range vision may be obscured by a million and one ideas that scatter attention, diffusing the focus we need to achieve long-term goals. Yes, this mind-opening transit stirs curiosity about a wide variety of subjects—but it may be difficult to concentrate and gain in-depth knowledge in any one area if we're skimming the surface. Expansive Jupiter in communicative Gemini can also be quite verbose, valuing the volume of information more than its substance. Nevertheless, we are able to assimilate large amounts of data and make interesting connections among previously unrelated points. Philosophical flexibility and mental versatility are gifts of this transit, while its less desirable qualities include inconsistency of beliefs and careless planning.

JUPITER IN CANCER: FEELING IS BELIEVING

June 25, 2013–July 16, 2014

Philosophical Jupiter provides understanding through emotions during its stay in sensitive Cancer. We're likely to reject ideas that do not correspond to gut instincts, applying a subjective check against concepts that sound good but just don't feel right. Returning to traditional sources of wisdom and reconnecting with nature and family deepens our roots in the past to provide a needed sense of stability in these tumultuous times. Yet looking back for answers to today's questions has its limitations; conditions are changing so rapidly now that old rules no longer apply. We gain a sense of safety by relying on time-tested principles, but we may lose the potential for envisioning a creative new tomorrow by following these well-worn paths. The sentimental nature of Jupiter in Cancer favors familiar circles to unfamiliar. Given this transit's protective qualities, this makes it easier to justify closing the door to new people and experiences. Racism, nationalism, and religious and ethnic prejudices are more prevalent when mental gates close to outsiders. Yet Jupiter in nurturing Cancer, at its highest potential, helps us recognize the living nature of truth in an ever-growing spiral that draws upon the best of the old to nourish new goals and aspirations.

JUPITER'S ASPECTS

Exuberant Jupiter in interactive Gemini forms stressful squares with Chiron the Wounded Healer on January 15 and March 27 in a series that began on July 24, 2012, raising our hopes for a solution to a long-standing problem. We may see progress around political tension centering on differences in religious views on national disputes that have continued for generations. Unfortunately, we may be all

too willing to reach for a quick fix that avoids dealing with the real issues. Forgiving an enemy sounds good in theory, yet it must be followed with concrete actions to cultivate trust and establish healthy relations. On May 28, visionary Jupiter forms a creative quintile with innovative Uranus, indicating that an exciting technological breakthrough is possible. However, it will remain to be seen if a product announced now ever comes to fruition: Jupiter and Uranus together are often more conceptual than practical.

Confident Jupiter in caring Cancer forms an anchoring Grand Water Trine with realistic Saturn and intuitive Neptune on July 17, empowering us to believe so strongly in dreams that we're willing to make a commitment based on feelings rather than the facts. Jupiter's uplifting nature can turn a difficult set of circumstances into a situation filled with opportunity. Saturn's involvement enables Neptune's visions to take form. For example, a politician's rhetoric might be turned into law, or the hopes of an entire nation could be expressed through a large-scale, coordinated social movement. However, Jupiter tensely opposes ruthless Pluto on August 7 and dynamically squares eruptive Uranus on August 21, unleashing energies that are nearly impossible to control. The Jupiter-Pluto alignment increases the strength of our convictions and encourages us to stand up and fight for our beliefs. Unfortunately, we're also less likely to compromise because we're so sure our way is the only way. The Jupiter-Uranus square can precipitate a surprising mass movement that catches on like wildfire. Impatience with the slow progress of social reform may reach an all-time high as people join together to bring about constructive change. Although this aspect can have a very positive outcome, it's important for everyone to be tolerant of others' beliefs or chaos may ensue.

On September 28 and December 17, giant Jupiter creates uneasy sesquisquares with compassionate Neptune, activating our most optimistic fantasies and idealistic dreams. Although this is a highly creative aspect, we can become confused if we're convinced everything we think is the absolute truth. Disillusionment follows: setting our expectations too high leads to disappointment or even discouragement. But we can just as easily be misled by political sound bites, corporate advertising, or someone's inflated promises when high hopes diminish our discernment. Turning lemons into lemonade in our imagination can be a useful skill as long as we're also willing to acknowledge the practical limits of reality.

SATURN IN SCORPIO: SHADOWBOXING

October 5, 2012–December 23, 2014
June 14, 2015–September 16, 2015

Responsible Saturn in formidable Scorpio tests our resolve. We are challenged to look into the dark corners of our psyches where fears about love, money, and mortality hide. It's tempting to turn away from these complicated subjects, yet the price of doing so is high because we are then controlled by unconscious impulses. Power struggles and relationship disappointments are common when we fail to face emotional issues, no matter how intense they may seem. Saturn in Scorpio reminds us that no one is entirely pure and simple. The complexities of giving and receiving affection, dealing with hidden desires, and working with manipulative people are numerous. But if we're willing to show up and do the work, Saturn also offers clarity and authority, enabling us to address these complicated matters. Taking responsibility for dark feelings doesn't mean that we must suppress them; it's a signal to engage them with patience rather than punishment. Discovering what we truly desire (and detest) is a powerful step toward creating healthier relationships. We may not get all our needs met, but acknowledging them makes it possible to have an honest discussion and to negotiate in good faith. Personal and professional alliances work more effectively when we stop keeping secrets from ourselves. Finally, with Saturn in Scorpio we could see even more consolidation of financial institutions as a result of bad loans.

SATURN'S ASPECTS

Taskmaster Saturn requires that we work hard for what we want. Its cooperative sextiles with unwavering Pluto—which began on December 26, 2012, and reoccur on March 8 and September 21—strengthen our resolve to accomplish even the most difficult tasks. Fortunately, it also gives us a deep reserve of energy to follow through on our plans over an extended period of time. On the political front, we're likely to see successful negotiations between previously opposing forces, with both sides satisfied about the outcome.

During Saturn's irritating quincunxes to irrepressible Uranus on April 12 and October 5, a seemingly unimportant event may come out of nowhere to dominate the news. When restrained Saturn meets up with spontaneous Uranus, sudden outbreaks of rebellion can occur, especially in response to heavy-handed political repression. Unfortunately, it's as hard to channel these forces as it is to contain them, so protests may not have the desired results.

Fortunately, steady Saturn forms sweet trines with spiritual Neptune on June 11 and July 19—in a series that began on October 10, 2012—combining unrelenting faith and commitment that can turn dreams into reality. Since these two aspects occur so close to each other and both planets move so slowly, the Saturn-Neptune trine acts as a stabilizing factor in world affairs throughout June and July. A newsworthy event may occur that synchronizes people's thoughts when quicksilver Mercury trines Saturn and Neptune on June 3. Friendly Venus steps into the picture on June 7, perhaps bringing general agreement among a diverse population. The Sun's trines to Saturn and Neptune on June 26 focus the energy on bringing idealistic visions into practical expression. Then, on July 17–20, opportunistic Jupiter and courageous Mars further open our minds to what is possible when we ground imagination in action.

URANUS IN ARIES: LET FREEDOM RING

May 27, 2010–August 13, 2010
March 11, 2011–May 15, 2018

Radical Uranus's visit to enterprising Aries fires up engines of change. We can expect the rapid acceleration of technological discoveries to continue. We get the sense that things will never be quite the same again during the Awakener's seven-year visit to this first sign of the zodiac: Both planet and sign favor innovation. When electrical Uranus was in Aries from 1843 to 1850, the first telegraph broke through the limitations of geography, enabling instantaneous communication over great distances. Uranus was again in Aries from 1927 to 1934, giving us the first transatlantic flight, the discovery of penicillin, the first television broadcasts, and significant developments in quantum physics. We can again expect exciting breakthroughs in a variety of scientific fields this time around, including discoveries that alter our understanding of the origins of the solar system and the development of life on Earth. We may make major strides in recognizing the nature of matter at more primal levels. It's also likely that we'll see significant advancements in the transmission of information, along with tapping new sources of energy that can finally reduce our dependence on petroleum products.

Individual rights—a primary concern of both Aries and Uranus—will take on greater importance as we balance the influences of excessive government and corporate power with humanitarian concerns and populist political movements. Perhaps a new model of human potential will begin to emerge as we explore our creative powers along with evolutionary concepts that alter the very nature of our identity. The process of merging human and machine should continue to accelerate as a new generation of prosthetic devices becomes commonplace. Uranus is associated with artificial intelligence, so we'll likely see microchip implants that extend our sensory mechanisms, an upsurge in robotics technologies, and another explosion in the ubiquity of computers. Nevertheless, something is missing. We are not satisfied with our modern world or with the kinds of work and consumerism that have replaced a more organic and soulful way of living. Yet it's in the awakening of an entirely new view of humanity and of human consciousness that futuristic Uranus in Aries will have the most impact. In 1931, when Uranus was last in Aries, Aldous Huxley wrote his prophetic novel *Brave New World.* Now, as this surprising planet is back in the first sign of the zodiac, we are truly standing at the edge of a brave new world of our own creation. As we step into an uncertain and unknowable future, we can expect some unusual experiments, discoveries, and inventions that are likely to dramatically alter the image we have of ourselves and our world.

NEPTUNE IN PISCES: LOVE WITHOUT BORDERS

April 4, 2011–August 4, 2011
February 3, 2012–March 30, 2025

Imaginative Neptune's entry into its watery home sign signals a spiritual awakening that transcends the threshold of our individual differences to reconnect all humanity in an integrative web of common awareness. Compassion shifts from an idealistic concept to an active energy that puts us directly in touch with one another in a more emotional way. The last time Neptune was in Pisces—from 1847 through 1862—concern for others was reflected in the abolitionist movement to end slavery in the United States and to free the serfs in Russia. It's very likely that this transit of Neptune will again put issues of injustice and inequality in the spotlight.

Dissolving boundaries on a personal level is both inspiring and confusing. As the great tide of humanity rises and falls, we can feel that we are being swept away by invisible forces beyond our control. These forces may, in fact, relax borders among nations in a long-term process that puts common concerns above separatist national interests, although we're also likely to see a fear-driven backlash. Religious differences might become less problematic as the faithful focus more on flexibility of spirit than rigidity of ritual. We may grow more psychically attuned with one another and with nature. The unifying forces of Neptune and Pisces remind us that *"All is One"* is not an abstraction, but the way the world really works.

The value of water is likely to increase, along with investments in conservation and desalinization. However, the effects of pollution will also grow painfully evident, leading to a scarcity of fresh, clean water. Neptune, the god of the seas, is the planetary ruler of oil. In fact, in 1859 when Neptune was last in Pisces, the very first oil well was drilled in Pennsylvania. Now the search for new fuel sources continues to grow in its urgency as the catastrophic ecological impact of the oil industry becomes inescapable. Neptune in Pisces increases sensitivity to toxins, requiring more thorough cleanup of existing waste and a more cautious approach to introducing new products into the environment. These may be the last days of environmentally disastrous plastics as we know them, with current chemical formulas replaced by biodegradable substitutes. The negative effects of prescription drugs—both personally and environmentally—become more obvious, precipitating radical changes in the manufacture and use of pharmaceuticals while increasing the demand for natural medicine and organic food.

PLUTO IN CAPRICORN: CHANGE FROM THE GROUND UP

January 25, 2008–June 14, 2008
November 26, 2008–March 23, 2023

Pluto takes about 245 years to complete one journey around the zodiac, but observations of its movement after its discovery in 1930 quickly revealed its power. This tiny but potent planet entered no-nonsense Capricorn in 2008, signaling major changes in the architecture of society. Capricorn is associated with established institutions such as government and business, so regenerative Pluto's visit indicates a drawn-out process that will ultimately alter the most fundamental organizational structures supporting our culture, including a major restructuring of the economy. While the short-term suffering of financial contraction is already apparent, this painful process is a necessary step as we overhaul our overextended, hyper-consumerist society into one in which humans and nature ultimately exist in greater harmony.

Capricorn is a practical earth sign, so we can expect growing urgency in the serious environmental crises we face. Global warming, for instance, will intensify pressures on corporations, governments, and individuals, forcing inevitable upheavals that will radically impact our modern way of life. Since Pluto is associated with the process of elimination, the accumulated effects of dumping toxins into the air, water, and soil will continue to become more evident during its long transit. All waste falls under Pluto's dominion, so we will likely continue our battles with the harmful fallout from oil spills, radioactive by-products, and other industrial garbage. Obviously, this could overpower all other issues and require a degree of change not seen since Pluto last transited Capricorn from 1762 to 1778. Democracy, like the mythological phoenix bird that flew from the ashes of ruins, arose from the destructive American and French Revolutions that ended monarchy. The same transit that gave birth to the individual freedoms we take for granted is now reenergizing a modern-day struggle to keep them.

The good news is that evolutionary events of this magnitude do not occur overnight. The corruption of existing institutions takes time—enough for those who can adapt to begin the necessary process of reform. Since Capricorn has to do with hierarchical rule from the top, this Pluto transit will continue to knock down those who have traditionally pulled the levers of power. Yet regardless of where state, church, banks, education, and industry go, there is constructive work we each can and must do as individuals at this time. Both Pluto and Capricorn are associated with power, so the application of personal will is critical and can make the difference between utopia and oblivion. Instead of merely relying on others to maintain and advance civilization, we each have the capacity—and, ultimately, the responsibility—to increase our own tangible contribution to the world.

The first step may be personally reexamining our career ambitions and individual life goals. Although this journey is likely to be the result of many interrelated events, for some it could grow out of dissatisfaction or a sense of impotence in life that's not limited to Pluto's transit this year. Among other people, it may be catalyzed by an economic downturn, the loss of a job, or a natural disaster. Of course, this can feel overwhelming; meeting increasing responsibilities is daunting. Thus it's best to address small but important issues as they surface, where we can see results more quickly and gain the confidence we need to continue moving forward. But we must remember that we won't necessarily be able to notice the changes day to day, because Pluto moves slowly. Although we cannot see a glacier moving, its relentless power relocates mountains that stand in its way. We are living at a special moment in history; this is a significant crossroads. Humanity has an unprecedented opportunity to become more empowered, allowing us to consciously create the future rather than unconsciously repeating mistakes of the past.

CHIRON IN PISCES: THE ART OF FORGIVENESS

April 20, 2010–July 20, 2010
February 8, 2011–April 17, 2018

Chiron's first foray into metaphysical Pisces since its discovery in 1977 increases the popularity of holistic forms of health care and subtle healing modalities. Although interest in mind-body medicine has been steadily growing for many years, it will receive a significant boost from breakthroughs in harnessing nonphysical energies that can positively impact our well-being. Alternative retirement homes and wellness communities will be in higher demand to address the growing needs of aging baby boomers. Since Chiron travels between the orbits of rational Saturn and radical Uranus, it ferries between the known and the unknown, working as a maverick outside traditional models. Its association with forgiveness while in spiritual Pisces reminds us that blame is never part of the solution; it merely perpetuates our problems. This isn't about avoiding the truth; it's about the power of unconditional love as a healing force that releases us from the pain of past wounds. The physical and mental well-being of individuals may be recognized as part of collective patterns, rather than separate experiences.

Ultimately we are more aware than ever of the human suffering all around the world. The role of spirituality in global healing will continue to grow as we see more shortcomings among organized religions—each one staking its claim as the only path to salvation. Although we are limited in what we can do on a personal level, we no longer have the option of leaving the work for someone else. The pain of standing by and doing nothing is greater than the frustration of not being able to fix everything.

THE MOON'S NODES

MOON'S NORTH NODE IN SCORPIO, SOUTH NODE IN TAURUS: GO DEEP

August 29, 2012–February 18, 2014

The Moon's North Node in Scorpio points us toward the growth and integration we experience when we encounter intense feelings and unfulfilled desires. It is tempting, though, to withdraw into the pleasurable comfort of the habit-driven South Node in Taurus, which tends to avoid complications and heavy emotions. Yet passion, not pacification, is the road to personal fulfillment now. Pushing beyond the boundaries of politeness can ruffle feathers, yet it will ultimately solve more problems than it creates. The key is to wed intensity with kindness so that we reach this deeper level of connecting without losing sensitivity to everyone's needs.

MERCURY RETROGRADES

All true planets appear to move backward from time to time, because we view them from the moving platform of Earth. The most noticeable and regular retrograde periods are those of Mercury, the communication planet. Occurring three or four times a year for roughly three weeks at a time, these are periods when difficulties with details, travel, communication, and technical matters are more common than usual.

Mercury's retrograde is often perceived as negative, but you can make this cycle work for you. Because personal and commercial interactions are emphasized, you can actually accomplish more than usual, especially if you stay focused on what you need to complete instead of initiating new projects. Still, you may feel as if you're treading water—or worse, being carried backward in an undertow of unfinished business. Worry less about making progress than about the quality of your work. Pay extra attention to all your communication exchanges. Avoiding misunderstandings and omissions is the ideal way to minimize complications. Retrograde Mercury is best used to tie up loose ends as you review, redo, reconsider, and, in general, revisit the past.

All three Mercury retrograde cycles occur in emotional water signs this year. This can make communication more difficult, because it's not easy to translate feelings into words. Our potential loss of objectivity, as well, can lead to even more misunderstandings than usual. Thankfully, these three periods give us the chance to reconnect with our emotions, which can inspire new waves of creativity.

FEBRUARY 23–MARCH 17 IN PISCES: DAYDREAM BELIEVER

Mercury's presence in sympathetic Pisces is more about feelings than facts. Its retrograde turn in this sign can pull a gauzy curtain of dreaminess across our eyes, fuzzing data and confusing conversations. This can be an inspiring period when psychic powers grow and creativity is freed from the fetters of reason. Still, Mercury's conjunctions with assertive Mars on February 26 and the radiant Sun on March 4 add punch to words and confidence to ideas that may sound too strong for overly sensitive individuals.

JUNE 26–JULY 20 IN CANCER: SENTIMENTAL JOURNEY

Mercury's backward turn in nostalgic Cancer sends us meandering down Memory Lane. It's tempting to remember the past as much brighter than the present, but don't forget that thinking can be a little cloudy now. Words hold weight; even innocent comments may be interpreted as aggressive remarks. The upside of this cycle is a greater capacity for introspection that can place personal history in a new light. Revising judgments about the past is an excellent way to untie psychological knots and create more freedom of response and reaction going forward in life.

OCTOBER 21–NOVEMBER 10 IN SCORPIO: TURNING DARK INTO RIGHT

Thoughts turn inward when Mercury retrogrades in mysterious Scorpio, and all this contemplation reduces the flow of information. Although this temporary respite gives us a chance to reevaluate relationships and investments, we risk becoming overly suspicious and focusing on what can go wrong instead of working to make things right. Mercury's conjunction with somber Saturn on October 29 underscores the dangers of looking only at the dark side of situations. However, the ringed planet helps us define complex issues in concrete terms, which could be a powerful step toward managing them with patience and discipline.

ECLIPSES

Solar and Lunar Eclipses are special New and Full Moons that indicate significant changes for individuals and groups. They are powerful markers of events, with influences that can appear up to three months in advance and last up to six months afterward. Eclipses occur when the New or Full Moon is conjunct with one of the Moon's Nodes. Solar Eclipses occur at the New Moon and are visible in narrow paths, but not everywhere that the Sun is visible. Locations where the eclipse can be seen feel its influence more strongly. Lunar Eclipses occur during Full Moons and are visible wherever the Moon is seen.

APRIL 25, LUNAR ECLIPSE IN SCORPIO: SINK OR SWIM

This Lunar Eclipse in passionate Scorpio tells us to let go of the past and start living in the present. Taskmaster Saturn's conjunction to the Moon, though, encourages a tenacious attitude that can keep us entangled in unrewarding relationships. Resentment, jealousy, and revenge aren't worth the effort they take to sustain. However, initiating Mars is conjunct with the sensible Taurus Sun, which favors simplifying life and making a fresh start instead of trying to fix an unresolvable problem.

MAY 9, SOLAR ECLIPSE IN TAURUS: TRIM THE FAT

The cost of comfort may become so high that we have to let go of laziness or some luxuries to make life more affordable. There's a self-indulgent side to Taurus, and with combative Mars and talkative Mercury joined with the Sun and Moon now, we can find ourselves aggressively defending our behavior. Yet trying to justify standing still and holding on to what we have may only increase the steep price we pay later for resisting the purging we need at this time.

MAY 25, LUNAR ECLIPSE IN SAGITTARIUS: LIFE'S AN ADVENTURE

An eclipse in farsighted Sagittarius reminds us to bring our attention back from some distant vision to focus on the here and now. We can discover alternative ways to make life work instead of acting as if there's only one road to fulfillment. Beliefs may not hold up in the face of changing circumstances that require flexibility instead of certainty. Asking questions reveals options that multiply choices, creating confusion for some but freeing most of us from rigid thinking and excessive judgment.

OCTOBER 18, LUNAR ECLIPSE IN ARIES: NO MAN IS AN ISLAND

Life is not a solo voyage even when we're feeling all alone. This eclipse emphasizes the need to work with others and demands some degree of compromise and accommodation. It's better to sit on the fence, gather more information, and mull things over than to race ahead impulsively now. While it may seem that sharing feelings with others hinders progress, it garners us support that overcomes the isolation of not accepting advice and assistance.

NOVEMBER 3, SOLAR ECLIPSE IN SCORPIO: BABY STEPS

Expect power struggles with controlling Saturn's conjunction to this New Moon Eclipse. It's not easy to trust people—and sometimes it's just as difficult to trust ourselves. This eclipse, however, is about backing away from pressure, reducing intensity, and seeking peaceful moments in our lives. Recognizing the gifts that we're given every day can alleviate a profound feeling of hunger, perhaps even despair, through small moments of joy and pleasure.

THE BOTTOM LINE: YELL FIRE!

The Mayan calendar may have turned over near the end of 2012, but the human story on this planet is far from complete. Nevertheless, we are still in the midst of a period of powerful change that began with the opposition of structural Saturn and explosive Uranus in late 2008 when we experienced the first wave of the worst financial crisis since the Great Depression, along with the subsequent election of Barack Obama.

The year 2012 brought the first of seven tense squares between Uranus and transformational Pluto that will recur through 2015, shaking the very foundations of societies around the world. The volatile Uranus-Pluto square is exact on May 20 and November 1, April 21 and December 15, 2014, and March 16, 2015. The long-lasting connection between revolutionary Uranus and volcanic Pluto is already fomenting change on a grand scale, and this will continue for years to come. The last time these two planets were squared to each other was in 1932–1934, when the United States was suffering from an economic depression and the rise of fascism was altering the political landscape of the world. Yet it's important to understand that these history-making alignments are just as much about discovering new aspects of human potential as they are about failing governments, social

revolutions, economic uncertainty, environmental stresses, and natural disasters. Uranus and Pluto are transpersonal planets that reshape consciousness, thrusting us into unfamiliar territory that is both inspiring and terrifying. This powerful planetary pair formed conjunctions in 1965–1966 and represent the radical cultural shifts of that period. Issues that arose then have sprung back into collective awareness with a renewed sense of urgency that is again waking the masses and inspiring social action. Hopefully we won't have to relive the hardships of the 1930s if we learned anything from the 1960s. Whatever happens, one thing is certain: We are now taking the next step in human evolution.

Futuristic Uranus in unstoppable Aries is pushing hard against the status quo, as represented by Pluto in Capricorn. But this isn't just a response to external authority; it's a significant shift in our sense of who we are. The mix of technology and medicine, coupled with advances in nanotechnology and genetics, makes it possible to alter the human body and actually redirect our own evolutionary path. Now, as we launch ourselves into a future of our own creation, we must expect resistance. Traditional institutions will condemn experimentation, and our own psyches will recoil against the unrelenting forward thrust of history. But it won't matter, for the powerful tides of change cannot be stopped. The wisest path is

to participate with a spirit of innovation and the flexibility to adapt to unexpected events as we enter the next stage of adventure and discovery.

It is tempting, though, to gaze back and seek to re-create the relative safety of the past. Joyful Jupiter's entry into cautious and conservative Cancer will bring waves of nostalgia for the "good old days," along with protectionist calls for stronger national borders. Yet the idea that we can return to the past is not a feasible one. The technological cats are out of the bag, and addressing environmental issues alone requires forward, not backward, thinking. Our challenge is to construct new realities based on bold visions and idealistic dreams of a world that does not yet exist. This takes courage in the face of confusion and confidence in the midst of chaos. It's tempting to call out to higher powers to rescue us from the consequences of our actions: Suffering evokes cries for help. And yet we are capable of healing ourselves if we finally

embrace the twenty-first century instead of retreating to mythical moments of an idealized past.

Inventive Uranus in pioneering Aries is opening new neural pathways that are reshaping our view of reality. Yes, we may encounter moments when thoughts are so strange that we may fear ourselves to be mad. But curious minds, flexible egos, and adaptable emotions allow us to glimpse a more enlightened, evolved, and competent humanity without breaking down. We are challenged to dance with the stranger who enters our heads with perceptions that don't readily fit into our existing intellectual framework. We must find new ways out of the dilemmas that we've created for ourselves. Embracing small discoveries and appreciating surprises are good training techniques: They prepare us to step up to the next level of human evolution and continue the remarkable journey of love and light on planet Earth.

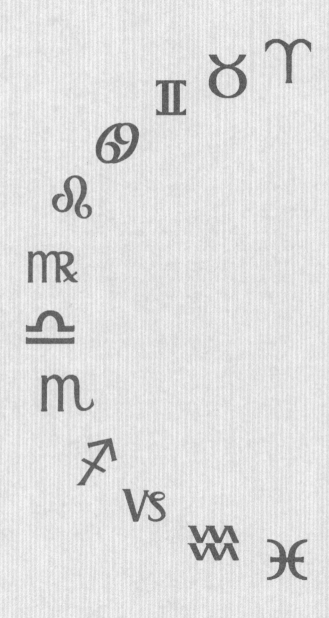

PART 2

AUGUST–DECEMBER

2012 OVERVIEW

2013 ASTROLOGICAL

FORECASTS

ARIES

MARCH 21–APRIL 19

ARIES

2012 SUMMARY

This year reveals even more changes that will rattle your windows and shake the foundations of your life. Your professional ambitions are suddenly electrified by the squares from high-voltage Uranus and unexpected developments require you to alter the course you thought would carry you into the future. Be patient as you move steadily toward your goals, even if you are tempted to bolt ahead without any second thoughts. Hard-earned stability begins to return by the end of 2012 if you can resist the temptation to aim higher than you can reach.

AUGUST—*a change will do you good*

Although you may feel stuck, it's crucial to keep your life in motion as the pressure for change mounts.

SEPTEMBER—*the cost of freedom*

Everything seems to be in a state of change, yet taking your time before reacting will work to your ultimate advantage.

OCTOBER—*dream the possible dream*

Give yourself permission to rest, but don't get too comfortable—you still have plenty to do while the cosmic tides are in your favor.

NOVEMBER—*anything can happen*

You cannot judge your success by external events. It's more important to consider your emotional and spiritual growth than what's occurring in the material world.

DECEMBER—*into the wild blue yonder*

Instead of trying to make major decisions that change the direction of your life, focus on doing whatever you can to make minor improvements day by day.

2012 CALENDAR

AUGUST

__WED 1–FRI 3__ ★ You won't know what's possible unless you try

__WED 8–SAT 11__ ★ Let your feelings guide you now

__WED 15–FRI 17__ ★ **SUPER NOVA DAYS** Remain calm in the face of turmoil

__SUN 19–MON 20__ ★ Be on guard against your own arrogance

__WED 29–FRI 31__ ★ There may be unexpected consequences to your actions

SEPTEMBER

__MON 3–WED 5__ ★ Clear and direct communication is your best bet

__FRI 7–MON 10__ ★ You will accomplish more if you can rein in your exuberance

__WED 12–SUN 16__ ★ You're ready to try something completely different

__TUE 18–THU 20__ ★ Connect with new people to bring more pleasure and prestige

__THU 29–FRI 30__ ★ Consider the impact of your words

__TUE 25–SAT 29__ ★ **SUPER NOVA DAYS** Your patience is tested

OCTOBER

__FRI 5–SUN 7__ ★ Serious relationship issues require your attention

__SUN 14–TUE 16__ ★ **SUPER NOVA DAYS** Observe sensible limits

__THU 25__ ★ Stop, look, and listen before you proceed any further

__SUN 28–MON 29__ ★ Act with common sense

NOVEMBER

__THU 1–SUN 4__ ★ A sudden twist on the partnership path creates excitement

__FRI 9__ ★ Pleasure is within your reach

__TUE 13–SAT 17__ ★ **SUPER NOVA DAYS** The stage is set for dramatic change

__WED 21–FRI 23__ ★ Taking decisive action can settle a matter

__MON 26–THU 29__ ★ Stand firm in your convictions

DECEMBER

__SAT 1–SUN 2__ ★ **SUPER NOVA DAYS** It's tough to establish limits

__MON 10–THU 13__ ★ Consider what makes the most sense before taking action

__SUN 16–TUE 18__ ★ Don't take on more than you should

__FRI 21–SAT 22__ ★ Incorporate the magic of your dreams into your plans

__FRI 28–MON 31__ ★ Trust your instincts

ARIES OVERVIEW

Your sign is on the cutting edge of change due to a dramatic cycle that took hold when revolutionary Uranus settled into fiery Aries on March 11, 2011, staying until May 15, 2018. This electrifying planet will shake, rattle, and roll with surprises, breakthroughs, and discoveries that are bound to keep you on your toes. Fortunately, your pioneering sign is made for exploring new ideas and experiences that will lead everyone else into the future. You typically find change an exciting adventure, but sometimes it's uncomfortable for others to be prodded into letting go of stale habits and outdated concepts. **It's up to you to blaze trails into unfamiliar territory, and you will continue to do so this year.** There are, however, two key periods when you must exercise extreme caution: Rebellious Uranus slams into tense squares with punitive Pluto on May 20 and November 1. Your margin for error is reduced within a week of these dates, making radical moves dangerous. Carefully calculate potential consequences, because once you've taken action, there may be no going back. On the positive side, these powerful transits can intensify your efforts and provide the force you need to overcome stubborn obstacles.

You may not have to venture far to connect with new people and open your eyes to fresh ways of thinking. Expansive Jupiter is in clever Gemini and your 3rd House of Immediate Environment for the first half of the year, increasing curiosity, spurring spontaneous conversations, and brightening most days with little discoveries that put a knowing smile on your face. Philosophical Jupiter shifts into caring Cancer and your 4th House of Roots on June 25. A deeper understanding of the family patterns that have shaped your behavior helps you recognize unconscious beliefs that may be hindering your progress. Diving into the emotions in which these memories are buried can leave you feeling vulnerable, but the process can also reward you with newfound clarity about your aspirations and how to fulfill them.

It's especially important to uncover the motives and desires hidden deep in your psyche with scrupulous Saturn's presence in penetrating Scorpio and your 8th House of Intimacy. This relationship-transforming transit began in October 2012 and will continue through 2014, testing your resolve when dealing with personal and professional partners. **The greatest challenge is to be honest with yourself about what you want and what you're willing to give to get it.** You probably prefer being relatively independent—not relying on others for much of anything. However, you can't discover the full potential of your relationships until after you realize that you can gain more love, money, and satisfaction by combining forces with passionate and powerful allies.

DOUBLE OR NOTHING

The transit of Saturn in your 8th House of Deep Sharing raises the stakes in your love life this year. If you're not totally committed to the relationship you're in, expect discontent to linger until you make some major changes. If you're single, be discriminating in your choice of companions, ruling out those individuals who can't take you as far as you want to go. Pleasure-seeking is pretty much out of the question when your ardent ruling planet, Mars, squares somber Saturn on January 7, but a fresh wave of excitement is coming with the warmth of spring. The Sun fires into irrepressible Aries on March 20 with flirty Venus following on the 21st, boosting your confidence and amplifying your sex appeal. Sassy Venus's conjunction with sexy Mars on April 7 is hot, hot, hot. Here's your chance to rekindle the spark with your current partner or jump into a new romance.

POTENT PARTNERSHIPS

Align yourself with powerful people this year; it could be the key to your success. It's better to work with a demanding individual who challenges you than with an easygoing person who lacks high standards. Saturn, the ruling planet of your 10th House of Career, forms favorable trines to visionary Jupiter on July 17 and December 12 that provide an ambitious, long-term picture of where you're going. These strategic aspects reward you for stepping back and planning your next move with patience and discipline, instead of rushing ahead with a poorly thought-out idea. Launching or expanding your own business is favored when lucky Jupiter crosses the bottom of your chart on June 25 and begins a six-year ascent toward a professional peak.

SAVE FOR A RAINY DAY

Manage your money carefully this year, because unexpected expenses or interruptions in your cash flow can put you in a tight spot. Your financial picture could suddenly change on March 28 when magnetic Venus and erratic Uranus join the Sun in impulsive Aries. Your hardworking planet, Mars, enters tight-fisted Taurus and your 2nd House of Income on April 20, making this a better time for saving money slowly than trying to make a fast buck. The intense Lunar Eclipse in your 8th House of Shared Resources on April 25 and a Solar Eclipse in your 2nd House on May 9 warn against reckless spending and unnecessary borrowing. If you need a loan or require an investment, fight hard for the best terms you can get. It's better to scrape by with less and pay it off sooner than to get trapped in debt.

CLAIM YOUR POWER

A new diet or exercise routine can work wonders for you when muscular Mars travels through your 1st House of Physicality on March 12–April 20. If you're already in good shape, exploring alternative forms of movement and experimenting with foods you've never tried are clever ways to avoid boredom. October is a key month for attending to your well-being, because the Aries Lunar Eclipse on the 18th highlights the physical aspects of your sign. Burning the candle at both ends could wear you out quickly, so make sure to get enough rest. If you're dealing with nervous tension, simplify what you eat to regain stability and make your life seem less hectic. Avoid risky sports and pushing your body to extremes to keep yourself safe throughout this time.

BUILDING FROM THE GROUND UP

A new chapter opens in your domestic life on June 25, when generous Jupiter enters your 4th House of Security for a yearlong visit. If your home already feels confining, you may now be convinced the walls are closing in. To gain some space, eliminate clutter; physical renovations or a move to a new location could also solve this problem. The deeper issues, though, are psychological; you may need to confront feelings about your childhood that you thought were already put to rest. As novelist Tom Robbins states, "It's never too late to have a happy childhood." Being kinder to yourself and accepting tenderness will establish a stronger and wider foundation upon which to build a more promising future.

HOME SWEET HOME

You don't have to travel far from home to feel like you're on an adventure this year. Jupiter, the ruler of your 9th House of Faraway Places, begins 2013 in your neighborly 3rd House, so you can find plenty of interesting ideas and exciting experiences right in your own backyard. The Sagittarius Lunar Eclipse rattles your 9th House on May 25, altering travel plans or interrupting your education. Yet the eclipsed Full Moon's trine to ingenious Uranus might redirect you in a more stimulating direction. Jupiter shifts into your familial 4th House on June 25, spurring interest in your origins. Consider scheduling a visit to your hometown or a trip to the country of your ancestors sometime over the next year.

HEAVEN ON EARTH

This could be a very important year in your spiritual life. The urge to pursue higher truth is nearly impossible to ignore when Mars travels through otherworldly Pisces and your 12th House of Divinity on February 1–March 12. In July, cosmic forces gather, giving you the discipline and inspiration to make your newfound faith last. On July 17, metaphysical Neptune aligns harmoniously with wise Jupiter and then forms the same favorable aspect with orderly Saturn on July 19. This rare Grand Water Trine unveils meaning and purpose that you can apply in concrete terms the rest of the year.

RICK & JEFF'S TIP FOR THE YEAR:
Pace Yourself

You tend to rush things, Aries, perhaps because you lack self-confidence, or you're unconsciously convinced you'll never reach your goals. Yes, acting impulsively makes life feel more exciting. Just remember that operating at high speed and leaping without looking are unlikely to produce the lasting results you want now. Instead, work this year on cultivating patience and planning strategically for your future. Slowing down to enjoy life's sweet moments is good practice for learning to take your time as you attack life's bigger challenges.

JANUARY

SHARE AND SHARE ALIKE

You can get 2013 off to a good start if you focus on being a cooperative member of the community. Mars, your energetic ruling planet, spends all of January in freedom-loving Aquarius and your 11th House of Groups, challenging you to integrate your independent spirit with collective goals. It's no easy task to express your individuality while remaining a supportive team player; you must find a healthy balance between self-determination and accommodation. This dilemma may grow even more difficult when you see the most competitive people rewarded as sociable Venus enters ambitious Capricorn and your 10th House of Public Responsibility on **January 8**. The Capricorn New Moon on **January 11** puts issues of authority and power in the foreground, intensifying your desire to reach the top of the mountain. However, an inelegant aspect from expansive Jupiter to this Sun-Moon conjunction can tempt you to push others out of the way in your desire to get ahead.

The pendulum swings in a friendlier direction when brainy Mercury and the heart-centered Sun enter your 11th House of Community on **January 19**. This extroverted trend receives a boost from the expressive Leo Full Moon in your 5th House of Fun and Games on **January 26**. You're ready to make a dramatic move in pursuit of love or to show off your creativity, but stern Saturn's square to the Moon reminds you to remain sensitive to others' limits. Still, your optimism grows thanks to joyous Jupiter's favorable aspects to this lunation. This giant planet of good fortune turns forward in your 3rd House of Communication on **January 30**, offering you ways to make new connections and promote your ideas.

KEEP IN MIND THIS MONTH

Sometimes your thinking is just too advanced for others to understand. Work to build a bridge from the old ways to your new vision so that your friends can get on board.

KEY DATES

JANUARY 4 ★ *supersize it*

A friction-free trine between assertive Mars and adventurous Jupiter infuses you with enthusiasm and innovation. The mood-setting Moon enters the picture with trines to both planets, making this a perfect day for sharing your ideas with excitement while remaining sensitive to the needs of your audience.

SUPER NOVA DAY

JANUARY 7 ★ *shoulder to the wheel*

You are being held to higher standards today with little margin for error as hard-driving Mars runs into a wall of resistance from a blocking square with obstinate Saturn. Purpose and discipline are essential. Deviating from the rules could produce immediate negative feedback. If you can patiently follow a well-defined plan, however, you can refine your skills and establish a strong foundation that provides enduring support for your long-term goals.

JANUARY 14–16 ★ *genius at work*

You come up with unconventional solutions to problems at work on **January 14** when clever Mercury in your 10th House of Career forms brilliant quintiles with conscientious Saturn and inventive Uranus. Yet your success can arouse jealousy or leave you feeling unfulfilled as appreciative Venus joins hungry Pluto in your 10th House on the **16th**. Take a deep look at your working relationships to find ways to repair them or discern which, if any, no longer meet your needs. This is also an opportune time to develop a neglected talent or an underutilized skill.

JANUARY 20 ★ *my way or the highway*

Mars forms an edgy semisquare with unruly Uranus, increasing your originality while lessening your willingness to follow anyone else's lead. This transit may show you a shortcut or two, leaving you excited with the brilliance of your discoveries. Yet a distinct need to do things your own way can be disconcerting to those around you who have different agendas. Watch out for reckless behavior and sudden anger, which can undercut trust and dry up tender feelings. If you're unwilling to make compromises, you may be better off on your own.

JANUARY 26 ★ *proceed with purpose*

Today you're tempted by indulgence—the dubious gift of a luxury-loving Venus-Jupiter sesquisquare. Yet the distractions of delight may be overpowered by a pressure-packed aspect between inexhaustible Mars and persistent Pluto that's useful for tackling daunting tasks. You have the strength and commitment to finally complete unfinished business. Cleaning up matters from the past is especially helpful because it supplies a constructive place to put your passion. Strong feelings of attraction or repulsion can rattle relationships, so it's wise to temper your reactions with a good dose of self-restraint.

FEBRUARY

FINDING FAITH

February is ideal for embarking on a spiritual quest—and you don't even have to leave home. The journey starts when Mars slips into magical Pisces and your 12th House of Soul Consciousness on **February 1**. Your potent ruling planet grows soft and tender in this dreamy part of your chart, which makes charging ahead with projects a bit more unappealing than usual. Investing time in metaphysical studies, prayer, and meditation allows you to take much-needed breaks from the demands of daily life and put your worldly ambitions in perspective. As cerebral Mercury shifts into your 12th House on **February 5**, you favor imagination over logic and intuition over reason. Mercury's conjunction with diaphanous Neptune on the **6th** diffuses your concentration and leads to confusing conversations, but it's bound to enhance your creativity.

Enjoy a fresh start with friends and colleagues on **February 10** with the Aquarius New Moon in your 11th House of Groups. If you've made commitments that no longer suit your needs, this lunation might motivate you to back out of them. The Sun's shift into gentle Pisces and your 12th House of Privacy on **February 18** takes you out of the spotlight or reduces your drive, yet it's a wonderful opportunity to recognize how much pleasure you receive from helping those less fortunate than you. A wave of compassion and forgiveness sweeps over you on the **21st** thanks to a solar conjunction with spiritual Neptune, dissolving any feelings of guilt and seeding future dreams. Mercury's retrograde turn on the **23rd** slows communication and muddles messages. But the industrious Virgo Full Moon in your 6th House of Work on the **25th** may reveal an unusual way to be more efficient on the job.

> **KEEP IN MIND THIS MONTH**
>
> *The work that's most meaningful to you may be invisible to others, but it still can nourish your soul and restore your spirit in powerful ways.*

KEY DATES

FEBRUARY 4 ★ *long and winding road*

It's a mushy Monday with mobile Mars in a wobbly conjunction with diffusive Neptune. This is useful for acting with great tenderness, following your feelings, or making a point in a gentle manner. At the same time, it's easy to wander off track, wasting time in pursuit of an illusion or wearing yourself out by forcing an issue that's not ripe for change. Avoid pushing straight ahead when taking the scenic route might save you time and energy in the long run.

SUPER NOVA DAYS

FEBRUARY 8–10 ★ *watch your words*

A hyperactive Mercury-Mars conjunction on **February 8** energizes your thoughts and conversations. Indeed, you may be reacting too quickly to consider the impact of your words and manner of expression. Some of what you say can be brilliant and insightful while other statements could provoke anger or lead to embarrassment. The day's edginess may leave you feeling off-balance and uncertain about when to push your message and when to keep your opinions to yourself. Taking a moment to organize your thoughts increases your chances of sharing something useful. You tend to shoot from the hip when Mercury and Mars square exaggerating Jupiter on **February 9–10**; watch out in case you misinterpret someone, overstate your case, or explode over petty issues. If you channel your passion into creative projects, though, you can tap into a virtually unlimited source of ideas.

FEBRUARY 15–16 ★ *cut to the chase*

This is a very constructive period; you're working more efficiently than you were earlier in the month. Mars in poetic Pisces picks up some muscle with a beneficial sextile to potent Pluto on **February 15**. Instead of meandering around lost in uncertainty, this aspect helps you to gather force and direct it with power and purpose. Mars is strengthened by a trine from responsible Saturn on the **16th**, adding a dose of discipline that also favors productivity. Quiet confidence gives you the clarity to simplify problems and solve them with relative ease.

FEBRUARY 25–26 ★ *rapid recovery*

Loving Venus moves into sentimental Pisces on **February 25**, arousing romantic longing on the same day that the analytical Virgo Full Moon might also stir up insecurity in relationships. Retrograde Mercury's second conjunction this month with testy Mars on the **26th** could incite you to fire off some harsh words or possibly to feel like the target of someone else's inappropriate aggression. Fortunately, Mars's reasonable trine with the integrative North Node of the Moon quickly shows you how to repair damage and restore trust.

MARCH

THE RACE IS ON

You can feel the heat rising this month as three planets fire into spontaneous Aries, inspiring you to take bold action. Pioneering Mars leads the parade on **March 12**, followed by the illuminating Sun on the **20th** and alluring Venus on the **21st**. Your irrepressible urge for new experiences tempts you to take chances—and you're happiest living on the cutting edge anyway. Still, it's possible to try some risky things while maintaining a backup plan so that you have a safety net to catch you if you fall. Stabilizing Saturn's sextile with profound Pluto on **March 8**—the second in a series that began on **December 26, 2012**, and finishes on **September 21**—can connect you with powerful allies who help you set appropriate boundaries and maximize the return on your efforts. Overblown Jupiter's quincunx with Pluto on **March 29** signals the need to simplify your plans by eliminating extraneous activities.

On **March 11**, the imaginative Pisces New Moon in your metaphysical 12th House joins Venus, adding beauty to your inner life and inspiring artistic expression. Mental Mercury's direct turn on the **17th** begins to solidify ideas that have been floating around looking for a place to land. The Sun enters fearless Aries on **March 20**, the Vernal Equinox, marking the start of a new astrological year and amplifying your taste for adventure. It's time to face the music in relationships on **March 27** with purging Pluto squaring the peace-seeking Libra Full Moon in your 7th House of Partners. Your reward for emotional honesty is more clarity about what you need and what you're willing to pay for it.

> ### KEEP IN MIND THIS MONTH
>
> *Give yourself permission to be a beginner when you try something new. Making mistakes is not a valid reason to give up if you're enjoying yourself and learning along the way.*

KEY DATES

MARCH 3 ★ *quiet strength*

Today you're able to cut through complexity to get to the core of a stubborn problem, with help from a subtle but powerful—and creative—Mars-Pluto quintile. It's possible now to take control of a situation without exhausting yourself or coming across as overly aggressive.

MARCH 7 ★ *against all odds*
Resistance from others slows you down with a stressful aspect between Mars and Saturn. If you are precise about what you want and modest in your goals, you can earn the support of a cautious person. But even if someone fails to cooperate with you, a brilliant Mars-Jupiter quintile could show you how to leap over an obstacle by approaching it from a totally different angle.

MARCH 11–12 ★ *you're number one*
The inspirational Pisces New Moon on **March 11** stirs dreams of love and creativity that might feel beyond your reach. But warrior Mars enters courageous Aries the next day, awakening your passion that can drive you to succeed. Use it to pursue your goals, both personal and professional; you have more to gain by applying this intensity to your own interests than by following someone else's lead. Playing second fiddle or simply trying to hold your ground may feel so confining that your frustration ignites a conflict.

SUPER NOVA DAYS
MARCH 20–22 ★ *lightning in a bottle*
You're filled with power and grace when the Sun's shift into confident Aries and your 1st House of Personality on **March 20** is followed by charming Venus on the **21st**. All eyes are turned in your direction as you shine your light with charisma and passion. But watch out, because dynamic Mars hooks up with wired Uranus on the **22nd**, shocking you with a jolt of electricity that turns a cool situation into an inferno of activity. Restlessness and rebellion could lead you to act impulsively, unsettling those around you. Still, this is also a highly inventive alignment that can be super-sexy when you experiment with new methods or unusual looks.

MARCH 25–28 ★ *liberation days*
Practice patience on **March 25** to handle rowdy Mars's quincunx to restrictive Saturn. Even if your enthusiasm rises with a high-octane Mars-Jupiter sextile on the **26th**, a Mars-Pluto square on the same day means you're better off concentrating on one task than spreading yourself too thin. The Sun and Venus conjoin Uranus on **March 28**, kicking up an urgent desire for freedom, and change leaves you teetering on the edge between genius and chaos.

APRIL

HIT THE GROUND RUNNING

Get excited about the first half of April because its cosmic energy can lift you to a higher level of happiness. The uncontainable Aries New Moon on **April 10** is an annual conjunction of the Sun and Moon in your sign, which usually brings a boost of energy and enthusiasm—and this one offers even more. Vivacious Venus and macho Mars join this New Moon, emphasizing playfulness, sex appeal, and creativity. This quartet of planets combines sensitivity with an inner fire that could make you more enchanting to others. But check your impulses when serious Saturn forms a constraining quincunx with spontaneous Uranus on **April 12**, the second of three aspects that began on **November 15, 2012**, and finishes on **October 5**. You may be expecting unanimous support for your escapades, but are more likely to be held back by a close friend or partner whose common sense exceeds your own.

Stability arrives with Venus's move into earthy Taurus and your 2nd House of Self-Worth on **April 15**, followed by the Sun on the **19th** and Mars on the **20th**. Slowing down to calculate expenditures of money and energy not only enables you to conserve now, but can lead to greater returns later. You may be surprised how much pleasure it brings to leisurely savor what you already have instead of racing toward the next object of desire. Responsible Saturn's conjunction with the relentless Scorpio Full Moon in your 8th House of Deep Sharing on **April 25** is further reminder to proceed with caution and respect the limits of others.

> ### KEEP IN MIND THIS MONTH
>
> *Putting your energy into cultivating the relationships and activities that have long-term value ensures that you will get to keep the best things that come your way.*

KEY DATES

APRIL 1 ★ *the power of your convictions*

You'll arouse enthusiasm in others today if you believe in what you say. The energetic Aries Sun's harmonious sextile with optimistic Jupiter expands your visions and empowers your words. If you speak from your heart, then you should have little difficulty connecting with positive people who encourage your growth.

APRIL 6–7 ★ *field of dreams*
You're living in either a state of grace or a world of illusion during these romantically charged days. Astrology's cosmic lovers, Venus and Mars, form sketchy semisquares with dreamy Neptune on **April 6** that can inspire desire and stimulate imagination. The upside of these transits is the sensitivity they bring to your relationships, giving you more compassion toward others. But on the downside, you could get lost in the fog of fantasy. Venus and Mars hook up in your sign on the **7th**, blessing you with the magic of attraction. Your confident charm enchants others to give you what you want, but you can also be content to enjoy the beauty of nature and art or be transported by the magic of music.

APRIL 13 ★ *mind on the run*
Messenger Mercury races into impetuous Aries to speed up your thinking and sharpen your mind. This is excellent for seeing the world with fresh eyes, discovering ideas and perspectives you never noticed before. Original concepts pop up quickly—and could burn out just as fast. Improvising is good in a pinch, but might lead to saying things that you regret. If you're dealing with a serious issue, reflect and do some research before making important statements.

SUPER NOVA DAY
APRIL 17 ★ *in the zone*
You are an unstoppable human laser beam today with the all-powerful Sun-Mars conjunction in aggressive Aries. This is a fireball of energy that triggers you to take immediate action. It helps if you already have a project you're trying to get off the ground or a new experience in which to pour your heart and soul. When you have a racetrack to run on you could be unbeatable, but if you're dealing with a humdrum day, your temper could get the best of you.

APRIL 26 ★ *gentle persuasion*
Adopt a softer approach to taking care of business today with instinctive Mars in a sweet sextile to compassionate Neptune. You instinctively know how to cajole people playfully instead of pushing them too hard. It's also beneficial to be less forceful with yourself, since tuning into your environment and catching the currents can take you where you want to go with less effort.

MAY

ON SHAKY GROUND

A pair of powerful eclipses this month takes you right to the precipice of change. On **May 9**, a Solar Eclipse in stubborn Taurus falls in your 2nd House of Resources, raising questions about finances and self-worth. If you've been sticking to an unrewarding job or investing too much in materials or skills that aren't paying off, it may be time to reassess your economic decisions. A Lunar Eclipse in adventurous Sagittarius on **May 25** rattles your 9th House of Travel and Higher Education. A stressful square to the Moon from imaginative Neptune can arouse fantasies of escape. Idealizing a place from your past might provide some inspiration, but it's more likely to distract you from discovering new ways to explore the world and broaden your mind. Yet even if you have your head in the clouds, your feet should remain on the ground when brainy Mercury travels through easygoing Taurus and your 2nd House on **May 1–15**.

Curiosity and flirtatiousness are part of the package when friendly Venus dances into lighthearted Gemini and your chatty 3rd House on **May 9**. You're more likely to appreciate people and activities in small doses now; boredom can set in very quickly. Mercury enters your 3rd House of Information on the **15th**, as does the Sun on the **20th**, brightening your days with a variety of experiences and people. Your willingness to talk about anything with just about anyone is excellent for opening new channels of communication. Just make sure that you're dealing with people who really understand a subject before you put your faith in what they say. Mars bounces into airy Gemini and Mercury swims into watery Cancer on the **31st**, encouraging casual behavior and subjective thinking.

> **KEEP IN MIND THIS MONTH**
>
> *You might find unfamiliar people and experiences so compelling that you (incorrectly) assume they will always intrigue you. Enjoy the moment without trying to make it last.*

KEY DATES

MAY 1 ★ *shoulder to the wheel*

Maintain a steady pace and focus on one job at a time if you hope to turn this frustrating day into a productive one. Active Mars's opposition to strict Saturn demands that you stick to a plan and not wander off track with clever improvisations. You have almost no room for error—and you will be reminded of this fact very quickly if you deviate from what's expected of you. Yet patiently attending to the toughest task can earn you some well-deserved respect.

SUPER NOVA DAYS
MAY 5–7 ★ *don't back down*
A Mercury-Saturn opposition on **May 5** could lead you into a confrontation with a negative person. Don't take no for an answer now since a potent Mars-Pluto trine gives you power and efficiency to overcome most obstacles. On **May 7,** you're filled with moneymaking ideas as a perceptive Mercury-Mars conjunction in your 2nd House of Resources urges you to fight for what you believe in with a combination of strength and persistence that's hard to resist. Your perspective is likely to prevail if your argument is based on reliable information.

MAY 13 ★ *dazed and confused*
Your emotions overcome your reason today as evaluating Venus forms a challenging square with fuzzy Neptune. Mars's conjunction with the karmic South Node of the Moon in Taurus provokes obstinate behavior when more creative perspectives are possible. A clever quintile between Mars and Neptune suggests that you may have more options at your disposal than you realize.

MAY 20 ★ *work in progress*
Two major outer planet aspects suggest that deeper changes are brewing. The last of three Jupiter-Saturn sesquisquares and the third of seven Uranus-Pluto squares lead you to adjust your long-range plans, especially those related to your career. Avoid rash decisions; external conditions are still in flux. Fortunately, the Sun's shift into adaptable Gemini indicates that there is more information coming. Remain flexible now until things settle down rather than forcing a showdown.

MAY 25–26 ★ *quick-change artist*
The fiery Sagittarius Lunar Eclipse on **May 25** supercharges the day while a stressful Mars-Pluto alignment intensifies the energy. The eclipse invites escapism, but Mars-Pluto plays for keeps. This is not the moment to fight; you may be standing on shifting ground. A squishy Sun-Neptune square on the **26th** is better suited for daydreaming than for arguing. Additionally, an excitable Mars-Uranus semisquare incites you to lash out against targets that aren't worthy of your attention. Adapting swiftly to suddenly changing circumstances works better than holding tightly to a rigid plan.

JUNE

BACK TO BASICS

The buzz you're feeling when June begins is likely to have you moving in many directions. Your ruling planet, Mars, along with the Sun in jumpy Gemini, incite you to flit restlessly from one activity to another. There's a subtle shift toward a more contemplative mood when lovely Venus enters caring Cancer and your 4th House of Home and Family on **June 2**. Nostalgia and domestic concerns pull on your heartstrings, leaving you more vulnerable. The jittery Gemini New Moon on the **8th** falls in your 3rd House of Communication, opening your mind to diverse people and subjects while increasing your distractions. On **June 11**, a subtle stabilizing force is the second of three trines between conscientious Saturn and idealistic Neptune that occurred on **October 10, 2012**, and will reoccur on **July 19**. Listen to an experienced individual whose hard-nosed pragmatism might help you make a dream come true.

Security is a top priority when the Sun shifts into protective Cancer on **June 21**, marking the Summer Solstice in your 4th House of Roots. Advancing your interests cautiously feels painfully ineffective, but it's healthier than forcing issues right now in your personal or professional life. The aspiring Capricorn Full Moon in your 10th House of Career on **June 23** could trigger a work-related crisis, yet is meant to highlight your long-term goals and push you to recognize the need for self-discipline. Lucky Jupiter's move into nurturing Cancer on the **25th** enriches your family life and encourages psychological development in the year ahead. However, it may take time to reach a deeper understanding of your desires, especially with fact-based Mercury turning retrograde on the **26th**. You'll need to do some backtracking before you are free to forge ahead.

> ### KEEP IN MIND THIS MONTH
>
> *You can't control what happens in the world, but you do have many options about how you manage your emotions. Attending to your inner needs makes everything else easier to handle.*

KEY DATES

JUNE 7–8 ★ *scenic detour*
You might drift off course on **June 7** when a fuzzy Mars-Neptune square favors fantasy and sacrifice over reason and ambition. Acting with compassion and

tapping into your imagination are desirable expressions of this tender transit. Although the antsy Gemini New Moon on the **8th** says *go*, a balky quincunx between forward-moving Mars and stand-still Saturn can block your progress. The point is not to stop completely but to redirect your efforts. If you encounter resistance, don't continue to push ahead or get bogged down in a battle. Navigating around (or adjusting your methods and expectations) is actually the most efficient way to get where you want to go.

JUNE 15–17 ★ *light at the end of the tunnel*
Mars in flighty Gemini likes to let you wander freely, but your ruling planet's clunky quincunx with fierce Pluto may extract a heavy price on **June 15**. Anger simmering below your surface could undermine a relationship—or erupt. Direct your attention to a single issue or emotion so you can address it with as much clarity and self-control as possible. Cleaning up clutter and finishing off minor tasks are beneficial ways to use this nervous energy. Pressure drops on the **17th** when Mars slides into an easy sextile with unconventional Uranus. This dynamic duo offers a sense of freedom that lets your intuition flow and your creativity shine.

JUNE 19–21 ★ *home sweet home*
Your brain is bursting with ideas and your inbox overflowing with messages when the Sun joins boundless Jupiter on **June 19**. This expansive event in your 3rd House of Information adds enthusiasm to your words and enhances your capacity for learning. Verbal Mercury's conjunction with affectionate Venus on the **20th** is in your private 4th House, creating an excellent moment for discussing personal matters with care and tenderness. The Sun's sweep into this intimate part of your chart on the **21st** lights the home fires and instills a sense of belonging that makes you feel more secure.

JUNE 27–28 ★ *all the world's your stage*
Stylish Venus sashays into loud Leo and your 5th House of Romance on **June 27** to lift your spirits and raise your personal profile. Your playful spirit and warmhearted generosity make you and whatever you propose more appealing. Recognizing the limits of others, though, is essential for avoiding stress when Mars tangles with authoritative Saturn on the **28th**.

JULY

STAIRWAY TO HEAVEN

You reach a more profound understanding of your life's purpose this month with a rare Grand Water Trine flooding your most sensitive houses. Philosophical Jupiter in your 4th House of Roots aligns harmoniously with pragmatic Saturn in your 8th House of Intimacy and metaphysical Neptune in your 12th House of Spirituality on **July 17–19**, giving you a broader vision of your past that helps you map out a clearer picture of the future. Your key planet, Mars, joins this planetary pattern on the **20th**, enabling you to turn these insights into constructive action. There are, though, some hurdles and some helpers along the way. The Sun's opposition to powerful Pluto on **July 1** and square to shocking Uranus on the **4th** could push you to a breaking point where you're ready to abandon your responsibilities. However, these aspects are meant to provoke a reassessment of your professional goals and family obligations. With a little patience and persistence, you can tap into unused resources and unmet desires that spur radically new approaches.

A subtle sense of order begins to take shape in your life with structuring Saturn's forward turn and a loving Cancer New Moon in your 4th House on the **8th**. You may not see exactly where you're going yet, but a slow-rising tide of hope lifts your spirits. Fleet-footed Mercury's shift to direct motion on **July 20** helps you gather scattered thoughts and pull them together into a coherent vision. The Sun strides into bold Leo and your 5th House of Self-Expression on the **22nd**, just before the Full Moon in socially conscious Aquarius. Learning how to navigate from being a star (Leo) to being a valuable teammate (Aquarius) is the challenge and gift of this lunation.

> **KEEP IN MIND THIS MONTH**
>
> *Think strategically; calibrating today's actions in terms of tomorrow's goals may seem less efficient now, but will pay big dividends later.*

KEY DATES

JULY 4–5 ★ *velvet revolution*

These are a couple of edgy days when your impatience and a desire to do things your own way could spark conflict. The Sun's harsh square to independent Uranus on **July 4** amplifies your hunger for freedom. You meet even the slightest hint of authority with a rebellious attitude and, perhaps, a desire to flee. Yet on the **5th**, Mars forms an imaginative quintile with Uranus that might give you the liberty you need without creating a ruckus. Trying unconventional approaches to problems can help you avoid a crisis. Still, a delicate semisquare between lovable Venus and aggressive Mars reflects social awkwardness or insecurity. If you can take criticism lightly and without judging others, your vulnerability will invite sweet connections instead of feelings of rejection.

JULY 12–13 ★ *try a little tenderness*

Mars's uncomfortable connection with the Moon's North Node on **July 12** can trigger irritable interactions with others. If you're feeling stressed or fatigued, it's best to put off serious discussions. Mars enters hesitant Cancer and your 4th House of Roots on the **13th**. You may be less available to the outer world while you attend to family matters and your own emotional needs. Your energy might not flow as freely since the spontaneity that allows you to act first and reflect later is frowned upon in this supersensitive sign.

SUPER NOVA DAYS
JULY 20–22 ★ *shoot for the stars*

Mars's trines to stabilizing Saturn and altruistic Neptune on **July 20** create a beautiful blend of structure and imagination. You can be productive in an easygoing way that allows you to enjoy whatever tasks you undertake when Mars joins opportunistic Jupiter on the **22nd** to arouse ambitious dreams of travel and adventure. But if you're constrained from thinking big, or don't get the physical exercise you need, you could be steaming with anger or resentment. Venus's entry into detail-oriented Virgo and your 6th House of Service might bog you down in petty tasks. However, if you want to launch a new enterprise and reach the heights of success, you'll need to master all the small steps along the way.

JULY 27 ★ *let go to grow*

It's better to do one thing with all your heart than to spread yourself too thin today. Mars's opposition to purging Pluto and the Sun's square to demanding Saturn reward you for your concentrated efforts. Your intense emotions could incite a heated battle; try to focus your passion on building something special, not tearing someone down.

AUGUST

TURN PLAY INTO PAY

You reach new heights of creativity with the Sun in dramatic Leo and your 5th House of Romance and Self-Expression until **August 22**. Remember, though, not to use this gift to play games when you could invest your energy in more important matters. The first of three powerful oppositions between enterprising Jupiter and transformational Pluto falls in your security-oriented 4th and 10th Houses on **August 7**. This can trigger a crisis at home or on the job that has you scrambling for safety—or, better, reviving an ambitious professional plan. This aspect recurs on **January 31** and **April 20, 2014**, providing two more chances to put these powerful planetary forces to practical use. The audacious Leo New Moon on the **6th** trines rebellious Uranus, triggering an urge for personal freedom and sparking originality. Communicative Mercury's move into your demonstrative 5th House on the **8th** makes your creative voice loud enough for everyone to hear.

Lovely Venus moves into relationship-oriented Libra and your 7th House of Partners on **August 16**, encouraging a sense of fair play in love and money. Keeping your allies on your side requires that you pay as much attention to their needs as your own. Your bright ideas may get your foot in the door, but without listening to others you won't be able to close the deal. The Aquarius Full Moon on the **20th** shines in your 11th House of Groups, challenging you to be a better friend and teammate. Learning how to adjust your methods of working is especially important with the Sun's move into modest Virgo and your 6th House of Service on **August 22**. Mental Mercury follows on the **23rd**, making this an excellent time to sharpen old skills and develop new ones.

> ### KEEP IN MIND THIS MONTH
>
> *Getting attention is not the same as getting results. When you make a good impression, follow it up with hard work to maximize the return on your efforts.*

KEY DATES

AUGUST 1–2 ★ *sweet and sour*

Your restless spirit and natural resistance to rules put you in a less-than-cooperative mood. You're still resonating from yesterday's explosive Mars-Uranus square, and now you face a manipulative Sun-Pluto quincunx on **August 1** that can stir up power struggles. Fortunately, Mars forms an efficient trine with the Moon's North Node that guides you to resolve relationship problems—as long as your head doesn't get in the way of your heart. In fact, you can be downright flirtatious on the **2nd**, with a saucy little Venus-Mars sextile adding delicious delight to your day.

AUGUST 11 ★ *changing currents*

Your work habits may be a little loose with a casual Mars-Neptune sesquisquare that's better for noodling around than being efficient. However, a sharp-eyed square between analytical Mercury and exacting Saturn helps you notice any errors and comment on them critically. Be perfectly clear with others about your intentions now to avoid hurt feelings later. Carefully choosing when to allow your mind to wander and when to concentrate inspires you to gracefully shift gears in response to these contrasting forces.

SUPER NOVA DAYS
AUGUST 19–21 ★ *embrace the unknown*

On **August 19**, the occasionally arrogant Leo Sun in your outgoing 5th House clashes with a square between bombastic Jupiter and wayward Uranus on the **21st**. These aspects can provoke reckless behavior and self-aggrandizing statements that may be difficult to substantiate. The idealistic Aquarius Full Moon on the **20th** also inspires you to work for an important cause, but circumstances are too volatile to be sure that your belief is well founded. Open your mind and start gathering information instead of making any serious promises or commitments. Philosophical Jupiter squares radical Uranus again on **February 26** and **April 20, 2014**, in a long-lasting process that can drastically change your perspective. Determine whether your expectations have a realistic chance of success before putting all your eggs in one basket.

AUGUST 27 ★ *love without limits*

Excess and self-indulgence entice you as your key planet, Mars, prances into your 5th House of Fun and Games while pleasure-loving Venus forms an unstable square with limitless Jupiter. You might overspend, oversell, or desire someone or something that costs a great deal more than it's worth. Stretching the boundaries of play and self-expression is fine as long as you don't push them beyond the breaking point.

SEPTEMBER

THE DEVIL'S IN THE DETAILS

Your success this month could hinge on your willingness to pay more attention to minor matters, even if they seem petty. The New Moon in precise Virgo occurs in your 6th House of Service on **September 5**, and you may feel picked on by overly critical people or stuck with boring tasks. But the New Moon's favorable sextile to benevolent Jupiter offers a world of opportunities if you become more conscientious about your work. Listening with an open mind becomes particularly valuable when verbal Mercury enters diplomatic Libra and your 7th House of Partners on the **9th**. Don't rush to respond to delicate questions; thinking through your answers lets you stand up for your side without alienating others. Relationship-conscious Venus's move into intense Scorpio and your 8th House of Deep Sharing on the **11th** is another signal to deal with people in a more thoughtful and considerate manner.

On **September 19**, the dreamy Pisces Full Moon in your 12th House of Secrets underscores the importance of discretion. You may want more time alone now, so make sure to monitor your energy levels and take breaks before you wear yourself out. Quiet communion with nature, contemplation of life's meaning, and other spiritual pursuits nourish your soul and enrich your inner world. You are able to accumulate professional power with subtlety and grace on the **21st** when ambitious Saturn makes its last sextile to generous Jupiter in a series that began on **December 26, 2012**, and repeated on **March 8**. The Sun's entry into cooperative Libra and your 7th House on **September 22** marks the Vernal Equinox, drawing creative, confident, and charming partners your way.

> **KEEP IN MIND THIS MONTH**
>
> *If you feel hemmed in by a million and one little tasks, make each one a tiny work of art and you'll weave together a rich tapestry of fulfillment.*

KEY DATES

SEPTEMBER 2 ★ *not so fast*

A cranky, impulsive Mercury-Mars semisquare can trigger thoughtless remarks that you may immediately regret. When you feel the heat of emotion rising, take a deep breath and consider the consequences before speaking. Mars's confusing quincunx with surreal Neptune tends to turn you around in circles instead of leading you where you want to go. Don't just push harder out of frustration; slowing down and rethinking your course is more likely to get you back on track.

SUPER NOVA DAYS
SEPTEMBER 9-11 ★ *all or nothing*

Patience, planning, and practice are needed on **September 9**, when rambunctious Mars in your 5th House of Play crosses paths in a tense square to humorless Saturn in your 8th House of Intimacy. No matter how entertaining you are now, your audience may not be in a responsive mood. Still, you can earn respect by working hard to complete one essential task— and gaining the trust of a demanding person may be worth the effort. The air is still thick on the **11th**, because a disturbing Mars-Pluto quincunx impedes your progress with power struggles. If you choose to engage in a battle and expect to win, be sure that you're ready to take it to the limit. However, you might suddenly realize that it's not worth the risk and wisely step aside.

SEPTEMBER 14 ★ *element of surprise*

An inventive Mars-Uranus trine reveals new and unusual ways to deal with adversaries or tackle tough jobs. Brilliant originality empowers you to perform what may look like a miracle to worriers and doubters who expect you to fail.

SEPTEMBER 17 ★ *smooth operator*

You are both clever and efficient today with a slick sextile between smart Mercury and speedy Mars on your side. Your sharp thinking and fresh insights enable you to express yourself with good-natured humor, making your messages easy to understand and delightful to hear.

SEPTEMBER 26-28 ★ *opposites attract*

The Sun forms an irritating semisquare to impatient Mars on **September 26**, stirring up trouble. You can, however, consciously apply this high-octane energy with a soft touch that works to your advantage. Try standing up for yourself with a smile, or gently pushing with a positive attitude. A sexy Venus-Mars square on the **28th** blurs the line between flirting and fighting, making it nearly impossible to know where you stand with someone. It's natural to have mixed feelings that might provoke irrational behavior, but avoid going too far and too fast too soon.

OCTOBER

THE PERILS AND PLEASURES OF PARTNERSHIP

Fasten your seat belt, because a wild New Moon in your 7th House of Partners on **October 4** can take you and your relationships on a roller-coaster ride. A Sun-Moon conjunction in lovely Libra is normally associated with making sweet alliances and comfortable new connections. This lunation, however, opposes disruptive Uranus and squares provocative Pluto, which can incite power struggles and sudden shifts of circumstances and moods. Remaining reasonable when you deal with emotionally inconsistent people and calming your own volcanic feelings can make the difference between war and peace now. You're tempted to run from demanding unions on the **7th** when romantic Venus enters carefree Sagittarius and your 9th House of Faraway Places. Pursuing interests in travel, higher learning, and people from different cultures will be rewarding as long as you're not using them to escape your current reality.

Once your ruling planet, Mars, moves into precise Virgo and your 6th House of Work on **October 15**, focus on refining old methods and applying your creativity in practical ways. If you're bored by your job, investing energy in a hobby or developing a new skill should perk you up. The independent Aries Full Moon on the **18th** lands in your 1st House of Personality as a reminder to address your own needs before worrying about others. The happier you are now, the more valuable you'll be to those around you. On **October 21**, rational Mercury's retrograde turn in your 8th House of Intimacy reminds you to back up and renegotiate your relationships. The Sun's shift into intuitive Scorpio and your 8th House on the **23rd** attracts strong partners and shows how teaming up with the right people will add power and passion to your life.

> ### KEEP IN MIND THIS MONTH
>
> *Expressing what you want from others is the essential first step to clearing the air and getting the most out of your alliances.*

KEY DATES

OCTOBER 2 ★ *fixer-upper*

A clever quintile between inquisitive Mercury and enterprising Mars reveals shortcuts and inspires creative problem-solving ideas. Now is the perfect time for untangling misunderstandings related to money and love. If you feel stuck in an unhappy situation, look a bit deeper—you'll probably find a surprising solution.

SUPER NOVA DAYS
OCTOBER 4-7 ★ *taking it up a notch*
If you feel suffocated by any external pressure right now, it's because Mars's strange sesquisquares to suspicious Pluto on **October 5** and nervous Uranus on the **7th** indicate serious irritations. These hard aspects with astrology's two most disruptive planets on the heels of the ambiguous Libra New Moon on the **4th** can intensify complex relationship issues. You're ready to push back with anger—which is understandable, but it's also more likely to aggravate the tension than resolve it. If you can instead apply these kinetic forces with conscious intent and originality, you could get out of a rut and create exciting new avenues of personal and professional expression.

OCTOBER 19 ★ *sweet surrender*
Today your ruling planet, hard-charging Mars, opposes spacey Neptune. It's a slippery aspect that can lead you astray, tricking you into chasing illusions or working with unreliable individuals. Demonstrating a tender touch, acting with compassion, following your intuition, and engaging in metaphysical activities are all ways to stay on your spiritual path.

OCTOBER 24 ★ *larger than life*
You're tempted to take on more than you can handle or promise more than you can deliver with active Mars's inelegant semisquare to exuberant Jupiter. There's nothing wrong with high aspirations, but your tendency to go too far or too fast won't help you reach your goals. If you're overflowing with energy, full of self-righteousness, or fed up and ready to fight, think carefully before firing the first shot. Retrograde Mercury's smart quintile with Mars is excellent for reviewing your current plans and tying up loose ends.

OCTOBER 31 ★ *keep your eyes on the prize*
Establish well-defined priorities and you'll have a highly productive day. A powerful Mars-Pluto trine is your sword for cutting through clutter, eliminating obstacles, and acting with quiet authority. You can finally complete unfinished business you've been avoiding. Don't lose sight of your primary objectives—a quirky Mars-Uranus quincunx is liable to interrupt you with unexpected distractions.

NOVEMBER

RELATIONSHIP REALIGNMENT

There are rumbles of change bubbling below the surface that could break through and alter the nature of an important partnership this month. November starts with the fourth of seven transformational squares between Uranus and Pluto on the **1st** that ratchets up tension between your need for independence and the heavy hand of authority that's thwarting your progress. On the **3rd**, a Solar Eclipse in power-sensitive Scorpio joins sobering Saturn in your 8th House of Intimacy, which forces you to make a tough decision. You can commit to work harder to keep a valuable alliance afloat—or recognize that you're not going to get what you want from it. Either way, it's better to make a choice than have one imposed upon you. Philosophical Jupiter's retrograde turn in your 4th House of Roots on **November 7** invites reflection as you look back to the past and reorient your plans for the future.

On **November 10**, mobile Mercury begins moving forward again in your 8th House to facilitate communication in critical collaborations. Think carefully before you speak or react to what others say since words have more impact than usual now. On the **17th**, the sensible Taurus Full Moon falls in your 2nd House of Self-Worth, spurring moneymaking ideas and encouraging resourceful behavior. The Sun shoots into visionary Sagittarius and your 9th House of Travel and Higher Education on the **21st**, lifting your focus above the normal fray of daily life to visualize a more expansive future. Aiming higher infuses you with hope, but the Sun's stressful square with nebulous Neptune on the **24th** could carry you beyond the bounds of reason.

> **KEEP IN MIND THIS MONTH**
>
> *Don't settle for less from the key people in your life. Define your needs and ask for what you want if you hope to be rewarded with greater returns.*

KEY DATES

SUPER NOVA DAYS
NOVEMBER 1–3 ★ *nothing ventured, nothing gained*
An alert sextile between curious Mercury and capable Mars on **November 1** can guide you through the rapids of intense emotions that are churning now. The creative consciousness of the Sun's sextile to Mars on the **3rd** helps you stay on course during the day's complicated New Moon Eclipse in passionate Scorpio. In fact, you might even be able to turn a loss into a gain if you are

persistent, persuasive, and know exactly what you want. It's understandable if frustration drives you to think about going it alone, but the challenge of working with a demanding colleague pays off if you don't give up.

NOVEMBER 9 ★ *efficiency expert*
This is a very productive day, for a hardworking Mars-Saturn sextile provides you with a perfect balance of effort and discipline. You can assess a task and complete it without wasting a single move. Make the time to sharpen your skills, especially when you have an experienced teacher to show you the ropes.

NOVEMBER 14–15 ★ *on-the-job jitters*
Expect the unexpected on **November 14–15**, when valuable Venus in your 10th House of Career forms hard aspects. You may experience upsets at work when an unpredictable square with Uranus brings surprises, and resentment may be evoked as Venus conjuncts punishing Pluto. But if you're willing to be flexible and handle awkward individuals and unexpected situations, you could earn new respect. On the other hand, boredom or unfair working conditions might provoke you to think about changing your place of employment.

NOVEMBER 19 ★ *lean on me*
Competent Mars in your 6th House of Skills cruises into a cool sextile with optimistic Jupiter, showcasing your ability to manage complex tasks with an easygoing attitude. Even if you're so busy that you feel pulled in several directions, you know how to prioritize your time and set a good example for others. If co-workers or customers are nervous and insecure, your calm steadiness under pressure can reduce everyone's stress.

NOVEMBER 29 ★ *in it to win it*
The confident Sun in upbeat Sagittarius sometimes leads you to promise more than you can deliver or raises your own expectations too high. But today's creative solar quintile to Mars in practical Virgo gives you the tools to expand your reach while keeping your feet firmly on the ground. If you have an idea to pitch, a product to sell, or a job you want, this dynamic Sun-Mars connection shows others that your high level of enthusiasm is rooted in a deep commitment and reinforced by your capability to justify it.

DECEMBER

OVER THE RAINBOW

You are drawn toward extreme adventure this month; distant places and mind-expanding activities are calling you to fly far away. On **December 2**, the restless Sagittarius New Moon falls in your 9th House of Big Ideas, arousing the desire to widen your horizons. Metaphysical Neptune's square to this lunation taps into a spiritual yearning or, less desirably, pulls you toward unrealistic fantasies that are likely to remain out of reach. Innovative Uranus, though, forms a favorable trine to this Sun-Moon conjunction, creating unexpected opportunities for travel and learning. This is perfect timing since intellectual Mercury launches into cavalier Sagittarius on the **4th** to open your mind and inspire bolder speech. Your ruling planet, Mars, enters diplomatic Libra and your 7th House of Partners on **December 7**, an excellent time for initiating new connections, taking a current relationship to a higher level, or going public with an important project. Still, be sure to tread lightly and listen to the feedback you receive rather than plunging ahead impulsively.

The Full Moon in versatile Gemini on **December 17** kicks up communication in your 3rd House of Data Collection. Chatting with others is useful for gathering information, especially when it comes to filling in the blanks where you have big ideas but lack some key data. The Winter Solstice is marked by the Sun's entry into responsible Capricorn and your 10th House of Career on the 21st, boosting your ambition and increasing your public responsibilities. Amicable Venus, also in the 10th House, turns retrograde later in the day, reminding you to repair professional relationships and perhaps reconnect with old colleagues. Mercury moves into your 10th House on the **24th**, challenging you to clear your mind and get busy organizing work-related projects.

KEEP IN MIND THIS MONTH

It's easy to find the motivation and discipline to persevere through thick and thin when you are reaching for a goal that passionately inspires you.

KEY DATES
DECEMBER 3 ★ *sharp as a tack*
Mercury in discerning Scorpio and your 8th House of Deep Sharing sextiles Mars in your practical 6th House of Habits, clarifying your thinking and adding powerful impact to your message. Today you're a more critical listener who quickly understands which information will be most useful and which to ignore. You'll find it easier now to nudge an ally in any direction you want her or him to go.

DECEMBER 9 ★ *give peace a chance*
You're able to stand up for yourself today in a pleasant, nonthreatening manner when Mars in gracious Libra forms a creative quintile with opinionated Jupiter in self-protective Cancer. If you're avoiding a confrontation because you're worried about starting a fight, this transit provides the finesse to make your points and gain the support of someone who might have been your adversary, but is now more likely to become your friend.

DECEMBER 13–15 ★ *stay on the straight and narrow*
You struggle to maintain your equilibrium with others when Mars slips on a banana peel of a quincunx to woozy Neptune on **December 13**. You might be able to work around a problem, but you're equally likely to waste time with distractions or avoidance techniques. If you happen to wander off course, a stressful aspect from exigent Saturn to Mars on the **14th** holds you accountable. However, your willingness to pay attention to external signals can work wonders on the **15th** thanks to the efficiency of an intelligent Mercury-Mars quintile.

DECEMBER 25 ★ *independence day*
Expect an explosive holiday with an electrifying Mars-Uranus opposition ready to unleash surprises and undercut cooperation. Your nervous energy and impatience could accumulate and mar your judgment, perhaps even leading to an argument or accident. But instead of acting rashly or rebelling against old rules and traditions just to be contrary, seek a fresh way to celebrate that captures the brilliance of this dynamic aspect in a positive manner.

SUPER NOVA DAYS
DECEMBER 30–31 ★ *yell fire!*
The year ends with a bang as an anti-authoritarian Sun-Uranus square and a ruthless Mars-Pluto square ignite rebellious feelings on **December 30**. It might not take much to push your buttons; powerful emotions have already been growing and are ripe for expression. Mouthy Mercury enters the picture on the **31st** with a conjunction to potent Pluto and a provocative square to combative Mars that could produce angry words. Taming your temper and saying what's on your mind with as much self-restraint as possible could avoid an end-of-the-year meltdown.

TAURUS

APRIL 20–MAY 20

TAURUS

2012 SUMMARY

Even when you're sure that you're right on track for love, fame, or fortune, a detour can lead you to a more rewarding path. Like a fine wine, you and your concepts will increase in value when you don't rush the process. One secret to cashing in on this journey is to develop additional skills and seek extra revenue streams. When your apprenticeship is over, it's time to face your allies and your adversaries from a position of greater authority.

AUGUST—*step up to the plate*
Although you may feel stuck, it's crucial to keep your life in motion as the pressure for change mounts.

SEPTEMBER—*it's showtime*
Acting more boldly in pursuit of your interests not only attracts attention, but also keeps you from worrying too much about the little things.

OCTOBER—*heart-to-heart*
It's okay to expect more from your relationships as long as you're willing to make the personal commitment necessary to reach common ground.

NOVEMBER—*life in the balance*
Changing your mind after serious reflection is a viable option right now. Admitting your mistakes is a sign of strength rather than weakness.

DECEMBER—*beyond the horizon*
You'll be much better off making thoughtful decisions based on where they will take you in the years ahead rather than shortsighted, random moves.

2012 CALENDAR

AUGUST

THU 2 ★	Take what you hear with a grain of salt
TUE 7–THU 9 ★	Set aside some time for pleasure
WED 15–FRI 17 ★	**SUPER NOVA DAYS** Secrets may surface that rock relationships
WED 22–THU 23 ★	Settling for less is not a viable option

SEPTEMBER

MON 3 ★	Heed the advice of an astute friend
WED 5–FRI 7 ★	Open your heart and mind, but don't go too far
THU 13 ★	Stretch your limits
THU 20–FRI 21 ★	Good humor keeps tension from getting out of hand
TUE 25–SAT 29 ★	**SUPER NOVA DAYS** Initiate an honest dialogue

OCTOBER

TUE 2–WED 3 ★	Don't lose touch with common sense
MON 8–WED 10 ★	Be very astute about people and money
TUE 16–WED 17 ★	A dose of reality is disappointing if you've gone too far
MON 22–THU 25 ★	**SUPER NOVA DAYS** Avoid making promises you can't keep
SUN 28–MON 29 ★	Your words are packed with more punch than you realize

NOVEMBER

THU 1–SUN 4 ★	Look before you leap
FRI 9 ★	Promise only what you can deliver
SAT 17–SUN 18 ★	Conversations reveal secrets that challenge relationships
WED 21–THU 22 ★	Desires can move beyond the bounds of reason
MON 26–THU 29 ★	**SUPER NOVA DAYS** Set relationship agendas with clarity

DECEMBER

SAT 1–SUN 2 ★	It's tempting to overdo just about everything
MON 10–WED 12 ★	**SUPER NOVA DAYS** Follow your heart bravely
SAT 15–SUN 16 ★	Be wary of impractical choices about love or money
FRI 21–SAT 22 ★	Find a healthy balance between hope and realism

TAURUS OVERVIEW

This year will demand a lot of flexibility from you. Change continues to accelerate, uncovering new interests, testing your current relationships, and altering the purpose of your life. It's natural for a steadfast Taurus to hold on to the status quo, rather than adapting to shifting circumstances. Fortunately, this process will grow easier once you realize that resistance is futile. **You can go kicking and screaming into a future that's different from the one you were anticipating, or you can use this year as an opportunity to reinvent yourself.** Neptune's entry into imaginative Pisces and your 11th House of Dreams and Wishes on February 3, 2012, began a protracted revisioning process of your long-term goals. Now it's time to weed out the impractical fantasies and transform your vision into reality. Fortunately, you receive constructive assistance from levelheaded Saturn's harmonious trines to illusory Neptune on June 11 and July 19 in an aspect series that began on October 10, 2012. Accurately separating fact from fancy now clarifies decisions that were previously unclear.

The greatest pressure for change comes on May 20 and November 1, when revolutionary Uranus forms dynamic squares with evolutionary Pluto in a recurring pattern that started on June 24, 2012, and finishes on March 16, 2015. Most likely, you have already encountered unexpected developments in your life since Uranus entered spontaneous Aries on March 11, 2011. Its seven-year visit to your 12th House of Destiny continues to bring sudden twists and turns on the road of life. **With Uranus's current squares to Pluto in your 9th House of Higher Truth, you may be questioning the ultimate meaning of your existence, reconsidering your priorities, and developing new goals.** Since you're usually quite practical in your thinking, the unconventional, conceptual, and theoretical realms you must now explore will certainly stretch your mind in ways you cannot yet imagine.

On a more pragmatic level, taskmaster Saturn in passionate Scorpio spends the entire year visiting your 7th House of Others. **Working in a partnership can bring challenges, but the rewards will follow if you're willing to set aside your fears, look deeply within for answers, and learn from those around you.** Saturn's cooperative sextiles with transformative Pluto on December 26, 2012, and March 8 and September 21 offer you chances to negotiate without compromising your basic values. Despite all the changes and challenges you must face, your confidence is high as jovial Jupiter moves through your 2nd

House of Self-Worth for the first half of the year. On June 25, Jupiter enters nurturing Cancer and your 3rd House of Immediate Environment, where it remains until July 16, 2014, giving you chances to learn without traveling far from home. Harmonious trines between expansive Jupiter and contractive Saturn on July 17 and December 12 enable you to see the big picture, create strategies for success, and execute your plans so you can reach your goals.

LABOR OF LOVE

Love may not be all fun and games this year, but your willingness to confront difficult issues can help strengthen a close relationship. Nevertheless, your patience will be tested as your 7th House of Companions plays host to Saturn the Tester. Learning by trial and error could help you discover how to keep an intimate relationship alive, even if it goes through a cooling period. A new romance might prove to be more enduring if you take it slow instead of rushing in. The emotionally intense Scorpio Lunar Eclipse on April 25 and the Scorpio Solar Eclipse on November 3 rattle your 7th House. Both eclipses conjunct Saturn, forcing you to clarify what you want and pushing you to work harder to get it. Your ruler, Venus, is the planet of love, and her conjunction with joyful Jupiter on May 28 can spark a new romance or rejuvenate an old one. Also, a positive Venus aspect to trustworthy Saturn on November 23 suggests a happy ending—as long as you don't take any shortcuts to pleasure along the way.

PARTNERS IN CRIME

Although you may have very specific ideas about your career objectives, other people can greatly contribute to your success this year. Ironically, hard-nosed Saturn in your 7th House of Partnerships leaves you feeling unsupported by your closest allies. But their negativity is not meant to discourage you; instead, use constructive criticism to spur you on to even bigger accomplishments. A stabilizing Grand Water Trine on July 17–20 is a perfect time to take on a new project or job, because Saturn harmonizes with optimistic Jupiter, visionary Neptune, and go-getter Mars. The Jupiter-Saturn trine recurs on December 12, bringing rewards for your hard work.

COUNT YOUR OPTIONS

Generous Jupiter in versatile Gemini visits your 2nd House of Money through June 25, offering a variety of ways for you to increase your income. The additional presence of value-conscious Venus on May 9–June 2 opens more doors, but a Taurus Solar Eclipse on May 9 cautions you against oversimplifying complex issues. Waiting to ask for a raise until May 27–28 when Mercury and Venus conjunct benevolent Jupiter could result in a financial windfall. You could make money from a creative venture when Venus visits your 5th House of Self-Expression on July 22–August 16. However, it's smart to tuck away some cash early in the year since you might experience a shortfall when luxury-loving Venus joins up with stingy Saturn on September 18.

CURB YOUR APPETITE

Managing unhealthy stress and establishing healthy limits may be your best insurance policies this year. Opulent Jupiter forms uneasy squares with wounded Chiron on January 15 and March 27, tempting you to ignore your limits and seek satisfaction by overindulging your senses. Such excess can tax your body, with fleeting pleasures leading to physical symptoms. Fortunately, it's easier to practice self-discipline when austere Saturn trines Chiron on March 21 and October 2. A Solar Eclipse in your normally steady sign on May 9 leaves you anxious about changes that seem to be beyond your control. But enrolling in a yoga class, practicing meditation, and exploring other methods of relaxation lessen the wear and tear on your body and can set new habits in motion that improve your health for life. Remember that proactive behavior, including regular exercise and a healthy diet, positively impacts your physical well-being.

QUIET ON THE HOME FRONT

There isn't a lot of planetary activity that directly influences your domestic life this year, prompting you to reach out into your community to augment your sense of family. Idealistic Neptune's long-term visit to your 11th House of Friends can inspire you to open your home to a wider network. Participating in a group offers practical benefits unless you sacrifice your identity for its benefit. The independent Sagittarius Full Moon Eclipse on May 25 activates your 8th House of Shared

Resources as it dynamically squares spacey Neptune. Don't rely on others to meet your needs—take initiative to create comfort at home. Pleasurable Venus visits your 4th House of Domestic Conditions on June 27–July 22, encouraging you to relax and indulge yourself with your friends and family.

ANYTHING IS POSSIBLE

Adventurous Jupiter's visit to your 3rd House of Short Trips from June 25 to July 16, 2014, suggests that you'll be more inclined to take a quick weekend getaway than go on an extended jungle safari. However, mysterious Pluto is camped out in your 9th House of Journeys, and the squares from unexpected Uranus on May 20 and November 1 could present sudden opportunities to go to more exotic destinations. Regardless of the distance involved, your experiences can profoundly transform your perspective, especially when Jupiter opposes Pluto on August 7 and squares Uranus on August 21.

EMBRACE THE UNKNOWN

Although you're more secure when you're in familiar intellectual and philosophical surroundings, this is your year to step out and dig into something new and different. This penchant for the unknown could have started when unconventional Uranus entered your 12th House of Imagination in 2011; regardless, accept that your old worldview has outlived its purpose. The pioneering Aries Lunar Eclipse on October 18 illuminates your spiritual 12th House, while self-directed Mars opposes otherworldly Neptune, making this an ideal time to go on a retreat to deepen your spirituality and self-understanding.

> ### RICK & JEFF'S TIP FOR THE YEAR:
> A Brand-New You
>
> The world is in a state of metamorphosis—and you have no choice but to evolve with it. Too much resistance will only heighten your frustration and leave you unhappy. In the long run, everything must change, including you. However, once you realize the inevitability of this break from the past, you'll see exciting opportunities and also grow enthusiastic about the new life that lies ahead.

JANUARY

STATE YOUR INTENTIONS

Starting the year with your feet firmly on the ground is important to you because three planets in orderly Capricorn emphasize your innate need for stability. The lingering effects of a cooperative sextile between persistent Saturn and potent Pluto that was exact on **December 26, 2012**, give you the stamina to take on a heavy workload this month. Your analytical skills are especially sharp on **January 6**, when logical Mercury joins Pluto in your 9th House of Future Vision. Your desire to achieve success grows stronger on **January 8** as your key planet, Venus, enters Capricorn. The calculating Capricorn New Moon on **January 11** plants a seed for the upcoming cycle, with five planets now congregating in your inspirational 9th House. However, reality can throw you an exciting yet destabilizing curveball on the **12th** when attractive Venus dynamically squares anything-can-happen Uranus.

Suppressed passions push into awareness on **January 16–17**, deepening the bonds of a partnership as loving Venus joins unwavering Pluto and is strengthened by stabilizing Saturn. Fortunately, you're able to put your theories into practice when brainy Mercury and the radiant Sun enter conceptual Aquarius and your 10th House of Career on **January 19**. Although harmonious aspects from Mercury and the Sun to independent Uranus and broad-minded Jupiter on **January 22–25** allow you to advance comfortably into new territory, stressful squares to restrictive Saturn on the **25th** and **30th** set obstacles in your path that could require you to make difficult decisions. Meanwhile, the self-centered Leo Full Moon on **January 26** illuminates your 4th House of Roots, shifting your attention away from your career and toward more personal concerns.

KEEP IN MIND THIS MONTH

Setting goals can be tricky if your aspirations are unrealistic, because you could end up disappointed. Still, you must stretch beyond your comfort zone to experience meaningful growth.

KEY DATES

JANUARY 3–4 ★ *think outside the box*

Your neurons are firing rapidly, connecting the facts in unexpected ways when mental Mercury squares electrifying Uranus on **January 3**. Just remember that your thinking may be unreliable, with ideas heading off in one direction, only to end up somewhere totally different. Instead of attempting to control the process, follow your intuition and enjoy unusual perspectives without too many expectations. Fortunately, propitious Jupiter forms a smooth trine to inexhaustible Mars in your 10th House of Status on **January 4**; you can expect a productive outcome from your mental gymnastics, no matter where you land.

JANUARY 11-14 ★ *stop and ask for directions*

You might believe you have it all together during the industrious Capricorn New Moon on **January 11** because you can make sense out of complex situations and work them to your advantage. However, your skillful calculations may not be enough to contain your impulsive desires when sensual Venus squares radical Uranus on the **12th**. A stressful Mercury-Jupiter aspect on **January 14** encourages you to gloss over the details, and Venus's ill-adjusted quincunx to indulgent Jupiter the same day reinforces your confidence that you're on track—when in truth you've most likely lost your way. Discussing your options with someone you trust can help you to find your bearings.

SUPER NOVA DAYS
JANUARY 22-26 ★ *a thrill a minute*

You can demonstrate your brilliance with new projects at work when clever Mercury forms a supportive sextile with erratic Uranus and a free-flowing trine with lucky Jupiter on **January 22**. However, you could feel as if you have so much information, you don't know where to begin. Exciting opportunities continue to come your way as the Sun follows suit with its sextile to Uranus on the **24th** and trine to Jupiter on the **25th**. Fortunately, you are able to move beyond your inclination to resist change and adapt to the transforming landscape. Nevertheless, you may reach your limit, announcing your intentions to return to stable ground as the dramatic Leo Full Moon on **January 26** overwhelms you with emotions. However, attempts to retreat will only lead to frustration. It's never wise to get off the ride while it's moving so fast.

JANUARY 30 ★ *dust yourself off*

You may experience a professional setback today as the light of the Sun in your 10th House of Public Responsibility is restricted by a square to Saturn the Tester. Your sense of defeat might tempt you to give up, but you would be wise to regroup, learn from your experience, and try again with a new and improved plan.

FEBRUARY

A FIELD OF DREAMS

Although you continue to focus on your career this month, your ambitions are less about getting ahead and more about pursuing your dreams when self-directed Mars enters your 11th House of Friends, Hopes, and Wishes on **February 1**. You're more likely to weave your fantasies into your conversations when communicator Mercury enters imaginative Pisces and your 11th House on **February 5**. Yet, your desire to advance professionally is still running strong, because your key planet, Venus, moves into your 10th House of Career and Responsibility on **February 1**. Harmonious aspects from valuable Venus to brilliant Uranus and beneficial Jupiter on **February 6–7** bring recognition at work or even a raise. But don't brag about your contribution to a group effort or expect something for nothing. If you do, sudden events around the unpredictable Aquarius New Moon on **February 10** could snatch success right out of your hands, teaching you an important lesson about practicing patience and humility.

The Sun joins the party in your social 11th House on **February 18**, shining light on more collective ideals rather than on your personal ambitions. You could be confused by a surprising lack of support at work with stressful aspects from friendly Venus to unstable Uranus on the **19th** and to domineering Pluto on the **22nd**. It may take time to untangle the events leading up to the analytical Virgo Full Moon on **February 25**, because thoughtful Mercury turned retrograde on the **23rd** for a three-week review in fuzzy Pisces. Venus is the last planet to leave your status-seeking 10th House, swimming into Pisces and your 11th House on **February 25** to tempt you with future possibilities, even if they seem out of reach.

KEEP IN MIND THIS MONTH

Give yourself permission to hope. Your happiness depends on creating a sensible balance between achieving realistic goals and entertaining your most implausible dreams.

KEY DATES

FEBRUARY 4–7 ★ *dare to believe*

You struggle to distinguish fact and fancy when imaginative Neptune joins insistent Mars on **February 4** and cerebral Mercury on **February 6**. Because these conjunctions activate your 11th House of Goals, your fantasies about the future are so convincing that you actually might believe them to be real. Although this can challenge your pragmatism, you now have the power to work toward making your dreams come true. You aren't as restrained by social convention when desirous Venus forms a supportive sextile with unorthodox Uranus on **February 6**, empowering you to take a risk to obtain something unusual or attract someone new. Fortunately, your gamble could lead to satisfaction beyond your expectations when lavish Venus trines auspicious Jupiter on **February 7**.

FEBRUARY 9–11 ★ *fool's gold*

Rational Mercury and superhero Mars form challenging squares to confident Jupiter on **February 9–10**, leading you to believe that you know the location of the legendary pot of gold. If you reach too far, however, you may be in for a reality check when you arrive at the end of the rainbow. Needy Venus in your 10th House of Status squares austere Saturn on **February 11**, indicating that you may not get what you want. Meanwhile, the futuristic Aquarius New Moon on the **10th** can act like a reset button in your professional 10th House, emphasizing your need to set new objectives if you fail to reach your current goals.

FEBRUARY 15–16 ★ *it takes a village*

This is a great time to execute your plans, since your actions demonstrate your determination and integrity. But you're more effective working as part of a team when warrior Mars in your 11th House of Community favors cooperation with a sextile to resolute Pluto on **February 15** and a smooth trine with karmic Saturn on **February 16**. Being honest about your intentions will encourage others to happily participate in your project now.

SUPER NOVA DAYS
FEBRUARY 25–28 ★ *dream weaver*

Your creativity is flowing strongly now, because the detail-oriented Virgo Full Moon on **February 25** illuminates your 5th House of Self-Expression and reflects the soulful Pisces Sun. Still, the Full Moon's dynamic square to overblown Jupiter empowers you to take your vision too far. Reaching for the ideal relationship seems more important than being real when romantic Venus conjuncts diaphanous Neptune on the **28th**. Fortunately, witty Mercury is supercharged by red-hot Mars on the **26th**, enabling you to conjure up a magical spell that can make something special happen.

MARCH

A PLETHORA OF PARADOXES

Although a series of positive aspects indicates smooth sailing through the watery Pisces New Moon on **March 11**, it still seems as if you're losing traction because interactive Mercury is retrograde until **March 17**. However, this is a great time for visualizing your ideal future while several planets cluster in dreamy Pisces and your 11th House of Long-Term Goals. You have the fortitude to transform your vision into reality when the Sun harmonizes with unrelenting Pluto and unwavering Saturn on **March 1**. Similarly, resourceful Venus and loquacious Mercury connect with Pluto and Saturn on **March 6–7**, gracing you with uncommon clarity and unflappable determination. But it's the Saturn-Pluto sextile that's exact on **March 8** that supplies you with inexhaustible energy and willpower all month. This long-lasting alignment enables you to exhibit discipline in the face of temptations and maintain a positive attitude in these challenging times.

You can feel your forward momentum building when enthusiastic Mars enters enterprising Aries on **March 12**. Mercury's direct turn on the **17th** feels like a booster rocket—and then additional propulsion arrives when the Sun and Venus blast into fiery Aries on **March 20–21**. Electrifying conjunctions to irrepressible Uranus from Mars on the **22nd** and from Venus and the Sun on the **28th** should launch you into orbit. Ironically, it's not that simple to stay on course, because expansive Jupiter creates irritating quincunxes with constrictive Saturn on **March 23** and heavy-handed Pluto on **March 29**. Although the objective Libra Full Moon on **March 27** helps you reestablish emotional equilibrium, squares to Pluto from Venus and the Sun on **March 31** can surprise you with the dramatic power of your feelings.

> ### KEEP IN MIND THIS MONTH
>
> *Even when things are going your way, there's still room for trouble. Stay cool, calm, and collected, because your persistence will pay off.*

KEY DATES

MARCH 4–6 ★ *making love work*

You overindulge or spend too much on **March 4** when your key planet, Venus, sparkles in your 11th House of Dreams as she squares opulent Jupiter. Thoughtful Mercury retrogrades back across the Sun on the **4th** and Venus on the **6th**, requiring you to rethink your communication strategies and reevaluate the distinctions between friends and lovers. Magnetic Venus cooperatively sextiles secretive Pluto on

March 6, drawing previously hidden feelings to the surface. Venus's easy trine with steadfast Saturn allows you to demonstrate your feelings in a very matter-of-fact manner, helping you regain the relationship security that you may have recently lost.

MARCH 9-11 ★ *lost in translation*
Your confidence soars—whether it's warranted or not—when quicksilver Mercury squares joyous Jupiter on **March 9**. You need to be very meticulous in your communication with friends because retrograde Mercury is visiting your 11th House of Social Networking; glossing over an apparently insignificant detail could lead to misunderstandings. The illusory Pisces New Moon on **March 11** is also in your 11th House, signifying a possible change of strategy in how you interact with others. Be careful; your current tendency toward fuzzy thinking could mislead others, including yourself. There's nothing wrong with daydreaming as long as you understand the difference between fantasy and reality.

MARCH 20-23 ★ *starting over*
The yearly astrological cycle begins anew at the Spring Equinox, which is marked by the entry of the Sun into Aries the Ram and your 12th House of Soul Consciousness on **March 20**. Your ruling planet, Venus, follows suit on the **21st,** attracting you to new spiritual pursuits. Meanwhile, messenger Mercury is speeding up, carrying your thoughts forward again. Your intuition can bring you a sudden flash of awareness when red-hot Mars conjuncts lightning-like Uranus on **March 22**. However, if you aren't paying attention to what's important, an uncomfortable aspect between promising Jupiter and demanding Saturn on the **23rd** will bring an important issue back into focus.

SUPER NOVA DAYS
MARCH 25-28 ★ *chaos theory*
Your top priority right now is to balance a multitude of apparently contradictory influences. You may be frustrated that adjustments you make in a relationship on **March 25** don't resolve the issue. Unwarranted fears on the **26th** might prompt you to overreact by escalating a power struggle with someone who's trying to control you. Fortunately, the lovely Libra Full Moon on **March 27** brightens your 6th House of Details, enabling you to create a new routine. Your logic is sound, but unrestrained desires might undo your good intentions when luxurious Venus parties with outrageous Uranus on **March 28**.

APRIL

BUILDING MOMENTUM

You're content to work behind the scenes during the first half of the month with the planetary emphasis on your 12th House of Privacy. On the surface it doesn't look like you're fully involved with what's happening in your life, because you are keeping your plans to yourself. Four planets in courageous Aries encourage you to take risks that others don't know about, yet your unexpressed enthusiasm is your secret weapon as you work toward unspoken goals. The excitable Aries New Moon on **April 10** reenergizes your mysterious 12th House. This fiery lunation's conjunction with artful Venus and ardent Mars kindles creativity and initiates a new cycle of personal expression. You are ready to bolt ahead on a pet project, but stern Saturn forms an unaccommodating quincunx to unstoppable Uranus on **April 12**, raising uncertainty. Should you buck the tide and push ahead or accept the annoying delays you now face? It's easier to justify your next move when mischievous Mercury skips into macho Aries on **April 13**, quickly convincing you to forge ahead with your plans.

You shine like a star during the second half of the month. Your power increases and you take center stage when your key planet, Venus, enters steady Taurus and your 1st House of Self on **April 15**, followed by the willful Sun on **April 19** and assertive Mars on **April 20**. Nevertheless, you may need to slow down, respond to someone's criticism, and regroup if necessary when naysaying Saturn in your 7th House of Relationships opposes Venus on **April 22** and the Sun on **April 28**. Additionally, the transformational Scorpio Full Moon Eclipse on **April 25** shakes your 7th House, requiring you to be realistic about the limitations of a partnership as you reevaluate its worth.

> **KEEP IN MIND THIS MONTH**
>
> *Don't be discouraged by obstacles that slow your progress. Think of them as lessons that allow you to hone your skills and improve your chances for success.*

KEY DATES

APRIL 6–8 ★ *some enchanted evening*

The cosmic lovers, sultry Venus and sexy Mars, join forces in your 12th House of Spirituality and Dreams on **April 7**, providing you with the desire and impetus to weave a rich tapestry of romance. But your fantasies may never see the light of day, for deceptive Neptune forms stressful semisquares with Venus and Mars on **April 6** and with the Sun on **April 8**. The thrill of amour is still alluring, even if it only exists within your imagination.

APRIL 14–15 ★ *more, more, more*
An indulgent Venus-Jupiter semisquare on **April 14** can trick you into believing that more of a good thing will only be better. Be careful; your unbridled enthusiasm can turn a lovely moment into a frustrating one if you crave quantity over quality. Fortunately, seductive Venus finds her way into her home sign of Taurus on the **15th**, quenching your desires and offering gratification through simple pleasures. Taking delight in your senses infuses your personality with an easygoing charm that makes you less needy and more fun to be around.

APRIL 21–24 ★ *roller coaster of love*
Pushy Mars in determined Taurus can lead to overbearing behavior as it forms a clunky semisquare with bombastic Jupiter on **April 21**. An obsessive Mercury-Pluto square the same day tempts you to wield power by making non-negotiable demands that are only covering your insecurities. Unreasonable stubbornness won't lead to happiness; it only isolates you further when affectionate Venus runs into the hard, cold wall of Saturn's opposition on the **22nd**. Thankfully, you can be more open-minded when interactive Mercury in fearless Aries aspects permissive Jupiter on the **23rd**. If you're able to roll with the dramatic emotional changes, Venus's synergetic trine to passionate Pluto on the **24th** rewards you by revitalizing a flagging relationship or stirring up a yearning for a new romance.

SUPER NOVA DAYS
APRIL 25–28 ★ *point of no return*
Expect drama in a close relationship on **April 25** thanks to an intense Scorpio Lunar Eclipse in your 7th House of Companions—especially if it feels like you've reached the end of a road. But aspects from rational Mercury and reckless Mars to metaphysical Neptune on the **26th** can reveal a higher path if you're ready to leave your old ways behind. The Sun's opposition to scrupulous Saturn on **April 28** can bring a final judgment; whatever happens, don't hold on to the past.

MAY

MONEY CAN'T BUY YOU LOVE

The spotlight is on you and your 1st House of Self when fleet-footed Mercury joins the practical Taurus party of Mars, the Sun, and Venus on **May 1**. You feel comfortable with your life now, but you barely have time to relax before the messenger planet speeds off to jittery Gemini on **May 15**. In fact you may grow restless even sooner, when your key planet, Venus, leaves her sweet home base of Taurus on **May 9** to evoke desires that aren't satisfied by standing still. Additional turbulence comes from a Taurus New Moon Eclipse, also on the **9th**, revealing personal issues that require your immediate attention. The brilliant Sun's shift into dualistic Gemini on **May 20** confirms the importance of making changes instead of stubbornly resisting them. You're left questioning your values during this phase since the Sun, Mercury, Venus, and Jupiter are clustered in your 2nd House of Self-Worth. On a more material level, expect money matters to move to the forefront as you consider making an expensive purchase or negotiating for a pay raise on **May 18–20** and **May 28**.

Although perceptive Pluto continues to transform your understanding of the bigger picture, explosive Uranus in your 12th House of Spirituality might bring a sudden change of perspective that can undermine more material pursuits. The real story this month is the tumultuous square from electric Uranus to volcanic Pluto on **May 20**— the third in a series of seven that began on **June 24, 2012**, reoccurs on **November 1**, and finishes on **March 16, 2015**. The Sagittarius Full Moon Eclipse on **May 25** activates your 8th House of Investments, bringing more surprises on the fiscal front.

> **KEEP IN MIND THIS MONTH**
>
> *Your natural impulse is to tightly hold on to what you already have, but letting go of what you no longer need makes room for meaningful new experiences.*

KEY DATES

MAY 1–5 ★ *heroic efforts*

Muster up all the patience you can if someone places an annoying obstacle in your way on **May 1**, when hot Mars opposes cold Saturn in your 7th House of Others. Your frustration may turn to self-doubt unless you can view this as a reason to improve your game. Fortunately, communicator Mercury's entry into persistent Taurus helps you say what you mean, and a powerful Sun-Pluto trine supplies you with enough energy to finish what you start. However, conversations can still get bogged down when Mercury opposes weighty Saturn on the **5th**. Relentless Pluto comes to the rescue as its trine to unstoppable Mars bestows you with uncommon courage and stamina.

MAY 9 ★ *know your limit*

Today's Solar Eclipse in Taurus and your 1st House of Self can bring a personal issue to a head. Others may think that you're being obstinate, but your apparent inflexibility only reflects your inner resolve. Nevertheless, you could reach a point where stubbornness becomes counterproductive. Thankfully, you are inclined toward compromise now that lovable Venus slips into Gemini the Twins, even if it doesn't come naturally. Displaying your determination shows your strength, but being open-minded can save the day.

MAY 16–20 ★ *into the great unknown*

Your fear of the future makes you nervous when the long-lasting Uranus-Pluto square becomes exact on **May 20**. The fixed Taurus Sun forms anxious aspects with high-strung Uranus and deep-diving Pluto on **May 16**, triggering a personal conflict that relates to larger evolving social issues. Although you might not understand everything that's going on, you're willing to take a chance for something you want when flirty Venus sextiles reactive Uranus on the **18th**. It's not necessary to explain your motives now; without risk there is no gain.

MAY 25–28 ★ *all's well that ends well*

The adventurous Sagittarius Lunar Eclipse on **May 25** shakes your 8th House of Intimacy and Transformation to the core. Relationship issues are not simply about promises and expectations now; they are about the profound influences that you and your partner have on each other and how you are irrevocably changed when you share deeply. Be careful about inadvertently making an incorrect assumption when the Sun squares confusing Neptune on the **26th**. Nevertheless, don't withdraw to protect your heart. Mercury and Venus propitiously conjunct with upbeat Jupiter on **May 27–28**, indicating a promising outcome to this little drama.

JUNE

BATTEN DOWN THE HATCHES

Two counteractive cosmic forces influence you this month. The first comes from the long-lasting effects of the Uranus-Pluto square that was exact on **May 20** and will reoccur on **November 1**. This dynamic pattern is a karmic wake-up call that can shatter your deepest convictions and alter the overall direction of your life. Although this metamorphosis will take years to complete, Mercury, Venus, and the Sun each has a turn now to oppose Pluto and square Uranus, dramatically increasing the pressure for change. On **June 7**, analytical Mercury stirs the stew as you worry about how much you have on your plate. On **June 11–12**, it's resourceful Venus's turn to stimulate your desire for comfort and safety in the midst of stormy seas.

The second cosmic force is a much-appreciated stabilizing effect you can feel all month from reliable Saturn's trine to magical Neptune that's exact on **June 11** and **July 19**. You know just what to do to achieve your dreams when your ruling planet, Venus, forms a graceful Grand Water Trine with Saturn and Neptune on **June 7**. The clever Gemini New Moon on **June 8** falls in your 2nd House of Self-Worth, enabling you to enjoy yourself with pleasurable distractions. Then, on **June 21**, the Sun's shift into self-protective Cancer marks the Summer Solstice, when your daily activities normally favor home and family. But the Capricorn Full Moon on **June 23** joins Pluto and squares Uranus, reactivating persistent problems that make it difficult for you to relax and find peace of mind. Fortunately, opportunity knocks close to home when Jupiter enters nurturing Cancer and your busy 3rd House on **June 25**.

KEEP IN MIND THIS MONTH
As the landscape changes all around you, rely on your inner strength to resist getting swept away by dramatic tides.

KEY DATES

JUNE 1–3 ★ *listen with your heart*

You may feel a bit scattered on **June 1** when the restless Gemini Sun cooperatively aligns with unsettling Uranus and anxiously aspects potent Pluto. You might attempt to avoid an important issue now because it feels too overwhelming to manage. But sweet Venus swims into receptive Cancer and your 3rd House of Communication on **June 2**, encouraging you to listen more and speak less. Messenger Mercury, also in watery Cancer, trines steady Saturn and visionary Neptune on **June 3**, inspiring you to work hard to realize your dreams.

SUPER NOVA DAYS
JUNE 7–8 ★ *sail away*
A gentle Venus-Neptune trine arouses romantic feelings or creative inspirations that can feel like a dream. But solid Saturn's trine to Venus supplies concrete support and structure to make these feelings last. Nevertheless, worries pull you into deep waters where you must face your fears as negotiator Mercury opposes shadowy Pluto. But Mercury's square to unconventional Uranus on **June 8**, along with the changeable Gemini New Moon, offers you a radical solution to a problem that has been bothering you, allowing you to move on with certainty.

JUNE 11–12 ★ *unstable ground*
Current circumstances make you question a recent decision. Possessive Venus in your 3rd House of Information opposes transformational Pluto on **June 11** and squares surprising Uranus on **June 12**, highlighting your need for security and revealing something that you didn't know about a close friend. Thankfully, you should be able to hold your position since serious Saturn's trine to compassionate Neptune on the **11th** acts as a stabilizing force.

JUNE 19–23 ★ *the good, the bad, and the patient*
You feel quite confident on **June 19** when the willful Sun hooks up with buoyant Jupiter in your 2nd House of Self-Worth. You'll believe nearly anything thanks to a Venus-Neptune alignment, even if you don't have all your facts right. Fortunately, the Sun's shift into contemplative Cancer on **June 21**, followed by the cautious Capricorn Full Moon on **June 23**, reminds you to cool your heels until you gather more information.

JUNE 26–27 ★ *don't sweat the small stuff*
Mercury's retrograde turn in your 3rd House of Immediate Environment on **June 26** heralds delays and misunderstandings during the next three weeks. Still, you can trust your instincts when dealing with others because the Sun trines sensible Saturn and psychic Neptune, making it unlikely that you will make a misstep. Sweet Venus pirouettes into showy Leo on the **27th**, encouraging you to be more open when sharing your love with those close to you.

JULY

THE EYE OF THE STORM

This month starts on a rough note as loving Venus in your 4th House of Domestic Conditions squares austere Saturn on **July 1**, creating feelings of isolation at home or within your family. Change is desirable when Venus trines progressive Uranus on **July 7**, but pushing for immediate satisfaction only brings frustration because retrograde Mercury backs into the nostalgic Cancer New Moon on **July 8**, reminding you of what you must complete prior to moving on. However, the stabilizing effects of an easy trine between hardworking Saturn and visionary Neptune that was exact on **June 11** and reoccurs on **July 19** act as ballast throughout the month to steady your progress. This is most notable on **July 17** when giant Jupiter—now in your 3rd House of Information—completes an emotionally empowering Grand Water Trine with Saturn and Neptune.

The storms of change are swirling around you, but somehow you're safe in what you know and secure in your place in the world. You are eager to reinforce your relationships with active nurturing on **July 20**, when active Mars reenergizes the grand trine with Saturn and Neptune. Meanwhile, expressive Mercury ends its retrograde phase on the same day, freeing up the lines of communication and giving you the opportunity to say exactly what you feel. Your desires turn practical when Venus enters earthy Virgo on **July 22**—then take flight as the futuristic Aquarius Full Moon brightens your professional 10th House. Temper your enthusiasm, though, or the Mars-Jupiter conjunction may carry you too far. On a personal note, stressful aspects on **July 26–31** turn expressing your feelings into hard work, but the promise of intimacy and pleasure make it all worthwhile.

> **KEEP IN MIND THIS MONTH**
>
> *You can be the master of your own fate by selectively choosing your battles. Creating healthy boundaries enables you to engage without becoming overwhelmed.*

KEY DATES

JULY 1–4 ★ *straight from the heart*

You wonder whether it's worth trying to smooth over a disagreement in a relationship when your key planet, Venus, creates difficult aspects with taskmaster Saturn and murky Neptune on **July 1**, producing feelings of insecurity. Additionally, the Sun in self-protective Cancer opposes domineering Pluto, intensifying a power struggle that you thought was already resolved. Although the Sun's unstable square with volatile Uranus on **July 4** indicates a breakdown or a breakdown in communication, the changes can be quite exciting if you are willing to take a risk and express yourself honestly.

JULY 7–9 ★ *sentimental journey*
Your desires grow increasingly unpredictable on **July 7** when beautiful Venus trines radical Uranus. Although you want everyone to know what you want because Venus is in lively Leo, her presence in your 4th House of Home and Family encourages discretion and retreat. Your fear of being vulnerable is affirmed by the timidity of the sensitive Cancer New Moon on **July 8,** which accentuates your 3rd House of Communication. Additionally, pensive Mercury retrogrades across the Sun on **July 9,** confirming that your thoughts are pulling you back into the past, rather than into the future.

JULY 12–13 ★ *guilty pleasures*
A challenging Sun-Neptune aspect on **July 12** seduces you into believing that your fantasies are real. And then a troubled semisquare between delicious Venus and extravagant Jupiter on the **13th** entices you to overindulge your senses. Fortunately, energetic Mars's shift into hesitant Cancer provides the caution that prevents you from going too far.

SUPER NOVA DAYS
JULY 17–20 ★ *bridge over troubled waters*
Meaningful relationships serve you well these days, acting like a solid foundation in a rather wobbly world. Persisting trines to dependable Saturn and inspirational Neptune from Jupiter on **July 17** and from Mars on **July 20** amplify the joy you feel when you're active within your community. Support from your friends adds emotional security, especially when trustworthy Saturn trines Neptune in your 11th House of Social Networking on the **19th.**

JULY 26–31 ★ *count to ten*
It's impossible to know what you want when hungry Venus opposes cloudy Neptune on **July 26**. A combative Mars-Pluto opposition and a restrictive Sun-Saturn square on the **27th** can precipitate a disagreement if someone questions your beliefs. Meanwhile, supportive Venus aspects on the **26th, 28th,** and **30th** increase your patience and endurance. Nevertheless, you may be tempted to lose your cool when hotheaded Mars squares reckless Uranus on **July 31**.

AUGUST

STUDENT OF LIFE

You're quite busy this month gathering information and exploring new ways to interact with others. You would love to relax at home when the playful Leo New Moon falls in your 4th House of Domestic Conditions on **August 6**, but a smooth trine with restless Uranus is stimulating enough to keep you on your toes. Bountiful Jupiter is moving through receptive Cancer and your 3rd House of Communication until **July 16, 2014**, increasing your appetite for learning and opening your mind to new ideas. Simple curiosity about a subject could morph into an obsessive need to collect more data if you think that having all the facts will help you gain power when Jupiter opposes heavy-handed Pluto on **August 7**. You are ambivalent about sharing your story because loquacious Mercury's shift into expressive Leo on **August 8** encourages you to talk, while its entry into your private 4th House motivates you to retreat.

You're ready to socialize at work when Venus moves into friendly Libra and your 6th House of Employment on **August 16**, but the intelligent Aquarius Full Moon on **August 20** falls in your 10th House of Career, reflecting your need to get ahead professionally. A lucky Jupiter-Uranus square on **August 21** is a wake-up call that provokes you to take a risk; just remember that knowing when to say no is always a useful skill. Make time for fun when the Sun enters virtuous Virgo and your 5th House of Spontaneity on **August 22**, followed by Mercury on the **23rd**. But you may need to postpone a getaway when plans are turned upside down on **August 24–27** as your key planet, Venus, forms a rare Grand Cardinal Square with Pluto, Uranus, and Jupiter.

> **KEEP IN MIND THIS MONTH**
>
> *While it's smart to have the right information at your fingertips, too much of it can weigh you down unless you learn to apply it wisely.*

KEY DATES

AUGUST 1–4 ★ *agent of change*

You feel domestic peace slipping away and may try to stabilize your environment by making one adjustment after another. Unfortunately, your attempts to fix a problem at home may meet with powerful resistance when the Sun quincunxes formidable Pluto on **August 1**. Relationship struggles settle down on **August 2** when sweet Venus in your 5th House of Love receives support from amorous Mars in caring Cancer. Thankfully, the Sun's harmonious trine to innovative Uranus on **August 4** sets your imagination free.

AUGUST 11–14 ★ *mind games*

You are eager to tell someone what's on your mind, but verbal Mercury's uneasy square to resistant Saturn in your 7th House of Others on **August 11** makes it difficult to share without feeling that you're being judged. Mercury's anxious quincunx to shrewd Pluto on **August 13** can make you seem more calculating than you actually are. Looking for answers outside of the box is exciting when the Trickster trines eccentric Uranus on the **14th**. However, trial and error is less efficient than thinking through the process in advance.

SUPER NOVA DAYS

AUGUST 20–24 ★ *fork in the road*

You struggle with stress on **August 20–22** when mental Mercury forms challenging aspects with Pluto, Uranus, and Jupiter. The Aquarius Full Moon on **August 20** shines in your public 10th House, bringing professional recognition that can lead to a promotion. A lightning bolt of opportunity is sparked on **August 21** by the surprising Jupiter-Uranus square that's reactivated by Mercury on the **22nd**. There is great potential every way you turn, yet, unfortunately, you can't just follow every whim. The Sun and Mercury enter exacting Virgo on **August 22–23**, enabling you to narrow your vision and make a difficult choice. Nevertheless, a Venus-Pluto square on **August 24** can raise fears that you made a wrong decision, forcing you to reevaluate your position.

AUGUST 26–30 ★ *reversal of fortune*

This is a time of frustration or breakthrough, depending on whether you're ruled by fear or love. Enriching Venus in your 6th House of Work opposes unpredictable Uranus on August 26 and squares excessive Jupiter on August 27, encouraging you to take an apparently lucrative offer. However, you could retreat to the safety of your comfort zone if you feel overwhelmed by the opportunity. Clear thinking and strategic planning smooth out rough roads with stabilizing aspects on **August 28–30**.

SEPTEMBER

THE PLOT THICKENS

Consolidate your energy this month and establish a regular routine that enables you to achieve satisfaction on the job and in your relationships. Thankfully, pleasant Venus's visit to sociable Libra and your 6th House of Work until **September 11** lightens the daily grind and makes it easier to put in the extra effort. The pragmatic Virgo New Moon on **September 5** plants seeds of inspiration in your 5th House of Self-Expression, arousing your creative instincts to help you to clarify your vision. This lunation's supportive sextile from cheerful Jupiter allows you to be very practical without getting bogged down in unnecessary details. Quicksilver Mercury travels through your 6th House on **September 9–29**, highlighting the specific steps you must take in order to get a job done as efficiently as possible.

On **September 11**, seductive Venus slips into sexy Scorpio and your 7th House of Partnerships and Public Life, shifting your attention away from yourself and onto deepening your relationships with others. The intuitive Pisces Full Moon on **September 19** illuminates your 11th House of Dreams and Wishes, creating a temporary escape from the more serious relationship issues you're presently facing. Your ability to limit your activities and focus your energy on making a partnership work is supported by responsible Saturn's sextile to perceptive Pluto on **September 21**. The Sun enters harmonizing Libra and your 6th House of Employment on the **22nd**, marking the Autumn Equinox and reminding you to balance work with play. Thankfully, a delicious Venus-Jupiter trine on **September 26** can bless you with a lucrative opportunity or sweet pleasure if your heart is in the right place.

> **KEEP IN MIND THIS MONTH**
>
> *Relationship dynamics may be more complex than you prefer right now, but avoiding the emotional intensity could create more problems than it solves.*

KEY DATES

SEPTEMBER 1–4 ★ *truth or consequences*

You can draw from a deep well of personal power on **September 1** when the Sun trines regenerative Pluto. You may even believe that you can overcome any obstacle, but you might waste time chasing illusions on **September 2** when vibrant Mars is confused by delusional Neptune. Restlessness follows on **September 3**, with a reckless Sun-Uranus quincunx urging you to suddenly change your plans, but acting impulsively has its drawbacks. You will be required to take responsibility for any ill-conceived actions when rational Mercury aligns with critical Saturn on **September 4**.

SEPTEMBER 9–11 ★ *anger management*
Energetic Mars in melodramatic Leo encourages you to express yourself, but his harsh square to authoritative Saturn in your 7th House of Others on **September 9** represents a formidable opponent. Instead of stubbornly plodding forward, understand that the current obstacles are really lessons you must learn before taking the next step. But it's difficult to acquiesce to someone else's power without feeling angry, especially on **September 11** as Mars uncomfortably aligns with suspicious Pluto. Still, hold your ground until you can proceed without engaging in conflict.

SEPTEMBER 14 ★ *incurable romantic*
You may lose yourself in a romantic fantasy when sultry Venus in your 7th House of Partners forms a magical trine to illusory Neptune in your 11th House of Dreams. Yet remember, your imagination can fuel an intimate relationship with the creative juice that it needs. It's less important to find love now than it is to express what's in your heart with tenderness and compassion.

SUPER NOVA DAYS
SEPTEMBER 18–21 ★ *get real*
Venus joins methodical Saturn and the karmic Lunar North Node in your 7th House on **September 18**, testing an existing commitment or enticing you to make a new one. Attractive Venus also sextiles provocative Pluto, empowering you to experience feelings on a very deep level. The psychic Pisces Full Moon on **September 19** allows you to be more receptive to your partner's emotions, even if their intensity makes you uncomfortable. Although a relationship can grow if you're willing to explore unfamiliar territory, you may be tempted to bolt when Venus aligns with maverick Uranus on **September 20**. Thankfully, you feel more secure when stabilizing Saturn sextiles profound Pluto on **September 21**.

SEPTEMBER 26–28 ★ *sweet satisfaction*
A harmonizing trine from affectionate Venus to effusive Jupiter on **September 26** brings easy sensual enjoyment, but a dynamic Venus-Mars square on the **28th** can create discord or cause sparks to fly. Fortunately, with the right chemistry this temporary friction can deepen the passion that grows out of conflict.

OCTOBER

THE CALL OF THE WILD

Your relationships remain top priority this month, but you encounter unexpected issues achieving a healthy balance between intimacy and independence. Although the next occurrence of the transformative Uranus-Pluto square isn't exact until **November 1**, you are already under pressure to redirect your life toward reaching more meaningful goals. The agreeable Libra New Moon on **October 4** falls in your 6th House of Employment, yet dynamic aspects to unrestrainable Uranus and unstoppable Pluto can make your job feel oppressive if it doesn't support a higher purpose. Even a normally comfortable relationship is more awkward now as strict Saturn in your 7th House of Partners forms an irritating aspect with rebellious Uranus on **October 5**. You want a soul connection rather than a simple romance when adorable Venus shifts into your 8th House of Intimacy on **October 7**, but her harsh aspects with diffusive Neptune and indulgent Jupiter on **October 10–11** make the path to love elusive.

The freedom-loving Aries Full Moon Eclipse on **October 18** overwhelms your 12th House of Destiny by firing up your imagination with exciting new plans. You have an urgent desire to make sudden changes at work in order to break out of a rut. Nevertheless, it's difficult to initiate action, and Mercury's retrograde turn on **October 21** makes it even tougher to gain the traction you need. Thankfully, on **October 25** an accommodating Sun-Neptune trine spreads a peaceful, easy feeling over your social life. Additionally, a profoundly restorative and regenerative Mars-Pluto trine on **October 31** pushes you to work hard and play hard. Although you are capable of great feats now, reserve some energy so you can gracefully ride the intensifying waves of change over the days ahead.

> **KEEP IN MIND THIS MONTH**
>
> *Whenever you're eager to head off on your own, remember that you'll be even more successful if you can work as part of a team.*

KEY DATES

OCTOBER 1–4 ★ *up in the air*
Right now you feel as if you're listening to several radio stations simultaneously, and it's hard to hear any of them clearly. You think that you

understand what someone is saying on **October 1**, when logical Mercury
in your 7th House of Others harmonizes with psychic Neptune. The Sun's
conflicting square with ruthless Pluto, however, locks you into a power
struggle with a formidable opponent. Even if you're sure you're ready for the
unexpected, the Sun's tug-of-war with surprising Uranus on **October 3** can still
catch you off guard. Meanwhile, pleasurable Venus in your 7th House forms
uneasy aspects with Pluto and Uranus on **October 2–3**, fomenting negativity
between you and your partner. Although there may be no quick fix for the
current stress, at least the diplomatic Libra New Moon on the **4th** assists you
in seeing the current situation from both points of view.

OCTOBER 10–12 ★ *larger than life*
You're confident as you head into unknown emotional territory, convinced that your
good intentions are enough to make everything turn out okay. However, charming
Venus squares fuzzy Neptune from your 8th House of Deep Sharing on **October 10**,
leading you to confuse an unrealistic fantasy with true love. The overindulgent Sun-
Jupiter square on the **12th** encourages flamboyant behavior as you attempt to act
out your dreams.

OCTOBER 16–19 ★ *pursuit of happiness*
You're ready for an extraordinary experience when exquisite Venus trines irreverent
Uranus on **October 16**. However, a fast-moving Aries Lunar Eclipse on the **18th**
suggests that events will unfold at a very rapid pace—and not necessarily according
to your agenda. Physical Mars in your 5th House of Love and Play encourages you
to pursue pleasure, but his opposition to elusive Neptune on the **19th** diffuses your
actions and diminishes your chances for material success. Nevertheless, following
a spiritual path now can bring you the satisfaction that you seek.

OCTOBER 29–31 ★ *reality check*
If you have made promises you cannot fulfill, you may need to face the facts and
lower your expectations on **October 29**, when retrograde Mercury runs backward
into Saturn the Taskmaster in your 7th House of Partnerships and Public Life.
Mars, moving through timid Virgo, anxiously aspects wild Uranus in rambunctious
Aries on **October 31**, tossing a bit of uncertainty into the social mix. Luckily, the
self-willed warrior planet forms a collaborative trine with tenacious Pluto, blessing
you with enough stamina and resolve to see you through the current changes.

TAURUS

NOVEMBER

FASTEN YOUR SEAT BELT

You can absorb a great deal of stress this month without showing any signs of wear and tear. The evolutionary Uranus-Pluto square on **November 1** is part of a continuing series of aspects that recurs three more times through **March 16, 2015**, irrevocably changing your view of the world. The transformative Scorpio Solar Eclipse on **November 3** falls in your 7th House of Partners, possibly shifting the dynamics of a significant relationship. This New Moon Eclipse joins conservative Saturn—and is followed by a Sun-Saturn conjunction on the **6th**—requiring you to follow the rules of engagement and demanding that you respond in a reliable manner. When your ruling planet, Venus, enters strategic Capricorn and your 9th House of Future Vision on **November 5**, you're willing to delay gratification because you believe that long-term success is sweeter than temporal pleasure. Additionally, communicator Mercury remains retrograde in your interactive 7th House until **November 10**, requiring you to reconsider recent decisions and revise your plans, if necessary.

However, Mercury turns direct on the **10th** to release you from your emotional ties to the past, while a joyful Sun-Jupiter trine on the **12th** infuses you with contentment. Optimism gives way to darker feelings that could include possessiveness, jealousy, or greed when stylish Venus conjuncts shrewd Pluto on **November 15**. The sensual Taurus Full Moon on **November 17** lights up your relationship houses, yet its harsh aspect to Pluto indicates that you still have residual negative feelings to resolve. Fortunately, a series of more supportive aspects that occur on **November 19–23** and **November 27–30** restores your self-confidence, increases your flexibility, and inspires you to follow through with positive actions to improve your life.

> **KEEP IN MIND THIS MONTH**
>
> *It may take a while for you to find your groove, but persistence and patience will pay off in steady gains by the end of the month.*

KEY DATES

SUPER NOVA DAYS
NOVEMBER 1–3 ★ *shift happens*
Your world may be a pressure cooker for change as revolutionary Uranus squares unrelenting Pluto on **November 1**, yet the support you receive from

124 ★ YOUR ASTROLOGY GUIDE 2013

others lets you withstand the duress with grace. Retrograde Mercury joins the Sun in your 7th House of Companions to deliver a message that you've heard before, but this time it finally clicks. The Sun-Mercury conjunction cooperates with fearless Mars, incisive Pluto, and therapeutic Chiron, blessing you with compassion and enough clarity to realize that a change in direction is inevitable. The powerful Scorpio Lunar Eclipse on **November 3** brings the point home once more; it's time to let go of an old relationship story that has served its purpose and open your heart to what's next.

NOVEMBER 7-9 ★ *the world is your oyster*
You want more from life now and probably have a concrete plan that will help you achieve your goals, even if they seem out of reach. Venus is currently visiting your 9th House of Big Ideas, and her collaborative sextiles with intuitive Neptune and brainy Mercury on **November 7-8** grace you with an uncanny ability to know which dreams make the most sense to pursue. Fortunately, you can manage a complex project and have the stamina to finish what you start on **November 9** when superhero Mars, now in detail-oriented Virgo, sextiles industrious Saturn.

NOVEMBER 14-15 ★ *jokers are wild*
You're ready to take a chance and try something radical on **November 14**, when enchanting Venus squares progressive Uranus. But the stakes are higher than you think, and your actions can stir up unexpectedly powerful emotions when Venus joins dark Pluto on the **15th**. The outcome is uncertain now; even if you believe truth is on your side, the rules of the game can change quickly.

NOVEMBER 27-30 ★ *lucky charms*
Be careful what you ask for because you're persuasive enough now to actually get what you want. Mischievous Mercury in your social 7th House forms a friendly sextile to flirtatious Venus in your 9th House of Adventure on **November 27**, heating up a casual conversation with someone you like. You can make a good situation sound even better when chatty Mercury trines jolly Jupiter on the **28th**. Indulgence isn't out of the question, either, since Venus opposes permissive Jupiter on the same day. Fortunately, the fun continues through the **30th**, when the optimistic Sagittarius Sun trines outrageous Uranus, convincing you to enjoy all that life currently has to offer.

DECEMBER

ACCENTUATE THE POSITIVE

An uplifting Sagittarius New Moon kicks off the month on **December 2**, inspiring you to set your goals higher while giving you the confidence you need to reach them. However, you won't be able to get away with false bravado because this New Moon occurs in your 8th House of Deep Sharing, sending you on an intense journey of self-discovery. Your sense of fairness wins out when assertive Mars enters objective Libra and your 6th House of Work on **December 7**. Being able to recognize your personal needs allows you to set them aside in order to do your job well. Fortunately, opportunistic Jupiter's coordinated trine to ambitious Saturn on **December 12** strengthens your resolve to make a realistic plan and execute it efficiently.

You may spend unwisely on indulgent gifts and holiday celebrations thanks to the scattered Gemini Full Moon on **December 17** lighting up your 2nd House of Money. You desire more than you currently have, but are cautious about exceeding reasonable limits with resourceful Venus in practical Capricorn camped out in your 9th House of Faraway Places. Although there's a lot of planetary activity throughout the month, you may feel sluggish or as if it's difficult to achieve satisfaction because your ruling planet, Venus, slows down to begin her 41-day retrograde cycle on **December 21**. This is also the Winter Solstice, another sign that it's time to retreat and journey inward. However, a shocking Mars-Uranus opposition on **December 25** and a fierce Mars-Pluto square on **December 30** indicate that you will end this year with a thrilling roller-coaster ride rather than a long and dreamy winter's sleep.

> **KEEP IN MIND THIS MONTH**
>
> *Psychological and spiritual transformation is your ultimate key to happiness. Instead of trying to control the external flow of events, focus on improving your inner game.*

KEY DATES

DECEMBER 2–4 ★ *learning to fly*

The inspirational Sagittarius New Moon on **December 2** coaxes you to imagine how it feels to soar like a bird in the cloudless blue sky. But dreaming about it isn't enough, because action-hero Mars forms a cooperative sextile with the winged messenger on **December 3**, enticing you to actually explore unfamiliar territory and then report back on your adventure. Mercury shifts into philosophical Sagittarius and your 8th House of Intimacy on **December 4**, endowing you with the gift of gab and enabling you to share complex feelings in a straightforward manner.

SUPER NOVA DAYS
DECEMBER 10–12 ★ *in it for the long haul*
You're attracted to the idea of something new and different on **December 10**, when alluring Venus forms a magical quintile to unorthodox Uranus. Her presence in your 9th House of Journeys makes it easier to stretch your limits by traveling to an exotic destination. Meanwhile, talkative Mercury in overconfident Sagittarius trines Uranus, helping you to rationalize your crazy idea. A long-lasting Jupiter-Saturn trine on **December 12** supplies you the street smarts that could turn your vision into an obtainable goal. Working with a partner or a friend is a win–win situation, with Jupiter and Saturn successfully collaborating on your behalf. A project that began around **July 17**, at the previous Jupiter-Saturn trine, may be right back on your plate now. Keep in mind that your current work might not reach fruition until the third and final occurrence of this aspect on **May 24, 2014**.

DECEMBER 21 ★ *spread your wings*
Widening your horizons mentally or physically is in your immediate future, so get your passport updated or enroll in that course you've been considering when the Sun enters ambitious Capricorn and your 9th House of Travel and Education. Your current wanderlust grows palpable as Venus turns retrograde today to extend her visit in your adventurous 9th House until **March 5, 2014**.

DECEMBER 29–31 ★ *curb your negativity*
You struggle to find that sweet spot between gradual change and spontaneous evolution as the year runs out. Mercury and the Sun square reactionary Uranus in your 12th House of Destiny on **December 29–30**, triggering your sense of urgency. You are driven to get to the bottom of an issue, and your curiosity can morph into an obsession by the **31st** when Mercury conjuncts mysterious Pluto in the 9th House of Higher Truth. But don't give in to anger if things aren't moving fast enough when warrior Mars squares Pluto and Mercury on **December 30–31**, spurring you to force a confrontation. However, taking the high road is your choice—a more peaceful way to end the year.

GEMINI

MAY 21–JUNE 20

GEMINI
2012 SUMMARY

It would be wise to use the first part of the year to finish up old business—you are being given a chance to see how previous successes and failures are connected to recurring patterns in your life. You can fine-tune your current ambitions with the insights you gain, empowering you to plan for the future with newfound confidence, although you may need to reevaluate your priorities and take bold action to establish new objectives.

AUGUST—*flying by the seat of your pants*
Although you can see that you're making progress again, you still must handle day-to-day situations as they arise before you think about what comes next.

SEPTEMBER—*storms of change*
It's necessary to think on two levels now. Take care of the most pressing issues while also considering the impact your current actions will have on your future.

OCTOBER—*change of pace*
Your newfound vision of the future eases your stress and gives you time to reconsider where you want your life to go.

NOVEMBER—*hurry up and wait*
If you're just spinning your wheels and getting nowhere fast, back up, catch your breath, reassess your approach, and try again.

DECEMBER—*over the rainbow*
It's easy for you to scatter your energy and have nothing to show for your efforts. Enjoying yourself is important, but keep some resources in reserve.

2012 CALENDAR

AUGUST

WED 1–SAT 4 ★ You could waste time and energy chasing your dreams

WED 8–THU 9 ★ Don't fool yourself about love or money

TUE 14–FRI 17 ★ **SUPER NOVA DAYS** Face current issues head-on

FRI 24–SUN 26 ★ Apply your passion to spiritual pursuits

SEPTEMBER

MON 3–WED 5 ★ Don't wallow in disappointment

FRI 7–SAT 8 ★ Be wise and exercise self-control

WED 12–SUN 16 ★ It's not easy to keep your desires in check

THU 20 ★ Enjoy yourself in the present moment

TUE 25–SAT 29 ★ **SUPER NOVA DAYS** The pressure to change continues to build

OCTOBER

WED 3–SUN 7 ★ It's difficult to find direction in your life

TUE 9–WED 10 ★ **SUPER NOVA DAYS** Blend material and spiritual pursuits

MON 15–WED 17 ★ Know your limitations

THU 25 ★ Face the facts

SUN 28–MON 29 ★ Make up your mind and stick to it

NOVEMBER

THU 1–SAT 3 ★ Seek innovative solutions

FRI 9–SUN 11 ★ Believe in your dreams

TUE 13–SAT 17 ★ **SUPER NOVA DAYS** Enter unfamiliar territory

THU 22–SAT 24 ★ Your uncertainty could provoke radical action

MON 26–THU 29 ★ Narrow your objectives

DECEMBER

SAT 1–SUN 2 ★ Believe in yourself

MON 10–FRI 14 ★ Your fantasies can stretch the bounds of your creativity

WED 19–SAT 22 ★ Success depends on finding a middle path

FRI 28–MON 31 ★ **SUPER NOVA DAYS** Keep the communication channels open

GEMINI OVERVIEW

This year is rich with opportunities for personal and professional growth; 2013 starts with propitious Jupiter in your sign, where it broadens your self-understanding and expands your vision of future possibilities. This growing perspective on how you might improve your life is likely to produce more ideas than even you can handle. Despite your mental dexterity, if you have too many balls in the air, you're bound to drop one or two. Don't let chance make the choice for you; let go of peripheral activities and interests so that you can focus on the most important ones. **You're planting conceptual seeds for career advancement or fulfilling relationships, and if you nourish them with care, they should take hold and show real growth in the second half of the year** when bountiful Jupiter enters nurturing Cancer and your 2nd House of Resources on June 25. Projects rooted in reality and watered by your attention can flourish, but ideas and plans tossed in the air without thought and commitment will soon be gone with the wind.

Slow down to master the nuts and bolts of your work; your extra effort can make the difference between professional success and failure now. One reason is that your ruling planet, Mercury, has three retrograde cycles in job-related houses this year, requiring you to make some adjustments, dig deeply to keep pace with the workload, and stay on track to reaching your goals. Mercury's reversals occur in your 10th House of Public Responsibility on February 23–March 17, your 2nd House of Income on June 26–July 20, and your 6th House of Employment on October 21–November 10. Being especially attentive to details during these periods not only helps you to avoid career complications but can also enhance your authority, increase your cash flow, and upgrade your skills.

Another reason concentration on the job is so important is that serious Saturn is spending this year roiling deep waters in passionate Scorpio and your 6th House of Service. If you truly care about what you're doing, intensifying your efforts can elevate your expertise. **Even the toughest challenges might seem like interesting puzzles for you to solve rather than sources of frustration that stop your progress.** But if you're just skimming the surface with a job that doesn't move you emotionally, developing new skills to change your career path is worth consideration. Fortunately, visionary Jupiter's favorable trines with ambitious Saturn and spiritual Neptune on July 17 conjure up pictures of a more fulfilling future. You should be able to connect the dots and recognize how to apply your resources and abilities to climb the professional ladder of success. It is essential, though, that your plan be something you feel strongly about, since mere ideas alone lack the power to make this magic happen.

ADDICTED TO LOVE

The love story of the year unfolds in late May with two significant events. A Lunar Eclipse in risk-taking Sagittarius falls in your 7th House of Partners on May 25. The Sun and Moon are in tense squares with imaginative Neptune, tempting you to run off to a romantic fantasyland. Dreams so delicious that reality seems to melt away can provide short-term relief from relationship woes, but the illusory nature of this eclipse is bound to lead to a rude awakening. Magnetic Venus's conjunction with magnanimous Jupiter on May 28 keeps sprinkling the fairy dust of hope that can make a thought or simple glance feel like an invitation to a lifetime of love. However, the long-term transit of mysterious Pluto in your 8th House of Intimacy is an ongoing reminder to look below the surface and only commit to someone when you're ready to fully engage your heart and soul.

ALL OR NOTHING

Professional transition is a major theme this year. You might hit the wall at work around the time of the Lunar Eclipse in Scorpio on April 25. This pressure-packed lunation in your 6th House of Employment is conjunct with scrupulous Saturn, which requires you to double your commitment to the tasks at hand—or to recognize that your current pathway won't lead you to fulfillment. Your current skills may not match the changing economic environment, requiring you to consider learning another line of work. But if you love what you're doing, investing in additional training should allow you to continue in the same field.

SAFETY COUNTS

The financial gods look on you favorably when lucky Jupiter begins a yearlong passage through your 2nd House of Money on June 25. Even though things seem to be rolling your way, cashing in on the opportunities this transit represents requires a safe and steady approach instead of a quick-buck attitude. Avoid costly mistakes by double-checking data during Mercury's June 26–July 20 retrograde in your 2nd House. Caution is also advised when Jupiter's overly optimistic square to reckless Uranus tempts you to take unreasonable risks on August 21. If you're smitten with a brilliant moneymaking idea, patiently do your research before placing your bet.

PREVENTION IS THE BEST MEDICINE

The good news is that wise Jupiter's presence in your 1st House of Self can increase your knowledge about diet and exercise in the first half of the year. There are plenty of sources out there to help you optimize your energy and well-being. However, your mind might be so filled with distractions that you sometimes fall into bad habits. Failure to attend to the mundane matters of regular upkeep can expose problems during the April 25 Lunar Eclipse in your 6th House of Health. In fact, hard-nosed Saturn's yearlong presence in this house of bodily maintenance rewards you for self-discipline, yet could make you pay a high price for a sloppy approach to self-care.

FAMILY FIRST

You could easily be distracted from domestic issues this year, thanks to idealistic Neptune's continuing transit in your 10th House of Career, leading to neglect on the home front. If you ignore family matters and maintenance of your living space, though, repairs may become urgent this summer. The Sun enters your 4th House of Roots on August 22, followed by your ruling planet, Mercury, on the 23rd. Their presence in eagle-eyed Virgo shines a bright light that exposes flaws in your household. Yet their oppositions to nebulous Neptune on August 25–26 invite evasive actions or misleading words that muddle matters. Showing up with heart in hand and integrity intact could heal emotional wounds and resolve material problems.

OVER THE EDGE

Your restless mind is always traveling in search of new information—and this year is no exception. Electrical Uranus, the ruler of your 9th House of Higher Thought and Faraway Places, forms powerful squares with transformational Pluto on May 20 and November 1 in a series that began last year and doesn't finish until 2015. These transits can turn your thinking in radical new directions. Your impatience with old ways of thinking is especially strong when unstoppable Mars and intellectual Mercury join progressive Uranus on March 22 and April 20, respectively. While you could experience brilliant breakthroughs, your inclination to go against the grain of convention can trigger conflicts. These are not the easiest times for travel since surprises are more likely to upset your plans than enliven them.

OUT OF YOUR ELEMENT

If your daily life doesn't correspond with your spiritual beliefs, the Solar Eclipse on May 9 is likely to expose these contradictions throughout the year. You may be inclined to hunker down in a state of denial with this lunation in stubborn Taurus and your 12th House of Soul Consciousness. Being comfortable with where you're at, though, isn't necessarily a signal that your thinking is correct. This eclipse is a reminder that facing emotional demons will teach you more about your higher purpose than sitting serenely on a meditation pillow. Examining your shadowy places of doubt and fear is not surrendering to the lesser parts of yourself, but a courageous way to test your faith.

RICK & JEFF'S TIP FOR THE YEAR:
Every Choice Matters

The many gifts of discovery that you receive this year can fill you with gratitude. But it's not giving thanks that will turn these presents into lasting sources of joy and fulfillment. You could easily lose your sense of priorities in a flood of information and experiences that tickle your curious fancy. A brief smile of recognition is generally sufficient. Work to quickly let go of trivial concepts, clearing your mind to focus on essential ideas that will positively change your life.

JANUARY

PERSISTENCE PAYS

It's not easy to define expectations or follow the rules in relationships, yet this is exactly what's demanded of you as the month begins with the willful Sun and thoughtful Mercury in serious Capricorn and your 8th House of Deep Sharing. These transits reward you for knowing what you want and sticking to your commitments, but may make life unpleasant when you are vague about your desires and let others take control. Be patient on **January 7** when aggressive Mars in your visionary 9th House slams into a tense square with restrictive Saturn in your 6th House of Habits. If your dreams of adventure or more creative work are stymied by the demands of your daily duties, don't give up; dig in with greater determination. You'll earn the freedom to explore new territory by taking care of business first. The earthy Capricorn New Moon in your 8th House on **January 11** marks a fresh start in your most significant relationships. Set clear goals and restructure responsibilities to strengthen these alliances.

Your mind and heart are open to fresh concepts and new experiences on **January 19** when the winged messenger Mercury and the radiant Sun fly into airy Aquarius and your 9th House of Travel and Higher Education. Pressure drops and hopes soar, lifting you above the dull predictability of your usual routine. You're buzzing with a million bright ideas and there's so much you want to say with the expressive Leo Full Moon in your 3rd House of Communication on the **26th**. Additionally, supportive aspects from effusive Jupiter in inquisitive Gemini and innovative Uranus in impulsive Aries can cheer you on. However, a lunar square to strict Saturn demands discretion, so choose your words carefully and back them up with facts to make them stick.

> ### KEEP IN MIND THIS MONTH
>
> *When you have a map in your mind of where you want to land in the future, your chances of success are infinitely greater than if you're making it up as you go along.*

KEY DATES

discerning the difference between a brilliant idea and a crazy one. Capable Mars's confident trine with optimistic Jupiter on the **4th** fills you with enthusiasm to tackle physical challenges, initiate projects, and impress people with your considerable charm. A careless Mercury-Jupiter quincunx on the **5th** could encourage you to make promises that you can't keep. But the messenger planet's conjunction with dark Pluto on the **6th** squeezes the fluff out of false dreams and forces you to focus on unforgiving facts. Facing reality's music, though, can empower you with intellectual certainty.

JANUARY 14 ★ *lost and found*
Your brainy ruling planet, Mercury, forms a squirrelly sesquisquare with inflationary Jupiter, raising expectations beyond reason. Yet if you're overwhelmed with data or out on an untenable limb, creative quintiles from Mercury to Saturn and Uranus will reel you back in. The brilliance of these aspects balances realism and innovation, helping you to solve almost any problem.

JANUARY 18 ★ *last chance*
Mercury joins the Sun in your 8th House of Shared Resources to sharpen your perceptions about relationships. This conjunction in calculating Capricorn allows you to sum up where you stand in a key personal or professional partnership. If this connection has reached the end of the road, you'll see it, but if you still have more to gain by the alliance, find out what you need to do to make it work.

JANUARY 22 ★ *genius at work*
You're bubbling over with insights as witty Mercury forms favorable aspects with unorthodox Uranus and far-seeing Jupiter while the Moon is in your clever sign. You have the flexibility to shift mental gears to grasp unfamiliar concepts or alter the way you speak to address the needs of your listener. Make some space in your schedule for brainstorming so ideas can flow freely.

JANUARY 25 ★ *incurable optimist*
Messages are decidedly mixed today as a square from controlling Saturn to mobile Mercury inhibits speech, delays messages, or slows you down with negative thinking. Yet a spirited trine between the expressive Sun and auspicious Jupiter raises flags of hope for the future despite current complications. Attending to minor matters now may be the toll you have to pay before you can get on the bridge to your beautifully imagined future.

FEBRUARY

PSYCHIC CONNECTION

It's slippery at the top, and managing your professional and public responsibilities can be pretty tricky this month. Your strong sense of compassion and overactive imagination may encourage you to take on tasks that aren't clearly defined when energetic Mars slips into abstract Pisces and your 10th House of Career on **February 1**. It's great to be inspired by a project or for your idealism to cast you in a leadership role, but don't overstretch yourself if you hope to maintain a modicum of control when others are relying on you. Another factor in this equation is Mercury's entry into dreamy Pisces and your responsible 10th House on **February 5**. Intuition tends to be stronger than logic, so learning to read the subtle signs between the lines may tell you much more than mere facts. Mischievous Mercury turns retrograde on the **23rd** and backpedals in your 10th House until **March 17**. Projects may go sideways or even stall during this period; you may need to readjust until your ruling planet goes direct and you find more solid footing.

Regardless of how much you already have on your plate, you may still be looking for answers with the inquisitive Aquarius New Moon stimulating your 9th House of Higher Mind on **February 10**. Pursuing knowledge, desirable as that sounds, can also distract you from your current obligations if you let your mind wander too far afield. The Sun's entry into spiritual Pisces and your dutiful 10th House on the **18th** supplies you with an abundance of faith, confidence, and creativity. The message of the earthy Virgo Full Moon in your 4th House of Roots on the **25th** is simple and straightforward: Get off your cloud and hunker down with the details.

> **KEEP IN MIND THIS MONTH**
>
> *You'll save time and energy if you can find ways around obstacles rather than trying to overcome them with persistence and force.*

KEY DATES

SUPER NOVA DAYS

FEBRUARY 6–9 ★ *more than meets the eye*

Your psychic powers are high on the **6th**, thanks to a Mercury-Neptune conjunction that enriches imagination and sensitizes speech. Indeed, your capacity to communicate in poetic and gentle ways can cool down heated adversaries. Nevertheless, what you're seeing might be more about wish fulfillment than reality, creating confusing conversations and muddling your mastery of details. A reliable ally can provide a dash of objectivity that keeps you from drifting off into fantasyland. On the **7th**, a benevolent Venus-Jupiter trine nourishes you with delicious ideas, sumptuous discussions, and playful flirtations. However, the pressure to get back to work is strong when Mercury joins pushy Mars on the **8th** and squares judgmental Jupiter on the **9th**. Irritability and impatience may provoke you to say something harsh when you really need the support of colleagues. The stress of trying to manage a fast-moving situation alone can feel overwhelming, which is why it's best to pull back, slow down, and devise a better strategy than hastily rushing ahead.

FEBRUARY 12 ★ *sharp as a tack*

Your thinking is crystal clear and you're not wasting words today. Even though Mercury is swimming through mystical Pisces, it forms harmonious aspects with no-nonsense Pluto and Saturn that provide islands of reason in the midst of foggy seas. Your powers of persuasion are very strong—you're able to present your points of view with enough warmth and charm to engage others without losing sight of your goals. A few well-chosen phrases targeted with narrow intention will be more effective than endless paragraphs of explanation.

FEBRUARY 21 ★ *destination unknown*

You might find yourself playing the role of a hero or a martyr today as the dramatic Sun joins sacrificial Neptune in your 10th House of Public Responsibility. You could be an inspiring leader whose vision of a better tomorrow rouses the support of your co-workers. It can be risky, though, to let passion get the best of you—selling your idealistic vision with emotional appeals might fail to provide it with the solid foundation that makes it last. If you're overly ambitious, you might wind up only chasing rainbows, returning empty-handed.

FEBRUARY 25-26 ★ *devil is in the details*

A hyperbolic Sun-Jupiter square on **February 25** encourages you to stretch your limits both personally and professionally. It's great to express yourself with such confidence and inspire others in the process. Yet retrograde Mercury backs over Mars on the **26th**, which can deflate big ideas with complications about mechanics and methods. Expansive plans will succeed or fail depending on the minor adjustments and details you choose to implement.

MARCH

PREPARE FOR LIFTOFF

Your top priority this month must be getting back on solid ground to address your personal and professional responsibilities. Tidy up loose ends and complete unfinished business to clear the decks so you can jump into new projects. On **March 8**, a sextile of industrious Saturn and incisive Pluto connects your 6th House of Employment and your 8th House of Deep Sharing to increase focus and efficiency. This stabilizing aspect first occurred on **December 26, 2012**, and will reoccur on **September 21** to ensure that you maintain a tight ship when working with others. The inspirational Pisces New Moon falls in your 10th House of Career on **March 11** to spawn creative ideas and activities in your professional life. Macho Mars's conjunction to this lunation kicks up enthusiasm, but could motivate you to take on tasks for which you're not properly prepared.

Your passion to spend time with friends and groups sharing new experiences is spurred when Mars moves into your collaborative 11th House and pioneering Aries on **March 12**. Continuing this buzz of social excitement, the Sun enters Aries on the **20th**—marking the Spring Equinox—followed by alluring Venus on the **21st**. But do be cautious about assuming additional obligations, because your ruling planet, Mercury, is retrograde until the **17th**, complicating communications and blurring details. The lovely Libra Full Moon on the **27th** opposes Venus and illuminates your 5th House of Romance, Children, and Creativity, which is a green light for opening your heart. However, lunar oppositions to macho Mars and erratic Uranus and a square with punishing Pluto can provoke extreme emotions. Fortunately, wise Jupiter's trine to the Moon from your flexible sign should help you quickly alter your course if you're heading into dangerous waters.

> ### KEEP IN MIND THIS MONTH
>
> *If you grab on to life with both hands, you could wind up holding nothing. Instead of scattering your forces, concentrate on what you value the most.*

KEY DATES

MARCH 4 ★ *for your eyes only*
Mercury backs over the Sun, which can either deepen your personal insights or allow you to get lost in a reality of your own making. This conjunction in your professional 10th House may stir up old business ideas, but it's best to keep mulling them over before sharing your thoughts with others. The awareness you're

gaining now is just for you; attempts to tell people about it can water down the message so much, you lose your thread of inspiration.

SUPER NOVA DAYS
MARCH 6-9 ★ *window of opportunity*
March 6 is ideal for patching over wounded relationships in your workplace and reestablishing peace. The sweet Mercury-Venus conjunction that day may stimulate creative concepts that aren't ready for prime time, but will take shape with Mercury's favorable aspects to ruthlessly efficient Saturn and Pluto on the **7th**. Pipe dreams will dissipate, but ideas worth pursuing may get the support of competent people. Verbose Mercury's square to Jupiter in chatty Gemini on the **9th** tempts you to say more than you should or overinflate a claim. It is, though, a wonderful opportunity to open your mind as long as you don't lose your sense of proportion.

MARCH 17 ★ *all aboard*
This is a pivotal time as your ruling planet Mercury stops its backward trek in your 10th House of Career and begins moving forward again. The Moon in your sign today increases your sensitivity to shifts in the wind, motivating you to take a more proactive approach to your job. Advancing your interests could be slow, though Mercury will pick up speed during the next couple of weeks.

MARCH 22 ★ *bombs bursting in air*
Rockets of rebellion, innovation, or conflict are firing when an irrepressible Mars-Uranus conjunction rattles your 11th House of Groups. This volatile planetary pair doesn't like to follow the rules, provoking erratic behavior among friends and colleagues or triggering an unexpected explosion in you. Finding positive ways to break out of your regular routine will reduce stress and, ideally, help you tap into the potential genius of this unpredictably inventive aspect.

MARCH 28 ★ *speak your mind*
Messenger Mercury creates a harmonious trine to reliable Saturn, giving greater credibility to your words. Today you can broach delicate subjects with sensitivity, delivering an important message without arousing mistrust or suspicion. Imaginative thoughts take root as you're able to connect them with the concrete steps needed to make them real.

APRIL

TIME OUT

Work feels like play this month as you participate in exciting projects with friends and co-workers. On **April 10**, the energizing New Moon in impetuous Aries occurs in your 11th House of Groups and is fired up with conjunctions to flirty Venus and sassy Mars. This creatively rich lineup brings originality and fun to much of what you do, especially when you're connected with imaginative allies. Just don't overlook other responsibilities and the limits of reality, because stern Saturn forms an annoying quincunx with unruly Uranus on the **12th**. This is the second of three alignments that began on **November 15, 2012**, and finishes on **October 5**, which requires impulse control, but can reward your discipline with the mastery of new skills. Your ruling planet, Mercury, zips into scrappy Aries on the **13th**, adding more fuel to your social fire and speeding up the pace of communication.

The tempo starts to slow on **April 15** when comfort-seeking Venus ambles into easygoing Taurus and your retiring 12th House. You're more interested in reducing social activities to find peace and privacy in the garden of your inner life than being the belle or beau of the ball. The Sun's shift into tranquil Taurus on the 19th, and Mars's similar move on the **20th**, both underscore the value of spiritual pursuits and less public exposure during the next few weeks. Work and health issues could grow tense with a Lunar Eclipse in your 6th House of Habits on **April 25**. The Full Moon in resolute Scorpio is conjunct to responsible Saturn, which can force you to alter your daily routine and invest more time and energy in nurturing yourself.

KEEP IN MIND THIS MONTH

No matter how flattering the attention you receive from others is now, recognize when you've had enough and leave before you're exhausted.

KEY DATES

APRIL 1 ★ *as good as gold*

It's your time to shine with a buoyant sextile between the Sun and Jupiter. Astrology's luckiest planet in your sign aligning favorably with the star of our solar system boosts confidence and adds an air of importance to everything you do. You don't need to struggle on your own when you have people ready to support you if you're willing to ask for their help. Selling yourself or a project is easy when you believe this strongly in what you're doing and what you say.

APRIL 7 ★ *life of the party*
You can be the leader of the pack today as a charming Venus-Mars conjunction in fearless Aries falls in your 11th House of Friends. Your playful personality lights up just about any room and inspires others to follow you to discover new forms of enjoyment. The Moon's presence in your 10th House of Public Responsibility naturally puts you in the spotlight, where your flirty and funny personality brightens the day of those fortunate enough to have you as a friend.

SUPER NOVA DAYS
APRIL 19–21 ★ *watch your tongue*
Slow down and think through situations before you act or speak impulsively on **April 19**, when talkative Mercury is sideswiped by a clunky quincunx from repressive Saturn. However, the reins of patience are not easy to find on the **20th** when Mercury joins volatile Uranus. Brilliant ideas and unconventional perspectives are gifts of this aspect, but restless feelings and provocative speech are its potential deficits. Sometimes you can get away with an inappropriate quip or shocking story—but not on the **21st**, when Mercury's tense square with investigative Pluto pushes past the surface to expose flaws in any argument while revealing previously hidden facts.

APRIL 23 ★ *the art of persuasion*
You can connect the dots and make sense of complex issues with a Mercury-Jupiter sextile, giving you the data to back up your beliefs and a big-picture overview to find meaning in seemingly separate ideas. Your verbal skills and capacity to convince others are exceptional when you have this high level of mental acuity.

APRIL 26 ★ *cloudy thoughts*
You lose sight of the line between reality and fantasy when the normally sharp vision of astute Mercury is blurred by a stressful semisquare with mythological Neptune. While this imaginative aspect is wonderful for speaking in poetic terms, be careful not to wander beyond the bounds of reason; a mental detour can be confusing to you and misleading to others.

MAY

IN OR OUT

Finding a consistent approach isn't easy this month as you vacillate between your need for privacy and your desire for attention. The month begins with the Sun in your secretive 12th House, indicating the value of escaping from people and responsibilities so that you can recharge your batteries. Yet sociable Venus's entry into Gemini on **May 9** makes you more popular than ever. Teasing may not be your intention, but it's what people perceive as you dance in and out of contact, one moment fully present and the next one gone somewhere else. A Taurus New Moon Eclipse, also on the **9th**, falls in your 12th House of Inner Peace, continuing the call to reconnect with your spiritual life through prayer or meditation. Yet on **May 15**, your curious ruling planet, Mercury, bounces into Gemini and your 1st House of Personality, where expressing yourself more openly pulls you out of the shadows once more.

The last remnants of your shyness and caution seem to wash away with the Sun's shift into Gemini on **May 20**, combined with the revolutionary Uranus-Pluto square. However, the expansive urges of outgoing Jupiter in your sign are constrained by a tense sesquisquare with sobering Saturn that inhibits enthusiasm, also on the **20th**. This transit is not meant to stop you in your tracks, but to remind you to proceed with caution, instead of recklessly rushing ahead. Unreliable partners or your confusion about someone else's intentions could create complications with the Sagittarius Full Moon Eclipse in your 7th House of Relationships on the **25th**. Sharing exciting dreams with others is delicious, but do your homework before assuming that a divine moment of inspiration will lead to a lasting alliance.

> **KEEP IN MIND THIS MONTH**
>
> *Freely choosing when to engage with others and when to withdraw reveals your strength and self-confidence rather than any lack of commitment.*

KEY DATES

MAY 4–7 ★ *applied intuition*

Your psychic powers awaken on the **4th**, when perceptive Mercury in your metaphysical 12th House forms a free-flowing sextile with otherworldly Neptune. But you're quickly called back to reality as expressive Mercury opposes earthbound Saturn on the **5th**, which can let some air out of your creative balloon. Fortunately, inspiration is not completely lost since mental Mercury's easy trine with regenerative Pluto on the **7th** recalls vital information and helps you tap into deeper meaning.

MAY 11 ★ *inner guidance*

A conjunction of the Sun and Mercury puts your heart and mind on the same track, producing clarity of vision and a greater sense of self-awareness. These insights, though, may not be ready for public expression—they are connected to an inner journey in your 12th House of Soul Consciousness rather than to worldly success. The answers you find can tell you more about your higher purpose, rather than simply providing you with data to help you achieve your material goals.

MAY 18 ★ *parallel universes*

Trickster Mercury in dualistic Gemini shows you the contrast between cold, hard reality and a rosy world of fantasies. Happily, you are well equipped to shift mental gears from the dreamscape of a Mercury-Neptune square to the pressing demands of a Mercury quincunx to Saturn. Avoid the disappointment that comes when hope is buried under the weight of duty. Breaking down a vision that seems out of reach into small steps will begin to make it more tangible.

SUPER NOVA DAYS
MAY 24–25 ★ *the price of peace*

You're at your most clever, playful, and charming best on **May 24** when captivating Venus joins your friendly ruling planet, Mercury. This aspect is ideal for discussing difficult subjects with graciousness that can smooth out the biggest bumps. The downside is that you tend to gloss over long-term differences in the name of short-term peace and harmony. Agreements that lack substance or sincerity, though, can melt away on the **25th** with a Solar Eclipse in your 7th House of Partners that squares squishy Neptune.

MAY 27–28 ★ *quality not quantity*

Your brain is running at warp speed and your mouth may be moving just as quickly on **May 27**. Communicator Mercury's conjunction with prosperous Jupiter hasn't occurred in your sign for more than a decade. You've hit a rich vein of ideas, a veritable treasure trove of information. Seductive Venus's conjunction with Jupiter on the **28th** could be equally bountiful when it comes to love, pleasure, and recognition. Use these powers selectively instead of believing that everything is for your pleasure.

JUNE

CHOOSE YOUR PRIORITIES WISELY

You're ready to take the initiative and run with it this month with the willful Sun and unstoppable Mars both traveling through your sign. Self-improvement is especially appealing with these planets in your 1st House of Personality—but hold on to your patience, since interactive Mercury is slowing down until **June 26**, when it stops dead in its tracks and begins its retrograde cycle. The cosmic messenger backpedals in your 1st House until **July 20**, requiring you to retrace your steps and redo tasks you may have done hastily. Valuable Venus's move into cautious Cancer and your 2nd House of Income on **June 2** also signals that you gain more when you progress at a measured pace. It's hard to stand still, though, with the jumpy Gemini New Moon on the **8th** within range of exuberant Jupiter. But, as is often the case, success hinges on choosing the best opportunity of the bunch before you.

Trust your intuition regarding work matters on **June 11** when stabilizing Saturn in your 6th House of Employment trines visionary Neptune in your 10th House of Career. Your imagination is a powerful tool that helps you make your professional dreams come true. This supportive aspect occurred on **October 10, 2012**, and will return on **July 19**. Financial matters are highlighted with the Sun's move into tenacious Cancer and your 2nd House of Money on the **21st**, marking the Summer Solstice. Solid Saturn sextiles the tightfisted Capricorn Full Moon in your 8th House of Shared Resources on the **23rd**, encouraging fiscal responsibility. Reliable partners can help you cash in on the long-term economic benefits of fortunate Jupiter's yearlong transit of your resourceful 2nd House starting on **June 25**.

> **KEEP IN MIND THIS MONTH**
>
> *Concentrate your energy where it counts most in order to enhance your self-worth and increase your net worth.*

KEY DATES

JUNE 3 ★ *dare to believe*

You can discuss delicate matters skillfully thanks to a combination of compassion and tact as verbal Mercury forms favorable trines to sensitive Neptune and mature Saturn. This supportive cosmic collaboration helps you bring a vague hope or dream down to earth with a perfect balance between practicality and inspiration.

JUNE 7–8 ★ *head in the clouds*

You're more interested in chasing dreams than addressing current realities today when impulsive Mars in scattered Gemini squares diffusive Neptune. Yet cerebral Mercury's opposition to potent Pluto indicates that such careless thinking could prove costly. Spilling secrets or failing to read the fine print might undercut the trust of a business associate and lead to unnecessary expenses. Allowing yourself a few moments to wander freely can provide some much-needed break time, but when it comes to critical issues, keep your mind focused on the bottom line.

JUNE 17 ★ *lost in translation*

Your fresh style and unique approach set you apart from the crowd thanks to a slick sextile between impromptu Mars and unconventional Uranus. Now that the Moon is hanging out in your playful and self-expressive 5th House, your infectious joy is turning heads in your direction. However, a slippery Mercury-Neptune sesquisquare colors communication with emotions that can mislead others or allow you to misinterpret someone else's message. Make sure you're on the same page before you assume your words have been understood.

SUPER NOVA DAYS
JUNE 19–20 ★ *happy days*

Your optimism soars with the Sun's conjunction to buoyant Jupiter on **June 19**, expanding your vision and opening your heart to possibilities beyond the limits that currently shape your life. It is possible, though, to turn a tiny problem into a gigantic cloud of doubt. Fortunately, fresh information inoculates you against fear and allows you to ride this rising tide to greater joy and recognition. Verbal Mercury and sociable Venus join in nurturing Cancer and your 2nd House of Income on the **20th**, helping you balance bombast with a tender touch that increases intimacy and earns you trust. A sharp eye for value is ideal for getting the most out of your abilities.

JUNE 26 ★ *playing it safe*

The Moon in futuristic Aquarius raises your eyes toward distant horizons in your 9th House of Faraway Places. But if you fail to pay attention to what's right in front of you, you could stumble. Mercury is turning retrograde in your 2nd House of Values, where holding on to what you have is worth more than buying a ticket to a land of make-believe.

JULY

BET ON YOURSELF

This is a great month for organizing your life, setting long-term goals, and establishing successful plans to reach them. Professional aspirations come into focus with a Grand Water Trine between Jupiter in your 2nd House of Income, Saturn in your 6th House of Employment, and Neptune in your 10th House of Career on **July 17–19**. These outer planets in sensitive water signs align your inner needs and your external ambitions with an almost perfect balance of optimism (Jupiter), realism (Saturn), and imagination (Neptune). Solidity and steadiness are also indicated by steadfast Saturn's direct turn on the **8th**, which puts work-related issues on a slow but productive path. Mercury's forward shift in your 2nd House on the **20th** gives you a clearer understanding of your self-worth that helps you to maximize your resources.

You're eager for changes in money matters when the Cancer New Moon occurs in your 2nd House on **July 8**. However, unforgiving Pluto's opposition to this lunation from your 8th House of Deep Sharing could mean that you're hitting a financial wall. You may need to reorganize debt, reduce expenses, or renegotiate an economic partnership before you can cash in on this potentially lucrative transit. Assertive Mars moves into your 2nd House of Finances on the **13th**, adding both motivation and muscle to your efforts at increasing your income. Mars joins opulent Jupiter on the **22nd** as the inventive Aquarius Full Moon lights up your 9th House of Big Ideas. You may be enthralled by an entrepreneurial spirit or develop a sudden thirst for additional education. While this is an appropriate time to consider grand schemes, value-setting Venus's entry into analytical Virgo reminds you to be thrifty and precise with your investments of time, money, and energy.

KEEP IN MIND THIS MONTH

Nurturing your natural talents and developing new ones are not only keys to material well-being, but can also become deep sources of satisfaction.

KEY DATES

JULY 4–5 ★ *silent fireworks*

You're extra jittery on **July 4** when the Sun squares unstable Uranus. Yet an inner call for freedom may suddenly urge you to discover how you hold yourself back from fulfilling your potential. Don't dissipate the power of this insight by trying to explain it to others. Communicative Mercury's spacey sesquisquare with cloudy Neptune on the **5th** is more likely to cause confusion than clarity.

JULY 9 ★ *self-reflection*
When retrograde Mercury backs over the Sun, you look deeply within to reconsider what you want most out of life. You probably won't fulfill those needs right away, but this is an excellent chance to align your head and heart—a key to expressing yourself with feeling and, perhaps, ultimately achieving your goals. When direct Mercury again conjuncts the Sun on **August 24**, you can put today's ideas into concrete form.

SUPER NOVA DAYS
JULY 17–20 ★ *master plan*
On **July 17**, opportunistic Jupiter's favorable trine with hardworking Saturn brings you a strategic vision for major growth that you'll refine when this aspect returns on **December 12** and **May 24, 2014**. But Jupiter's trine to Neptune on the **17th** is a onetime transit that inspires professional dreams— and may show you a more meaningful way to contribute to society. Speedy Mars provides motivation and efficiency with his trines to Neptune and Saturn on the **20th**. Reaching these imaginative heights requires real, on-the-ground action instead of pie-in-the-sky speculations. Making the most of your resources with Mars in your 2nd House of Self-Worth includes taking care of yourself as well as continuing to augment your skills.

JULY 22 ★ *run a tight ship*
You're filled with confidence as the wind whips through your sails with a super-dynamic Mars-Jupiter conjunction in your 2nd House of Personal Resources. The Sun's shift into dramatic Leo and your 3rd House of Communication emboldens your words and enhances your creativity while artistic Venus dances into your 4th House of Roots, either supporting your aspirations with competence or holding you back with unfinished business on the home front.

JULY 27 ★ *integrity counts*
You work hard for what you receive today, yet these honest efforts produce enduring results. The Sun's square to prudent Saturn reminds you to avoid overreaching. An intense Mars-Pluto opposition in your financial 2nd and 8th Houses requires total concentration and careful spending. Although you can't buy your way to happiness, you can fight for what you need.

AUGUST

ZEN WARRIOR

It's tempting to overlook details when you're enthused about a major project, but focusing on the little things can help you avoid being sideswiped by surprises this month. Gigantic Jupiter, astrology's most optimistic planet, opposes penetrating Pluto on **August 7**, a pattern that returns on **January 31** and **April 20, 2014**. Brace yourself: A cynical person or withdrawal of expected support from others could puncture your balloon of ambition or self-importance. Limiting your reach and concentrating on one step at a time helps you through a potential minefield of mistrust and manipulation. Stressful squares from explosive Uranus to Jupiter in your 2nd House of Income on the **21st** can produce financial shocks. However, this aspect, which repeats on **February 26** and **April 20, 2014**, could also bring you original moneymaking ideas.

Your active mind is especially fertile now as the creative Leo New Moon in your 3rd House of Information trines inventive Uranus on **August 6**. Confident communication and bright ideas glow with excitement when candid Mercury moves into entertaining Leo on the **8th**. Graceful Venus enhances your charms as she glides into irresistible Libra and your 5th House of Romance on the **16th**. The call of freedom is in the air on the **20th**, when the independent Aquarius Full Moon brightens your 9th House of Adventure. A lunar conjunction with intoxicating Neptune evokes fantasies about getting away from it all. You return to reality on **August 22–23** when the Sun and Mercury enter fastidious Virgo and your domestic 4th House. Refining the ways that you run your home and live with your family entails a complicated mix of thinking and feeling. Nevertheless, observing how your unconscious operates can help you turn anxiety into opportunity.

> **KEEP IN MIND THIS MONTH**
>
> *Recognizing and respecting the line between enthusiasm and hyperactivity makes it possible to enjoy the thrills of discovery without your energy getting lost or scattered.*

KEY DATES

AUGUST 4 ★ *emotional authenticity*

It's courageous to reveal your vulnerability instead of just showing off the positive side of your personality. The bighearted Leo Sun shining in your 5th House of Self-Expression motivates you to take chances in demonstrating your feelings with its liberating trine to spontaneous Uranus in your 12th House of Secrets. Honesty can be tricky, but you earn trust when you come straight from your heart.

SUPER NOVA DAYS
AUGUST 11-14 ★ *silence is golden*
You may be frustrated when you don't get the answers you're seeking on **August 11**, as unyielding Saturn forms a blocking square to inquisitive Mercury. But think about keeping silent for a change, rather than feeling compelled to talk when you don't have anything to say. Mercury's clunky quincunx with discreet Pluto on the **13th** also inhibits the conversational flow. But a benefit of these restrictive transits is that they can force you to do some deep, perhaps life-changing, thinking. The stopper comes out of the bottle on the **14th** when mouthy Mercury in your 3rd House of Communication is freed to speak spontaneously by a fiery trine to uncontainable Uranus.

AUGUST 19-22 ★ *politically incorrect*
You resist rules and authority as philosophical Jupiter's square to radical Uranus on the **21st** kicks in early with hard solar aspects to both planets on **August 19**. Still, you might be reluctant to express your feelings openly with Mercury's sesquisquare to underground Pluto on the **20th**. But holding your tongue isn't easy when Mercury makes stressful aspects to opinionated Jupiter and irreverent Uranus on the **22nd**. You may be exploding with brilliance, but you risk using provocative language and behavior that upsets others.

AUGUST 25 ★ *mental holiday*
This is a perfect day to relax and let your mind wander. Mercury's opposition to surreal Neptune sets the stage for storytelling, daydreaming, and escaping reality. Avoid serious business or initiating conversations where you're seeking facts and figures. Minor irritations at home can surface, but practicing compassion and forgiveness are better uses of your time now than trying to take corrective action.

AUGUST 27-30 ★ *practical pursuits*
Your clarity returns on the heels of a logical Mercury-Saturn sextile on **August 27**. Trust earned by hard work and accountability invite deeper discussions and insights with Mercury's trine to penetrating Pluto on the **28th**. The solidity you gain pays off in expansive vision and unwavering optimism from the Mercury-Jupiter sextile on the **30th**. Yet the communication planet's presence in your pragmatic 6th House means you need to apply ideas in the real world rather than simply playing in the conceptual realms.

SEPTEMBER

FROM THE GROUND UP

Turn your attention inward to examine your personal needs this month as you build a more solid foundation for the future. The skillful Virgo New Moon falls in your 4th House of Roots on **September 5**, signaling the importance of maintaining a healthy home and family life. This lunation's harmonious aspects to farseeing Jupiter and surgical Pluto help you to cut away the fat of unrealistic expectations to focus your efforts on an ambitious plan that's within your reach. This is not, however, an enterprise to be taken lightly; you must carefully attend to every detail and even cultivate new skill sets to achieve your goal. Concentration at work is especially valuable with resourceful Venus's entry into insightful Scorpio and your 6th House of Employment on **September 11**. If you can exercise discretion with colleagues, you'll earn and avoid potential jealousy and mistrust.

The inspired Pisces Full Moon on **September 19** illuminates your 10th House of Career, arousing enthusiasm about your job or public service. Yet you may also take on responsibilities that stretch you beyond the limits of your experience, time, or energy. Don't be shy about asking for support if you need it or declining an opportunity for which you aren't adequately trained. A savvy Saturn-Pluto sextile on the 21st provides a reality check that helps you recognize your boundaries and shows you where you must apply more effort. Your heart starts to sing when the Sun shifts into sociable Libra and your 5th House of Love and Play on the **22nd**. This is the Autumn Equinox and heralds a new season for personal pleasure and creative expression.

> **KEEP IN MIND THIS MONTH**
>
> *Aiming for the sky is exhilarating when you're fully fueled for the journey and have the necessary support system to ensure a successful experience.*

KEY DATES

SEPTEMBER 2–4 ★ *facts trump feelings*

Jumping to conclusions puts you in a precarious position as Mercury's stressful semisquare to impatient Mars provokes fast answers on the **2nd**. Defending your ideas, especially new ones, can spur arguments if you lose your cool. Mercury semisquares karmic Saturn on the **4th**, requiring you to support your position with solid data. If your words are based on reality, patiently making your point will build a stronger case than being pushy or withdrawing out of frustration.

SEPTEMBER 9–11 ★ *duty calls*

Emotions are decidedly mixed on the **9th** when chatty Mercury glides into lovely Libra and your 5th House of Romance. You're eager to entice others to come out and play and could sweet-talk your way into someone's heart. However, bold Mars in Leo in your verbal 3rd House slams into a square with naysaying Saturn that loads you down with work or deflates you with a frustrating task. You may be tempted to shirk your responsibilities when Mercury skids on a quincunx with slippery Neptune on the **11th**, but using your imagination to help you find solutions is more creative than making endless excuses.

SUPER NOVA DAYS
SEPTEMBER 14–17 ★ *adrenaline rush*

Relationship negotiations grow intense with Mercury's square to Pluto in your 8th House of Intimacy on **September 14**. Don't just put a pretty face on a disturbing union; honest conversation—painful as it might be—is a strong step toward healing. If you're locked into a repetitive loop of negative thinking, an innovative Mars-Uranus trine can open the way to unexpected solutions. A high-frequency Mercury-Uranus opposition on the **16th** tests your patience and agitates your nerves. Still, an experimental attitude makes you a fascinating source of fresh ideas. Mercury's harmonious sextile with insistent Mars on the **17th** offers both passionate speech and a sensitive delivery that helps you send strong messages in a reassuring manner.

SEPTEMBER 19–20 ★ *stairway to heaven*

Imagination carries you over the rainbow thanks to Mercury's square to overblown Jupiter on the **19th** and sesquisquare with illusory Neptune on the **20th**. Go ahead and dream the impossible dream, but don't try to sell others on your vision until you're certain that it's real.

SEPTEMBER 27–29 ★ *the art of seduction*

You mesmerize others on **September 27** when a clever Mercury-Pluto quintile deepens your perceptions and infuses your words with subtle power. Mercury's entry into profound Scorpio and your systematic 6th House on the **29th** increases your understanding of how to use language to get your way.

OCTOBER

HEAD OVER HEELS

Your relationship life should be exciting, inspiring, and maybe even a bit dangerous this month. The urge to open your heart and experience love in different forms can provoke risky behavior with the lovely Libra New Moon in your 5th House of Romance on **October 4**. This charming lunation increases opportunities to freely express yourself and attract plenty of attention for it. But the smooth sailing associated with socially skillful Libra may be interrupted by unexpected events, power struggles, and excessive reactions as the New Moon opposes rebellious Uranus and squares controlling Pluto and bombastic Jupiter. Your passion for pushing the limits of partnership is underscored with amorous Venus's move into adventurous Sagittarius and your 7th House of Others on **October 7th**. The love planet tempts you to toss caution to the wind and pursue pleasure with unreliable individuals.

A partial retreat may be in order when normally aggressive Mars minces into meticulous Virgo and your 4th House of Roots on the **15th**. Attending to minor domestic problems and home maintenance isn't nearly as much fun as running with the wind. However, turning critical thoughts into constructive actions transforms self-doubt and irritability into greater competence and efficiency. Friends may distract you from your duties with the Lunar Eclipse in your 11th House of Groups on the **18th**. This impatient Aries Full Moon propels you into starting new projects when a logical look at the costs of participation should make you think twice. The need to reconsider your commitments and make adjustments on the job comes with Mercury's retrograde turn in your 6th House of Employment on **October 21**. You may have to double back and redo some tasks at work, but more streamlined methods will increase productivity in the long run.

KEEP IN MIND THIS MONTH

Riding an emotional wave of excitement makes your life interesting now, but a little bit of caution can keep you from wiping out.

KEY DATES
OCTOBER 1–2 ★ *psychic hotline*
On **October 1** crafty Mercury in your job-related 6th House forms a favorable trine to metaphysical Neptune in your 10th House of Career, tuning you in to clever ways to handle colleagues and customers and solve problems. Trust your instincts even if you don't have the facts to back them up right now. Mercury's creative quintile to

speedy Mars in your heady 3rd House on **October 2** supplies original thinking and subtlety, helping you to gently make points that overcome opposition and doubt.

SUPER NOVA DAY
OCTOBER 8 ★ *face the music*
Expect to feel edgy today, as quicksilver Mercury rubs against quirky Uranus in an awkward quincunx. Minds and messages run amok, challenging you to maintain focus and keep facts in order. However, Mercury's subsequent conjunction with taskmaster Saturn in your 6th House of Details demands concentration and might punish you if you deviate even slightly from the rules. Positively, this aspect can motivate you to do some deep thinking that reveals essential information about your health or your job. Mercury backs into this union with Saturn again on **October 29** and **November 25**, giving you two more chances to put your intellectual ducks in a row.

OCTOBER 10–12 ★ *fantasy island*
Your compassion and imagination overrule your common sense on **October 10** when vivacious Venus and the radiant Sun form hard aspects with ungrounded Neptune, spurring you to pursue fantasies and overlook falsehoods. Opening your heart to others is fine as long as you're not making a serious investment of time, money, or energy. Evaluative Venus's unbalanced sesquisquare with expansive Jupiter on the **11th**, followed by the Sun's square to this excessively optimistic giant planet on the **12th**, reinforces the likelihood of seeing things and people as you wish them to be rather than as they really are.

OCTOBER 24 ★ *no more drama*
Minor matters at home could blow up into major issues if you allow the heat of a Mars-Jupiter semisquare to push you to extremes. Retrograde Mercury's quintile with Mars reminds you to focus on facts and keep an open mind if you want to deflate inappropriate anger and direct your emotions more effectively.

OCTOBER 29 ★ *think again*
You feel trapped in routine tasks or daily obligations thanks to Mercury's second conjunction—the first was on the **8th**—with rule-bound Saturn. But don't let delays in getting the information you seek or doubts about your ability to learn stop you cold; they're simply meant to slow you down until you have all the facts.

NOVEMBER

DEVILISH DETAILS

This month is all about improving your life by eliminating unhealthy habits and developing greater efficiency in your daily routine. November begins with perceptive Mercury in your 6th House of Work, where it's moving backward to bring your attention to unfinished business until **November 10**. Minor matters at your job could become major issues if you don't start fixing them quickly. The fourth of seven transformational Uranus-Pluto squares occurs in your sensitive 12th and 8th Houses on **November 1**, awakening volcanic emotions that could rock your world. Pay close attention to your feelings, but think carefully before you act on them. The Scorpio New Moon on the **3rd** is a Solar Eclipse in your 6th House that signals fresh challenges in your place of employment. Happily, industrious Mars in Virgo sextiles this Sun-Moon conjunction, enhancing your ability to handle any unexpected changes.

Reliable allies are a must when enterprising Venus enters disciplined Capricorn and your 8th House of Deep Sharing on **November 5**. It's better to have demanding partners with high standards than easygoing ones who lack commitment, loyalty, or professionalism. Exercise financial restraint when extravagant Jupiter turns retrograde in your 2nd House of Money on **November 7**. Methodical management of your material and emotional resources gives you the staying power to achieve your most ambitious goals. On the **17th**, the pastoral Taurus Full Moon shines in your metaphysical 12th House, reminding you that peace and quiet are essential for recharging your batteries and lifting your spirits. The Sun fires into outgoing Sagittarius and your 7th House of Others on the **21st**, attracting adventurous partners and enabling you to be a more dynamic spokesperson for your beliefs.

> **KEEP IN MIND THIS MONTH**
>
> *Tackling small but essential tasks is tedious work, but will help you weave a web of efficiency that ultimately allows you to get more done in less time.*

KEY DATES

NOVEMBER 1 ★ cut to the chase

You can put your finger on a key idea and express it with power and precision today as retrograde Mercury joins the Sun and forms a clear-thinking sextile with incisive Mars. Take time to reflect upon your heart's desires, especially related to work, since Mercury's solar conjunction occurs in your 6th House of Employment.

However, some personal thoughts are not yet ready for prime time and don't need to be shared with others.

SUPER NOVA DAYS

NOVEMBER 8-11 ★ *into the mystic*

Your vivid imagination allows you to talk your way around a tricky situation. Sweet conversations are supported by expressive Mercury's gentle sextile with pleasing Venus on the **8th**. This transit is ideal for patching up a misunderstanding with a close friend or colleague. On the **9th**, a cooperative sextile from action-planet Mars to systematic Saturn in your 6th House of Service raises your productivity without burning you out. Your creativity soars as Mercury forms harmonious trines to intuitive Neptune the day before and after its shift to forward motion on **November 10**. This is like sprinkling a little fairy dust, showing you just how to send strong messages wrapped up in subtle packages.

NOVEMBER 20 ★ *turn the tables*

Don't fret if your day gets off to a rough start; you'll have enough self-awareness to put it back on track before it's over. An uncomfortable early-morning quincunx between Mercury and Uranus makes you nervous with odd thoughts and unusual events. Yet the evening's supportive sextile between Mercury and ruthless Pluto helps you brush aside distractions, set your priorities, and communicate with power and purpose.

NOVEMBER 24-25 ★ *reality check*

Confusing partners complicate your life on the **24th** when the Sun in your 7th House of Relationships squares irrational Neptune. Inspiring connections are wonderful as long as you realize that what you're hearing may be pipe dreams. Reality lands with a thud on the **25th** when Mercury connects with somber Saturn. Eliminate bad ideas forever, but examine those concepts that have a scintilla of potential; perhaps one of them will prove worthy of further study.

NOVEMBER 27-28 ★ *smarty-pants*

Mercury's sextile to stylish Venus on **November 27** aligns you with people of good taste. But the promises of profit or pleasure will grow even stronger when the messenger planet trines infectious Jupiter on the **28th**. Your capacity to learn, teach, and communicate is at a peak, enabling you to motivate others and inspire them with your wisdom.

DECEMBER

ATTITUDE ADJUSTMENT

Take a second look at relationships this month—and maybe even a third or fourth—as new partnerships and old alliances are put to the test. On **December 2,** the New Moon in Sagittarius falls in your 7th House of Others, sprouting seeds of opportunity for making connections or taking a current union to a higher level. A supportive trine from surprising Uranus adds excitement and innovation, but a challenging square to this lunation from spacey Neptune can take your enthusiasm beyond the bounds of reason. Loquacious Mercury's launch into friendly Sagittarius on the **4th** expands your social circles and is excellent for selling and teaching as long as you don't stretch the truth too far. Visionary Jupiter's trine with practical Saturn on **December 12** is the second in a series that began on **July 17** and ends on **May 24, 2014.** This strategic alignment in your 2nd House of Income and 6th House of Work provides a balanced perspective on professional matters that helps you make sensible long-term decisions.

You see the contrast between your own needs and those of others clearly under the bright light of the restless Gemini Full Moon on **December 17.** Consistency may elude you in this flexible sign, but allowing yourself to shift gears according to your moods nourishes your changeable soul. Order comes with the Sun's entry into traditional Capricorn and your 8th House of Intimacy on the **21st.** This turn of the season is the Winter Solstice, demanding accountability in relationships, constraining you with rigid rules, or helping you reach a higher level of engagement. Yet Venus's retrograde shift in the 8th House on the same day reminds you to reexamine your partnership expectations until this lovable planet turns forward on **January 31, 2014.**

> **KEEP IN MIND THIS MONTH**
>
> *Don't expect to find a single right answer to partnership questions now. Keep an open mind and try different approaches according to each situation.*

KEY DATES

DECEMBER 6–7 ★ *pie in the sky*

It's hard to know what's real as Mercury squares ephemeral Neptune on **December 6** and forms a clumsy sesquisquare with exaggerating Jupiter on the **7th.** You could find yourself sharing inaccurate information, buying into someone else's fantasy, or promising more than you can deliver. Exploring unconventional ideas is fine as long as you study them further prior to acting on them. You are likely, though, to become more alluring with passionate Mars's entry into likable Libra and your 5th House of Romance, also on the **7th**.

DECEMBER 10 ★ *intellectual pursuits*
There are no limits to how far your mind can travel today. Brainy Mercury's creative trine to brilliant Uranus in your 9th House of Faraway Places inspires original concepts that can help you overcome an impasse with someone stuck in the past. But try to be patient with conservative thinkers who may require more time to catch on to what you're proposing.

DECEMBER 15–16 ★ *less is more*
Your mental adeptness is off the charts on **December 15** with the Moon in your sign, while articulate Mercury makes a clever quintile with energetic Mars. But instead of relying on fast-talking now, you have the social skills to express yourself with elegance and grace. Yet on the **16th**, Mercury skids into an unstable quincunx with Jupiter; you might say more than you should or become overwhelmed by too much information.

DECEMBER 26–27 ★ *return to reason*
You can be so sweet on **December 26** with Mercury's sextile to compassionate Neptune. Kindness comes easily; you see the bright side of almost any situation and the best in almost every person. However, a Mercury-Saturn semisquare demands patience and pragmatism the next day, putting an end to silly thoughts and trivial communications.

SUPER NOVA DAYS
DECEMBER 29–31 ★ *fast-and-furious finish*
You may reach a breaking point with someone on **December 29** as Mercury connects with the principled Capricorn Sun in your 8th House of Transformation just before making a tense square to reactive Uranus. The Sun-Uranus square on the **30th** can suddenly alter the course of a relationship. Your need for freedom may be greater than your hunger for closeness, but it's healthier to take some time off or to reinvigorate a partnership with conscious intent than to let your emotions explode. Pressure continues to build through the **31st** as Mercury hooks up with steamy Pluto while both square combative Mars, a combination that can spark heated discussions. Focus on the facts to produce desirable change instead of letting negative feelings spur hurtful remarks.

CANCER

JUNE 21–JULY 22

CANCER

2012 SUMMARY

Observing the world and your own thoughts without making judgments is a powerful way to enhance your learning and expand your mind. It's terrific to be enthusiastic about broadening your horizons, yet care should be taken to avoid spreading yourself so thin that the costs exceed the benefits. If you spend all of your time trying to make your mark in the world, your foundation may become shaky, so don't lose sight of the importance of maintaining a happy home life that will support your ambitions.

AUGUST—*aim for the stars*
There is too much energy available to you now to use it on anything less important than striving to reach your highest aspirations.

SEPTEMBER—*stick to the facts*
Managing the minor details of your daily life more efficiently frees up time, energy, and mindshare for addressing bigger issues.

OCTOBER—*home is where the heart is*
Doing the challenging work of understanding other people's points of view will bring you the freedom to express your own more effectively.

NOVEMBER—*release and catch*
Addition by subtraction could be your theme this month, so try simplifying your life to exchange quantity for quality.

DECEMBER—*take charge*
It's better to be perceived as bossy—if that's what it takes to get what you want—than to come across as indecisive and weak.

2012 CALENDAR

AUGUST

THU 2–FRI 3 ★	Channel your frustration into an inspiring project
TUE 7–WED 8 ★	Stop worrying so much
THU 16–FRI 17 ★	Manipulation is a major hindrance to trust
WED 22–FRI 24 ★	**SUPER NOVA DAYS** Your energy continues to deepen and grow
SUN 26 ★	Join up with an ally in pursuit of a mutual dream

SEPTEMBER

MON 3 ★	Take a stand on your own behalf
THU 6–SAT 8 ★	Calculate the costs of fulfilling your dreams
SAT 17–SUN 18 ★	The price of emotional freedom is higher than you expect
SAT 15–SUN 16 ★	You may feel pulled in several directions
TUE 25–WED 26 ★	You are tempted to suddenly pick up and run away
SAT 29 ★	**SUPER NOVA DAY** You're ready for immediate change

OCTOBER

FRI 5–SUN 7 ★	Keep your actions rooted in reality
TUE 9–WED 10 ★	**SUPER NOVA DAYS** Make your dreams come true
MON 15–TUE 16 ★	Experiment at your job and in your daily routine
TUE 23–THU 25 ★	Hold on to your common sense
SUN 28–MON 29 ★	Beware of taking on more than you can handle

NOVEMBER

THU 1–SAT 3 ★	Reevaluate your needs and commit to fulfilling them
FRI 9 ★	You receive approval from unexpected sources today
FRI 16–SAT 17 ★	Take the initiative in relationships
WED 21–THU 22 ★	Stretch your boundaries
MON 26–WED 28 ★	**SUPER NOVA DAYS** Patience and persistence bring satisfaction

DECEMBER

SUN 2 ★	Don't fall for a story that sounds too good to be true
FRI 7 ★	Be open to new forms of fun today
MON 10–WED 12 ★	You're itching to speak your mind
FRI 21–SAT 22 ★	Present yourself with a newfound sense of authority
FRI 28–SUN 30 ★	**SUPER NOVA DAYS** Don't waste time doing battle

CANCER OVERVIEW

Y ou can't hide from the powerful changes that continue to rock your world this year. **In the past, you might have found safety by withdrawing into your protective shell, but now you must step outside the security of your home and family to engage the transformational forces that are asking you to evolve.** Your sign is known for its tendency to hold on to the past, but intense pressures to break away from the status quo began when revolutionary Uranus formed dynamic squares with relentless Pluto on June 24 and September 19, 2012. Your personal journey of metamorphosis continues to surprise you as the recurring Uranus-Pluto squares on May 20 and November 1 shake things up.

You are likely to become more deeply involved in a professional or personal relationship that has a compulsive element to it, since Pluto is in your 7th House of Partners. Pluto's regenerative process can overwhelm you at times, because something must come to an end before the new cycle can begin, but things should work out for the best as long as you're willing to meet others halfway. **Unexpected twists and turns on your career path are likely consequences of your entanglement with an influential person,** with unconventional Uranus holding court in your 10th House of Public Responsibility. Remember, although this long-lasting evolutionary process extends through 2015, it's easier to address the issues as they arise than to wait until a crisis forces you to change.

Benevolent Jupiter enters your sign on June 25 for a yearlong visit, blessing you with a wave of self-confidence. **Your optimistic attitude enables you to see the positive potential in even the most challenging situations.** Maximize the upcoming opportunities by finishing old business during the first half of the year when Jupiter is still in your 12th House of Endings. Although you're typically more comfortable waiting for something to happen and then reacting, Jupiter's shift into your 1st House of Self gives you more control over the events of your life. Circumstances are particularly favorable for turning your fantasies into reality when Jupiter forms a highly favorable Grand Water Trine with visionary Neptune and ambitious Saturn on July 17. A project or relationship that starts now could grow more permanent when the strategic Jupiter-Saturn trine reoccurs on December 12 and May 24, 2014. However, you may be tempted to take on more than you can handle or get involved in a conflict when Jupiter triggers the lingering Uranus-Pluto square on August 7 and August 21. Taskmaster Saturn, traveling through your 5th House of Self-Expression this year, requires a measure of self-discipline. **Learning to say no to pleasurable distractions demonstrates your depth of character and improves your chances for success.** Saturn's harmonious trines to imaginative Neptune on June 11 and July 19 help you establish a workable balance between your unreachable dreams and what's actually attainable.

SLOW AND STEADY

Impulsive romantic moves are frowned upon by stern Saturn in your 5th House of Love this year. A spring romance may stir your desires, but the intense Scorpio Lunar Eclipse on April 25 adds frustration because it conjuncts restrictive Saturn and opposes physical Mars. It will take time to overcome obstacles and reach lasting satisfaction in a relationship. Fortunately, your fantasy may come true when affectionate Venus visits your emotional sign on June 2–27 to warm your heart. Although love is in the spotlight when Venus moves through your playful 5th House on September 11–October 7, her conjunction with wary Saturn on September 18 cools your passion. Be clear about your commitments or Mercury's retrograde in your 5th House on October 21–November 10 may unravel an apparently stable partnership. Additionally, the Scorpio Solar Eclipse on November 3 is conjunct to Saturn the Tester, punishing reckless spontaneity while rewarding methodical planning and follow-through.

EXPECT THE UNEXPECTED

Radical Uranus continues its journey through your 10th House of Career this year, unleashing change when you least expect it. Its stressful squares to powerful Pluto on May 20 and November 1 suddenly reveal your need for freedom as you struggle with those who might be trying to control you. Nevertheless, you may begin planning an escape from your job even earlier, when active Mars runs through your 10th House on March 12–April 20. Unfortunately, showstopping Saturn restrains wild Uranus on April 12 and October 5, thwarting your efforts to take your plans to the next level. Thankfully, you can make progress more successfully when the Sun, Mercury, and Mars each take turns harmonizing with ingenious Uranus on August 4, August 14, and September 14.

 ## NO SHORTCUTS

You can make more money this year if you're willing to sweat for it. Hard-nosed Saturn is dampening the spirit of your 5th House of Play, limiting your profits from creative projects and risky enterprises. Forming an alliance with a competent person can help when enriching Venus visits your 7th House of Partners on January 8–February 1, especially on January 16–17. Taking initiative on the job or asking for a raise can put a few extra dollars in your bank account on March 28. Don't fall into the trap of buying unnecessary luxuries on May 28, even if you feel confident about your ability to pay for them. Saving money is advised through the summer; you may need the extra cash when Venus joins stingy Saturn on September 18.

 ## KNOW YOUR LIMITS

You're sure you can overcome nearly any infirmity simply through the healing power of positive thought on May 25, when the overconfident Sagittarius Lunar Eclipse activates your 6th House of Health and Habits. However, it's crucial to recognize the limits of mind over matter and to obtain qualified medical help if needed. Of course, practicing self-restraint while you are healthy can also be an aid to your well-being, especially once opulent Jupiter enters your sign on June 25.

 ## HOMEWARD BOUND

Many aspects of your life feel unstable this year and it's only natural that you counterbalance outward pressure by retreating inwardly. Thankfully, you won't need to wait until propitious Jupiter begins its yearlong visit to self-protective Cancer on June 25—although it does become easier for you to withdraw and recharge your emotional batteries. Venus leads the planetary parade into your 12th House of Privacy on May 9, encouraging you to step back from the chaos of everyday life. Entertaining at home is rewarding when pleasurable Venus visits your 4th House of Home and Family on August 16–

September 11. However, overcommitting can produce anxiety when Venus forms a Grand Square on August 24–27, causing plans to go awry.

THE SKY'S THE LIMIT

Neptune's long-term visit to your 9th House of Faraway Places colors your travel plans with an idealized, romantic air this year. Still, turning these fantasies of an ideal vacation into the journey of a lifetime is actually possible when realistic Saturn harmoniously trines magical Neptune on June 11. Additionally, journeying Jupiter swings into the picture to form a Grand Water Trine with Saturn and Neptune on July 17. Finalize your plans in June and hit the road in July. Your first wave of wanderlust occurs when restless Mars enters your adventurous 9th House on February 1; however, Mercury's retrograde on February 23–March 17 means that unforeseen complications could require your intervention, so make sure that all details are in place before you leave.

A LEAP OF FAITH

More than ever your dreams hold the key to your future. However, the danger isn't that you'll lose yourself in your fantasies; it's that you might hold yourself back because of old fears that have little to do with your present situation. Hopeful Jupiter is in your 12th House of Soul Consciousness until June 25, prompting you to question what's real as you seek the meaning of life. But Jupiter's shift into your 1st House of Self and its sweet trines to pragmatic Saturn and imaginative Neptune on July 17 enable you to manifest your visions. Enhance your spiritual growth by firm convictions and committed actions.

RICK & JEFF'S TIP FOR THE YEAR:
Reach Out and Receive

Nourish your personal growth this year by allowing yourself to have new experiences. Although you long to feel safe and secure, receiving what you want requires you to broaden your horizons. Be prepared to step outside your comfort zone instead of waiting for good things to come to your doorstep. You don't have to take major risks, but you can greatly benefit by going beyond your normal limits, even when it's scary.

JANUARY

THE POWER OF TWO

You are ready to take risks at work if you spot a chance to get ahead this month. Unfortunately, the results of your impulsive actions may not live up to your expectations. Collaborating with others, though, can bring slower, yet more reliable, advancement without jeopardizing your current stability. The Sun and logical Mercury remain in dependable Capricorn and your 7th House of Partners until **January 19**, indicating that someone has a steadying effect on you. But trickster Mercury squares erratic Uranus in your 10th House of Career on **January 3**, tempting you to stake your future on a fleeting idea. When peacekeeping Venus visits your 7th House on **January 8–February 1**, you realize what you must do to get along with others. Unfortunately, a sudden desire for immediate results on the **12th** may lead you into radical behavior that creates problems you don't anticipate. Nevertheless, your incisive thinking and relentless follow-though are valuable assets when relationships become intense as passionate Pluto conjuncts insistent Mercury on **January 6** and amorous Venus on **January 16**.

Rely on the conservative advice of a wise friend, business partner, or spouse on **January 11**, as the disciplined Capricorn New Moon falls in your 7th House of Companions. But the New Moon's disquieting aspect with pompous Jupiter encourages you to override common sense and step out on your own. Relationships may grow more complex as the Sun and Mercury enter your 8th House of Deep Sharing on the **19th**, but good fortune lightens the load on **January 22–25**. Still, be ready to rein in an extravagant purchase or a carefree lifestyle when the lavish Leo Full Moon on the **26th** squares austere Saturn.

> **KEEP IN MIND THIS MONTH**
>
> *Although you're typically cautious, you may be itching to make your move now. Thankfully, listening to another person's perspective shows you the value in a more moderate approach.*

KEY DATES

JANUARY 1–4 ★ *haste makes waste*

Someone may talk you into believing a fairy tale on **January 1** when cunning Mercury in your 7th House of Others aligns with fanciful Neptune. But you could be overwhelmed from too much information on **January 3** as Mercury's dynamic square with brilliant Uranus fills your head with streams of new ideas. The fast pace of conversations, emails, texts, and phone calls can be so exciting that success seems close enough to touch. The buoyant Mars-Jupiter trine on the **4th** urges you to act with confidence. A fortunate outcome is likely if you avoid rash behavior, make a sensible plan, and conserve your energy so you can finish what you start.

JANUARY 7-8 ★ *patience is a virtue*
Your efforts to cooperate with others may be thwarted when resistant Saturn squares assertive Mars in your 8th House of Deep Sharing on **January 7**. It's particularly frustrating if a trusted friend or business ally is the one who's blocking your progress. However, you're able to meet the challenges with a smile as gracious Venus enters hardworking Capricorn and your 7th House of Partnerships on the **8th**. Don't give up now; withdraw, regroup, and retry when you're ready.

JANUARY 16-18 ★ *talk it out*
Give relationships top priority now with four planets congregating in your 7th House of Companions. Sultry Venus bumps into shadowy Pluto on **January 16**, revealing hidden desires and secret agendas. The intense emotions that are expressed can be overwhelming, yet you could also build intimacy if you're willing to go deep. Fortunately, communicator Mercury joins the radiant Sun on **January 18**, clarifying your thoughts and enabling you to stick with a conversation until the issue is resolved.

SUPER NOVA DAYS
JANUARY 22-26 ★ *integrity counts*
Whatever you think right now can come true as long as you remain flexible with the details. Smooth trines to abundant Jupiter from Mercury on the **22nd** and from the Sun on the **25th** turn the days prior to the theatrical Leo Full Moon into a show of their own. Additional aspects from Mercury and the Sun to irrepressible Uranus on the **22nd** and **24th** can't help but increase the air of unpredictability. However, on the **26th** the Full Moon in your 2nd House of Values urges you not to compromise your core beliefs for the sake of fleeting success.

JANUARY 30 ★ *necessary detour*
A constrictive Sun-Saturn square prevents you from racing through a critical life intersection today. You may feel as if a wall is blocking your creativity, but it's really just a reminder that you cannot continue on your merry way until your previous responsibilities have been fulfilled.

FEBRUARY

FANTASY ISLAND

You dream about a journey to an exotic destination this month as a parade of planets enters imaginative Pisces and your 9th House of Faraway Places. Impulsive Mars leads the pack on **February 1**, adding a sense of urgency to your plans while giving you the drive to pursue an ambitious aspiration. On the **5th**, poetic Mercury enters your 9th House, inspiring you to think of your future on a grander scale than ever before. However, turning your thoughts into reality may take longer than you expect since Mercury retrogrades on **February 23**. Although the details of your itinerary could change dramatically during Mercury's three-week reversal, you are being given extra time to put all the pieces in order. The Sun's shift into your 9th House of Travel and Higher Education on the **18th** is yet another sign to reach beyond your normal boundaries. Your metaphysical horizons grow wider; even if there are no travel plans in your immediate future, enrolling in a new course of study is another way to satisfy the adventurous nature of the 9th House. On **February 25**, lovely Venus joins the pod of Pisces planets, turning up the volume on your escapist fantasies.

The intellectual Aquarius New Moon on **February 10** activates your 8th House of Intimacy and Transformation, prompting you to weigh the pros and cons of deepening a romance, rather than actually jumping in and doing it. On **February 25** the analytical Virgo Full Moon illuminates your 3rd House of Information, but her square to giant Jupiter pressures you to reach further than ever before. Fortunately, you have the tools to turn your vision into reality as long as you balance faith with reason.

> **KEEP IN MIND THIS MONTH**
>
> *Go ahead and follow your bliss—as long as you're clear about your intentions. Remember, pursuing magical experiences isn't enough; you also must seek meaning.*

KEY DATES

FEBRUARY 4–7 ★ *through the looking glass*

You don't know where to turn when dynamic Mars joins surreal Neptune on **February 4**. This conjunction occurs in your 9th House of Future Vision, allowing confusing dreams to replace specific goals. Mental Mercury shifts into phantasmagorical Pisces on the **5th** and conjuncts Neptune on the **6th**, further luring you into a chimeric world of possibilities and potentials. Hang tight rather than wandering too far; you're likely to experience joy when sweet Venus harmoniously trines lucky Jupiter on **February 7**.

SUPER NOVA DAYS
FEBRUARY 9–12 ★ *slow down*
Saying yes is easy when sassy Mercury and superhero Mars square strident Jupiter on **February 9–10**. The futuristic Aquarius New Moon on the **10th** is another signal to start something new. But you may not be very upbeat as congenial Venus crosses paths with naysaying Saturn on the **11th**. Sometimes hearing no is a blessing in disguise, because practicing self-restraint is helpful in the long run. Fortunately, a realistic Mercury-Saturn trine on the **12th** tells you that obstacles will fade if you take your time and methodically apply what you learn.

FEBRUARY 15–16 ★ *don't back down*
Expect success as enterprising Mars aligns smoothly with unrelenting Pluto and hardworking Saturn. You're wise to gratefully accept a powerful ally's assistance on **February 15** when Mars sextiles Pluto in your 7th House of Others. But you must not change horses midrace if you're to reach your goals, even if the going gets rough. Thankfully, Mars trines Saturn in your 5th House of Self-Expression on the **16th**, supplying you with plenty of determination and endurance, assuring that your actions will have the impact that you desire.

FEBRUARY 21–23 ★ *wishful thinking*
The ethereal Sun-Neptune conjunction in your 9th House of Big Ideas on **February 21** is mystifying, making it difficult to discern the truth. Your fantasies aren't real just because you can see them in vivid colors. Nevertheless, it's empowering to honor these glimpses of your ideal future. Just remember that mischievous Mercury's retrograde turn on **February 23–March 17** can create delays, so don't be surprised if you get lost trying to find the pot of gold at the rainbow's end.

FEBRUARY 25–28 ★ *incurable romantic*
Realism and idealism stand in stark contrast when the discerning Virgo Full Moon counterbalances five planets floating in dreamy Pisces on **February 25**. Although it isn't wise to escape reality, you may not be able to ignore the temptations of the overindulgent Sun-Jupiter square. However, don't fall victim to extravagant desires, even if Venus's shift into mystical Pisces on the **25th** and her conjunction with delusional Neptune on the **28th** make them hard to resist.

MARCH

BREAK OUT OF YOUR SHELL

Although social activities are keeping you busy, you feel safe in your cozy little world for the first part of the month. Even if a personal or professional relationship is stressful, you have a chance now to reestablish equilibrium while addressing critical issues. If both parties are willing to show up with authenticity, Saturn's stabilizing sextile to resolute Pluto in your 7th House of Others on **March 8** empowers you to solve a difficult relationship problem. Additionally, harmonious Pluto's aspects to the Sun on the **1st**, amicable Venus on the **6th**, and interactive Mercury on the **7th** create additional opportunities to make enduring connections with someone who is willing to be your mentor. However, the clairvoyant Pisces New Moon on **March 11** is a turning point that marks the beginning of a fresh cycle of outward, rather than inward, movement and exploration. This contemplative New Moon in your 9th House of Future Vision—as noted by seven planets in emotional Pisces—is your chance to look ahead with optimism while still holding on to the security of your past.

On **March 12**, courageous Mars fires into spontaneous Aries and your 10th House of Public Responsibility, pushing you to get ahead. Mercury ends its retrograde phase in your 9th House of Big Ideas on the **17th**, as ideas that have been on hold begin to come together. You may act uncharacteristically reckless when the Sun and Venus shift into impatient Aries on **March 20–21**, followed by a shocking Mars-Uranus conjunction on the **22nd**. Your life is on the move again, yet the Libra Full Moon on **March 27** gently reminds you that progress does not come without compromise.

> **KEEP IN MIND THIS MONTH**
>
> *Make smart use of the free time you have. You want to be well rested and well prepared when circumstances demand all your attention.*

KEY DATES

MARCH 1–4 ★ *to thine own self be true*

Your psychic powers are strong, yet it can be challenging to distinguish your feelings from those of a passionate friend on **March 1** when the empathic Pisces Sun-Pluto sextile emphasizes your 7th House of Others. Fortunately, the Sun's smooth trine with ethical Saturn in your 5th House of Creativity means that your emotional honesty is more important than anything else. You're tempted to take the easy way out, but succumbing to the indulgent Venus-Jupiter square on the **4th** will only distract you from the important work of being yourself.

MARCH 9–12 ★ *out of bounds*
Your intuition works overtime when witty Mercury forms a dynamic square with inflationary Jupiter in your 12th House of Fantasy on **March 9**. You are tempted to stretch the truth or to believe that your dreams are real. Either way, the New Moon in imaginary Pisces on the **11th** is the beginning of a more action-oriented cycle— which is confirmed when macho Mars blasts into unstoppable Aries on **March 12**.

SUPER NOVA DAYS
MARCH 20–23 ★ *claim your power*
Don't hide your true intentions right now, even if it's scary to take a chance by revealing what you want. The Sun's shift into headstrong Aries on **March 20** marks the Spring Equinox and the beginning of the astrological New Year, spurring you to take professional risks. Good-natured Venus joins the Sun, Mars, and Uranus in your 10th House of Career on the **21st**, enabling you to turn up the charm and present a more dynamic side of your personality at work, even while under stress. However, being friendly won't prevent you from insisting on getting your way when fearless Mars conjuncts rebellious Uranus on the **22nd**.

MARCH 25–28 ★ *no turning back*
You wrestle with mixed messages during the days prior to the ambivalent Libra Full Moon on **March 27**. A frustrating Mars-Saturn quincunx on the **25th** may have you doubting a recent decision, but Mars's sassy sextile to cheerful Jupiter on the **26th** quickly restores your self-confidence. Although the wisdom of the Mercury-Saturn trine on **March 28** calms your uncertainty, the Sun and Venus hook up with rowdy Uranus to entice you into acting recklessly in the pursuit of pleasure.

MARCH 31 ★ *in the name of love*
You may find yourself swimming in deep waters as Venus and the Sun both square formidable Pluto. You might need to defend your feelings or apologize for overstepping your limits. Thankfully, support from generous Jupiter indicates that your honorable intentions and honest approach can tip the odds in your favor.

APRIL

THE CALL OF THE WILD

This month gets off to a fiery start with four planets ramming through rowdy Aries and your 10th House of Career and Public Life. Although you are normally cautious about asserting yourself at work, you are growing more impatient every passing day and want your perspective taken into immediate consideration. It's exciting to forge ahead boldly as an uncharacteristic desire to take risks pulls you outside your comfort zone. Mercury adds to the uncertainty as it swims through murky Pisces in your 9th House of Adventure and into unexplored territory. The action picks up on **April 7** as creative Venus conjuncts with hyperactive Mars in your 10th House. You're challenged to keep up the frenetic pace, yet when the powerhouse Aries New Moon on **April 10** joins Venus and Mars, your enthusiasm prompts you to show off your leadership skills.

You may have doubts about your professional objectives on **April 12** as restraining Saturn forms an anxious quincunx to unsettling Uranus in your 10th House of Status. You might secretly wish that you could retreat into the safety of anonymity, but persuasive Mercury helps you talk your way back into the public eye on the **13th** as it enters your 10th House. You long for peace and quiet when Venus shifts into pastoral Taurus on **April 15** and may actually find time to relax when the Sun slips into easygoing Taurus and your 11th House of Community on **April 19**, followed by Mars on the **20th**. Although you may worry about the changes foretold with karmic Saturn's conjunction to the Scorpio Lunar Eclipse on **April 25**, you can handle them successfully if you rely on your common sense . . . and a little help from your friends.

> ### KEEP IN MIND THIS MONTH
>
> *Marshal your courage, let go of the shore, and head out to sea. The swiftly moving currents of change will carry you to your destination.*

KEY DATES

APRIL 1 ★ *dare to believe*

Confident Jupiter's supportive sextile to the audacious Aries Sun is enough to temporarily turn you, a cautious crustacean, into a fearless Ram. Further contemplation now won't make you any wiser. Forget about gathering additional facts or relying on logic. Follow your intuition and move ahead with unwavering certainty.

APRIL 6–8 ★ *waves of temptation*

You feel the subtle yet powerful pull of enchanting Neptune these days as it creates stressful aspects with sexy Mars, sensual Venus, and the brilliant Sun. Your creativity is irrepressible, especially when cosmic lovers Venus and Mars hook up on **April 7**. But Neptune's presence in your 9th House of Big Ideas indicates that the dream of starting a project or embarking on an adventure might be better than actually doing it. See how you feel in a few days before getting in over your head.

APRIL 10–12 ★ *make love, not war*

You jump into action furthering your career objectives when the combative Aries New Moon on **April 10** falls in your 10th House of Status. The New Moon's conjunction with warrior Mars gets your adrenaline pumping, but you could inadvertently escalate a heated conflict if you're not careful. Fortunately, captivating Venus is nearby to remind you that charm is a better weapon than aggression. Luckily, you will have a chance to put things back in order on the **12th** if you went too far. Conservative Saturn's alignment with progressive Uranus may feel awkward at first, yet it's crucial to overcome your embarrassment, make the necessary apologies, and move on.

APRIL 19–21 ★ *bite your tongue*

You finally gain traction toward your objectives when the Sun and Mars plow their way into grounded Taurus on the **19th** and **20th**. But watch what you say because messenger Mercury joins surprising Uranus on **April 20**, prompting you to speak before thinking. Temper your tone, or you might find yourself in an intense argument when Mercury squares forceful Pluto on the **21st**.

SUPER NOVA DAY
APRIL 25 ★ *stop and go*

You don't know whether to step on the gas or slam on the brake today due to the passionate Scorpio Lunar Eclipse aligning with hot Mars and cold Saturn. The Moon is eclipsed in your 5th House of Love and Creativity, so you find it challenging to express yourself in the moment. Fortunately, a smooth trine to compassionate Neptune enables you to take the high road as long as you remember that faith has helped you overcome obstacles in the past and will do so again in the future.

MAY

EMBRACE THE UNKNOWN

Although you start this month with your feet on the ground managing your responsibilities, you grow more reflective as the days wear on. However, it seems as if your progress is being thwarted at every turn, but your strong resolve enables you to prevail. Four planets traveling through determined Taurus and your 11th House of Long-Term Goals can make you stubborn, encouraging you to resist the pressure to change. However, adaptability becomes your secret weapon when magnetic Venus enters inquisitive Gemini and your 12th House of Soul Consciousness on **May 9**, stimulating your curiosity about spiritual practices. Meanwhile, a Taurus Solar Eclipse the same day reveals the instability of your current plans, suggesting that maintaining the status quo is no longer working.

The direction of your life is shifting, and transformations also occur on a more subconscious level as thoughtful Mercury joins visionary Jupiter and desirous Venus in your spiritual 12th House on **May 15**, followed by the Sun on the **20th** and Mars on the **31st**. Although these planets in restless Gemini increase the noise level in your head, these are not conversations that you want to have with anyone else. You are given a chance to contemplate your inner journey and its impact on your daily routine when the freedom-loving Sagittarius Lunar Eclipse shakes up your 6th House of Habits on the **25th**. There's plenty of change in your professional world, too, as the long-lasting Uranus-Pluto square on **May 20** influences your 7th House of Relationships and your 10th House of Career. This dynamic aspect isn't only about a single event, but rather the continuation of a metamorphosis that began on **June 24, 2012**, and lasts through **March 16, 2015**.

> ### KEEP IN MIND THIS MONTH
>
> *You're good at hiding your evolving feelings behind your protective outer shell. While you're actively working on your issues, others may be fooled by your apparent stillness.*

KEY DATES

MAY 1–5 ★ *in it to win it*

When you run into an obstacle, you often prefer to retreat rather than confront the situation directly. Right now, however, you have the willpower to overcome formidable odds and defend your position, thanks to constrictive Saturn in your 5th House of Self-Expression opposing aggressive Mars on **May 1** and expressive

Mercury on **May 5**. Fierce Pluto is your ally now as it harmonizes with the illuminating Sun on **May 1** and Mars on the **5th**, strengthening your spirit with unshakable convictions. Instead of withdrawing in defeat, hold your ground until the resistance begins to dissipate.

MAY 9–11 ★ *up in the air*

An easygoing Taurus New Moon is usually quite stabilizing, but on **May 9** a Solar Eclipse in your 11th House of Community indicates a sudden shift in your social life. Even if everything seems to be fine with your friends, trouble may be brewing—especially if you don't agree with your peers about an important issue. Your unwillingness to negotiate stems from five planets gathering in fixed Taurus and your future-minded 11th House. Fortunately, a creative quintile between communicator Mercury and altruistic Neptune allows you to make a deal that works for everyone. A focused Mercury-Sun conjunction on **May 11** aligns your words with your will, enabling you to say exactly what you mean.

SUPER NOVA DAYS
MAY 20–25 ★ *yell fire!*

Your words spill over with urgency as the revolutionary Uranus-Pluto square blasts articulate Mercury on **May 20**. Although powerful people are in your life to help you evolve now, Mercury's awkward aspect to Pluto means that you might not know what to say to them. Meanwhile, Mercury's easy sextile to uncontainable Uranus provokes you to make sudden exclamations that overstate your beliefs. You may find a gentler voice on the **24th** when Mercury conjuncts lyrical Venus in your 12th House of Inner Peace. However, the Sagittarius Full Moon Eclipse on **May 25** reignites your unexpressed fears of the unknown as it squares otherworldly Neptune. Remember that you're currently in a long-term process of change and it's not necessary yet to have all the answers.

MAY 31 ★ *don't worry, be happy*

Mars sneaks into your 12th House of Privacy today, giving you the sign that it's okay to keep a few secrets. And although Mercury the Messenger is shifting into your 1st House of Personality, you need to feel emotionally safe before revealing your thoughts. Thankfully, your concern about how others may react is likely unwarranted.

JUNE

HOME SWEET HOME

This extraordinary month affirms your inward focus, allows you to balance your dreams with reality, and begins a long-term cycle of opportunity. Emotional security is always important for you, so it's good news that steadfast Saturn's trine to spiritual Neptune spreads a magical safety net under you all month. Reflective Mercury—now in nurturing Cancer—completes a Grand Water Trine with Saturn and Neptune on **June 3**, enabling you to talk about your highest hopes in a concrete manner. These romantic fantasies come gently down to earth as affectionate Venus enters Cancer on **June 2** and reactivates the grand trine on **June 7**. On the **21st**, the Sun's entry into Cancer marks the Summer Solstice, enriching the present moment with childhood memories. The Sun's subsequent trines with Saturn and Neptune on the **26th** renew the persistent power of the Grand Water Trine that's motivating you to follow your dreams. Bountiful Jupiter's shift into your sign on the **25th** indicates a year of substantial growth.

Nevertheless, you also have your share of stress this month. Pressure from relationships and work tempts you to withdraw from the discomfort and hide out at home when Mercury harshly aspects relentless Pluto and reactive Uranus on **June 7–8**. The dualistic Gemini New Moon opens your mind to alternative perspectives, yet its occurrence in your 12th House of Escapism on the **8th** also reinforces your tendency to retreat. Receiving help from a friend or partner is likely on the **23rd** when the Capricorn Full Moon lights up your 7th House of Companions. Pay attention to every detail, because unfinished business creates complications when introspective Mercury turns retrograde in Cancer on **June 26** for three weeks of mental backtracking.

> ### KEEP IN MIND THIS MONTH
>
> *This is no time to get lazy, even if everything seems to be under control. Don't miss this rare opportunity to set the stage for what's ahead.*

KEY DATES

JUNE 2–3 ★ *beautiful dreamer*

You are blessed with extra charm this month as alluring Venus visits your sign on **June 2–27**, enticing you to put pleasure at the top of your agenda. Artistic creativity is supported on the **3rd** by clever Mercury's smooth trines to whimsical Neptune in your 9th House of Big Ideas and strategic Saturn in your 5th House of Self-Expression. Sharing your ideas with someone you trust is a good first step toward manifesting your dreams.

SUPER NOVA DAYS
JUNE 7-8 ★ *home is where your heart is*
Seductive Venus in tender Cancer relaxes into an emotionally grounded Grand Water Trine on **June 7**, inviting you to be vulnerable enough to share your feelings in supportive situations. Conversations may grow intense as verbose Mercury opposes passionate Pluto, yet you are securely anchored to safety with immutable Saturn's involvement in the grand trine. However, acting on your feelings can increase confusion with bold Mars squaring bewildering Neptune. The interactive Gemini New Moon on the **8th** helps to lighten the mood, but things may not turn out exactly as you expect with Mercury tensely squaring unpredictable Uranus. Thankfully, you are able to stay calm and centered as long as you are honest about what you want.

JUNE 11-12 ★ *between heaven and earth*
The exact trine between practical Saturn and magical Neptune on **June 11** enables you to keep your balance, even with one foot on the ground and the other floating in a higher dimension. This profound support can prevent you from destabilizing your love life when needy Venus squares wild and crazy Uranus on the **12th**. Inappropriate desires may catch you by surprise in a professional setting with Uranus in your 10th House of Career, but dependable Saturn's support empowers you to express yourself within reason.

JUNE 19-23 ★ *law of prosperity*
It's a lucky day when the Sun meets up with propitious Jupiter on **June 19** in your 12th House of Destiny. One phase of spiritual growth is culminating, with the next cycle starting when the Sun shifts into your sign on **June 21**. Act with confidence during the ambitious Capricorn Moon on the **23rd**, but remember that you're not invincible.

JUNE 25-26 ★ *sentimental journey*
Jupiter shifts into nostalgic Cancer on **June 25**—a cosmic blessing that increases your faith in yourself. It may take a while to see how the opportunities unfold because of Mercury's retrograde period on **June 26–July 20**. Still, the Sun's fabulous trines with Saturn and Neptune will lead you in the right direction.

JULY

SMOOTH SAILING

Positive feelings wash magically into your life this month as a persistent Grand Water Trine that first occurred in June continues to flow. However, tension that stems from conflicts between your personal or professional needs and the demands of others indicates a rough start to the month. Mischievous Mercury is retrograde in your 1st House of Self until **July 20**, obstructing your progress with delays that arise from mixed messages or sloppy thinking. It may require extra concentration to overcome your fears of rejection or being misunderstood on **July 8** when the supersensitive Cancer New Moon conjuncts retrograde Mercury.

Somber Saturn casts a dark cloud over your summer fun as it continues through your 5th House of Play. Still, you'll feel satisfied as long as you're focusing on your long-term goals, thanks to its fluid trine to dreamy Neptune in your 9th House of Future Vision. Practicing self-discipline became a priority on **June 11** when Saturn previously trined Neptune, and this helpful aspect repeats on **July 19**, allowing you to perfect your strategy. Meanwhile, on the **17th**, expansive Jupiter—now in your sign for a one-year visit—extends your vision even further as it forms a self-sufficient grand trine with Saturn and Neptune. Opportunities abound, and your quiet confidence spurs you to move ahead with your plans. Additionally, energetic Mars shifts into your 1st House on the **13th**, giving you more courage to initiate decisive action. Mars trines Saturn and Neptune on **July 20** and conjuncts Jupiter on **July 22** to strengthen your resolve, increase your enthusiasm, and raise the chances for your success. The intelligent Aquarius Full Moon, also on the **22nd**, fosters emotional detachment so you aren't swept away by delusions of grandeur.

> **KEEP IN MIND THIS MONTH**
>
> *Patience is a virtue as long as you don't wait forever. Eventually you must set your plans into motion, even if you struggle to overcome your own resistance.*

KEY DATES

JULY 1–4 ★ *catch and release*

You are hooked by your own desires on **July 1** as attractive Venus forms tough alignments with restrictive Saturn and addictive Neptune. Although your self-esteem can suffer if you don't get what you want right away, an unrelenting Sun-Pluto opposition forces you to fight for what you think is yours. Win or lose, a shocking Sun-Uranus square on the **4th** opens your eyes, radically alters your perspective, and turns your head in a different direction.

SUPER NOVA DAYS
JULY 7–8 ★ *free to be you*
You aren't restrained by your usual habitual concerns when adorable Venus aligns with radical Uranus on **July 7**. Your eccentric tastes may seem endearing to others, allowing you to say what you want, even if it's more than you intended to share. On the **8th**, the overly cautious Cancer New Moon joins communicator Mercury, retrograde in your 1st House of Personality, prompting you to withdraw into the security of your emotional shell. Instead of worrying about what others think, use this time for constructive self-reflection.

JULY 13 ★ *born to run*
Zippy Mars enters your sign today and fires you up for action, and although he remains in your 1st House of Physicality until **August 27**, your initial reaction may be a mixture of excitement and apprehension. However, if you try to suppress the impulsive expression of Mars, your emotions could turn self-destructive. There's no reason to hold yourself back now if your intentions are pure, but choose your battles carefully.

JULY 20–22 ★ *soldier of fortune*
Mental Mercury's direct turn on **July 20** restarts a project that's been stuck. Militant Mars marches into the scene, motivating you to apply your carefully constructed strategy while making your dreams come true. Your exhilaration is high as invincible Mars hooks up with cavalier Jupiter on the **22nd**; it feels as if you can't fail. The Sun's shift into self-centered Leo encourages you to act solo while the community-minded Aquarian Full Moon shining in your 8th House of Shared Resources reminds you that working with others lets you accomplish more.

JULY 27–31 ★ *dangerous liaisons*
You're sure the odds are stacked against you when an intense Mars-Pluto opposition on **July 27** rattles your 7th House of Relationships, dragging a power struggle out into the light. Even if you try to avoid extreme measures, an unruly Mars-Uranus square on the **31st** provokes reckless behavior. Fortunately, gentle Venus aspects to Jupiter and Pluto on the **28th** and **30th** allow you to process deep feelings without upsetting the status quo.

AUGUST

A CHANGE WILL DO YOU GOOD

If you've been tenaciously holding on to old patterns and unhealthy habits, it's time to let go. Optimistic Jupiter continues to play an active role in expanding your world all month, aspecting transformative Pluto in your 7th House of Partners on **August 7** and volatile Uranus in your 10th House of Career on **August 21**. You may be driven by such a compulsive desire to succeed that you exaggerate your actions and possibly stir up an extreme reaction in a jealous competitor. Sudden opportunities for advancement place additional stress on relationships, especially if you believe that you must wrestle control from a powerful person standing in your way. All these issues intensify when the melodramatic Leo New Moon falls in your 2nd House of Finances on the **6th**. Getting a raise or receiving a promotion may seem more important now than working out the kinks in a partnership.

You find it easier to talk confidently about what you want when chatty Mercury struts into proud Leo and your 2nd House of Possessions on **August 8**. Venus's shift into cooperative Libra and your comfortable 4th House on the **16th** reminds you that it's okay to relax while enjoying yourself with your family at home. But you may feel the need to express your individuality on **August 20** as the nonconformist Aquarius Full Moon illuminates your 8th House of Intimacy. There's no time to rest as the Sun and Mercury rush into your 3rd House of Immediate Environment on **August 22–23**, making it nearly impossible to keep up with everything that's happening. Thankfully you can finally find a moment to catch your breath on **August 27–30**, when Mercury and the Sun align nicely with several other planets to end the month on a sweet note.

KEEP IN MIND THIS MONTH

Be ready to pass up a chance for career advancement to keep your life in balance. Every lucrative possibility that comes along isn't necessarily right for you.

KEY DATES

AUGUST 4–7 ★ *money can't buy you love*

You could suddenly forget that you're a sensitive Crab when the Sun forms a superconductive trine with electric Uranus on **August 4**, revealing innovative ways to increase your income and obtain more freedom at work. You feel unstoppable because boisterous Jupiter opposes indefatigable Pluto on the **7th**. The extravagant

Leo New Moon on **August 6** activates your 2nd House of Money, tempting you to believe that acquiring the right things will buy you happiness. However, accumulating more possessions might actually distract you from a significant opportunity for personal growth.

AUGUST 11-14 ★ *reversal of fortune*
A sobering Mercury-Saturn square on **August 11** leaves you doubting your competence or questioning your strategy, but it's really a call to a higher level of excellence. You resist compromising your beliefs with Mercury in your 2nd House of Values, but be open to negotiation on everything else. It's difficult to know what's important enough to fight for when argumentative Mercury forms an anxious quincunx with suspicious Pluto on the **13th**. Don't let your wounded pride become an obstacle in your path. Fortunately, a brilliant Mercury-Uranus trine on the **14th** clears away your uncertainty with one lightning-like flash of awareness. You'll know what to do once you see the situation in this bright new light.

SUPER NOVA DAYS
AUGUST 20-23 ★ *no easy way out*
The Aquarius Full Moon on **August 20** pulls you away from your heart and into your head, where you can rationalize risky strategies to advance your interests. Opportunistic Jupiter squares shaky Uranus in your 10th House of Status on **August 21**, possibly indicating a sudden change in fortune, but it can also make a long shot look like a sure thing. Quicksilver Mercury's tense alignments with Uranus and Jupiter on the **22nd** coax you to take the bait, yet the Sun's shift into practical Virgo the same day, followed by a shift into Mercury on the **23rd**, require you to use your common sense.

AUGUST 26-30 ★ *call a friend*
You may not be able to see your future clearly now, but you're unhappy and stressed and something must give. Vulnerable Venus in your 4th House of Security is under duress, creating difficult aspects with wayward Uranus and loud Jupiter on **August 26-27**, and you're ready to do whatever's necessary to reestablish equilibrium. Fortunately, a series of supportive Mercury aspects on **August 28-30** opens communication channels so you don't feel so alone.

SEPTEMBER

BUSY AS A BEAVER

This month is bustling with things to do, and you must manage your time carefully so you don't become overwhelmed or exhausted. But don't sit on the sidelines; critically analyze your current situation, set priorities, eliminate unnecessary activities, and get busy taking care of what's essential. Brainy Mercury and the bright Sun are activating your 3rd House of Immediate Environment, scattering your energy with a million minor tasks. The industrious Virgo New Moon on **September 5** falls in your busy 3rd House, shifting your drive into high gear so you can meet all your obligations. Nevertheless, hard work doesn't seem to accomplish much since pushy Mars squares unresponsive Saturn on **September 9**, while Mercury's entry into ambiguous Libra could add to your indecisiveness. You may be spinning your wheels on the **11th** when physical Mars and mental Mercury form unsettling quincunxes with mysterious Pluto and meandering Neptune, but Venus swims into the powerful waters of Scorpio to help you process your emotions.

Brace yourself for unforeseen changes at work, which could cause concern on the home front. Taking radical action on **September 14**—when active Mars trines ingenious Uranus in your 10th House of Career—can alleviate the tension. The visionary Pisces Full Moon on the **19th** illuminates your 9th House of Big Ideas, restoring your confidence and possibly provoking you to say more than you intend. If you stretch the truth, an unforgiving Saturn-Pluto sextile on the **21st** could force you to be more realistic. However, if you can focus on one task at a time, you can increase your productivity. A long-lasting Jupiter-Neptune alignment on **September 28** reminds you that success can be yours if your aspirations are supported by a workable strategy.

> **KEEP IN MIND THIS MONTH**
>
> *Don't try to do everything at once. You can move your life forward on a few well-chosen fronts if you're willing to limit extraneous activities.*

KEY DATES

SEPTEMBER 1 ★ *charge your batteries*

You may be feeling your oats as the radiant Sun's power is reinforced by its regenerative trine to Pluto. But rather than putting your physical resources to work, the methodical Virgo Sun tells you to save your strength. Fortunately, potent Pluto in your 7th House of Companions means that collaborating with others can fuel your passion to work even harder. Be smart: By using your brains and not your brawn today, you can conserve the energy you will need tomorrow.

SEPTEMBER 5–7 ★ *make your own luck*

You filter out unnecessary noise on **September 5** when the discriminating Virgo New Moon activates your 3rd House of Data Collection. However, the cooperative Sun-Jupiter sextile on the **7th** helps you assimilate all the new information. Your current good fortune stems from your positive attitude and your keen ability to spot a good opportunity when you see one.

SEPTEMBER 14–16 ★ *twisted logic*

You're extremely wired as interactive Mercury squares stormy Pluto on **September 14** and opposes cataclysmic Uranus on the **16th**, rocking your 4th House of Foundations. A soothing Venus-Neptune trine on the **14th** allows you to calmly hold a vision of your ideal future, however, while a radical Mars-Uranus trine provokes you to do something about it. Be careful not to overreact—you may waste time worrying about things that will never happen.

SUPER NOVA DAYS
SEPTEMBER 18–22 ★ *make it work*

A sobering Venus-Saturn conjunction on **September 18** raises real concerns about a relationship, yet the poetic Pisces Full Moon on **September 19** entices you to escape into your fantasies. Fortunately, you're able to overcome difficult odds as Venus and Saturn form supportive sextiles with powerful Pluto in your 7th House of Partners on the **18th** and the **21st**, respectively. Pay careful attention to the needs of others and don't make assumptions, because a Mercury-Jupiter square on the **19th** urges you to accept sloppy thinking and messy shortcuts. The Sun's move into fair-minded Libra on the **22nd** marks the Autumn Equinox, altering your perspective by enabling you to see things from an entirely different point of view.

SEPTEMBER 26–28 ★ *take a chance on love*

Look for romance, pleasure, or at least a lovely sense of contentment to light up your world when sensual Venus trines joyful Jupiter on **September 26**. A sexy Venus-Mars square on the **28th** can arouse your passion in someone or create discord in a relationship. Either way, resolving the tension can be an exciting and enjoyable process.

OCTOBER

RISE TO THE CHALLENGE

Stressful relationships push you one way and then suddenly pull you another this month. Although it's unwise to let go of control at work and allow others to change the direction of your life, it's even more foolish to think that you can ignore the demands being placed on you. Ultimately, your smartest strategy is to seek an effective balance between holding on to the way things are and being open to positive change. Nevertheless, destabilizing forces on the job require you to respond when the diplomatic Libra New Moon squares provocative Pluto and opposes disruptive Uranus on **October 4**. Handling the current situation doesn't necessarily resolve the deeper dilemma, which has its roots in a complicated Saturn-Uranus quincunx that first occurred on **April 12**. Stabilizing Saturn repeats this uncomfortable aspect to unmanageable Uranus on the **5th**, making it difficult to maintain your creative integrity while also trying to forge a new vision of your future. You may need to acknowledge that your plans need serious revision when fleet-footed Mercury runs into stern Saturn on **October 8**.

You're quickly convinced that you have little to worry about when pretty Venus and the radiant Sun aspect illusory Neptune and sanguine Jupiter on **October 10–12**. The incorrigible Aries Full Moon Eclipse on the **18th** shakes your public 10th House, catalyzing much-needed professional change while sweeping away the accumulated tension. Mercury's retrograde turn on **October 21**, along with the Sun's shift into resolute Scorpio on the **23rd**, reminds you that patience is one of your greatest strengths. Although you cannot deny that these are serious times, the Sun-Neptune trine on the **25th** and the Mars-Pluto trine on the **31st** give you the courage to smile as you move through these days with unflappable resolve.

> **KEEP IN MIND THIS MONTH**
>
> *Instead of worrying about meeting unrealistic timetables and deadlines, just stay on course. You will make more progress than you ever thought possible.*

KEY DATES

SUPER NOVA DAYS
OCTOBER 1–4 ★ *never a dull moment*
Your creative juices flow when cerebral Mercury in your 5th House of Self-Expression forms a synergetic trine with intuitive Neptune on **October 1**.

Beautiful Venus, tough-guy Pluto, and inventive Uranus gang up on **October 2–3** to convince you to express your feelings more freely or to take a creative risk. However, you may first need to stand up to someone's negativity or handle a difficult situation in order to prove your worthiness when the Sun squares Pluto on the **1st**. You may be surprised by events at work on the **3rd** when the Sun opposes Uranus, prompting you to overreact. Try not to get too caught up in a drama, especially one that isn't yours. Thankfully, the Libra New Moon in your 4th House of Security on **October 4** allows you to navigate the rough emotional waters, soothe frayed feelings, and finally move forward with your plans.

OCTOBER 10–12 ★ *too good to be true*
You are able to retreat from the pressures of everyday life when irresistible Venus in your 6th House of Daily Routines forms a dynamic square with intoxicating Neptune in your 9th House of Future Vision on **October 10**. An inflationary Sun-Jupiter square on the **12th** fills you with confidence, even if you must ignore some of the facts to maintain your optimism. Go ahead and enjoy yourself without overindulging, but delay major decisions until you have a more realistic outlook.

OCTOBER 16–19 ★ *fast and furious*
You can't repress your desires, and your co-workers may be quite surprised with your unconventional behavior on **October 16** when flirty Venus trines wild-child Uranus. The reckless Aries Full Moon Eclipse on the **18th** dares you to come out of your shell. But on the **19th**, active Mars in your 3rd House of Communication opposes dispersive Neptune to raise self-doubt and weaken your message. Don't be overly concerned if you can't put your finger on the source of your angst; the uncertainty won't last long.

OCTOBER 29–31 ★ *seal the deal*
Put your thoughts in writing when retrograde Mercury conjuncts authoritative Saturn in your 5th House of Spontaneity on **October 29**. Fortunately, your persistence can overcome the resistance you encounter as superhero Mars harmoniously aligns in a happy trine to omnipotent Pluto on the **31st**. However, Mars also forms a disquieting quincunx with explosive Uranus the same day, making it wise to tread lightly. You can accomplish your goals without trying to tempt fate.

NOVEMBER

There's plenty of action on the romantic front this month with the Sun in seductive Scorpio and your 5th House of Love and Play until **November 21**. But you're still faced with a misunderstanding to untangle, because expressive Mercury is retrograde until **November 10**, remaining in your 5th House all month. The Scorpio Solar Eclipse on the **3rd** joins karmic Saturn, indicating that you'll get what you deserve in an intimate relationship. If you've been attentive and loving, the bonds of your connection now have a strong chance of deepening. But if you've been restless or emotionally distant, it's time to change your behavior and recommit to your partner or consider taking your heart in another direction. Love turns into serious business when Venus enters calculating Capricorn and your 7th House of Partnerships on the **5th**. The Sun's conjunction with responsible Saturn on **November 6** demands that you honor your promises and should expect the same in return.

Your emotions are on the line in a personal or business relationship on **November 14–16**, when Venus and the Sun form tough aspects with independent Uranus in your 10th House of Career and intense Pluto in your 7th House of Others. If situations are too complex, the simplistic Taurus Full Moon on the **17th** reminds you to reestablish your priorities and get back to the basics. On **November 21**, the Sun enters uplifting Sagittarius and your 6th House of Self-Improvement, restoring your self-confidence and inspiring you to set new goals at work. Although the Mercury-Saturn conjunction on the **25th** requires you to manage information more carefully, sweet aspects from Mercury to delicious Venus and magnanimous Jupiter on **November 27–28** suggest a more pleasurable end of the month.

> **KEEP IN MIND THIS MONTH**
>
> *If you're honest with yourself and others, you can turn an unpleasant melodrama into a chance to receive support from those you love.*

KEY DATES

SUPER NOVA DAYS
NOVEMBER 1–3 ★ *against all odds*
A methodical approach to achieving your goals limits your potential now, unless you're willing to revise your plans and make adjustments on the fly.

Retrograde Mercury and the Sun align with unstoppable Pluto and proactive Mars on **November 1–3**, empowering you to handle difficult challenges. The fourth recurrence of the evolutionary Uranus-Pluto square that began in **2012** and repeats three more times through **2015** also occurs on **November 1**, triggering intense reactions to whatever you do. However, awkward aspects from Mercury and the Sun to Uranus the Awakener in your 10th House of Status mean that you could encounter a surprise or two as you work toward achieving your goals. Don't wait for the transformational Scorpio Solar Eclipse on the **3rd** to catch you off guard in your personal life; take the initiative to balance your career objectives with your relationship needs.

NOVEMBER 10–12 ★ *blue skies*
November 10 is a turning point— you're finally able to let go of the same old issues you've been mentally stuck in. It's because thoughtful Mercury has been covering old ground in your 5th House of Self-Expression since it turned retrograde on **October 21**, and with today's direct turn you can take what you recently learned and start applying it toward a creative venture. Fortunately, an enthusiastic Sun-Jupiter trine on the **12th** provides confidence and helps to embolden your vision. Trust your instincts because they will guide you to greater heights now.

NOVEMBER 17–19 ★ *social butterfly*
The Taurus Full Moon on **November 17** brightens your 11th House of Social Networking, reflecting your deep need for community. Even if you've been wrapped up in your own inner world, this is a call to reconnect with your friends, instead of concentrating your attention only on one person or project. An excitable Mars-Jupiter sextile on the **19th** has you saying yes to invitations that you might otherwise pass up.

NOVEMBER 27–30 ★ *the edge of glory*
You may be putting too much emphasis on relationships as your main source of joy now: That's the message when a tug-of-war between pleasure-seeking Venus in your 7th House of Others and promising Jupiter in your 1st House of Self culminates on **November 28**. Fortunately, words flow as loquacious Mercury in your 5th House of Spontaneity forms harmonious aspects with Venus and Jupiter on **November 27–28**, enabling you to easily discuss a touchy issue. This is no time to hold back, especially when a thrilling Sun-Uranus trine on the **30th** empowers you to be boldly innovative and break out of your familiar shell.

DECEMBER

OUT LIKE A LION

This has been a year of personal opportunities and profound growth, and it fittingly ends as the momentum rises to a crescendo. Although you may try to contain yourself as challenging events begin to stack up throughout the month, you realize that you must manage your reactions to those closest to you. Process your frustration and transform negative emotions into constructive actions. The inspirational Sagittarius New Moon on **December 2** stirs your desire for adventure while your long-term planning is assisted by logical Mercury's move into farsighted Sagittarius on the **4th**. Still, you might become ambivalent about doing too much work through the holiday season when ardent Mars pushes its way into sociable Libra on the **7th** to enhance your 4th House of Home and Family.

No matter how caught up you are in the hustle and bustle of the season, the diversity-seeking Gemini Full Moon on **December 17** lights up your 12th House of Privacy, gently reminding you to save time for spiritual development. On the **21st**, the Sun's shift into traditional Capricorn and your 7th House of Companions marks the Winter Solstice, a time to settle into the safety of your most secure relationships. But anxiety over a past event or an old partnership can complicate alliances when loving Venus begins her retrograde cycle in your 7th House on the same day. Unresolved domestic tension may heat up on **December 25–31** as cranky Mars, talkative Mercury, and the willful Sun stress punishing Pluto and shocking Uranus. Tempers could flare unless you're willing to discuss your concerns in an objective manner without blaming anyone else for your unhappiness.

> **KEEP IN MIND THIS MONTH**
>
> *Conserve some energy for what's most important to you instead of getting hooked by your need to demonstrate your love by constantly pleasing others.*

KEY DATES

SUPER NOVA DAYS
DECEMBER 2–3 ★ *fearless leader*
Broaden your horizons at your job on **December 2**, when the optimistic Sagittarius New Moon falls in your 6th House of Self-Improvement. At the same time, however, the Moon's smooth trine with irrepressible Uranus in your 10th House of Career indicates unexpected twists on your career path.

A surprise can still lead you to success, but in a different way than planned. Fortunately, you can find a way to get what you want with intelligent Mercury's cooperative sextile to insistent Mars on the **3rd**. Mercury is in precise Virgo, so get your facts straight before trying to convince someone to follow your plan.

DECEMBER 10–12 ★ *sustainable growth*

Overconfidence could prompt you to overstep your bounds at work on **December 10** when the Sun in the 6th House of Employment forms a crunchy quincunx with excessive Jupiter. Talkative Mercury's flowing trine with innovative Uranus activates your professional 10th House, giving you the right words to further your ambitions. Thankfully, you're able to balance your personal and professional worlds when Jupiter harmoniously trines ambitious Saturn on **December 12**. It may be time to reactivate a creative project that you thought about on **July 17**, when Jupiter trined Saturn in the first of a series of aspects that completes on **May 24, 2014**. Take a strategic view and give yourself time to reach your goals.

DECEMBER 17 ★ *follow your bliss*

The lighthearted Gemini Full Moon brightens your 12th House of Soul Consciousness on **December 17**, tuning you into the magic of the holiday season. An idealistic Jupiter-Neptune alignment awakens your spiritual awareness to reveal a higher meaning to your hopes and dreams.

DECEMBER 25 ★ *proactive measures*

A minor disagreement could escalate into a major conflict today, because impetuous Mars in your 4th House of Domestic Conditions opposes unrestrainable Uranus. Letting others know what you want in advance helps ameliorate your stress before it explodes.

DECEMBER 29–30 ★ *power play*

Your agenda does not match everyone else's expectations on **December 29**, when a mentally focused Sun-Mercury conjunction in your 7th House of Others activates the long-lasting Uranus-Pluto square. You might not like the advice you're receiving with an authoritarian Sun-Mercury conjunction in Capricorn—and its tense aspects to Uranus and Pluto can provoke strong reactions to whatever is said. However, if you can calmly focus your attention on one issue at a time, a tense Mars-Pluto square on the **30th** can help you clear the air once and for all.

LEO

JULY 23–AUGUST 22

LEO

2012 SUMMARY

The parts of your life that are not meeting your expectations need to be revamped or eliminated, for you are being called to concentrate your ambitions on what could be most productive through the coming years. Be ready to embrace career opportunities that come your way, even if they take longer than expected to manifest. Throughout the entire year, your life continues to evolve in ways that you might not expect, so it's wise to pace yourself for the long haul rather than exhausting your reserves too soon.

AUGUST—*through the eye of a needle*

Although your progress can raise expectations about what you could accomplish, don't bite off more than you can chew just to prove that you can do it.

SEPTEMBER—*no turning back*

Although moments of sudden insight offer glimpses of your future, you still must come back to the present and live your life as it is right now.

OCTOBER—*from the ground up*

If you take the time to strengthen your family relationships and fulfill your domestic obligations, you will also build an enduring foundation for the years ahead.

NOVEMBER—*so close, yet so far away*

The ebbs and flows of time can be frustrating, especially when your progress is impeded by circumstances that seem to be beyond your control.

DECEMBER—*count your blessings*

An abundance of social activities helps to keep your spirits high. Just make sure that your enthusiasm to spread joy doesn't spread you too thin.

2012 CALENDAR

AUGUST

WED 1–THU 2 ★ Give those you love the independence they now require

TUE 7–THU 9 ★ Be vigilant about staying honest

WED 15–FRI 17 ★ **SUPER NOVA DAYS** Minor irritations could turn to anger

FRI 24–SUN 26 ★ Sharing your dreams is worth the effort

WED 29 ★ Don't be afraid to defend your ideas

SEPTEMBER

SAT 1–WED 5 ★ A reality check brings fantasies down to earth

THU 13– SUN 16 ★ Take a chance and reinvent your image

SAT 22–SUN 23 ★ Your thirst for knowledge grows

TUE 25–THU 27 ★ Suppressed feelings are released when the unexpected happens

SAT 29 ★ **SUPER NOVA DAY** A much-needed breakthrough is possible

OCTOBER

TUE 2–WED 3 ★ Reconnect with your soul's purpose

SUN 7–WED 10 ★ **SUPER NOVA DAYS** Ground your fanciful flights in reality

MON 15–TUE 16 ★ It's tough to find a point of balance

SUN 28–MON 29 ★ Your enthusiasm could be a bit too much

NOVEMBER

THU 1–SAT 3 ★ Take care of family responsibilities first

FRI 9 ★ Your dreams can come true

TUE 13–SAT 17 ★ **SUPER NOVA DAYS** Rely on your intuition

MON 26–THU 29 ★ Your domestic life is at a turning point

DECEMBER

SAT 1–SUN 2 ★ Focus on one thing at a time

MON 10–FRI 14 ★ Let your imagination run wild

WED 19–SAT 22 ★ **SUPER NOVA DAYS** Explore new ways to enjoy yourself

FRI 28–MON 31 ★ Expect a thrilling ending to this transformational year

LEO OVERVIEW

The year starts with your focus on group activities as expansive Jupiter in chatty Gemini occupies your 11th House of Community until June 25. **You'll gain opportunities to advance professionally and to enliven your personal life by participating in organizations and working as a member of a team.** Diversity can be a key to your success, since spending time with different kinds of people increases the number of contacts you can call upon as needed. Your desire to become involved in causes isn't necessarily rooted in the purity of your beliefs. Philosophical Jupiter in multifaceted Gemini can inspire a wide variety of interests that are more about the pleasure of being part of a movement than being 100 percent committed to the ideals of an organization itself.

On June 25 Jupiter shifts into sentimental Cancer and your 12th House of Divinity, making spirituality a significant theme for the second half of the year. You can develop a deeper understanding of the meaning of your life without necessarily being able to put it into words. Jupiter in Cancer represents wisdom that is emotional rather than intellectual. **However, a profound sense of belonging to something larger than the material world can comfort you in inexpressible ways.** On July 17, Jupiter forms the most favorable astrological pattern, a Grand Water Trine, with rational Saturn and inspirational Neptune, connecting these planets in the most sensitive parts of your chart. Saturn in your 4th House of Family and Neptune in your 8th House of Intimacy align with visionary Jupiter to create a framework of understanding that helps you appreciate where you are now and hints at where opportunities for growth will come next. The communication planet, Mercury, turns retrograde three times this year: February 23–March 17, June 26–July 20, and October 21–November 10. These backward periods activate the same houses as the grand trine, helping you to reflect on the past and untangle old knots of misunderstanding so that you're free to advance emotionally and spiritually.

A continuing pattern that directly affects your career comes from the challenging squares between revolutionary Uranus in Aries in your 9th House of Beliefs and evolutionary Pluto's presence in Capricorn in your 6th House of Work. The third and fourth of the seven aspects occur on May 20 and November 1 in a slow transformational process that began last year and culminates on March 16, 2015. **These life-changing transits spur deeper questions about your current**

employment and future professional plans. Pluto in your 6th House represents the effort you must expend to stay on top of your obligations on the job; these demands may feel excessive if you're not sufficiently rewarded for what you do. When new interests are sparked by restless Uranus's transit, you might find it difficult to spend much of your time and energy on tasks that lack meaning. Nevertheless, altering your professional path only makes sense when you calculate the risks involved and plan the steps you need to take.

SWEET SURRENDER

You continue to want love to take you beyond the limits of ordinary emotions with transcendental Neptune in your 8th House of Intimacy all year. This long-term transit increases your sensitivity and desire for a compassionate partner. Passionate Mars blasts through your 7th House of Others until February 1, starting your year off with a strong emphasis on relationships. He leaves your sociable 7th House just as alluring Venus arrives to keep interpersonal activity at a high level through February 25. You may find it easy to attract interesting people or spice up an ongoing alliance, yet an independent person might keep you from getting as close as you want. A Sagittarius Lunar Eclipse in your 5th House of Romance on May 25 can mark a key transition in matters of the heart, inspiring you with new dreams of love but also revealing where fantasies have marred your judgment and changes are required.

A CHANGE IS GONNA COME

You're either excited by what you do for a living or chafing with boredom in your current job this year, because electric Uranus continues to square extreme Pluto in your 6th House of Employment. A Taurus Solar Eclipse in your 10th House of Career on May 9 could trigger an event that propels you in a new direction. If the weight of your responsibilities doesn't match your paycheck, learning how to delegate your duties to others can lighten your load. Holding on to a position out of fear or loyalty will only prolong your dissatisfaction, so think about looking elsewhere for fulfillment, even if it takes you into an entirely different field. The dependable Taurus Full Moon on November 17 also brightens your 10th House, awakening you to more practical and lucrative ways to work.

A NEW DEAL

It's a financial wake-up call when the analytical Virgo Full Moon falls in your 2nd House of Resources on February 25. Lavish Jupiter and capricious Uranus's stressful lunar aspects could spur a desire for spontaneous spending. Fortunately, penny-pinching Pluto forms a favorable trine with the Moon, helping you move toward a more solid financial foundation. You might want to rethink investments or restructure debt while your 2nd House ruler, Mercury, is retrograde in your 8th House of Shared Resources on February 23–March 17. Changing the terms of an unsatisfying business partnership, or backing out of it completely, is wiser than vainly holding on with blind faith.

PATTERN RECOGNITION

Unresolved health issues and undesirable habits demand your undivided attention with the proud Leo Full Moon on January 26. A stressful square to this lunation from Saturn could slow you down, but is meant to motivate you to take better care of yourself. Informative Jupiter in Gemini's supportive sextile reveals alternative approaches to well-being that you may find less difficult to follow than you expect. The fiery Leo New Moon on August 6 boosts your energy, and you're ready to roar with muscular Mars in Leo and your 1st House of Physicality on August 27–October 15. Just don't let this wave of increased vitality and passion for movement push you too far too fast.

FROM THE GROUND UP

Major work can be expected in domestic matters with responsible Saturn in Scorpio in your 4th House of Family this year. Secret pasts could be exposed, allowing you to understand the root causes of mistrust or the reasons why you haven't reached your full potential. Your willingness to dig deeply into these uncomfortable areas should reward you with greater awareness of your needs and how best to fulfill them. The Scorpio Full Moon Eclipse in your 4th House on April 25 is a critical turning point when housing and personal concerns come to a head. A helpful trine to this eclipse from forgiving Neptune offers inspiration and compassion for your own failures and for the shortcomings of others.

FRESH FRONTIERS

Your long-term itch for travel will continue this year as freedom-loving Uranus transits your 9th House of Faraway Places. On April 10, the antsy Aries New Moon in this restless part of your chart kicks up excitement about visiting unusual places or beginning a new course of studies. However, the impatient Aries Full Moon Eclipse on October 18 can interrupt educational plans or complicate a trip. If you committed yourself too quickly and have a change of heart, it's better to pay the price and cancel than to force yourself down a road that no longer holds your interest.

ANSWERS FROM WITHIN

Your spiritual path unfolds before you this year. It starts with accepting your place in the universe when wise Jupiter enters your 12th House of Destiny on June 25. You can gain a sense of belonging that's stronger than any external influences. Whether you're respected and loved by the outer world or not, your inner feeling of tranquility can put you at ease. The contemplative Cancer New Moon in your metaphysical 12th House on July 8 is joined with cerebral Mercury to help initiate you into a higher state of awareness. Learning to look inside to observe your reactions is a powerful step toward self-awakening.

RICK & JEFF'S TIP FOR THE YEAR:
Wise Beyond Words

Magic happens as you watch more and say less. When you quiet yourself and drop the need to impress others, rivers of information flow in your direction. These are connections from the world to your innermost self, which weave a fabric of meaning and purpose that requires no explanation. This awareness is the silent knowing that cannot be found in any book, but has been streaming through your veins since the day you were born and now reappears to illuminate your soul and inspire your ambitions.

LEO

JANUARY

The year begins with the radiant Sun in your 6th House of Health and Habits, sending strong signals to apply some post-holiday discipline to your personal and professional lives. Vivacious Venus is in Sagittarius and your 5th House of Fun and Games until **January 8**, making you more than a little reluctant to cut back on pleasure and settle down to work. Yet putting more effort into your job and taking better care of your body will pay dividends throughout the year. The ambitious Capricorn New Moon in your 6th House on **January 11** is another push to be more serious about your career. Right now sharpening your skills can help you climb the ladder of success—or a lack of training may keep you spinning your wheels with less fulfilling tasks. A steady and persistent approach to self-improvement is more effective than sporadic bursts of activity, so make a plan and stick to it.

Brainy Mercury's conjunction with the Sun focuses your thinking and empowers communication on **January 18**. A clear picture of what works in your life and where you need to make adjustments helps you map out a strategy to get the most out of your abilities. On **January 19**, Mercury and the Sun enter your 7th House of Partnerships and Public Life to put more juice into relationships. Your bright ideas are more likely to land on receptive ears now, attracting open-minded and intelligent people. The audacious Leo Full Moon on the **26th** tempts you to boldly put all your cards on the table, yet savvy Saturn's stressful square indicates the importance of sharing information selectively rather than naively exposing your unfiltered feelings to everyone.

> **KEEP IN MIND THIS MONTH**
>
> *Buckling down and studying hard to be a good student of your craft may be humbling now, but you'll be proud of your accomplishments later.*

KEY DATES

SUPER NOVA DAYS
JANUARY 4–7 ★ *building your base*

Expect a little help from your friends on **January 4** when energetic Mars in your 7th House of Partners forms an enterprising trine with magnanimous Jupiter in your 11th House of Colleagues. You'll find it essential to balance high expectations with an eye for details, because a scrutinizing Mercury-Pluto conjunction on the **6th** can cause failure due to a minor matter. Stern

Saturn either slams the brakes on your ambitions with a harsh square to Mars on **January 7** or carefully establishes a rock-solid foundation built on strict guidelines and meticulous methods.

JANUARY 12–13 ★ *technical wizardry*
On **January 12**, your brilliant blend of practicality and originality reveals new ways to solve old problems thanks to ingenious quintiles from the Sun to solid Saturn and innovative Uranus. Intuition spurs unconventional insights that might radically alter your work life. The Sun's favorable sextile to the Moon's North Node on the **13th** attracts confident individuals and helps you share your enthusiasm in ways that inspire others.

JANUARY 16 ★ *efficiency expert*
Appreciation for your efforts may not come easily as evaluating Venus joins insatiable Pluto in your 6th House of Employment. Relationships on the job may be undermined by mistrust or manipulation, especially when secrecy is involved. Expressing discontent doesn't help morale unless your recognition of what's wrong drives you to come up with answers. The upside of this transit is that you can discover how to get the most out of your resources by streamlining ways to cooperate with others and maximizing the use of time and materials.

JANUARY 25 ★ *a variety of options*
You may feel stuck in the negative thinking pattern that a Mercury-Saturn square prompts, but you can easily overcome it by finding alternative routes around obstacles. The Sun's supportive trine to optimistic Jupiter in versatile Gemini enriches you with bright ideas that come from conversations with friends and co-workers. If you're experiencing a mental block, step back for a moment, have a friendly chat with someone you trust, and your mind will be refreshed and ready to try again.

JANUARY 30 ★ *reality check*
Creative projects and friendly relations grind to a halt as the Sun forms a tense square with restrictive Saturn. Perhaps you were too hopeful about an arrangement and didn't fully consider its emotional consequences. If you're unsatisfied, it's better to stop now rather than forcing yourself to go ahead out of a sense of obligation. Propitious Jupiter is turning direct today, which is a reminder that other opportunities lie ahead, making it easier to learn and accept hard lessons right now.

FEBRUARY

LOVE VERSUS LOGIC

A dramatic dance between romance and reason this month plunges you into an emotional fantasyland one moment and cools you down with logic the next. The fun starts on **February 1** with incorrigible Mars entering fantasy-driven Pisces and your 8th House of Intimacy, followed by airy Venus's shift into intellectual Aquarius and your 7th House of Others. Though you long to erase boundaries and jump in with your heart or into a business alliance, you'll find this countered by an equally urgent need for breathing space. On the **5th**, interactive Mercury's plunge into Pisces and your 8th House tilts the balance toward a total merger, especially when you're dealing with an imaginative talker. Yet no matter how tight you are with someone, the New Moon in nonconformist Aquarius on **February 10** can snap you back to a place where you value your independence more than anything else.

The rhythm shifts again with the Sun's entry into Pisces on **February 18**, reviving dreams of idyllic relationships. These unrealistic desires can blur your judgment and pull you into an unhealthy alliance. Playing the rescuer role or sacrificing yourself for another's illusions is obviously an undesirable way to go. Mercury's retrograde turn on the **23rd** might help you review recent events and clear up a misunderstanding, yet it's more likely to lure you into alliances where facts are fuzzy and deception is possible. Venus drifts into poetic Pisces and your 8th House on **February 25**, enticing you to fall in love with love. Life is dreamily delicious and ripe for romance, yet the rationality of the earthy Virgo Full Moon the same day signals the need for a little discrimination and a more careful investment of your resources.

> **KEEP IN MIND THIS MONTH**
>
> *It's perfectly acceptable to change your mind and renegotiate the terms of a partnership instead of silently enduring an unsatisfying situation. Being honest is truly the best policy.*

KEY DATES

FEBRUARY 7 ★ *lovable you*

Whatever you're selling is very appealing to others today. Charming Venus in your 7th House of Partners forms a free-flowing trine with joyful Jupiter that makes you extremely desirable company for work or play. While it's tempting to say yes to every invitation, being choosy in a friendly way keeps you from spreading yourself too thin and missing out on the most useful connections.

FEBRUARY 9–11 ★ *not so fast*

Breaking rules and thumbing your nose at authority sounds exciting when the Sun makes an edgy semisquare with rebellious Uranus on **February 9**. Strong opinions charged up by a tense square between uncontainable Mars and strident Jupiter can fuel further conflict on the **10th**. A boost of enthusiasm is welcome as long as you don't overpower innocent bystanders or promise more than you can deliver. Restrain yourself on the **11th**, when a heavy-handed square between Venus and Saturn weighs down relationships with responsibility. You might find yourself feeling underappreciated, but you can earn love and respect with patience and persistence.

SUPER NOVA DAYS

FEBRUARY 14–16 ★ *no pain, no gain*

Valentine's Day is bittersweet when an uncomfortable Sun-Pluto semisquare on **February 14** brings secret concerns out into the open. If you're able to move beyond mistrust or resentment, you'll find that you can extract rewards from even the most difficult situation. A laser-like Mars-Pluto sextile on the **15th** can transform relationship wounds into passionate moments that deepen connections. This aspect creates an ideal moment for addressing delicate issues with focus and purpose, and facilitating change without stirring up irrelevant side issues. The competence of this planetary pair is reinforced by a highly productive trine between enterprising Mars and orderly Saturn on **February 16** that helps you manage delicate tasks with gentle efficiency.

FEBRUARY 21 ★ *fantasy island*

Your tenderness is both a blessing and a curse as the Sun joins compassionate Neptune in your 8th House of Deep Sharing. Others inspire you with their dreams of emotional or financial riches, yet what you're seeing and hearing may not reflect reality. Outright fraud, or simply misplaced faith, can take more from you than you wish to give. It's fine to share a vulnerable space—but don't make any serious long-term commitments.

FEBRUARY 25 ★ *larger than life*

You're blessed with abundant professional opportunities when the industrious Virgo Full Moon and the imaginative Pisces Sun form expansive squares to excessive Jupiter in your 10th House of Career. Go ahead and take on additional tasks—but remember that if they turn out to be more than you can handle, your reputation could suffer.

MARCH

SLOW START, FAST FINISH

The month rolls out tenderly as the gentle Pisces Sun swims through your 8th House of Intimacy until **March 20**. You could take a major step forward in a relationship with the Pisces New Moon in the 8th House and conjunct to romantic Venus on **March 11**. The love planet's presence at this lunation sprinkles magic fairy dust on your partnerships, making even less-than-satisfying connections seem wonderful. Your belief in a personal or professional alliance raises hopes that might not be supported by facts. Tempering your urge to merge with a strong dose of common sense can help turn magic into reality or keep you from overestimating others. On the **12th**, however, the heat of anticipation starts to burn away dependency as irrepressible Mars enters headstrong Aries and readies you to take action on your own. This energizing transit occurs in your 9th House of Faraway Places and Higher Mind, stimulating desires for traveling, learning, and connecting with people from different cultures.

Your desire for adventure is stoked even higher when the Sun and Venus enter dashing Aries and your 9th House on **March 20–21**. Moving too fast, though, looks risky on the **23rd** and **25th**, when permissive Jupiter and Mars form misaligned quincunxes with wary Saturn. If you shoot from the hip, you're likely to meet resistance or run off course, so plan your moves carefully and be ready to make minor corrections as you go. The accommodating Libra Full Moon on **March 27** falls in your 3rd House of Communication, spurring bright ideas when you slow down long enough to listen to others. Expect intense negotiations with demanding Pluto's square to the Moon, and count on surprises—some of them pleasant—with Uranus, Venus, and Mars opposite it.

> **KEEP IN MIND THIS MONTH**
>
> *Avoid promising too much to others, as these commitments can become burdensome when your need for freedom grows as the month marches on.*

KEY DATES

MARCH 1 ★ *lead with your heart*

You have a perfect combination of softness and strength when the compassionate Pisces Sun makes favorable aspects to powerful Pluto and steadfast Saturn. Trust your judgment in relationships—you're capable of attracting responsible partners who are in it for the long haul. You can get what you want from people when you're clear about your needs and sensitive in expressing them.

MARCH 4–7 ★ *second time around*

Make a careful review of your relationships on **March 4**, when retrograde Mercury backs over the Sun in your 8th House of Deep Sharing. This is not a time to initiate new partnerships or business deals, but it might be useful for making adjustments to an existing agreement. It's best to set priorities and focus on one subject at a time rather than letting conversations ramble as data-oriented Mercury moves toward a constructive trine with serious Saturn in Scorpio on the **7th**.

MARCH 16–17 ★ *every word counts*

You may not get the cooperation you want on **March 16**—especially if you come on too strong. The Sun's stressful alignment with somber Saturn that day makes for emotionally cloudy weather. Slowing down and tuning in to the mood of others, however, prepares you to express your needs more effectively. Precise communication is critical on the **17th** when verbal Mercury shifts into forward gear in your intimate 8th House. Words leave a lasting impact when the communication planet stops to change directions.

SUPER NOVA DAYS
MARCH 20–22 ★ *break on through*

Expect rockets of enthusiasm to fire at the Spring Equinox when the Sun shifts into Aries and your visionary 9th House on **March 20**, followed by sassy Venus's entry into this opinionated house on the **21st**. Your hunger for fresh experiences can motivate you to take chances, yet it's appropriate to experiment with new activities and let go of those that don't work. In fact, an electrifying Mars-Uranus conjunction in excitable Aries on the **22nd** could find you twitching with anticipation and restless for change. However, if you behave impulsively, you can upset others and spur an unnecessary conflict. Innovation doesn't have to be disruptive, especially when your methods are as original as your ideas.

MARCH 28 ★ *call of the wild*

Break free of social expectations today, and let unconventional tastes and exotic attractions spice up your personal life. The fresh and feisty spirit of spring runs strong as the bright Sun and flirty Venus join wayward Uranus in your 9th House of Beliefs. Rebelling against the status quo is less productive than simply reinventing yourself.

APRIL

AIM FOR THE STARS

You're excited by your aspirations for new personal and professional experiences during the first half of the month. The Sun's dynamic presence in your 9th House of Adventure is kicked into a higher gear with the rowdy Aries New Moon on **April 10**. This energizing union of the Sun and Moon in Aries ignites your passion for adventure, encourages you to break out of your usual routine, and widens your intellectual horizons. The cosmic lovers, Venus and Mars, join this lunation to charge up your creative and romantic interests while they inspire social and artistic endeavors. Responsibilities on the home front, though, could slow you down with reliable Saturn's uncomfortable quincunx with unstable Uranus on the **12th**. This aspect occurred on **November 15, 2012**, and finishes on **October 5**, giving you more time to find a healthy balance between taking care of business and being free to pursue your wildest dreams.

Expect new ideas and intellectual impulsiveness with quicksilver Mercury's entry into speedy Aries on **April 13**. However, the pace slows with Venus's shift into laid back Taurus and your 10th House of Career on the **15th**, followed there by the Sun on **April 19**, and by Mars on the **20th**. It's time to put potentials into practice by recommitting to your professional goals and working with steadiness to help you earn dollars and respect. You may hit a bump in the road with the secretive Scorpio Full Moon Eclipse in your 4th House of Roots on **April 25**. A lunar conjunction with pessimistic Saturn could darken your mood with self-doubt or delay your public progress until you complete unfinished personal business.

> **KEEP IN MIND THIS MONTH**
>
> *Scattering your forces is fun for a while, but it won't produce the lasting results you desire. Save your best shot for the target you really want to hit.*

KEY DATES

APRIL 1 ★ *two-way street*
An opportunistic Sun-Jupiter sextile activates your community-oriented 11th House, boosting your self-confidence and your public profile. You're enthusiastic about becoming more involved in something larger than yourself and, fortunately, your friends and colleagues encourage your growth. Making your point and making connections come easily when you're as interested in listening as you are in talking.

APRIL 7 ⋆ *nothing ventured, nothing gained*
Your social life sizzles today as sensual Venus and physical Mars join together in red-hot Aries. You may be especially attractive in new situations with this conjunction in your 9th House of Faraway Places. People from different backgrounds may also be more desirable now—you're ready to enjoy the cultural pleasures of foreigners and their food, art, and music. A minor risk is that you're so good at charming people, you can give someone the impression that you're interested in romance when you're just being friendly.

APRIL 17 ⋆ *claim your power*
You have the drive to start new projects and forcefully advance your ideas with today's potent conjunction of the willful Sun and unstoppable Mars in Aries. This is usually associated with initiating enterprises, physical activity, and even being a little aggressive. However, the Moon's presence in shy Cancer and your 12th House of Escapism can trick you into wasting your efforts on unachievable goals or allowing you to feel weak even if your mind and muscles ripple with strength.

SUPER NOVA DAYS
APRIL 20–23 ⋆ *prove your worth*
You're revved up on **April 20**—despite energetic Mars's entry into docile Taurus—thanks to a high-frequency Mercury-Uranus conjunction. Speaking without considering the consequences of your words can prove costly when Mercury squares punishing Pluto on the **21st**. Don't hold on to unworkable ideas or intellectual positions unless you're certain of their ultimate value. You may feel as if the isolating Venus-Saturn opposition on **April 22** is testing you, as the week starts on a sobering note. If you can handle money and relationships with care, you'll earn respect and avoid expensive mistakes. Happily, Mercury's smart sextile with noble Jupiter on the **23rd** garners support from pals or colleagues when you take the time to describe what you need from them.

APRIL 28 ⋆ *duty calls*
You're torn between your public and personal responsibilities as the Sun in your 10th House of Career opposes exigent Saturn in your family-oriented 4th House. Fortunately, your newfound sense of urgency requires you to recognize your limits and reconfigure your priorities. Although you might be overwhelmed by your obligations, you should be able to overcome difficulties and achieve success.

MAY

YOU'RE THE BOSS

Two polarizing eclipses this month influence the ways you express yourself both creatively and professionally. On **May 9**, the determined Taurus New Moon is a Solar Eclipse in your 10th House of Career that's likely to amplify your ambitions. Contentious Mars's conjunction with the eclipse could provoke conflict with authorities and drive you to seek employment elsewhere. The desire to run your own business is understandable, yet whether you stay in your current position or go somewhere else, learning how to delegate duties and motivate others to share the load makes the difference between fulfillment and frustration. The adventurous Sagittarius Full Moon Eclipse on **May 25** occurs in your 5th House of Love and Creativity to stimulate hunger for new forms of pleasure and self-expression. Empathic Neptune's square to the eclipse inspires your imagination and heightens your sensitivity to your audience. But this dreamy planet may also lure you into pursuing fantasies that are unlikely to become realities.

Getting along with friends and colleagues is another key concern with four planets flitting into diverse Gemini and your 11th House of Groups this month. Vibrant Venus leads the parade to enliven your social life on **May 9**, followed by chatty Mercury on the **15th**, the radiant Sun on the **20th**, and rowdy Mars on the **31st**. Connecting with a wide variety of people is exciting but could scatter your intellectual, emotional, and physical resources. The third of seven unstable squares between transformational outer planets Uranus and Pluto on **May 20** is a reminder to keep your eyes on the big prize of long-term change instead of being distracted by trivial events.

> **KEEP IN MIND THIS MONTH**
>
> *Success is more likely when you take the long road to the top now instead of seeking out shortcuts that won't get you as far.*

KEY DATES

MAY 1 ★ *inch by inch*

You may feel bullied or overloaded by the formidable obstacles you face at home and at work. A stressful opposition between active Mars and static Saturn is pouring on all this pressure. Fortunately, a powerful Sun-Pluto trine helps you concentrate your efforts and manage a difficult task with patience and maturity. Mental Mercury's entry into earthy Taurus signals the need to seek simple solutions to handle what's already on your plate instead of piling on additional obligations.

MAY 7 ★ *karma rules*

Watch out today lest you hold on to the past or fall back into a stubborn habit. The Sun's passage over the Lunar South Node in resistant Taurus and your professional 10th House favors laziness over innovation. Working with passionate people or committing to solve a tough problem may be difficult at first, but will eventually prove to be worth the effort. A creative Sun-Neptune quintile supplies the imagination you need to perform miracles as long as you have a little faith in yourself.

MAY 11 ★ *back to basics*

Clear thinking and effective communication are on tap today with crafty Mercury joining the Sun in practical Taurus. Their alignment in your 10th House of Career gives you a platform for reasonable ideas, especially when your information is rock-solid. Build credibility by addressing core issues, avoiding big promises, and working with a pragmatic point of view. Concrete plans with a direct path to implementation are appreciated while pie-in-the-sky concepts will likely fall flat.

MAY 16 ★ *exit strategy*

You feel a little edgy and struggle to cooperate with people in positions of power today as the Sun forms tense aspects with reactive Uranus and imposing Pluto. Work can be challenging if you're bored with the routine and stuck in a stagnant situation. The urge to rebel is strong, but it's smarter to have a viable escape plan in place before you act hastily. Slow down to reconsider your long-term job prospects and you just might discover a radically different way to use your talents.

SUPER NOVA DAYS
MAY 25–27 ★ *out of bounds*

You're tempted to play risky games on the **25th** with the Sagittarius Full Moon Eclipse in your frolicsome 5th House. Mars's tense aspects with ruthless Pluto and volatile Uranus on **May 25–26** increase the likelihood of danger. A Mercury-Saturn aspect sharpens your perceptions, but a foggy Sun-Neptune square can lead you to overlook details or ignore good advice. Adjust your course on the **27th,** when the Sun aligns with disciplined Saturn and an adaptable Mercury-Jupiter conjunction opens your mind to new ways of thinking.

JUNE

HEAVEN'S GATE

Your awareness of worlds beyond this one grows this month with significant planetary activity in your 12th House of Spirituality. Magnetic Venus's shift into cuddly Cancer and this private part of your chart on **June 2** attracts you to prayer, meditation, and contemplation, which can quiet and comfort your heart. The nourishment of nature and the tranquility that comes from being less ambitious enable you to reduce your expectations of others and find a larger purpose and meaning in your life. The Sun's entry into Cancer on **June 21** is the Summer Solstice, which is another signal to turn inward and get away from it all. You may uncharacteristically long to be out of the spotlight on this introspective journey. Benevolent Jupiter's move into protective Cancer on the **25th** for a yearlong stay in your soulful 12th House is like having an angel on your shoulder whispering words of wisdom and encouragement in your ear.

Commitment to your highest hopes can turn inspiration into reality with realistic Saturn's constructive trine to idealistic Neptune on **June 11**. This is the second of three aspects—the first was **October 10, 2012**, and the last is on **July 19**. Saturn in Scorpio is deep in your ancestral 4th House, where addressing your greatest fears and desires can reduce the former and give shape to the latter. Before then, on **June 8**, the scattered Gemini New Moon in your 11th House of Groups sows innumerable seeds of ideas with friends or colleagues, but don't allow others' schemes to distract you from your own dreams. The dutiful Capricorn Full Moon lands in your work-related 6th House on the **23rd**, reminding you that patience and discipline pay long-term dividends.

> **KEEP IN MIND THIS MONTH**
>
> *What you do out of sight of others will not attract attention, but it can fill your soul with joyful self-awareness that can serve you for the rest of your life.*

KEY DATES

JUNE 1 ★ *untangling knots*

Your morning might be marred by a power struggle or vexing task due to an uncomfortable Sun-Pluto quincunx. Then a brilliant Sun-Uranus sextile lightens the latter part of the day with bright ideas teaching you to let go and seeking alternative ways of dealing with difficulties. What first seemed like an unwinnable battle can suddenly be resolved with a radical change of perspective.

JUNE 7–8 ★ *lost in translation*
Beware following a friend or colleague's misplaced idea on **June 7**, which features a slippery square between misdirected Mars and confusing Neptune. A perceptive Mercury-Pluto opposition should send up warning signals, but you may be thinking too narrowly to see the big picture. On the **8th**, an awkward quincunx between insistent Mars and stubborn Saturn could leave you stuck with someone else's dirty work. Either do the job with as much grace and efficiency as you can or just say no, because an intellectually unstable Mercury-Uranus square could trigger a verbal explosion that undercuts effective communication.

JUNE 14–15 ★ *clear the path*
On **June 14** an innovative Sun-Uranus quintile in your 9th House of Big Ideas awakens your mind to a surprising vision of your future. However, in order to explore the possibilities you may have to eliminate other commitments with a pesky Mars-Pluto quincunx on the **15th**. Original concepts require better management of your resources and precise execution to fulfill your expectations.

SUPER NOVA DAY
JUNE 19 ★ *open heart, open mind*
Optimism rises as a result of gaining support from colleagues, making new connections, and finding more joyful ways to express yourself. The Sun, your creative ruling planet, joins farsighted Jupiter in your 11th House of Friends, Hopes, and Wishes, inspiring a broader vision for a group. Your contribution to an organization can garner respect and cast you into a leadership position. It's easy to see that helping others, even humanity as a whole, is the best way to help yourself. The more you give, the more you get back in return.

JUNE 26–27 ★ *shining star*
The Sun forms a Grand Water Trine with Saturn and Neptune on **June 26**, providing power for your dream-making machinery. Your ability to combine imagination and pragmatism builds a solid foundation to support your loftiest ambitions. Your high-level organizational skills mix perfectly with compassion that entices people to follow your lead. On the **27th**, sparkling Venus enters bighearted Leo and your 1st House of Personality to enhance your self-image and increase your charisma, making you nearly impossible to resist.

JULY

BACK IN THE GAME

The deep inner work you began last month now leads you toward a renewed sense of purpose. Your focus is decidedly inward with messenger Mercury backpedaling in your spiritual 12th House, which is also occupied by philosophical Jupiter and the Sun. Putting truth into action and strategically bringing your dreams down to earth are supported by an emotionally enriching Grand Water Trine of Jupiter, Saturn, and Neptune on **July 17–19**. These outer planets align in your most intimate houses, so you may not be able to articulate your insights very well at first. But the vision that arises this month should take more concrete form when Jupiter and Saturn make favorable trines with each other again on **December 12** and **May 24, 2014**. However, a break with the past could leave you restless or disoriented as shocking Uranus forms an explosive square with the supersensitive Cancer New Moon on **July 8** in your 12th House of Destiny.

You may retreat in search of safety when warrior Mars becomes more spiritual and softens your approach upon entering nurturing Cancer and your 12th House on **July 13**, but this should only be a short period of respite. Mercury's forward turn on **July 20** and the Sun's entry into your creative sign on the **22nd** signal your readiness to put ideas into action. The solar presence in your 1st House of Personality raises your confidence and restores your sociability. Still, you may encounter obstacles when personal or professional partners are resistant to changes in relationships. Stodgy Saturn squares the futuristic Aquarius Full Moon on the **22nd** to brighten your 7th House of Others. Slow down and earn credibility before advancing your interests.

KEEP IN MIND THIS MONTH

Sketching a rough outline of a major goal gives you a strong base upon which to build your future—but don't worry about filling in every little detail.

KEY DATES

JULY 1 ★ *down and dirty*

Tense issues at work bog you down in a power struggle—and trust is elusive with the blinding Sun's opposition to suspicious Pluto. However, if you're willing to face the root cause of your discontent instead of simply blaming others, you not only will avoid a battle but can also permanently eliminate an irritating obstacle.

JULY 4–7 ★ *quick-change artist*

Your nerves are taut when a Sun-Uranus square on **July 4** puts you on edge and springs surprises. However, trust your first reactions on the **5th** when impulsive Mars's creative quintile to Uranus sharpens your instincts, allowing you to swiftly adjust to changing conditions. On the other hand, Venus in Leo's awkward quincunx with manipulative Pluto represents a lack of appreciation that could make you question your value. But the tide turns quickly again with needy Venus's thrilling trine to experimental Uranus on **July 7** that rapidly replaces feelings of rejection with new forms of pleasure and unexpectedly delightful connections.

JULY 13 ★ *luxury tax*

Going overboard with spending, consumption, or expectations of others is likely with indulgent Venus's irresponsible semisquare to extravagant Jupiter. The dramatic Leo Moon adds another log to the fires of excess, encouraging exaggeration and increasing your need for approval. Thankfully, stretching your social, artistic, and financial limits just a little bit can fill you up without emptying your bank account or demanding an exorbitant emotional price.

SUPER NOVA DAY
JULY 22 ★ *carpe diem*

Planets are popping on this high-frequency day, which kicks off with an exuberant Mars-Jupiter conjunction in your fateful 12th House. The motivation to take on fresh challenges is strong, but patience and preparation are required to reach new heights. Making a realistic self-assessment of your abilities, along with refining your skills and obtaining the right tools, increases your income when Venus enters pragmatic Virgo and your 2nd House of Money. The Sun's move into lively Leo is a morale booster, although snarky Saturn's square to the Aquarius Full Moon may reduce the support you get from others. The truth is that the only one holding you back is you; if you have passion and a strong sense of purpose, there's no mountain you can't climb.

JULY 27 ★ *running on empty*

If you try to go faster today, you'll actually use up more time and energy than you would by finding a steady pace and sticking to it. Sobering Saturn's square to the Sun from your domestic 4th House reminds you to resolve issues on the home front instead of running away from responsibilities.

AUGUST

LIGHT MY FIRE

You burn with enthusiasm this month with the fiery Leo Sun illuminating your 1st House of Personality until **August 22**. This energizing solar transit boosts your self-esteem, empowering you to make changes in your appearance and emboldening your approach to others. Grabbing the spotlight comes more easily now, but you may not push hard for it until aggressive Mars leaves your secretive 12th House and enters expressive Leo on **August 27**. You still have some behind-the-scenes work to complete before you're ready to play your hand. The playful Leo New Moon on the **6th** trines irreverent Uranus, encouraging you to try out a different look and to take yourself less seriously. However, this lunation's square to the Moon's Nodes suggests that these modifications may not appeal to everyone. The first of three Jupiter-Pluto oppositions on **August 7**—reoccurring on **January 31** and **April 20, 2014**—can arouse discontent and a deep desire to make major improvements at work. Jupiter's tense square to impulsive Uranus on the **21st**, which repeats on **February 26** and **April 20, 2014**, spurs you to take immediate action, even if exercising caution would produce more favorable results.

Be ready to go public with new projects and address relationship issues openly on **August 20**, with the intellectual Aquarius Full Moon in your 7th House of Partners. The best way to collaborate with individuals who have ideas contrary to yours is to balance your creativity with objectivity and common sense. The Sun's shift into prudent Virgo and your 2nd House of Resources on the **22nd**, followed by calculating Mercury on the **23rd**, reminds you to attend to financial matters. Being thrifty helps, but investing in refining your present skills or developing new ones is even more financially beneficial in the long run.

KEEP IN MIND THIS MONTH

A big performance requires plenty of preparation. Don't jump the gun and start your show until you've carefully rehearsed your part.

KEY DATES

AUGUST 4 ★ *learning to fly*

Allow yourself as much freedom as you can today as a liberating Sun-Uranus trine opens your mind. Temporarily letting go of responsibilities gives you the space you need to see your life with a fresh perspective. This is an ideal time to release your old self-image, making way for a more amazing you with an adventurous future.

AUGUST 8–11 ★ *face the music*

Brainy Mercury brightens your thoughts with its entry into sunny Leo on **August 8**. Yet bold ideas and brash statements can lead you astray with the Winged Messenger's unsettling quincunx with deceptive Neptune on the **10th**. Making unrealistic promises ends when restrictive Saturn squares Mercury on the **11th**. Nevertheless, you can turn negative comments into useful information by taking what you hear into serious consideration instead of defensively going into denial. Hard facts can build a solid foundation when you're willing to address them honestly.

SUPER NOVA DAYS
AUGUST 16–19 ★ *the truth will set you free*

Enjoy sweet social conversations on **August 16** thanks to luscious Venus's move into lovely Libra and your 3rd House of Communication. Your interactions with authorities, though, could be complicated by an untrusting Sun-Pluto sesquisquare. Luckily, a clever Sun-Saturn quintile shows you where to stand firm and where to let others lead. You're itching for change on the **19th**, sparking conflict if you're bored or feeling confined. The Sun's hard aspects to boundless Jupiter and independent Uranus stir up restlessness; you're yearning to break free. Yet these electrifying forces also enrich you with originality and honesty that can suddenly end a deadlock and open doors of opportunity.

AUGUST 26 ★ *the high cost of faith*

Protect your material resources today by doing some serious research before making a major purchase. That's because your financial decisions could be flaky with the Sun in your 2nd House of Money opposite blurry Neptune in your 8th House of Deep Sharing. Investing in someone else's fantasy can be a costly experience economically and emotionally. Developing respect for yourself helps prevent another person's neediness from draining your bank account or damaging your self-esteem.

AUGUST 30 ★ *wise beyond your years*

You make tough decisions graciously today as the Sun forms a harmonious sextile with ethical Saturn. This favorable alignment with the Sun in your fiscal 2nd House brings a strong sense of self-discipline that allows you to make sound choices about saving and spending. Your calm and self-controlled manner motivates you to concentrate on the details, leaving no stone unturned. Maturity shows you the big picture and supplies you with the patience to work toward long-term solutions.

SEPTEMBER

MONEY MATTERS

Managing your finances with greater care should pay off handsomely this month. This focus on material resources is triggered by the Sun's presence in the practical earth sign of Virgo and your 2nd House of Possessions until **September 22**. Reduce frivolous expenses to channel more time and money into cultivating skills that contribute to your future income. The conscientious Virgo New Moon on the **5th** is powered by a trine to unrelenting Pluto in your 6th House of Employment to help you eliminate distractions and increase your efficiency. A supportive sextile from Jupiter in your imaginative 12th House provides the inspiration you need to raise your hopes and work harder to reach your dreams. Interactive Mercury glides into diplomatic Libra and your 3rd House of Communication on **September 9**, enhancing your ability to listen with an open mind and express your ideas pleasantly.

Expect emotional issues to intensify when Venus dives deeply into Scorpio and your 4th House of Personal History on **September 11**. You may experience jealousy and power struggles when Venus joins controlling Saturn in your private 4th House on the **18th**. Fear of rejection might inhibit you from addressing these matters until the **19th**, when the sympathetic Pisces Full Moon floods your 8th House of Deep Sharing. This flow of unrestrained emotions washes away mistrust, giving rise to compassion and allowing you to grow closer with an influential ally. Saturn's sextile with Pluto on **September 21** is excellent for channeling passion into your work, and the Sun's entry into artistic Libra and your 3rd House of Information on the **22nd**, the Autumn Equinox, favors creative thinking.

> **KEEP IN MIND THIS MONTH**
>
> *Focus on learning valuable new skills rather than merely showing off talents you already have. Additional training maximizes your strengths and creates noticeable improvement where you're weakest.*

KEY DATES

SEPTEMBER 1–3 ★ *dangerous curves ahead*

Everyone's ready to cooperate with you on **September 1**, with a potent Sun-Pluto trine and a solar sextile to the Lunar North Node. Yet slippery aspects to illusory Neptune from Venus on the **1st** and Mars on the **2nd** suggest that you may overestimate others' abilities or waste your time chasing rainbows. Forcing issues on the **3rd** might only carry you further off course as a hard-to-manage

Sun-Uranus quincunx indicates that making subtle adjustments will be more productive than driving hard and fast.

SUPER NOVA DAYS
SEPTEMBER 7–9 ★ *the tortoise beats the hare*
You're filled with cheerful optimism now with a buoyant Sun-Jupiter sextile on **September 7**, while Mercury's creative quintile with the jovial planet can show you how to live up to your high expectations. Yet even the best-laid plans run into snags on the **9th** when reckless Mars in valiant Leo slams into a roadblock with stingy Saturn. The warrior planet in your physical 1st House makes you impatient and urges you to muscle your way through obstacles. Remember, although slowing down or even stopping to modify your methods may be frustrating, it will save you time and effort and increase your chances for success in the long run.

SEPTEMBER 14 ★ *reckless abandon*
You see radical new ways to get things done today thanks to go-getter Mars's harmonious trine with inventive Uranus. You can be assertive with a lighter touch when you don't take yourself so seriously. Don't let your pride keep you from exploring unconventional ways of acting, even at the risk of looking foolish. Running away from it all is also very tempting since dealing with routine tasks and predictable situations is especially boring now.

SEPTEMBER 21–22 ★ *the big picture show*
You see your life in a larger perspective on **September 21**, when the creative Sun's brilliant quintile with visionary Jupiter reveals meaning about you and your goals that previously escaped your notice. This vision can reward you with faith and reinforce your sense of purpose. The Sun's move into socially astute Libra and your communicative 3rd House on the **22nd** helps you present your ideas in a more inviting manner.

SEPTEMBER 25–26 ★ *the wobbly warrior*
You're battling for a lost cause given sticky solar aspects to misguided Neptune on **September 25** and combative Mars on the **26th**. Fighting for the underdog and struggling to live up to your ideals are worthy expressions of these complex transits. However, if you feel like a victim or martyr, it's probably better to rebuild your inner strength than to strike out at an external enemy.

OCTOBER

INFORMATION OVERLOAD

You'll spend a lot of time expanding your mind this month, because October starts with the Sun in objective Libra and your 3rd House of Learning. However, gathering information that clashes with what you already know may create as many problems as it solves. The airy Libra New Moon on **October 4** blows in a breeze of fresh ideas that can rock your world. Volatile Uranus's opposition to this lunation and tense squares from probing Pluto and global Jupiter can deliver shocking news, provoke explosive debates, and stimulate radical insights. Giving yourself enough time to assimilate this input helps you work out contradictions internally, instead of striking back or reacting hastily. Trickster Mercury in slow-cooking Scorpio turns retrograde in your 4th House of Roots on the **21st**, favoring a more contemplative approach to processing data over the next three weeks. Your social life, on the other hand, accelerates with affectionate Venus's move into adventurous Sagittarius and your 5th House of Romance on **October 7**. Containing your thoughts is one thing, but restraining your heart's desire for fun may be almost impossible with this risk-taking transit.

Mars's move into logical Virgo and your 2nd House of Resources on **October 15** reminds you to manage your time, money, and energy more carefully. But you'll find it hard to be prudent when the blazing Aries Full Moon Eclipse on the **18th** polarizes your 9th House of Truth, Travel, and Higher Education. While this could signal the cancellation of a trip or a revision of long-standing beliefs and educational plans, Jupiter's overly optimistic square makes it difficult to take a step back. Fortunately, the Sun's shift into your foundational 4th House and emotionally complex Scorpio on the **23rd** is bound to bring you back to your roots.

> **KEEP IN MIND THIS MONTH**
>
> *Be sure you're standing on solid emotional ground before making critical decisions. Your feelings determine where your mind travels now.*

KEY DATES

OCTOBER 1–3 ★ *embrace the unknown*

You may encounter conflict on the job as the Sun, your planetary ruler, forms a squeezing square with unwavering Pluto on **October 1** and an opposition with stormy Uranus on the **3rd**. The former forces you to make a tough decision, but the latter compels you to suddenly change your mind. The upside of these transformational transits can be a breakthrough in your professional life. Newfound power and freedom can be yours if you're willing to let go of whatever isn't working and take a chance on experimenting with something completely different.

OCTOBER 7–8 ★ *revolution for the hell of it*

You're in a less-than-cooperative mood on **October 7** when the exhilaration of Venus's arrival into your playful 5th House is kicked into higher gear by a rambunctious Mars-Uranus sesquisquare. Impatience, boredom, and built-up resentment surge to the surface. Mercury's edgy quincunx with progressive Uranus on the **8th** continues this anti-authoritarian theme. However, the consequences of reckless behavior arrive quickly when Saturn the Tester meets up with Mercury the Trickster, while the rewards of appropriate experimentation may also become evident.

SUPER NOVA DAYS

OCTOBER 10–12 ★ *curb your enthusiasm*

Sacrificing yourself for love or loot can be much more expensive than you expect if you let your hope, imagination, or desire exceed the bounds of reason. A romantic Venus-Neptune square on **October 10** evokes compassion, but a squishy Sun-Neptune sesquisquare can weaken your will and further skew your judgment about a person or a purchase. Venus's anxious sesquisquare to effusive Jupiter on the **11th** and the Sun's square to this giant planet on the **12th** continue to favor faith over facts. Nevertheless, opening your heart wider is healthy if you recognize your limits.

OCTOBER 25 ★ *state of grace*

Let go of negative judgments about yourself or someone close to you today when an inspiring Sun-Neptune trine activates your intimate 4th and 8th Houses. Forgiveness is a beautiful thing, freeing you from failures of the past and creating unencumbered visions of the future.

OCTOBER 30–31 ★ *mining for gold*

You connect with your deepest desires on **October 30**, due to the Sun's conjunction with the Moon's North Node in shadowy Scorpio—though you may have to work through repressed family-related issues to get in touch with your feelings first. On **October 31**, angry Mars activates the intense Uranus-Pluto square that's exact on **November 1**, creating an air of electricity and suspense. Facing fears and old failures can be your ticket to finding the passion required to process these emotions.

NOVEMBER

WALK ON THE WILD SIDE

Ironically, Leo, the best way to create a more rewarding future for yourself is to dig into the past. Retrograde Mercury burrows into your 4th House of Roots until **November 10**, challenging you to revisit some emotionally charged issues. Dealing with old patterns of doubt, self-criticism, or family dynamics is hard work but will cost less and earn you more than ignoring your past. On **November 1**, the fourth of seven earthshaking Uranus-Pluto squares sets the stage for seismic shifts that could eventually alter the course of your career. The intense Scorpio New Moon on **November 3** is a Solar Eclipse conjunct with serious Saturn in your 4th House that leaves little doubt about your priorities. Even though weird Uranus's quincunx to this special lunation might spring some surprises, favorable sextiles from Mars and Pluto provide persistence and power to transform personal pain into professional gain.

Focus on managing ongoing tasks in an organized manner—rather than charming others on the job—when valuable Venus enters responsible Capricorn and your 6th House of Employment on **November 5**. The Full Moon in stubborn Taurus and your professional 10th House on the **17th** highlights places where you're stuck in your work life yet might also cool your ambitions if you're in a comfortable situation. But don't worry about becoming so content that you settle for less because the Sun's entry into extroverted Sagittarius and your 5th House of Self-Expression on the **21st** increases your willingness to take risks. Romantic interests, the pursuit of pleasure, and your creative spirit are spiked with optimism and childlike delight that put you in the mood to play.

KEEP IN MIND THIS MONTH

Engage your darkest feelings with logic and reason so you can finally close the door on a difficult chapter of your life.

KEY DATES

NOVEMBER 1–3 ★ *bundle of nerves*

The Sun's erratic quincunx to Uranus triggers anxious feelings on **November 1**, but it's quickly followed by a sextile to Pluto that helps you regain your sense of equilibrium. Retrograde Mercury's conjunction to the Sun in your domestic 4th House reminds you of unfinished family business, yet it's best not to obsess about it if you can't bring any fresh ideas to the situation. On the **3rd**, the Scorpio New Moon Eclipse sextiles dynamic Mars, giving you the energy to develop new skills.

NOVEMBER 6 ★ *the long road home*
Dark clouds of doubt and delay overshadow you today with the expressive Sun's conjunction with somber Saturn in your 4th House of Roots. Yet you can also find your resolve by recognizing what you're missing and acknowledging the sustained effort required to make yourself whole. The key to happiness may be fixing problems on the home front, but don't expect solutions overnight. Real answers require you to make an honest assessment of your own role in the situation and commit yourself to sustaining a long course of corrective action.

NOVEMBER 12 ★ *calling all angels*
You feel your spirits lift when you receive faith and support from an unexpected source today—or perhaps when you assist someone in need yourself. The Sun's harmonious trine with sage Jupiter in your 12th House of Divinity broadens your perspective enough to dilute the wounds of past failures and current struggles. Taking some time away from routine tasks to absorb the healing powers of nature and meditation allows you to soak in the gifts of this bountiful transit.

SUPER NOVA DAYS
NOVEMBER 14–17 ★ *tipping point*
Venus's tense aspects with unreliable Uranus on **November 14** and temperamental Pluto on the **15th** shake up your relationships—especially those at work. Boredom, pushy people, and the pressure to perform unfamiliar tasks could unsettle your daily routine. The self-directed Sun's stressful connections with Uranus and Pluto on the **16th** and the Taurus Full Moon in your professional 10th House on the **17th** could bring you to a boiling point. Exploding or withdrawing in anger is only useful if it awakens new ideas that motivate you to take charge and initiate change instead of letting it lead you.

NOVEMBER 24–26 ★ *count your blessings*
The exuberance of the Sun lighting up your 5th House of Fun is heightened by its square to imaginative Neptune on **November 24** and sesquisquare to bountiful Jupiter on the **26th**. These visionary aspects fuel creative and romantic dreams that tempt you to overreach, so open your heart but don't leap without looking.

DECEMBER

LIFE OF THE PARTY

You're in a celebratory mood as December starts thanks to the Sun's presence in effervescent Sagittarius and your 5th House of Fun and Games. The holiday spirit is amplified by the Sagittarius New Moon on **December 2** that inspires playful behavior, creative self-expression, and romantic impulses. However, some people may have difficulty telling when you're teasing and when your intentions are real, so make a point of sending clear signals. Gregarious Mercury adds color to your communication when it enters fun-loving Sagittarius on the **4th**. Your sense of humor and outspoken opinions are likely to attract plenty of attention. Helpfully, your ability to press a point in a gracious manner is enhanced with Mars's shift into stylish Libra and your communicative 3rd House on **December 7**. The warrior planet wears velvet gloves in this diplomatic sign to refine your negotiating skills.

On **December 12**, Jupiter repeats a trine with Saturn that first occurred on **July 17** and will return on **May 24, 2014**. The strategic alignment between the planets of future vision and current reality can give shape to your dreams and set you on a course toward making them come true. Group activities can reach a critical point with the busy Gemini Full Moon in your team-oriented 11th House on the **17th**. You may be stretched so thin that you'll need to back out of an obligation; or you could find yourself at odds with the philosophy of an organization. The Sun's shift into ambitious Capricorn on **December 21**, the Winter Solstice, compels you to set priorities at work to get the most out of your abilities. Resourceful Venus's retrograde turn in your 6th House of Employment on the same day kicks off six weeks of job-related review and reevaluation.

> **KEEP IN MIND THIS MONTH**
>
> *Having a good time is a holiday gift to yourself, but generously sharing the joy you're feeling with others is a present that will last much longer than this season.*

KEY DATES

DECEMBER 2–4 ★ *incurable optimist*

It may be difficult to contain your excitement when you're fired up by the boisterous Sagittarius New Moon in your 5th House of Creativity on **December 2**. Luckily, if you have a delicate message to share, an articulate Mercury-Mars sextile on the **3rd** cuts through mental clutter to help you get straight to the point. But then Mercury's blast into farseeing Sagittarius on the **4th** lifts your head from the minor details of daily life so you can see the big picture and visualize a more inspiring future.

DECEMBER 10-12 ★ *for your eyes only*
Too much enthusiasm and excessive honesty can get the best of you as exaggerating Jupiter forms an unstable quincunx with the Sun on **December 10**. Think twice before sharing information that's not ready for prime time. Fortunately, if you do spill the beans, a subtle Sun-Neptune quintile on the **12th** provides sensitivity, compassion, and forgiveness to smooth out any rough spots.

DECEMBER 17-18 ★ *trust your instincts*
People are pulling you in several directions when the jittery Gemini Full Moon on the **17th** raises your social game to another level. Reactionary Uranus turns direct, tempting you to make quick decisions—but waiting until things calm down will produce more thoughtful results. Luckily, flashes of intuition arrive with a Jupiter-Neptune sesquisquare on December **17th**, followed by Mercury's clever quintile with psychic Neptune on the **18th**. Using your imagination should allow you to understand issues that facts alone cannot explain.

DECEMBER 25-26 ★ *give peace a chance*
Staying sweet and spiritual on **December 25** may be challenging with assertive Mars's opposition to disruptive Uranus. This tense alignment between your 3rd House of Communication and 9th House of Philosophy can trigger a battle over competing ideas. Happily, a sensitive Mercury-Neptune sextile on the **26th** is excellent for healing hurt feelings and backing away from extreme positions. If you're not feeling as appreciated as you wish, you'll need a mature attitude to accept the limits imposed on you by a strict Sun-Saturn semisquare.

SUPER NOVA DAYS
DECEMBER 29-31 ★ *inevitable change*
You end the year with a strong desire to take your professional life in a different direction. Messenger Mercury and the Sun join in your 6th House of Employment and square revolutionary Uranus on **December 29-30**. Tense connections among Mercury, Mars, and Pluto on the **30th** and **31st** add an intensity that can be destructive unless you apply your creativity and passion to seek more stimulating work.

♍

VIRGO

AUGUST 23–SEPTEMBER 22

VIRGO

2012 SUMMARY

Use this time as a period of retraining and readjusting to step back and reexamine where old habits are no longer useful and to adopt new ways of managing your health and lifestyle. Repairing relationships starts by demonstrating flexibility and a friendly attitude that's open to new and different points of view. Grasping basic principles is your ladder to the stars, rewarding you with a richer sense of meaning and purpose.

AUGUST—*starting over*
You don't need to know every step that you will be taking in advance to begin a successful journey that can enrich your life.

SEPTEMBER—*organized chaos*
Being mentally flexible enables you to adjust your thinking, shift your priorities, and adapt your methods to handle unanticipated events effectively.

OCTOBER—*beauty and the bottom line*
Taking an objective look at what you've accomplished in life will show you how to get more money, respect, and pleasure from your work.

NOVEMBER—*useful u-turn*
Eliminating the clutter that fills your day, your calendar, and your mind's bandwidth frees you from distractions that take more from you than they give.

DECEMBER—*spread your wings and fly*
You don't have to settle for less in life when you open your mind and think about the many alternatives beyond the limits of your current situation.

2012 CALENDAR

AUGUST

WED 1 ★ Develop new skills and interests

WED 8–THU 9 ★ Feelings are more important than facts

WED 15 ★ Dig below the surface to uncover hidden resources

WED 22–FRI 24 ★ **SUPER NOVA DAYS** Overlook petty differences

WED 29 ★ Put a positive spin on a negative situation

SEPTEMBER

SAT 1 ★ Explore your imagination

FRI 7– MON 10 ★ You might raise expectations beyond reason

THU 20– SAT 22 ★ **SUPER NOVA DAYS** Conversations grow convoluted

TUE 25–WED 26 ★ Your extreme desires could prompt risky behavior

SAT 29 ★ Create an escape plan that's both safe and stimulating

OCTOBER

FRI 5–SUN 7 ★ Words take on extra significance

MON 15 ★ Restrain the urge to splurge

SAT 20– SUN 21 ★ Don't stress if you can't put your thoughts into words

THU 25 ★ **SUPER NOVA DAY** Withholding information can undermine trust

SUN 28–MON 29 ★ Keep your head in the clouds and your feet on the ground

NOVEMBER

THU 1–SAT 3 ★ Finances take a sudden turn

SUN 11–TUE 13 ★ Avoid paranoia by keeping your beliefs grounded in reality

FRI 16–SAT 17 ★ Concentrate on activities that have the most impact

THU 22–SAT 24 ★ Follow standard operating procedures

MON 26–WED 28 ★ **SUPER NOVA DAYS** Harsh judgment demands strong action

DECEMBER

SAT 1–SUN 2 ★ You're likely to go too far or expect too much

MON 10–WED 12 ★ Your imagination soars as communications grow confusing

SUN 16–MON 17 ★ Strong messages conflict with hypersensitivity

FRI 21–SAT 22 ★ Take the lead in romantic matters

FRI 28–SUN 30 ★ **SUPER NOVA DAYS** You may go to extremes of self-expression

VIRGO OVERVIEW

Start small and work your way up to the bigger issues this year; you'll make great strides in your journey of self-improvement. Responsible Saturn is in your 3rd House of Immediate Environment, requiring you to restructure your day-to-day life and how you interact with those closest to you. **Instead of letting your philosophical perspective dictate your daily agenda, be mindful of every little thing you do.** Pay attention to how you manage the flow of information in your communication with others and be more conscious of your own mental patterns and habitual behaviors. You become more serious about this process when transformational Pluto forms a supportive sextile to Saturn on March 8 and September 21 in a series that began on December 26, 2012.

Other people are a source of inspiration this year, although you need to establish boundaries if you're to remain clear about your goals. With imaginative Neptune camped out in your 7th House of Relationships, those closest to you can act as mirrors, reflecting your own fantasies. However, confusion dissipates on June 11 and July 19 when hardworking Saturn harmoniously trines Neptune, enabling you to take practical steps toward realizing your dreams. Additional emotional support comes from five other planets moving through your 11th House of Friends during June and July, creating a series of auspicious grand trines. On June 3–7, communicator Mercury and sweet Venus complete a Grand Water Trine with Saturn and Neptune, turning on your charisma and prompting others to support your aspirations. The Sun radiates emotional security as it trines Saturn and Neptune on June 26. Your confidence and enthusiasm are off the charts when buoyant Jupiter and impulsive Mars reactivate this magical planetary pattern on July 17–20. During this phase, your overall sense of well-being can be very satisfying—but don't grow complacent, because this is a propitious time to put your plans into motion.

Personal relationships remain in the spotlight as the long-lasting square between wayward Uranus in your 8th House of Regeneration and passionate Pluto in your 5th House of Love and Creativity is exact on May 20 and November 1. This aspect series, which began on June 24, 2012, and completes on March 16, 2015, can revitalize a flagging partnership if you're willing to engage in deep psychological transformation. However, it can also signal the end of a relationship if you are fearfully clinging to the past and unwilling to make any changes. In either case, your desire for independence will be strong enough to make waves when honorable Saturn forms an irritable quincunx with irrepressible Uranus on April 12 and October 5 in a series that began on November 15, 2012.

HOUSE OF MIRRORS

Mystical Neptune's presence in your 7th House of Others can put an enchanting spell on any partnership. However, it can also create an impenetrable layer of fog between you and someone else. There are a total of seven planets in your 7th House on March 11 when the empathetic Pisces New Moon makes it difficult to distinguish your feelings from the ones you pick up from another person—and you're likely to misread signals thanks to trickster Mercury's retrograde on February 23–March 17. With Venus the Lover also in your 7th House on February 25–March 21, you might find yourself drawn to someone, only to discover that he or she isn't what you'd imagined. A series of planetary oppositions to perceptive Pluto in your 5th House of Romance on June 7, June 11, July 1, July 27, and August 7 creates tension, yet offers a clearer reflection of what's happening. The Venus-Pluto conjunction in your 5th House on November 15 brings to the surface intense feelings that have the power to transform the dynamics of your love life.

ROOM AT THE TOP

You're at the peak of your professional game with prosperous Jupiter in your 10th House of Career until June 25. In fact, the year begins on a high note with an energetic Mars-Jupiter trine in your 6th House of Work on January 4. The good news gets even better on February 6–7 as enterprising Venus and surprising Uranus align harmoniously with Jupiter, producing unexpected recognition for your hard work, boosting your self-esteem, or bringing a cash bonus. However, it's time to look further into the future on June 25 when Jupiter shifts into your 11th House of Long-Term Goals, where it remains until July 16, 2014. Cultivate new connections within your community, develop social networks, and grow more trusting and appreciative of friends who support you.

EASY COME, EASY GO

You struggle to hold on to your cash this year with erratic Uranus in your 8th House of Investments and Shared Resources. The Libra Full Moon on March 27 illuminates your 2nd House of Finances and opposes Uranus and the money planet Venus, emphasizing your financial instability. The Libra New Moon on October 4 again opposes volatile Uranus, possibly catalyzing much-needed changes in a business relationship. The Aries Lunar Eclipse on October 18 rattles your 8th House of Joint Holdings and is another not-so-gentle reminder to keep your fiscal policy conservative right now.

LEAN ON ME

You're naturally inclined to maintain a healthy lifestyle, but you may have to learn how to ask for help when you need it this year. Chiron the Wounded Healer remains in your 7th House of Others until 2018, but trines from trustworthy Saturn on March 21 and October 2 can alleviate your fear of being vulnerable, especially if a friend comes through with the support you need. Consult a health care provider about a chronic problem around March 28–29 when interactive Mercury trines Saturn and conjuncts Chiron. Also, it's wise to increase the intensity of your workouts during macho Mars's visit to your sign on October 15–December 7.

WINDOW OF OPPORTUNITY

You'll have more fun at home—whether you're alone, with family, or with guests—when pleasurable Venus is in your 4th House of Domestic Conditions through January 8 and then again on October 7–November 5. Although you're inclined to stay close to your place of residence, Venus in high-spirited Sagittarius encourages you to turn your home into a place of adventure by hosting people from faraway places, listening to music from other cultures, or expanding your culinary skills to include other national cuisines. A boisterous Sagittarius Lunar Eclipse on May 25 shakes up your household by emboldening you to take a risk and start a remodeling project, redecorate a room, or throw a party to remember.

FLEXIBLE FLYER

You tend to travel for business purposes while opportunistic Jupiter is visiting your 10th House of Career until June 25. If possible, avoid going on a trip March 23–29 when Jupiter forms uneasy quincunxes with restrictive Saturn and formidable Pluto. Once Jupiter enters your 11th House of Friends on June 25, you're more likely to embark on an excursion for social reasons rather than for work. Even if you pay attention to every little detail when Mercury is retrograde on February 23–March 17, June 26–July 20, or October 21–November 10, prepare to make last-minute changes due to unforeseen circumstances.

GUIDING LIGHT

You are very serious about acquiring practical tools that advance your spiritual development. But study will only take you so far, even with ambitious Saturn's presence in your 3rd House of Learning. A key to your metaphysical growth is finding a teacher or guru who can take you further along the path than you could go on your own. Inspirational Neptune, making a long-term visit to your 7th House of Others, can cause you to idealize someone who seems to know more than you. Thankfully, synergetic Saturn-Neptune trines on June 11 and July 19 give you a mix of intuition and sensibility that enables you to choose a reliable guide to take you to the next level.

RICK & JEFF'S TIP FOR THE YEAR:
Keep Your Eyes on the Prize

You normally prefer a more objective view of the world, so you may feel a bit disoriented with so many planets in emotional water signs this year. However, resistance to powerful waves of feelings is futile and will only bring frustration and exhaustion. Instead of fearfully holding onto the status quo, trust the wisdom of the cosmos by pushing away from the shore and into the strong currents. If you lose your bearings once you leave solid ground, the best way to prevent instability is to focus on the horizon and your future goals rather than looking back to the past.

JANUARY

POWER PLAY

You are ready to hit the ground running this month as a heightened sense of practicality enables you to express yourself methodically and advance steadily toward your goals. You're in a serious mood when your ruling planet, Mercury, in ambitious Capricorn hooks up with ruthless Pluto in your 5th House of Creativity on **January 6**, prompting you to think about getting ahead even when you're engaging in play. Valuable Venus enters calculating Capricorn and your 5th House on **January 8**, which allows you to have a good time as long as you manage to be productive, too. Since the gathering of planets in results-oriented Capricorn requires you to make a concrete plan for your success, the New Moon in the sign of the climbing Mountain Goat on the **11th** is a great time to put it into action.

The energy shifts on **January 19** as Mercury and the Sun enter conceptual Aquarius and your 6th House of Self-Improvement, giving you more freedom to adapt your daily routine to your unique way of doing business. Luckily, on **January 22–25** Mercury and the Sun form supportive aspects with innovative Uranus and fortuitous Jupiter, creating the potential for an unexpected breakthrough at work or public recognition for a job well done. These auspicious days can increase your self-confidence, which is great as long as you don't get too cocky. If you do assume that everything is copacetic, the dramatic Leo Full Moon in your 12th House of Destiny on the **26th** could be a sobering reality check as it squares karmic Saturn. The challenging Sun-Saturn square on **January 30** presents obstacles that can slow you down until you've learned your spiritual lesson.

> **KEEP IN MIND THIS MONTH**
>
> *In the midst of all your obligations to others and commitments to yourself, schedule some playtime when you can kick back and enjoy yourself.*

KEY DATES

JANUARY 1-4 ★ *lost in your mind*

You're able to share your ideas more creatively while messenger Mercury visits your 5th House of Self-Expression. You strive to be practical in your thinking, but a Mercury-Neptune sextile on **January 1** infuses your thoughts with fantasy. Although Mercury's creative square with inventive Uranus on the **3rd** can trigger intellectual brilliance, you're not interested in conforming to other people's expectations. Nevertheless, you're motivated to achieve your professional objectives on **January 4**, when assertive Mars in your 6th House of Work trines far-reaching Jupiter in your 10th House of Career.

SUPER NOVA DAYS
JANUARY 7–11 ★ *turning point*
January 7 can be a rather frustrating day at work. Impatient Mars in your 6th House of Details squares restraining Saturn, so you may have to wait a little longer before taking action. Fortunately, Venus enters conservative Capricorn on **January 8** and connects with spacey Neptune on the **10th**, cultivating patience as a more attractive strategy than just bolting ahead. The Capricorn New Moon on **January 11** begins a monthlong cycle of activity as it stimulates your 5th House of Love and Creativity. The New Moon's magical quintiles to brilliant Uranus and earnest Saturn bless you with an extra dose of ingenuity and charisma, emboldening you to start the next phase of your journey with renewed self-confidence.

JANUARY 16–18 ★ *you get what you need*
Your emotional intensity is strong enough to heat up an intimate relationship or strengthen your resolve in a business negotiation on **January 16**, when seductive Venus joins persuasive Pluto in your 5th House of Romance and Self-Expression. You become even more determined to satisfy your desires on the **17th** when Venus supportively sextiles persistent Saturn. Fortunately, communicator Mercury hooks up with the radiant Sun on the **18th** to give your words enough power to convince others that you're speaking the truth.

JANUARY 24–26 ★ *the sky is the limit*
Expect a great deal of excitement at work on **January 24** with the high-frequency electricity of the Sun's supportive sextile to eye-opening Uranus. The Sun's trine to expansive Jupiter on the **25th** broadens your vision, encourages you to set your goals higher than ever, and instills you with enough enthusiasm to fuel a journey to the stars. However, a methodical Mercury-Saturn square requires you to make certain that you've addressed all details prior to blastoff. Your sense of invincibility culminates with the proud Leo Full Moon on **January 26** that illuminates your 12th House of Endings, alerting you that it's now time to slow down and integrate the recent changes.

FEBRUARY

PERCEPTION IS REALITY

It's difficult to know what's real in your relationships this month as planets cluster in fanciful Pisces and your 7th House of Partnerships and Public Life. Your personal and professional interactions are top priority when spontaneous Mars begins the parade into your 7th House on **February 1**, followed by communicator Mercury on **February 5**, the Sun on **February 18**, and loving Venus on **February 25**. Even with this growing emphasis on others, however, you might not know where you stand with them, because each of these planets joins fuzzy Neptune after it enters Pisces, confusing your desires with reality. Excessive self-confidence can overinflate your expectations when pompous Jupiter squares Mercury on the **9th**, Mars on the **10th**, and the Sun on the **25th**. Fortunately, common sense prevails when serious Saturn trines thoughtful Mercury on the **12th** and Mars on the **16th**.

You may be more assertive than usual as your key planet, Mercury, conjuncts Mars in your interactive 7th House on **February 8**. An uncharacteristic intensity can permeate conversations throughout the month because speedy Mercury slows down—along with your progress—until it turns retrograde on the **23rd**, tracking closely with Mars the entire time. A second Mercury-Mars conjunction on the **26th** can reactivate an old argument, even if you thought the conflict was resolved. Meanwhile, the futuristic Aquarius New Moon on **February 10** plants a seed of intention in your 6th House of Self-Improvement, encouraging you to think of new and different ways to change your everyday life for the better. The exacting Virgo Full Moon on **February 25** reminds you to pay attention to your feelings, even though practical considerations may require you to keep them to yourself to avoid conflict.

> **KEEP IN MIND THIS MONTH**
>
> *People sometimes show up in your life to reflect issues that you need to work on. Instead of trying to fix anyone else, remember that real change starts within you.*

KEY DATES

FEBRUARY 5–7 ★ *top of the world*

When cerebral Mercury enters your 7th House of Companions on **February 5**, you shift your analytical attention from the details of daily life to how you interact with others. It's hard to separate your expectations from reality, however, because Mercury joins dreamy Neptune on **February 6**, which can be inspiring if you remember to keep your facts and fantasies in their proper places. You're more willing to experiment as desirable Venus forms a supportive sextile with unconventional Uranus. Although you may be inclined to try something new and different in your relationships, Venus in your 6th House of Work happily trines propitious Jupiter in your 10th House of Status on the **7th**, indicating that you could be rewarded for your ingenuity on the job instead.

FEBRUARY 10–12 ★ *inch by inch*
The quirky Aquarius New Moon on **February 10** reveals silver linings in dark clouds because it's accompanied by an upbeat Mars-Jupiter square that infuses you with excitement. But take things slowly, because severe Saturn in your 3rd House of Communication aspects Venus and Mercury on **February 11–12**, bringing delays and even setbacks if you impulsively rush ahead. Rather than wallowing in self-doubt, concentrate on what needs to be done, make a concrete plan, and then move resolutely toward your goal one step at a time.

FEBRUARY 15–16 ★ *in the zone*
Warrior Mars is your ally now, gracing you with a deep reservoir of energy and the ability to collaborate effectively with others to achieve success. Mars in your 7th House of Partnerships cooperatively sextiles potent Pluto on **February 15** and trines reliable Saturn on the **16th**, empowering you to express yourself creatively while still working closely with someone else. Fortunately, your co-workers can be of great help because your high level of organization makes it easier for them to contribute their skills to the project.

SUPER NOVA DAYS
FEBRUARY 23–25 ★ *the devil is in the details*
Although the hardworking Virgo Full Moon on **February 25** falls in your 1st House of Physicality, it may not be easy to accomplish your goals now. Your ruling planet, Mercury, begins its retrograde phase on **February 23** in your 7th House of Partners, possibly unraveling a working relationship. If necessary, renegotiate the details of an agreement prior to Mercury's direct turn on **March 17**. But don't push too hard for final resolution in a conflict; the Full Moon and the Sun dynamically square grandiose Jupiter, allowing you to overlook important details and possibly promise more than you can deliver.

MARCH

LOST AND FOUND

You can barely keep your thoughts distinct from those of the people around you this month. It's because six planets congregating in hypersensitive Pisces and your 7th House of Others soften the hard edges that normally separate you from the rest of the world. A heightened state of empathy turns your mind into an emotional sponge, absorbing the feelings of those closest to you. Thankfully, a long-lasting sextile between stabilizing Saturn and surgical Pluto on **March 8** enables you to cut through the noise and make enduring changes to the way you process information. However, trusting your intuition is difficult because you naturally still want the details, even when the psychic Pisces New Moon on **March 11** falls in your social 7th House.

You're likely to misread the intentions of a partner or misunderstand a conversation while Mercury the Trickster is retrograde in fantasy-prone Pisces and your 7th House of Companions until **March 17**. You may struggle with staying motivated because your previous goals appear to lose some of their importance. Happily, the cobwebs of confusion begin to dissipate once clever Mercury turns direct. The pace of change picks up steam when three planets each shift into fiery Aries in your 8th House of Regeneration—Mars on the **12th**, the Sun on the **20th**, and Venus on the **21st**. But your forward motion isn't so steady on **March 23** when an anxious quincunx between optimistic Jupiter and pessimistic Saturn leaves you doubtful. The diplomatic Libra Full Moon on **March 27** brightens your 2nd House of Values, reminding you that having to make compromises doesn't mean that you must sacrifice any of your core beliefs.

> **KEEP IN MIND THIS MONTH**
>
> *It's never easy to let go of old agendas, especially if you don't know what will replace them. Yet this step is necessary before you can start the next phase of your journey.*

KEY DATES

MARCH 1 ★ *deep thoughts*

You may not use many words today, but you still get your point across succinctly. This no-frills attitude is courtesy of the Sun trining somber Saturn in your 3rd House of Communication. A powerful Sun–Pluto sextile strengthens your resolve and compels you to express yourself creatively, even while you fulfill your responsibilities.

MARCH 4–7 ★ *make love work*

Rational Mercury's retrograde in your 7th House of Companions is a great time to revisit interpersonal issues, and on **March 4** its conjunction with the Sun focuses your thinking on relationships. Yet it's not easy being logical as sensual Venus squares indulgent Jupiter, increasing your desires and encouraging you to ask for more than usual. The topic of conversation is love when talkative Mercury conjuncts romantic Venus on the **6th**. Discussing difficult subjects can lead to lasting progress toward resolving your differences as Venus and Mercury trine trustworthy Saturn and sextile insightful Pluto on **March 6–7**.

MARCH 9–12 ★ *fools rush in*

You say something that might be better left unsaid on **March 9**, when loquacious Mercury squares bombastic Jupiter. Although you may pause to consider other people's feelings when the compassionate Pisces New Moon lands in your 7th House of Relationships on **March 11**, you're not likely to think twice before doing something reckless when impetuous Mars blasts into dauntless Aries on **March 12**. Just remember that exercising a little caution can save the day.

MARCH 20–22 ★ *yell fire!*

The Spring Equinox, marked by the Sun's move into pioneering Aries and your 8th House of Deep Sharing on **March 20**, empowers you to take a risk to increase the level of intimacy in a meaningful relationship. Venus enters vibrant Aries on the **21st**, reinforcing your desire for an intense connection with someone special. Combustible Mars hooks up with uncontainable Uranus on the **22nd**, setting off emotional fireworks or triggering a conflict.

SUPER NOVA DAYS
MARCH 27–31 ★ *navigating rough waters*

You crave more harmony in your relationships with the peace-seeking Libra Full Moon on the **27th** lighting up your sociable 7th House. But you can't decide on a course of action, because aspects to adventurous Jupiter, cautious Saturn, and thrilling Uranus on **March 28–29** have you seeking stability and excitement at the same time. Uncomfortable alignments with suspicious Pluto on **March 29–31** stir up feelings of jealousy or resentment, making it difficult to relax, but facing these challenges can transform you into a better person if you remember to be kind and honest in your dealings with others.

APRIL

SUSTAINABLE GROWTH

Although you begin April with a surge of progress, by midmonth the noise begins to settle down, enabling you to sustain your enthusiasm while seeking new ways to widen your horizons. Your normally cautious approach to change is at odds with the challenges you face with a cluster of planets in impulsive Aries and your 8th House of Transformation. You bring an especially creative approach to relationships on **April 6-8** when animated Mars, amorous Venus, and the Sun aspect poetic Neptune in your 7th House of Partners. The assertive Aries New Moon on the **April 10** conjuncts Mars and Venus in your 8th House, motivating you to move beyond the status quo by embracing the future rather than holding on to the past. However, resistant Saturn in your 3rd House of Immediate Environment forms an irritating quincunx with uncontrollable Uranus on **April 12**, escalating your discomfort with any transitions that are unfolding too fast. Fortunately, quicksilver Mercury dashes into trailblazing Aries on the **13th**, giving you a much-needed new perspective to handle current developments.

On **April 15** resourceful Venus enters your 9th House of Higher Thought and Faraway Places, raising your interest in subjects and activities that expand your mind and broaden your view of the world. The Sun enters dependable Taurus and your 9th House on **April 19**, followed by Mars on the **20th**, reinforcing your pragmatic approach to growth. Taskmaster Saturn's opposition to Venus on **April 22** and the Sun on **April 28** may slow your progress substantially by placing obstacles in your path, compelling you to work hard without necessarily seeing immediate gain. The enigmatic Scorpio Full Moon on **April 25** is a Lunar Eclipse that conjuncts Saturn in your 3rd House of Communication, requiring you to concentrate on one task at a time.

> **KEEP IN MIND THIS MONTH**
>
> *Reaching your goals may depend upon your ability to turn your passion at the beginning of a project into sheer determination and willpower later on.*

KEY DATES

APRIL 1 ★ *sunny-side up*

It's easy to imagine that you can accomplish nearly anything today because exuberant Jupiter in your 10th House of Career and Public Life is illuminated by a supportive sextile from the Sun in fearless Aries. Others may think that you're lucky, but it's your positive attitude that's at the root of your current good fortune.

APRIL 9–13 ★ *closer to free*

Mercury's magical quintile to dark Pluto on **April 9** adds depth and intensity to your messages. But when the Communicator runs into critical Saturn on the **10th**, you'll need facts to support your point of view. Tension builds as the unpremeditated Aries New Moon in your 8th House of Intimacy on the same day prompts you to reveal secrets that leave you feeling vulnerable. The conflict between sharing your emotions now and waiting for a better time is exacerbated by Saturn's maladjusted quincunx to reckless Uranus on **April 12**. Although there may be sensible reasons to respect the confines of the current situation, Mercury's shift into headstrong Aries on the **13th** might convince you to say what's on your mind anyway.

APRIL 20–23 ★ *truth and consequences*

You're compelled to express yourself—even if it will ruffle someone's feathers— when intelligent Mercury joins rebellious Uranus in your 8th House of Deep Sharing on **April 20**. Although Mars's move into steady Taurus on the same day encourages complacency, its active semisquare to opinionated Jupiter on the **21st** provokes dramatic action. Assuming that you speak your piece, an isolating Venus-Saturn opposition on **April 22** can bring harsh judgment from someone who is normally supportive. Fortunately, a cooperative Mercury-Jupiter sextile on the **23rd** helps you find the words to regain trust and earn recognition for taking an unconventional stand on an important subject.

SUPER NOVA DAYS
APRIL 25–28 ★ *practical magic*

Your life feels unpredictable right now. Even though the Sun, Venus, and Mars are all in down-to-earth Taurus, a magnetic Scorpio Lunar Eclipse on **April 25** in your 3rd House of Immediate Environment infuses you with a sense of instability. The Full Moon Eclipse conjuncts concrete Saturn, enchanting you with the power of your desires and the possibility of concentrating your emotional intensity to get what you want. Your fascination with what lies beyond the real world is encouraged by an illusory Mars-Neptune sextile on the **26th**. However, the karmic Sun-Saturn opposition on the **28th** indicates that you won't get away with outsmarting reality if you try to stretch it too far.

MAY

WORK IN PROGRESS

You may be frustrated by setbacks to your plans this month, but you can rebound quickly and establish new goals based on a deeper awareness of who you are and how you want to express yourself. Your ability to make long-term plans is quite sound, with incisive Pluto in your 5th House of Self-Expression creating a harmonious trine with the Sun on **May 1**, Mars on **May 5**, and Mercury on **May 7**— all in your 9th House of Future Vision. A Taurus Solar Eclipse in your 9th House on **May 9** is a harbinger of unexpected change, though, even if everything seems stable in the moment. Venus's entry into your 10th House of Public Responsibility, also on the **9th**, shifts your focus to seeking recognition on the job. Your thoughts turn to more immediate career concerns when analytical Mercury steps into your 10th House on **May 15**. The Sun and Mars follow suit on **May 20** and **May 31**, further emphasizing the transition from planning for the future to dealing with the present. All of these planets—plus opportunistic Jupiter—traveling through diverse Gemini may present so many options that narrowing your focus can be problematic.

Nevertheless, bigger changes are afoot, stemming from a long-lasting square between revolutionary Uranus and evolutionary Pluto that began on **June 24, 2012**, and culminates on **March 16, 2015**. This powerful aspect is exact on **May 20**, deepening an inner conflict between your urgent need to express yourself more passionately and the growing stress it places on your personal relationships. On **May 25**, a Sagittarius Lunar Eclipse lands in your 4th House of Roots, which can put an end to unrealistic dreams about your home and family.

> **KEEP IN MIND THIS MONTH**
>
> *Although you prefer having a concrete plan to get ahead at work, too much structure can limit your ability to adapt to changing circumstances.*

KEY DATES

MAY 1–5 ★ *heroic efforts*

You're ready to methodically set your strategy into motion, but may lack sufficient information as Saturn the Tester opposes Mars the Warrior in your 9th House of Big Ideas on **May 1**. Your key planet, Mercury, enters practical Taurus on the same day to help you clarify your long-range goals. Additionally, a powerful Sun-Pluto trine gives you the stamina to overcome the resistance you face. If you don't have all your facts in order, thoughtful Mercury's opposition to unforgiving Saturn on

May 5 sends you back to the drawing board until you've learned what you need to know. Again, a trine to unrelenting Pluto—this time from Mars—enables you to act on your resolve with unflappable determination.

MAY 9 ★ *lighten up*

There's a sense of playfulness in the air when flirty Venus enters whimsical Gemini on **May 9**. Yes, you're motivated to accomplish your goals, but you like the idea of having a variety of ways to reach them. The sensible Taurus New Moon Eclipse reminds you that the simplest approach is still the best one, while cautioning you against becoming so stuck in your ways that you lose your ability to adapt to the big changes coming your way.

SUPER NOVA DAYS
MAY 18–20 ★ *tricky currents*

While you're great at analyzing a situation to make a smart decision, Virgo, a lot of uncertainty is packed into these days. Brainy Mercury is in your 10th House of Status and its square to deceptive Neptune on **May 18** can be confusing if you're under pressure to make an immediate choice, especially when others are depending on you to lead the way. An unorthodox Venus-Uranus sextile encourages you to try a new route to reach your destination, and Mercury's sextile to Uranus on the **20th** is ready to reward your originality. Yet all your well-intended efforts may be for naught in light of large-scale social changes that stem from the life-changing Uranus-Pluto square that's exact on **May 20**.

MAY 25–28 ★ *the time to hesitate is through*

Just as you begin to gain traction, a confusing Sun-Neptune square on the **26th** starts you wondering whether or not you're heading in the right direction. Thankfully, any self-doubt quickly dissipates when Mercury and Venus conjunct sanguine Jupiter, inspiring you with new ideas and a greater sense of worth on **May 27–28**. Don't be afraid to take a risk—as long as you bring along some of your famous common sense.

JUNE

THE PERSISTENCE OF ILLUSION

The pressure for change doesn't let up this month, but you will have days when your uncertainty vanishes and even the most fleeting dreams appear vividly real. These moments, however brief, are not meant to confuse you; rather, they are opportunities to make your wishes come true. Industrious Saturn in your 3rd House of Data Collection forms a trine to elusive Neptune in your 7th House of Partnerships on **June 11**, empowering you to build new structures that support your vision, ground your intuition, and sharpen your instincts in business and personal relationships. However, this Saturn-Neptune trine is strengthened on **June 3** when cunning Mercury creates a stabilizing Grand Water Trine with these two slow-moving planets, enabling you to make a concrete plan that can stand the test of time. On **June 7**, glamorous Venus follows the pattern to trine Saturn and Neptune, enhancing the possibilities before you while giving you the patience and follow-through to see your aspirations materialize. It's the radiant Sun's turn to illuminate and crystallize your opportunities when it completes the grand trine on **June 26**, sustaining this constructive pattern throughout the month.

Meanwhile, you're eager to seek recognition in your chosen field thanks to the restless Gemini New Moon on **June 8** that emphasizes your 10th House of Career and Responsibility. The earthy Capricorn Full Moon on **June 23** lands in your 5th House of Self-Expression, encouraging you to carve out some time for creative endeavors and enjoy playtime with your inner child or the children in your world. Mercury's retrograde turn in your 11th House of Pals on **June 26** begins a three-week period of introspection, prompting you to review recent social events, reevaluate your role in organizations, and rethink your goals for the rest of the year.

> ### KEEP IN MIND THIS MONTH
>
> *You can minimize the stress associated with big changes by focusing your attention on a single goal and relentlessly keeping your eyes on the prize.*

KEY DATES

JUNE 2–3 ★ *you've got a friend*

You long to cultivate more nurturing relationships when lovable Venus meanders into sensitive Cancer and your 11th House of Friends and Associates on **June 2**. You could greatly benefit from participating in a group activity when interactive Mercury, also in your 11th House, forms a Grand Water Trine with Saturn and Neptune on

June 3. Although you may be tempted to keep your feelings to yourself, sharing them can lead to increased relationship stability in your everyday life.

SUPER NOVA DAYS
JUNE 7–8 ★ *embrace the unknown*
There is more going on than meets the eye when curious Mercury opposes secretive Pluto on **June 7** and squares shocking Uranus on the **8th**, creating some excitement and turmoil. However, procrastination abounds when forceful Mars squares confusing Neptune on the **7th**, dissipating your energy and reducing your ability to take decisive action. Happily, you feel loved by your friends as appreciative Venus in your 11th House of Community harmonizes with enduring Saturn and idealistic Neptune. The adaptable Gemini New Moon on **June 8** showcases your ability to move back and forth between stressful periods of uncertainty and relaxing moments of peaceful coexistence.

JUNE 11–15 ★ *building a mystery*
Needy Venus opposes punishing Pluto on **June 11** and squares volatile Uranus on the **12th**, fomenting emotional conflict that can make romance feel like a battlefield. But a powerful trine between solid Saturn and surreal Neptune on the **11th** enables you to ground even your most unrealistic ideas. On **June 14**, a snappy Sun-Uranus quintile activates your inner nerd and sparks flashes of ingenuity that move you closer to your goals. However, a crunchy Mars-Pluto quincunx on the **15th** can stymie your progress toward your objectives, especially if you mistakenly think that manipulative behavior will take you where you want to go.

JUNE 19–23 ★ *simply irresistible*
You may see opportunity everywhere you look on **June 19** when the Sun conjuncts cheerful Jupiter in your 10th House of Career. You are extraordinarily persuasive and can sweet-talk your way into someone's heart on the **20th** as chatty Mercury hooks up with charming Venus. The Sun's entry into self-protective Cancer and your 11th House of Groups on **June 21** marks the Summer Solstice, a time when your friends and associates assume an increasingly important role in your life. However, the crafty Capricorn Full Moon in your 5th House of Love on **June 23** reveals emotions that test the boundaries separating a romance from a friendship.

JULY

FIELD OF DREAMS

Explore the outer limits this month by imagining the possibilities ahead rather than solely focusing on concrete objectives. The planetary gathering in your 11th House of Long-Term Goals inspires you to seek the pot of gold at rainbow's end, even if you don't know how to get there just yet. You're likely to reexamine old expectations before thinking about your new mission as your ruling planet, Mercury, retrogrades through reflective Cancer and your 11th House until **July 20**. State your intentions as clearly as possible on **July 8** when the caring Cancer New Moon, also in your 11th House, invites you to plant a seed of intention that you can nurture to fruition over the weeks ahead.

Fortunately, you can easily crystallize the best parts of your diaphanous visions because of a long-lasting holding pattern between disciplined Saturn in resourceful Scorpio and magical Neptune in creative Pisces. This Saturn-Neptune trine is exact on **July 19** and is the final occurrence of a series that began on **October 10, 2012**, empowering you to manifest your dreams. Luckily, bountiful Jupiter and competent Mars trine Saturn and Neptune on **July 17** and **July 20**, helping to make your wishes come true. This consolidating Grand Water Trine reminds you that steady progress is possible and allows you to integrate a deeper spiritual perspective into your life. On **July 22**, a boisterous Mars-Jupiter conjunction in your futuristic 11th House raises your confidence and increases your zest, motivating you to strive for perfection. However, Venus's shift into discerning Virgo, along with an intelligent Aquarius Full Moon that brightens your 6th House of Details, place you on familiar ground and remind you that working smarter is better than working harder.

KEEP IN MIND THIS MONTH

Don't just rely on your sharp perceptions and cool logic; try sinking into your feelings and letting intuition be your guide.

KEY DATES

JULY 1 ★ *against all odds*

You may feel deprived of emotional satisfaction on **July 1** when affectionate Venus squares austere Saturn in your 3rd House of Communication. Trying to build bridges just creates frustration; the gulf between you and others only seems to widen. Suffering is a tough teacher, especially when an unflinching Sun-Pluto opposition adds tension to the mix. An unrealistic Venus-Neptune quincunx may encourage escapist behavior, but the gift of resolution is hidden in the storm clouds if you're brave enough to penetrate the fog that separates you from the truth.

JULY 4–7 ★ *free bird*

Your rebellious behavior puts others on notice that you're not willing to play by their arbitrary rules on **July 4**, when the Sun in defensive Cancer dynamically squares Uranus in disruptive Aries. This electric combo allows you to see things differently, but you might lose objectivity when mental Mercury runs into fuzzy Neptune the next day, distracting you from your tasks and prompting absentmindedness. You're attracted to the unusual as lovely Venus conspires with quirky Uranus in your 8th House of Intimacy and Shared Resources on the **7th**. Instead of clinging to past memories, find exhilaration in recognizing that you're emotionally free to express your true desires.

SUPER NOVA DAYS
JULY 17–20 ★ *the power of now*

Your imagination expands on **July 17** when philosophical Jupiter harmoniously aligns with planetary heavyweights Saturn and Neptune, and then you receive a blast of assertive energy as warrior Mars marches into the picture on **July 20**. Saturn adds realism to transcendent Neptune and hopeful Jupiter, inspiring practical speculation and authentic altruism. Mercury's direct turn on the **20th** is another signal to start working on a new project. Although your creativity may be off the charts, ultimately it is your patient perseverance that ensures enduring success.

JULY 22 ★ *adrenaline rush*

Action-hero Mars and jovial Jupiter meet up today, turning you into an enthusiastic dynamo of energy. If you can't channel your excitement into creative activities, at least go to the gym and work some of it off. The eclectic Aquarius Full Moon illuminates your 6th House of Self-Improvement, offering you an opportunity to balance your fastidious attention to details with a more lighthearted approach.

JULY 27 ★ *dangerous curves ahead*

Pessimism or fear can alter your perceptions on **July 27** when contentious Mars in your 11th House of Social Networking opposes underhanded Pluto, making it hard to know who's on your team and who may be undermining your work. Additionally, a critical Sun-Saturn square can weigh you down with responsibility. Don't be discouraged; drive carefully and wait until the road straightens out before resuming your speed.

AUGUST

THE SHOW MUST GO ON

This month of exciting opportunities comes when you're ready to push hard for success—and it's appropriate to establish new behaviors that help you to realize your dreams. Just don't waste your energy filling in too many details of your action plan; there will be many surprising twists and turns along the way. Being flexible may be as important now as being prepared. Overblown Jupiter, moving through your 11th House of Long-Term Goals, is a significant player as it opposes scheming Pluto on **August 7** and squares radical Uranus on **August 21**. You may feel as if Easy Street is just around the next corner, tempting you to take a shortcut and make a mad dash for the finish line. Unfortunately, this is not a wise strategy—opposing forces may be stronger than you realize. Proceed with caution instead of trying to take advantage of every situation and force progress before its time.

Meanwhile, you're torn between expression and silence. The Sun is shining in dramatic Leo until **August 22**, urging you to share what's in your heart. However, the showy Leo Sun is hiding out in your 12th House of Privacy, so your shyness or humility could make you reluctant to say what you feel. You may worry about what others think of you or feel nervous about speaking in front of a group on **August 6**, when the theatrical Leo New Moon activates your quiet 12th House. The eccentric Aquarius Full Moon on **August 20** illuminates your 6th House of Self-Improvement, opening your mind to new ways of handling your daily routine.

> **KEEP IN MIND THIS MONTH**
>
> *When you make decisions by rationally eliminating unrealistic choices, you limit your options. Instead, try entertaining each possibility on its own merits as it appears.*

KEY DATES

AUGUST 1–4 ★ *playing on the edge*

You struggle to decide what you want on **August 1**, when a difficult Sun-Pluto quincunx lowers your vitality but a jumpy Venus-Uranus aspect provokes you to take a risk. Independent Uranus in your 8th House of Deep Sharing exacerbates the contradiction between your yearning for affection and your search for freedom. However, the cosmic lovers ignite passion as feminine Venus and masculine Mars seductively dance on **August 2**. A thrilling Sun-Uranus trine on **August 4** opens doors that were previously locked, but it's still up to you to take advantage of the more permissive environment.

AUGUST 7 ★ *top dog*
You want to stretch the envelope with your big ideas now that giant Jupiter in your 11th House of Goals opposes powerful Pluto. You may feel ten feet tall and bulletproof with a strong desire to control other people—or at least strongly influence them. But if you are too forceful today, some unexpected consequences will soon need your attention.

AUGUST 11-14 ★ *every cloud has a silver lining*
You doubt yourself after an encounter with a hypercritical person thanks to Mercury's square to sobering Saturn on **August 11**. Unfortunately, it's easy to get stuck in a negative mental groove on **August 13**, when compulsive Pluto irritates overanalytical Mercury in your 12th House of Spirituality. However, despair is short-lived because Mercury's fluid trine to ingenious Uranus on **August 14** hands you the keys of innovation that let you escape from your self-designed box.

SUPER NOVA DAYS
AUGUST 20-23 ★ *anything goes*
You're sure that you can achieve unrealistic goals if you just make enough plans on **August 20**, when the radical Aquarius Full Moon highlights your 6th House of Details. The next day, though, a jolting Jupiter-Uranus square blasts open a window of opportunity that suddenly reveals a variety of new options. On **August 22**, witty Mercury aligns with Jupiter and Uranus, sparking even more creative thoughts, so take the time to write down your inspirations before they fade. Thankfully, the Sun enters methodical Virgo on the **22nd**, followed by Mercury on the **23rd**, enabling you to put your best ideas to practical use.

AUGUST 26-27 ★ *shake, rattle, and roll*
You're ready to do something totally different on **August 26** when a titillating Venus-Uranus opposition awakens unusual interests, yet a bewildering Sun-Neptune opposition in your relationship houses adds confusion and chaos to the mix. Still, a quick departure from the norm will do wonders for your psyche. Just make sure you don't overdo it; an indulgent Venus-Jupiter square on **August 27** can tempt you with excess.

SEPTEMBER

SHINE YOUR LIGHT

You're eager to show others how competent you are with the bright Sun in your efficient sign and your 1st House of Self until **September 22**. Thankfully, you can express yourself clearly with your ruling planet, Mercury, also in precise Virgo until **September 9**. The problem is that sometimes you might as well be pushing a boulder up a steep hill, while at other times circumstances move so quickly you can't keep up with them. A number of awkward quincunxes throughout the month—on the **2nd, 3rd, 11th, 20th,** and **25th**—make it difficult to find your groove and sustain a steady pace of progress. But positive aspects to beneficial Jupiter in your 11th House of Goals on **September 7, 21,** and **26** suggest that your current efforts will pay off if you worry less about your day-to-day accomplishments and just focus on your ultimate destination.

The analytical Virgo New Moon on **September 5** lands in your physical 1st House, and its supportive sextile from effusive Jupiter gives you an extra boost of energy. However, the Moon's anxious quincunx with irrepressible Uranus in your 8th House of Shared Resources can trigger an unexpected disagreement with a close friend or business partner. Mercury's entry into fair-minded Libra and your 2nd House of Self-Worth on **September 9** enables you to discuss your needs objectively and make compromises without lowering your self-esteem. Your attention shifts toward the needs of others on **September 19**, when the empathetic Pisces Full Moon brightens your 7th House of Partnerships. The Sun's shift into diplomatic Libra and your 2nd House of Values marks the Autumn Equinox on **September 22**, reminding you to be fair and gentle when you criticize yourself or others.

> **KEEP IN MIND THIS MONTH**
>
> *Although it may feel as if you're spending a lot of time putting out fires, you're actually making more progress than you realize.*

KEY DATES

SEPTEMBER 1–3 ★ *destination unknown*

Because you understand how to express your personal power and creativity, you can have a profound impact on others by simply showing up and being yourself. On **September 1**, the willful Sun in your 1st House of Self forms a trine with mysterious Pluto in your 5th House of Romance, enabling you to make a lasting impression on someone you admire. However, you could lose focus when fearless

Mars aligns with foggy Neptune on **September 2**. Adjust your course of action as necessary when the Sun forms an uneasy quincunx to erratic Uranus on the **3rd**. Instead of going in with a rigid plan, prepare to make as many minor modifications as necessary as you travel forward.

SUPER NOVA DAYS
SEPTEMBER 5–9 ★ *cool your jets*
Focus your attention on practical matters during the earthy Virgo New Moon on **September 5**. Your precise concentration fades, your horizons expand, and you begin to entertain alternative strategies on **September 7**, as the Sun sextiles visionary Jupiter in your 11th House of Dreams and Wishes. Rational thinking gives way to a rising tide of desires on the **8th**, when sensual Venus forms a creative quintile with provocative Pluto. You might try to restore emotional balance when Mercury enters objective Libra on the **9th**, but hot Mars's stressful square to cold Saturn forces you to slam on the brakes. You haven't run into a wall; this is simply a reminder for you to pay attention to external conditions and not just your inner needs.

SEPTEMBER 16–19 ★ *no escape*
Your thoughts are unconstrained by reason when quicksilver Mercury opposes electric Uranus on **September 16** and squares effervescent Jupiter on the **19th**. But you still may feel isolated or undeserving of love on the **18th** when receptive Venus joins doubting Saturn in your 3rd House of Communication. You may have to control your feelings, but you still must deal with other people's emotional dramas precipitated by the hypersensitive Pisces Full Moon on the **19th**, illuminating your 7th House of Companions.

SEPTEMBER 26–28 ★ *on a wing and a prayer*
All is well on **September 26** as enchanting Venus harmonizes with auspicious Jupiter, enabling you to see beauty and opportunity everywhere you look. An edgy Venus-Mars square on the **28th** can fuel a lovers' spat or a sexy encounter. Either way, Jupiter's alignment with bewitching Neptune in your 7th House of Relationships places your fantasies in the pilot's seat, revealing the infinite possibilities of an unobstructed, cloudless sky.

OCTOBER

CHASING THE BOTTOM LINE

Your finances are your primary concern this month as the Libra Sun moves through your 2nd House of Money until **October 23**. The Sun's stressful aspects with heavy-handed Pluto on **October 1** and unpredictable Uranus on **October 3** can catch you off guard and send you scrambling to get your cash flow back under control. Problems with a business partner may be disruptive during the normally even-tempered Libra New Moon on **October 4** as it opposes Uranus in your 8th House of Shared Resources. You would really like to establish stability in your daily affairs, but when steady Saturn forms an anxious quincunx with chaotic Uranus on **October 5**, you can't seem to regain a sense of order no matter how hard you try. This unstable connection with Uranus is reactivated by mischievous Mercury on **October 8** and **November 1**, yet you're more serious when the Winged Messenger conjuncts Saturn on **October 29**, prompting you to focus on the details that will ultimately make or break your plans.

Action-hero Mars rushes into your 1st House of Self on **October 15**, heating up your sign and pushing you to be more assertive than usual. It's time to take charge, define your boundaries, and defend them against anyone who might try to boss you around. But staying centered can be challenging now, especially around the reckless Aries Full Moon Eclipse on **October 18** that zaps your 2nd and 8th Houses of Resources, evoking contradictory feelings about your personal core values, what you own, and what you share. Gaining clarity isn't easy when Mars opposes dreamy Neptune on **October 19** and thoughtful Mercury begins its three-week retrograde cycle on **October 21**.

> ### KEEP IN MIND THIS MONTH
>
> *Be patient with yourself if your priorities seem to change as you get closer to making a major decision. Reconsider what's negotiable and what's not.*

KEY DATES

OCTOBER 1–4 ★ *stand up for your rights*

An inspirational person motivates you to take the high road as communicator Mercury forms a fluid trine with spiritual Neptune in your 7th House of Others on **October 1**. Don't let your idealism turn into escapist behavior, though, because someone may be testing your ability to defend yourself when unyielding Pluto squares the Sun in your 2nd House of Values. A conflict can grow out of hand by

October 3 as the Sun opposes wild Uranus. An extreme position won't lead to a resolution, so use the diplomacy skills of the peace-keeping Libra New Moon on the 4th to find middle ground.

OCTOBER 10-12 ★ *who's on first?*

You're so confused that you don't even know who is pulling the strings when Venus and the Sun create critical aspects to dizzy Neptune in your 7th House of Companions on October 10. You're tempted to overreact or turn a molehill into a mountain on October 11-12 as Venus and the Sun are stressed by overbearing Jupiter. Things are neither as bad nor as good as they seem. Trying to force an answer to an unclear question will only make matters worse, so let the energy settle back down on its own instead.

OCTOBER 16-19 ★ *call of the wild*

You're ready to step outside the box and try something completely new and different on October 16, thanks to a trine between pleasure-seeking Venus and unconventional Uranus. On October 18, the impetuous Aries Full Moon Eclipse lands in your 8th House of Intimacy, provoking you to take a risk by expressing your innermost feelings without thinking about the consequences. But exercise a little self-restraint and self-reflection, because independent Mars opposes intoxicating Neptune on the 19th, possibly muddling your actions. You may think you know where you're heading, but your actions may not reflect your intentions; proceed with extreme caution.

SUPER NOVA DAYS
OCTOBER 29-31 ★ *the buck stops here*

You've been reviewing your plans since your ruling planet, Mercury, turned retrograde on October 21; now it's time to apply what you've learned. On October 29, Mercury's conjunction with authoritative Saturn in your 3rd House of Communication demands that you say what you mean and mean what you say. There's very little margin for error, so decide what makes the most sense and then be precise as you inform others of your choice. A potent Mars-Pluto trine fortifies your actions on the 31st, but don't be too aggressive or wild, or crazy Uranus will undo the gains you've made.

NOVEMBER

Your relationship to the children in your world and to your own playful spirit is in the midst of a deep and lasting shift as revolutionary Uranus forms a dynamic square to evolutionary Pluto in your 5th House of Fun. Although this powerful aspect—the fourth in a series that began on **June 24, 2012**, and finishes on **March 16, 2015**—is exact on **November 1**, expect personal and business interactions to be stressed throughout the month as you weigh what you want against what you can realistically expect. On **November 14–15**, charming Venus squares unbridled Uranus and joins passionate Pluto in your 8th House of Deep Sharing, intensifying your desires and prompting reckless behavior. Make a plan and stick with it, even if it requires all your discipline and self-restraint, especially when the Scorpio Solar Eclipse conjuncts exacting Saturn in your 3rd House of Communication on **November 3**. You might even receive a bit of help from trickster Mercury—retrograde in your 3rd House until **November 10**—requiring you to reprioritize your daily schedule so you can be even more efficient once it turns direct.

Later in the month you're eager to widen your horizons and open your mind to new experiences when the Taurus Full Moon on **November 17** lights up your 9th House of Travel and Education. At the same time, the Moon's harsh aspects to Uranus and Pluto reactivate an unresolved interpersonal conflict from earlier this month, making it more difficult for you to spread your wings. Although the Sun's entry into adventurous Sagittarius on **November 21** gives you the confidence to set lofty goals, Mercury's conjunction with stern Saturn on **November 25** slows you down long enough to make sure that you have all your facts straight before continuing on your way.

> **KEEP IN MIND THIS MONTH**
>
> *There is a more serious side to play that allows you to explore your creativity productively while also having fun.*

KEY DATES

SUPER NOVA DAYS
NOVEMBER 1–3 ★ *now or never*
Sudden changes in a relationship take you by surprise and send you back to the drawing board to figure out a new game plan as shocking Uranus squares purging Pluto on **November 1**. Fortunately, expressive Mercury helps

you switch up your strategy—if you're willing to say what's on your mind. Mercury is retrograde now, encouraging you to look back and reconsider your expectations. Its conjunction with the investigative Scorpio Sun in your 3rd House of Immediate Environment motivates you to dig beneath the surface to get to the core of what's going on. Initiating a difficult conversation can clear the air of negativity and permit you to move ahead in the following weeks. The Scorpio Solar Eclipse on **November 3** acts as a point of no return, thrusting you forward whether you're ready or not.

NOVEMBER 8–12 ★ *smooth operator*
A sparkling Mercury-Venus sextile on **November 8** helps you to turn on the charm, while a hardworking Mars-Saturn sextile on the **9th** gives you the energy to finish whatever project you start. Thankfully, recent planning will soon begin to pay off as enterprising Mercury turns direct on **November 10**. Your chances for success are greatly improved on **November 12** by the Sun's lucky trine to abundant Jupiter in your 11th House of Goals.

NOVEMBER 17–20 ★ *great expectations*
On **November 17**, the Taurus Full Moon brightens your 9th House of Big Ideas, suggesting that you could improve your prospects for advancement by enrolling in a course of study. Self-directed Mars in your sign forms a cooperative sextile with propitious Jupiter on the **19th**, inspiring you to reach higher than ever before. Although Mercury's crunchy quincunx to edgy Uranus on the **20th** nudges you to share your ideas before they're fully developed, its sextile to unrelenting Pluto gives you the determination to keep trying until you get it right.

NOVEMBER 27–30 ★ *too clever for your own good*
You can communicate your ideas with ease on **November 27–28**, when gregarious Mercury in your 3rd House of Information forms positive aspects to friendly Venus and confident Jupiter. But an overindulgent Venus-Jupiter opposition on the **28th** entices you to focus only on the good stuff, which can make others question your motives. Although an ingenious Sun-Uranus trine makes you sound smart on the **30th**, an annoying Mercury-Uranus alignment means that others may not be able to understand what you're saying unless you simplify your concept and explain everything very carefully.

DECEMBER

NO REST FOR THE WEARY

The theme of home and family looms large this holiday month, which begins with an inspirational Sagittarius New Moon on **December 2**, activating your 4th House of Foundations. Friendly Mercury enters forward-looking Sagittarius on **December 4**, motivating you to think ahead and make plans to enjoy this special season with those you love. Reckless Mars shifts into logical Libra and your 2nd House of Money on **December 7**, requiring you to maintain a balanced approach to your finances when considering your upcoming expenses. Fortunately, on **December 12** an ambitious Saturn-Jupiter trine offers you an opportunity to reach your goals if you're willing to restrict your personal time so you can work unencumbered by distractions.

The dualistic Gemini Full Moon on **December 17** illuminates your 10th House of Career, encouraging you to keep your options open at work. Although an unrestrained Jupiter-Neptune alignment allows you to see possibilities you might normally miss, it can be difficult to choose one path when you have so many alternatives. The Sun's entry into traditional Capricorn and your 5th House of Fun and Games on **December 21**—the Winter Solstice—favors you with a keen sense of organization, especially when celebrations are involved. However, loving Venus turns retrograde the same day, initiating an emotional cycle of delayed satisfaction that lasts until **January 31, 2014**. Don't let your frustration turn into a temper tantrum when angry Mars opposes volatile Uranus on **December 25** and squares unforgiving Pluto on **December 30**. Rational Mercury creates stressful alignments with Uranus, Pluto, and Mars on **December 29–31**, setting the stage for a tumultuous end of the year. Your willingness to communicate honestly without blaming others turns a chaotic time into an exciting New Year's Eve.

KEEP IN MIND THIS MONTH

You won't have to travel to some exotic place to bring a little fun and adventure into your life. You can enjoy the best times while staying right at home.

KEY DATES

DECEMBER 1–3 ★ *light at the end of the tunnel*

You may have trouble sleeping on **December 1** when an anxious Mercury-Pluto semisquare keeps you awake. You could hopelessly spin your mental wheels, trying to figure out a way around an unpleasant situation. Thankfully, the visionary Sagittarius New Moon on **December 2** broadens your perspective to discover a solution to a long-standing problem. Trust your intuition; an otherworldly Mercury-Mars sextile on the **3rd** will lead you in the right direction.

DECEMBER 10–12 ★ *time is on your side*

Your mind lights up with fireworks on **December 10** as Mercury in exuberant Sagittarius creates a superconductive trine with explosive Uranus. Although you can figure out how to get what you want now, your impatience creates problems if others can't keep up with your lightning-fast thinking. Luckily, your persistence elicits the support you need from friends and associates when generous Jupiter in your 11th House of Community trines steadfast Saturn on **December 12**.

DECEMBER 16–17 ★ *curb your enthusiasm*

You might say too much about a family matter when gossipy Mercury in your domestic 4th House quincunxes excessive Jupiter on **December 16**. The flighty Gemini Full Moon on **December 17** makes it tough to get much accomplished if you're scattering your energy by trying to do too many things at once. Finally, a dynamic sesquisquare between Jupiter and nebulous Neptune makes it a challenge to bring your dreams down to earth. Nevertheless, consciously focusing on one task at a time is an antidote to haphazardly mismanaging your calendar.

DECEMBER 24–25 ★ *a house of cards*

Relationships take an unexpected twist, but Mercury's shift into conservative Capricorn and your 5th House of Spontaneity on **December 24** should help you manage it. However, an irrepressible Mars-Uranus opposition on **December 25** can bring a thrilling surprise—or a sudden disappointment. Be adaptable and prepare to change your plans at a moment's notice.

SUPER NOVA DAYS
DECEMBER 29–31 ★ *give peace a chance*

Your self-esteem is tested as Mars in your 2nd House of Self-Worth forms a difficult square with ruthless Pluto on **December 30**. The Sun and Mercury bring additional stress on **December 29–31** when they cross paths with Pluto and Uranus, provoking you to stand up for your beliefs even against great odds. Don't let your emotions get the best of you, or you may say or do something you'll later regret. Fortunately, the Sun and Mercury sextile Chiron the Wounded Healer on **December 30–31**, teaching you that forgiveness is all that's truly important now.

LIBRA

SEPTEMBER 23–OCTOBER 22

LIBRA

2012 SUMMARY

There's no time to waste complaining or feeling sorry for yourself. One way or the other, unfinished business from your past is recycled and brought into your current experience. In the long run, it's better for those you love if you organize your life now in a way that will allow you to give of yourself more freely over the years to come. Taking more risks and living closer to the edge of unconventionality can actually reduce the likelihood of unexpected surprises.

AUGUST—*long and winding road*

A wide spectrum of experiences may be exciting, worrisome, challenging, empowering, frustrating, and satisfying. Instead of focusing on any single event, pay attention to the entire mix.

SEPTEMBER—*change is in the air*

Although you must focus your attention on the present, you also will greatly benefit from carefully considering the long-term consequences of your current activities.

OCTOBER—*time to shine*

You may feel as if a weight has been lifted from your shoulders. Instead of just celebrating, spend time contemplating how you want to use your newfound sense of freedom.

NOVEMBER—*a stitch in time saves nine*

The future is not written in stone. If you anticipate tomorrow's challenges, you can either just worry about them or do something proactive before they manifest.

DECEMBER—*leap of faith*

You will be more likely to sustain the joyful spirit of this season if you set healthy boundaries when it's appropriate.

2012 CALENDAR

AUGUST

WED 1–THU 2 ★ You're the life of the party

TUE 7–THU 9 ★ Turn your fantasies into reality

WED 15–FRI 17 ★ **SUPER NOVA DAYS** Slow down to increase your efficiency

MON 27–FRI 31 ★ Don't let down your guard just yet

SEPTEMBER

SAT 1–TUE 4 ★ Reevaluate your relationships

THU 6–SAT 8 ★ Spend more time with others

WED 12–THU 13 ★ Don't believe everything you are told

TUE 25–WED 26 ★ **SUPER NOVA DAYS** Satisfaction will likely elude you

OCTOBER

TUE 2–FRI 5 ★ There are important matters to consider

TUE 9–WED 10 ★ **SUPER NOVA DAYS** Expand your vision of the future

MON 15–TUE 16 ★ You're challenged to reestablish your balance

SUN 28–TUE 30 ★ Curbing your enthusiasm can be tricky

NOVEMBER

THU 1–SUN 5 ★ You have big ideas about what you want

FRI 9 ★ Live as if you will assuredly reach the stars

TUE 13–SAT 17 ★ **SUPER NOVA DAYS** Buried emotions bubble up into awareness

MON 26–THU 29 ★ Your conversations lead to exciting plans

DECEMBER

SAT 1–SUN 2 ★ Opportunities appear too good to be true

MON 10–FRI 14 ★ **SUPER NOVA DAYS** Get in touch with your heart

SUN 16–MON 17 ★ A friend catches you off guard with a brilliant move

WED 19–SAT 22 ★ Direct your thoughts toward your home and family

FRI 28–MON 31 ★ Stand up for something that really matters

LIBRA OVERVIEW

Your desire for more fulfilling relationships continues to take you on a journey to the depths of your own being this year. While you'll find moments of contentment, you have much more to gain by reaching beyond the status quo. The transformational squares of electric Uranus and powerful Pluto that began shaking your life last year are back on May 20 and November 1 to keep the wheels of change turning. **Stepping into the shadows of your personal history and uncovering buried memories can be a scary process.** Pluto's presence in your 4th House of Roots may tempt you to ignore uncomfortable feelings in an attempt to maintain the harmony you value so much. However, bringing these suppressed parts of yourself into the light empowers you personally and professionally. Irrepressible Uranus in your 7th House of Partners keeps you dancing to the beat of someone else's heart until you're willing to break free of your people-pleasing mode and focus on satisfying yourself.

Your personal life is popping with surprises, but progress at work occurs at a steadier pace. Lucky Jupiter settles into your 10th House of Career on June 25 for a yearlong stay, multiplying your opportunities for advancement. Being comfortable with the mission of the business or organization you work for and with your specific duties is essential to making the most out of this beneficial transit. Jupiter in sensitive Cancer nourishes your soul when your job corresponds with your personal values. **You can advance in a situation that doesn't resonate with your life purpose, but the drain on your physical and emotional energies is likely to be greater.** Self-employment may be more appealing now and could work out well if you've carefully studied the situation, are very clear about your goals, and have a well-defined strategy for achieving them.

You're a natural peacemaker because you know how to remain cool on the outside, even under pressure. However, pushing yourself to be more productive is a good investment of your time and energy this year. There's hard work to be done if you hope to make the most of your abilities with industrious Saturn in Scorpio in your 2nd House of Resources. **Your willingness to sweat and strain to maximize your talents can make the difference between struggling to just get by and increasing your income and self-worth.** It's time to resurrect talents that you haven't fully developed in the past—and may have abandoned—and take them to a new level. It might require some selfishness on your part, though, to put less effort into pleasing others so that you can fulfill your own potential. Visionary Jupiter's favorable trines to ambitious Saturn on July 17 and December 12 grace you with keen professional judgment and the ability to establish a successful long-term strategy, enabling you to lay down the framework for the future.

FUTURE SHOCK

Brace yourself for sudden shifts of mood and changing circumstances this year with the ongoing transit of radical Uranus through your 7th House of Companions. Look to new forms of freedom and stimulation to enliven your relationships. Your ruling planet, Venus, joins the Sun and Uranus on March 28, enticing you to take risks in the pursuit of unfamiliar pleasures and unconventional people, rather than idly sitting by while your partner behaves irresponsibly. A Solar Eclipse in your 8th House of Intimacy on May 9 reminds you to reevaluate your expectations of others and what you're willing to give back in return. Digging in your heels to address your own needs is a better choice than compromising to maintain a less-than-satisfying situation. A Lunar Eclipse in independent Aries on October 18 fires up your 7th House with a fresh attitude and a sense of urgency. Whether you make a dramatic move right away or simply recognize that you're ready to turn the page, you'll be aiming toward the future instead of clinging to the past.

LADDER OF SUCCESS

Opportunity starts knocking on your career door when optimistic Jupiter takes out a one-year lease in your 10th House of Profession on June 25. Its constructive trines with realistic Saturn on July 17, December 12, and May 24, 2014, are excellent for making strategic decisions and starting long-term projects. Try to adapt to surprises with grace on August 21, when volatile Uranus squares Jupiter, suddenly altering your trajectory at work. However, your innovative thinking can transform uncertainty about a problem into a brilliant insight that frees you from dull tasks with limited potential for advancement. Just be careful about taking on too much too fast during detail-oriented

Mercury's reversal in your 10th House on June 26–July 20. Digesting new information and managing communications can be full of complications.

 LEAN AND MEAN

Stingy Saturn's presence in your 2nd House of Money may put a squeeze on your income, so pay closer attention to how you spend your cash and the value you place on your own work. Saturn is in economically astute Scorpio, which teaches you ways to get the most bang for your buck and the highest return on your efforts. The Scorpio Full Moon Eclipse on April 25 could mark a time when you're ready to let go of habitual fears and self-doubts to bring more discipline and focus into your life. Cutting the fat of wasted time and talent to use your power more effectively reflects the spirit of the no-nonsense Mars-Saturn opposition accompanying this eclipse. Mercury's retrograde cycle in your 2nd House on October 21–November 10 is a perfect time for a personal audit of your resources to ensure that you're making the most of your assets.

 TENDER LOVING CARE

You're tempted to avoid responsibility for your physical well-being thanks to the long-term transit of evasive Neptune in your 6th House of Health. Luckily, assertive Mars's presence in this part of your chart on February 1–March 12 pushes to initiate a new exercise program—though gentle forms of activity like yoga or t'ai chi that also have spiritual components may suit you best. Mercury's overlapping retrograde in your 6th House on February 23–March 17 motivates you to be more conscious of your diet or revives interest in soulful activities like meditation or dance. Avoid extremes and monitor your energy level to make subtle, healthy adjustments throughout the year.

 CONSTRUCTION ZONE

Your ongoing excavation of your personal history, spurred by Pluto's presence in your 4th House of Roots, takes a delightful turn when Venus transits this intimate area on January 8–February 1. This is an excellent time to resolve family strife and diminish the wounds of past disappointments. The Capricorn

Full Moon in your 4th House on June 23 is supported by insightful aspects from compassionate Neptune and stabilizing Saturn that help you define your domestic dreams and take constructive steps to make them real.

ALL OVER THE MAP

Joyful Jupiter in jaunty Gemini and your 9th House of Getaways until June 25 fills you with a sense of adventure, inspiring you to make a multitude of travel and education plans. Just watch out—you might also experience mental overload as your mind is pulled in a million directions. Alluring Venus's conjunction with Jupiter on May 28 magnifies your love of learning and attraction to foreign cultures. But don't let a flirtation distract you from higher aspirations.

PRACTICE MAKES PERFECT

You'll make a deeper connection with the divine part of your daily routine with inspirational Neptune in your 6th House of Habits all year. Integrating metaphysical ideas into your work raises consciousness while still taking care of business. On July 26 your ruling planet, Venus, in your 12th House of Destiny opposes Neptune, bridging the gap between the ideal and the real, and warming you with unconditional love. The Virgo New Moon in your 12th House on September 5 inspires you to focus on a spiritual practice that reinforces your faith with action.

RICK & JEFF'S TIP FOR THE YEAR:
Use Your Sixth Sense

Don't let the limits of logic and your need to explain yourself to others get in the way of the rising wave of intuition that's accessible to you this year. Emotion and instinct can teach you more and take you further than facts alone. Your most meaningful discoveries may not be translatable into words, but this doesn't make them less real. There is a well of wisdom beyond language available now that can enrich your body, mind, and soul.

JANUARY

FROM THE GROUND UP

The key to getting this year off to a good start is taking care of personal business and attending to home and family matters. Turn some of your attention away from the outer world to address inner issues with the transits of fast-moving Mercury, Venus, and the Sun in your 4th House of Roots this month. Resourceful Venus, your magnetic ruling planet, enters responsible Capricorn on **January 8**, reminding you to be more disciplined and patient. Love and approval may not be given easily now, but you can earn them with hard work and commitment. On **January 11**, the Capricorn New Moon lands in your 4th House, inspiring you to be more ambitious and set higher goals for yourself. Managing your time more effectively and bringing order to your home establishes the solid foundation you need to fulfill those aspirations.

You're in a playful mood on **January 19**, when the confident Sun and chatty Mercury shift into quirky Aquarius and your 5th House of Self-Expression. Your creativity grows when you're willing to try out new ideas and risk looking foolish. Romance could arrive in unexpected ways, like falling for someone who seems totally inappropriate for you. Yet love flourishes when you open your heart in situations that seem strange. Experimenting with your current partner or with someone new gives you the freedom to explore feelings without needing to control the outcome. The bold Leo Full Moon shines in your team-oriented 11th House on **January 26**, pushing you into prominence in a group situation or bringing a conflict with a friend or colleague to a head.

KEEP IN MIND THIS MONTH

If you can avoid the rush to instant gratification, you've reached a higher level of maturity, and you'll be rewarded with greater satisfaction down the road.

KEY DATES

JANUARY 6–7 ★ *buried treasure*

Focus on healing an old wound right now, rather than wallowing in the pain of denial or dishonesty. Certainly, dealing with such complex emotional issues isn't easy, but analytical Mercury's conjunction with penetrating Pluto on **January 6** creates a good time to face hard facts that have been hidden from view. The communication planet's supportive sextile with reliable Saturn indicates that insight into your personal history can untangle knots of mistrust that have blocked your progress. Yet awareness means nothing without action, and energetic Mars's stressful square to Saturn on the **7th** shows you where to concentrate your effort. A deeper understanding of your untapped talent can supply the devotion required to bear down and begin to fulfill this potential.

JANUARY 10–12 ★ *wake up!*

You're lost in fantasies on **January 10** as pleasure-seeking Venus aligns with dreamy Neptune. Yet the images arising in your mind could prove misleading, because a slippery Mercury-Neptune semisquare muddles your thinking. You may overreact to a critical conversation, but you are gifted with the ability to discuss delicate subjects in a compassionate manner. Venus's tense square with spontaneous Uranus on the **12th** could spur a sudden attraction or a radical shift in style or taste. A pair of clever solar quintiles to Saturn and Uranus, though, empowers you to repair shattered alliances and recover from shocking relationship news.

SUPER NOVA DAYS
JANUARY 16–17 ★ *basic instincts*

Your peacemaking planet Venus runs into provocative Pluto on **January 16** to strip away politeness and lead you to the heart of desire. Harmony at home and the approval of others are less important than connecting with your deepest needs and recognizing what you must do to fulfill them. Your ability to tap into underused personal resources is reinforced with Venus's favorable sextile to disciplined Saturn on the **17th**. Passion and reason align to increase your efficiency and put you on a more productive path.

JANUARY 22 ★ *out of focus*

Self-sacrifice and chasing illusions can prove costly with a blurry Venus-Neptune semisquare that makes someone or something appear more worthwhile than it actually is. Yet a smart Mercury-Jupiter trine clears away clouds of confusion and enriches your relationships with clever communication.

JANUARY 25 ★ *just say yes*

You swing between pessimism and optimism with a naysaying Mercury-Saturn square on **January 25**, followed by a hopeful Sun-Jupiter trine. Don't let another person's doubts undermine your big dreams. Ideally, your mastery of details and realistic assessment of the current circumstances will provide you with a solid framework to support a more expansive view of the future.

FEBRUARY

LISTEN TO YOUR HEART

Romance—one of your favorite subjects—gets top billing for much of this month. Venus, the planet of love, enters witty Aquarius and your amorous 5th House on **February 1**, putting you in a playful mood and inviting plenty of attention. Your innovative ways of expressing your feelings and exposing your talents are bound to garner you admiration without making you look like a show-off. But finding time to play can be difficult with active Mars diving into altruistic Pisces and your 6th House of Service on the **1st**. It's easy to sacrifice yourself for a task that never ends, so think twice before taking on any new responsibilities. However, renewed inspiration in your work is a potential benefit as long as you don't waste your time daydreaming. The unconventional Aquarius New Moon on **February 10** falls in your 5th House of Play, creating an excellent moment for initiating creative projects and being spontaneously friendly and flirty. You may discover delight in unexpected places and share your joy with others.

Your progress on projects may start to slow when productive Saturn turns retrograde and the Sun slips into whimsical Pisces on **February 18**. Cerebral Mercury turns backward in your systematic 6th House on the **23rd**, reminding you to simplify your life, revise your methods, and complete unfinished tasks. Yet you could find pleasure, and maybe even an emotional attraction, on the job with lovely Venus's move into dreamy Pisces on the **25th**. Beware spreading your energy too thin—you might wear yourself out if you don't take care of yourself. The Full Moon in health-oriented Virgo brightens your 12th House of Escapism on **February 25**, squaring excessive Jupiter in multifaceted Gemini. It's time to pull in the reins and be more discriminating about your commitments.

> **KEEP IN MIND THIS MONTH**
>
> *Burning your candle at both ends brings you a short-term buzz of excitement, but managing your schedule wisely produces a lasting balance between work and play.*

KEY DATES

SUPER NOVA DAYS
FEBRUARY 6–7 ★ *object of desire*
A sweet sextile between sexy Venus and irreverent Uranus spices up your personal life on **February 6**. Your saucy attitude and fresh approach to

relationships provide pleasure in a light, noncommittal way. This is a chance to gently stretch the limits of social behavior without risking your reputation. A murky Mercury-Neptune conjunction could create communication confusion, but is also a rich source of imaginative thinking. Unbridled pleasure is a potential gift of a lucky Venus-Jupiter trine on the **7th**. Your charm flows so easily that affection and attention naturally come your way. Gentle persuasion is much more effective now than acting needy or applying pressure on others.

FEBRUARY 11 ★ *due diligence*

If you encounter disappointment or disapproval today, don't even think about shutting down and running away; it's time to show up and face the music. Evaluative Venus runs into a stressful square with resistant Saturn, which can frustrate your aspirations, complicate relationships, and even undermine your sense of self-worth. While gifts may not be offered to you freely now, this aspect shows you where you're lacking the resources necessary to get what you want. Don't let yourself be blocked by doubt, insufficient funds, or a reluctant partner; take stock of your needs and commit to doing what's necessary to fulfill them. You probably won't see quick results, but Saturn will eventually reward you for your patience, persistence, and clear sense of purpose.

FEBRUARY 19–22 ★ *sink or swim*

Unreliable individuals wreak havoc with your plans as Venus forms an edgy semisquare with unpredictable Uranus on **February 19**. Flexibility helps you adapt to surprises and also makes it possible to appreciate people who act in unexpected ways. The metaphysical Sun-Neptune conjunction on the **21st** is excellent for beginning a spiritual practice and seeking more meaning in your work. Purging Pluto's semisquare with Venus on the **22nd** squeezes out ambiguous feelings, forcing you to make a difficult choice. If you don't trust someone, either clear the air or consider cutting this person loose. It's healthier to deal with the consequences of being truthful than to avoid a confrontation.

FEBRUARY 28 ★ *altered states*

There's magic in the air that can carry you on wings of romantic love, dreams of fulfilling work, or faith in the power of healing. Your ruling planet, Venus, joins otherworldly Neptune to dissolve the limits of ordinary reality and engender hope— or to lure you into a fantasyland of illusion.

MARCH

STEP UP TO THE PLATE

This month marks your transition from a period of preparation—almost an apprenticeship—to your quest for a higher level of recognition from others. March begins with the Sun in adaptable Pisces and your 6th House of Employment. The New Moon in this pliable sign on **March 11** can spur you to develop new skills or take the ones you have even further. This lunation brings artistry and charm to the workplace with its conjunctions to the creative cosmic couple of Venus and Mars. However, your willingness to sacrifice yourself to please others begins to slip with go-getter Mars's move into independent Aries and your 7th House of Partnerships on **March 12**. You're more likely to achieve the equality you desire and the attention you deserve when you stand up and claim them for yourself instead of passively waiting for others to notice you.

Mental Mercury's forward turn in your 6th House on **March 17** rejuvenates your thinking and increases efficiency in your daily life. The Sun blazes into Aries, marking the Spring Equinox and firing up relationships in your 7th House on the **20th**. This solar shift kicks up your confidence, empowering you to be more assertive with others. It's also a good time to go public with projects, seek a job, and pursue love. It's critical that you take the initiative around the **March 27** Libra Full Moon, which falls in your 1st House of Personality. The Sun, Venus, Uranus, and Mars face the Moon from your 7th House, which can keep you dancing to someone else's tune unless you take up the baton and start leading the band yourself.

> **KEEP IN MIND THIS MONTH**
>
> *The comfort of others is not your primary responsibility now. You have the most to gain if you put your own interests first.*

KEY DATES

MARCH 4-6 ★ *attitude adjustment*

Your expectations may be too high with an overly optimistic Venus-Jupiter square on **March 4**. Stretch your perspective to understand how someone else thinks—but don't lose sight of your own core values. You'll make more grounded assessments of the worth of people and things on the **6th** thanks to Venus's favorable aspects with tough guys Saturn and Pluto. Maturity and patience solidify your buying decisions and your stance with others. Messenger Mercury's conjunction with charming Venus serves up some sweet talk that helps you express your needs in nonthreatening ways.

MARCH 12 ★ *take charge*

Expressive Mars wakes up from sleepy Pisces and emerges from your deferential 6th House today to invigorate your relationships with his move into pioneering Aries. Aggressive individuals or crises might require rapid response. Still, it's better to take chances and push your own agenda with passion than to spend your energy trying to put out someone else's fires.

MARCH 16–18 ★ *the things we do for love*

On **March 16** a crafty quintile between Venus in gentle Pisces and Pluto in ambitious Capricorn helps you untangle social knots, motivate others, and get what you need without ruffling feathers. Venus's ungainly sesquisquare with stern Saturn on the **18th**, however, is a call for self-restraint and might create frustration with partners. You must first define expectations if you hope to establish trust and find true satisfaction.

MARCH 21–22 ★ *blast off!*

Your patience grows short as Venus enters reckless Aries and your 7th House of Others on **March 21**. Your attempts to cover up disagreements are likely to fail with a volatile Mars-Uranus conjunction turning the heat up even higher on the **22nd**. Happily, both planetary patterns can motivate you to be bolder and more direct with people. Less sweetness and more sass is bound to get you noticed in a big way. Look to innovative alliances and original methods to break through obstacles and get projects and partnerships moving at a faster pace.

SUPER NOVA DAYS

MARCH 28–31 ★ *rock-and-roll star*

You are especially captivating now with a beautiful Sun-Venus conjunction on **March 28**. Unconventional Uranus amplifies the power of this alignment of will and wiles with a fresh attitude or unique appearance. You may be surprised by unexpected personal and professional connections. Their ultimate value will be tested when Venus has challenging encounters with super-serious Saturn on the **30th** and perceptive Pluto on the **31st**. Yet even if you have to lower your expectations in one situation, a rich Venus-Jupiter sextile promises bigger emotional or material rewards somewhere else.

APRIL

RELATIONSHIPS 2.0

Your uncharacteristically bold approach to interacting with others continues this month with the confidence-building Sun in energetic Aries heating up your 7th House of Partners. Your considerable social skills may reach an unprecedented level of effectiveness with the enterprising Aries New Moon on **April 10**. This exceptional union of the Sun and Moon is joined by vivacious Venus and macho Mars to send your charm, creativity, and sex appeal into the stratosphere. Watch out, though, lest you project all this goodness onto someone else and make him or her the object of your desire. A high-intensity attraction is healthy as long as you receive as much appreciation as you give. Prepare for verbal duels when sharp-tongued Mercury enters combative Aries on the **13th**. Provocative speech can stir up conflict, but might also open minds to bright new ideas with Mercury's tense aspects to shocking Uranus on the **20th** and insightful Pluto on the **21st**.

You can begin a slower and more pragmatic assessment of alliances when your ruling planet, Venus, enters earthy Taurus and your 8th House of Deep Sharing on **April 15**. Steadiness and reliability are worth more to you now than excitement and freedom. This practical perspective grows with the Sun's entry into dependable Taurus on the **19th**, followed by Mars on the **20th**. Don't give in to stubborn individuals, even when holding your ground produces tension. It's vital to trust yourself if you're going to create the personal intimacy or professional cooperation that you desire. If the intense Scorpio Full Moon conjunct to severe Saturn in your 2nd House of Resources on **April 25** causes you to question your worth, concentrating your efforts on what you do best can restore your confidence.

> **KEEP IN MIND THIS MONTH**
>
> *Taking a more realistic view of others now may dim some of the stars in your eyes, but it will ensure that you have more rewarding alliances in the future.*

KEY DATES

SUPER NOVA DAYS

APRIL 6–7 ★ *take a chance on love*

You can veer off into fantasyland on **April 6** as Venus and Mars form slippery semisquares with illusory Neptune. Questionable decisions come from letting hope overcome logic. Nevertheless, artistic and romantic inspiration enhances your power of attraction when Venus and Mars hook up in your 7th House of Partners on **April 7**. An exciting connection happens when you make the first move and bring something new to the table. Rekindling passion in a current union or striking a spark for a new one requires a little risk taking rather than playing it safe or sitting on the fence.

APRIL 14 ★ *a little goes a long way*

Your eyes are bigger than your stomach when an indulgent semisquare between sensual Venus and boundless Jupiter expands your appetites. Being adventurous by opening your heart brings you pleasure—but it may come with a high price tag. Yet playing, spending, and ingesting just a little more than usual could fill you with joy without costing too much.

APRIL 17–18 ★ *make love, not war*

Passion pops on **April 17** as the willful Sun and angry Mars meet up in red-hot Aries and your 7th House of Others. You could be bullied or motivated by a pushy person, but can make better use of this energy bomb by boldly going after who or what you want on your own terms. If you stir up discomfort by coming on stronger than someone else expects, a delicate Venus-Neptune sextile on the **18th** blesses you with the diplomacy and grace to smooth things over.

APRIL 22–24 ★ *reversal of fortune*

Don't despair if you encounter feelings of rejection on **April 22** when innocent Venus opposes mean old Saturn, indicating financial or social contraction. The good news is that you can recognize what you need to do to earn love, respect, or money. Fortunately, your recovery could be rapid; Venus's restorative trine to resurrecting Pluto on the **24th** shows you how you might heal relationships and apply underused assets more effectively.

APRIL 28 ★ *no easy way out*

Only your total commitment to hard work will bring you respect with a demanding Sun-Saturn opposition in your resource and economic houses. Venus's passage over the karmic South Node of the Moon in Taurus, though, can be like a skulking child who doesn't take responsibility for his or her actions. Don't freeze up out of fear or laziness; dive in to resolve a crisis once and for all.

MAY

FLAGS OF FREEDOM

You may feel pulled in two very different directions during the first half of the month. Brainy Mercury and the Sun are settled in stabilizing Taurus and your 8th House of Deep Sharing, testing your commitment to others. Prepare to compromise and accept the limits of predictability if you want reliable partnerships. Yet on **May 9,** magnetic Venus enters flirtatious and curious Gemini and your adventurous 9th House, attracting you to new people and distant places. The Taurus New Moon, also on the **9th,** is a Solar Eclipse that can undermine a financial alliance or a cozy personal connection. Its conjunction with the karmic Lunar South Node in loyal Taurus tempts you to hang on to someone even if you're not getting much from the connection. Let go; it's healthier than resisting change out of habit or a misplaced sense of obligation.

Mercury flutters into Gemini on **May 15,** filling your mind with so many interests that your thoughts become scattered. Then, on the **20th,** the Sun follows the messenger planet into the sign of the Twins and your focus makes a definitive turn away from placating others toward expanding your horizons. Education and travel are high on your list of priorities, and learning for the pleasure of it, rather than only to advance your career, is rewarding. The third of seven Uranus-Pluto squares on the **20th** sends deep shock waves through your personal life, reminding you that making a radical change might be your best option. The effusive Sagittarius Full Moon in your communicative 3rd House on **May 25** is a Lunar Eclipse square with Neptune, which can muddle messages or promote unrealistic thinking, so it's critical to discern the difference between facts and fantasies.

> ## KEEP IN MIND THIS MONTH
>
> *Sticking with a relationship that has lost its juice will wear you both down in the long run. Bring new life to it or consider moving on.*

KEY DATES

MAY 5–7 ★ *adrenaline rush*

Your endurance is admirable with a persistent Mars-Pluto trine on **May 5,** but even that might not be enough to calm agitated allies. Venus's hard aspects to disruptive Uranus on the **5th** and perturbing Pluto on the **6th** can rattle relationships and shake up your sense of self-worth. On the other hand, you might also break social patterns and discover deeper personal needs. Your assessment of others and your ability to make your points with power and precision are supported by a smart Mercury-Mars conjunction in your 8th House of Shared Resources on **May 7**.

MAY 13–15 ★ *no nonsense*
Your judgment could be skewed with a fuzzy Venus-Neptune square on **May 13**. Yes, magical moments of delight inspire romantic feelings and stimulate your imagination; just don't commit to anything without making a more sober assessment. Reality returns soon enough when lovable Venus rubs up against severe Saturn with an awkward quincunx on the **15th**. Reducing expenses, temporarily lowering your expectations, and adjusting to short-term limits will save you time and money in the long run.

MAY 18 ★ *time out*
Your taste for freedom grows with a sextile between creative Venus and restless Uranus. You might gain more satisfaction by walking away from social commitments—even if it means being alone—than adhering to someone else's agenda. Venus's harsh quincunx to Pluto represents coercive forces you are wise to avoid rather than getting bogged down in a relentless power struggle.

MAY 24–26 ★ *crazy love*
You can charm the birds out of the trees with a verbally compelling Mercury-Venus conjunction on **May 24**. Just be careful about what you ask for, because forceful Mars in determined Taurus forms stressful aspects with controlling Pluto on the **25th** and erratic Uranus on the **26th** that are likely to complicate relationships. Sure, you may prefer to live in a dreamland with the Sun's square to drifty Neptune on the **26th**, but pragmatic Saturn's tense aspect to Venus requires restraint and realism.

SUPER NOVA DAY
MAY 28 ★ *lucky charms*
This delicious day is brought to you by a generous conjunction of captivating Venus and cheerful Jupiter in your visionary 9th House. Cooking up plans for an inspiring trip or engaging in stimulating conversation links your head and your heart in delightful ways. Additionally, Venus and Jupiter form creative quintiles with brilliant Uranus in your 7th House of Others. If you have something to sell—make your pitch. Just don't go overboard with superfluous data. Keep it lively and entertaining for your intended audience.

JUNE

WHISTLE WHILE YOU WORK

The late-spring breezes of the Sun in Gemini stir your 9th House of Adventure with visions of escape to faraway places, but professional opportunities suggest that business should come first this month. Socially skillful Venus enters conservative Cancer and your 10th House of Career on **June 2**, which can pay handsome dividends at work. Handling people with your characteristic charm can ingratiate you with colleagues and customers and earn the respect of authority figures. If you're artistic, revealing your creations should bring more recognition now, as well. On **June 8**, the versatile Gemini New Moon could scatter your attention by stimulating curiosity about people of other cultures and travel to distant lands. On the **11th**, the second of three harmonious trines between ambitious Saturn in your 2nd House of Income and imaginative Neptune in your 6th House of Employment shows you how to earn money while pursuing your dreams.

The Sun's entry into Cancer on **June 21** marks the Summer Solstice in your professional 10th House, encouraging you to assume more public responsibilities. The competent Capricorn Full Moon in your 4th House of Home and Family on the **23rd** favorably aligns with no-nonsense Saturn to help you find the order and discipline you need to pursue your goals. Auspicious Jupiter's shift into Cancer on the **25th** begins a one-year stay in your 10th House, which increases your chances for success. Beware of taking on more work than you can handle when Mercury turns retrograde in Cancer on the **26th**, complicating communications and big projects with minor snafus. Reduce errors by using caution and seeking the advice of experienced individuals.

> **KEEP IN MIND THIS MONTH**
>
> *Tuning into your emotions and understanding your deepest needs can provide you with more effective guidance than bright ideas that don't feel right.*

KEY DATES

JUNE 7–8 ★ *stormy weather*

You can balance imagination and realism perfectly on **June 7** as Venus forms harmonious trines with irrational Neptune and rational Saturn. Use this moment to serve your professional aspirations—but remember that others may not be forthcoming, since trickster Mercury opposes secretive Pluto and Mars squares slippery Neptune. Apply some healthy skepticism to any promises to avoid buying into someone else's fairy tale. Originality and accountability arrive on the **8th** with an ingenious but unstable Mercury-Uranus square and a hard-edged quincunx between physical Mars and practical Saturn. Brilliant thinking may be thwarted by the limits of tools and systems; adjust your skills or plans as necessary.

SUPER NOVA DAYS
JUNE 11–12 ★ *calm under pressure*
You can tame short-term relationship and financial crises with long-term thinking as valuable Venus opposes pressurized Pluto on **June 11** and squares electric Uranus on the **12th**. The steadying Saturn-Neptune trine on the **11th** provides a broader perspective that helps you navigate the treacherous waters of manipulative people, social instability, and a possible cash crunch. Problems arising now don't have to be resolved immediately unless your intuition brings a sudden awakening that puts your situation in a totally new and different light.

JUNE 16 ★ *heart of gold*
Diplomatic Venus's friction-free trine with the integrative North Node of the Moon in emotional Scorpio brings peace to chaos or getting what you need from someone who's reluctant to give it. Your sensitivity to others' desires and fears can make for quick yet deep connections that build trust and intimacy.

JUNE 19–20 ★ *somewhere over the rainbow*
Your vision of the future expands with an overly optimistic conjunction of the expressive Sun and limitless Jupiter on **June 19**. However, this union in your farseeing 9th House may lack practicality as it's accompanied by a starry-eyed Venus-Neptune sesquisquare. Unrealistic expectations about travel and education can quickly go up in smoke. A sharper analysis of your resources and an ability to communicate with tender persuasion are provided by the conjunction of mental Mercury and sensual Venus on **June 20**.

JUNE 27 ★ *leader of the pack*
Your confidence shines and your social life is likely to be enhanced as artful Venus dances into lively Leo. This transit in your 11th House of Groups increases your popularity among friends and could put you in a leadership position in an organization. Allow yourself a small feeling of self-importance; it'll provide you with the inner authority that enables you to do your job.

JULY

WINDOW OF OPPORTUNITY

Summer may be a time for fun in the sun for many people, but there are too many professional opportunities for you this month to miss out on while relaxing on the beach. A subtle shift toward productivity starts when constructive Saturn turns forward in your 2nd House of Resources on **July 7**, reminding you to invest in the skills you need to increase your income. On **July 8**, the New Moon in normally cautious Cancer falls in your 10th House of Career to initiate bold action. This lunation is opposite unrelenting Pluto and square to unruly Uranus, which can spawn a work-related crisis. Yet it could be a powerful launching pad for career transformation if you hope to make a major change. Warrior Mars stirs things up on the **13th** when he enters Cancer and trines Neptune and Saturn on the **20th**. Fortunately, your strong emotions and potentially impulsive behavior are tempered by a strategic Grand Water Trine on **July 17–20**. Expansive Jupiter, constrictive Saturn, and intuitive Neptune align favorably, providing a balance of vision, reason, and faith to help assess and advance your professional interests.

Business-related information flows more easily and suspended projects get back on track when communicative Mercury turns direct in your 10th House on **July 20**. The intelligent Aquarius Full Moon shines in your 5th House of Creativity on **July 22**. This innovative event encourages originality, yet its stressful square to cautious Saturn and clumsy quincunx with sweet Venus can inhibit you with shyness. It's a day of contrasts as Venus moves into prim Virgo while the Sun strides into boisterous Leo and your 11th House of Friends, increasing your visibility in your community.

> ### KEEP IN MIND THIS MONTH
>
> *Pursue your long-term goals by focusing on the big picture. Don't waste your energy on the minor details of your daily life.*

KEY DATES

JULY 1 ★ *face the music*

You're in for an intense day as a Sun-Pluto opposition brings up irksome issues at home or at work. You might feel less appreciated than you should with vulnerable Venus's square with harsh Saturn. Venus also forms an unstable quincunx with squishy Neptune that could lead you to act evasively. It's healthier, though, to address issues directly with the patience and maturity that's necessary to commit to correcting mistakes.

JULY 5–7 ★ *the edge of love*
Seductive Venus's spiky semisquare to sexy Mars spices up your social life on
July 5. Still, you might also take flirting too far or have an emotional outburst due
to your lovely ruling planet's quincunx to volcanic Pluto. Thankfully, you regain
freedom in relationships and original forms of entertainment on the **7th** by a trine
from enchanting Venus to unorthodox Uranus.

JULY 13 ★ *larger than life*
Too much is not enough for you today with magnanimous Jupiter's semisquare
to pleasure-loving Venus. You could find yourself acting self-indulgently—or, on
the other hand, expanding your tastes to appreciate new experiences. You can
also overestimate the appeal of someone or something and wind up expecting or
paying more than you should. If you have the slightest doubt about an emotional
or financial commitment, consider delaying your decision until you have more
information.

JULY 26 ★ *dare to believe*
Your heart and soul are opening with an inspiring opposition of delightful Venus to
magical Neptune. This aspect is often associated with fantasy, but you're unlikely
to get lost in the mists of illusion today because Venus also forms a sensible sextile
with stable Saturn, keeping your feet on the ground while your head's in the clouds.
Don't be afraid to dream; instead of looking toward a distant horizon with no idea
how to reach it, you've got an inner map that can show you the way.

SUPER NOVA DAYS
JULY 27–31 ★ *claim your power*
Quiet confidence comes from within on **July 28** as Venus in your private 12th
House sextiles optimistic Jupiter. Low-key pleasures and relaxed relationships
allow you to enjoy yourself. However, stressful aspects from Mars to Pluto on
the **27th** and Uranus on the **31st** still add tension. Fortunately, you're able to
take care of business calmly but productively on the **30th** when Venus forms a
creative trine with shrewd Pluto. You can uncover underappreciated resources
and get the most out of your money. This favorable alignment of your socially
sensitive planet with tiny but powerful Pluto can also make you highly
persuasive without seeming the least bit pushy.

AUGUST

WORK, PLAY, PRAY

Social activities fill your time this month with the Sun in demonstrative Leo and your 11th House of Friends until **August 22**. The gregarious Leo New Moon's trine to eccentric Uranus on the **6th** may initiate you into an unconventional group where you could play a leadership role. Even your adorable ruling planet, Venus, gets in the act when she shifts into lovely Libra and your 1st House of Personality on the **16th**, magnifying your appeal to others and supporting your pursuit of pleasure. However, Jupiter, the planet of opportunity, tells a very different tale as it transits through your 10th House of Career, prompting a deep examination of your long-term plans. On **August 7**, Jupiter makes the first of three oppositions to transformational Pluto that will return on **January 31** and **April 20, 2014**. These transits can disrupt your sense of security, yet their higher purpose is to instill more passion in your work. The urge to take chances in your professional life is triggered by Jupiter's kinetic square with thrill-seeking Uranus on **August 21** that will recur on **February 26** and **April 20, 2014**.

The brainy Aquarius Full Moon on **August 20** illuminates your 5th House of Love and Creativity with revelations about romance and fresh ways to warm your heart. However, more serious matters require attention with the Sun's shift into methodical Virgo and your 12th House of Privacy on **August 22**, followed by thoughtful Mercury on the **23rd**. Taking some alone time for self-reflection and engaging in a spiritual practice will help you balance the high levels of personal and professional activity that are bound to keep you busy all month.

> **KEEP IN MIND THIS MONTH**
>
> *Make adjustments if you're helping others without getting anything in return. Mutual support is vital for healthy relationships.*

KEY DATES

AUGUST 2–4 ★ *under the radar*

You can motivate people with the gentlest touch on **August 2** as graceful Venus forms a smart sextile with assertive Mars. There's also a quiet flirtatious quality to this alignment that lets you send subtle signals of interest in someone without being noticed by others. Unusual characters and new forms of fun may enter your life on the **4th** as the heartfelt Sun in your sociable 11th House trines outlandish Uranus in your 7th House of Partners.

AUGUST 8-9 ★ *surprising solution*
Your bold words put you in a tight spot on **August 8**, when expressive Mercury enters charismatic Leo, encouraging bravado, while Venus is in a stifling semisquare with Saturn. Make sure you have all the resources you'll need—and the agreement of others—before you make promises you could have a tough time keeping. But even if you get yourself into a jam, you can discover an unexpected way out as Venus makes a creative quintile with visionary Jupiter on the **9th**.

AUGUST 14-16 ★ *it takes a village*
Everyone's working in harmony on **August 14**, when Mercury in your 11th House of Groups trines revolutionary Uranus in your 7th House of Partners. All this collaboration can produce brilliant results as free-flowing conversations break down barriers and open the door to more cutting-edge alliances. A thin-skinned Mercury-Venus semisquare on the **16th** can leave you or others super-sensitive to words and tone of voice; fortunately, Venus's move into your gracious sign helps you smooth over any misunderstandings.

AUGUST 21-22 ★ *genius at work*
Your brain is buzzing on **August 22** with outrageous thoughts that may be too convoluted to explain as smart-guy Mercury makes tense aspects to the **August 21** Jupiter-Uranus square. Electrifying ideas and crazy conversations break through outmoded views of reality to provide glimpses of the future. Still, you might be so far ahead of your time that you have to slow down, back up, and rethink your strategy to put these new concepts into a usable form.

SUPER NOVA DAYS
AUGUST 24-27 ★ *runaway relationships*
Close connections are complicated by a mistrusting Venus-Pluto square on **August 24** that's better at concealing feelings than expressing them. The slightest hint of influence could be interpreted as an attempt at manipulation. While Venus's beguiling quintile with passionate Mars can patch over some partnership problems on the **25th**, it will take more than a good time to resolve the underlying issues. Hidden concerns could surface with Venus's explosive opposition to impulsive Uranus on the **26th**, yet an escapist Venus-Jupiter square on the **27th** is better for weaving fantasies than facing facts.

SEPTEMBER

SHINE YOUR LIGHT

The little things you do in private will go a long way toward making you more successful in public this month. Focus on completing unfinished projects with the Sun in fastidious Virgo and your 12th House of Endings until **September 22**. The efficiency of this hyper-competent earth sign is kicked up another notch with the Virgo New Moon's harmonious aspects to strategic Jupiter and formidable Pluto on **September 5**. Your commitment to developing your talent grows as you recognize the long-term opportunities a stronger skill set will bring. You express yourself more eloquently than ever thanks to messenger Mercury's entry into diplomatic Libra on the **9th**. You can soothe some people and stimulate others with a clear presentation of your ideas. Your charming and cooperative ways serve a deeper purpose with Venus's descent into shadowy Scorpio and your 2nd House of Resources on the **11th**. An acute awareness of your emotional and material needs prompts you to seek better returns on your investments of time and energy.

You could be overly distracted at work on **September 19** when the quixotic Pisces Full Moon brightens your 6th House of Employment. If you're underappreciated or exhausted by your obligations, you may be flooded with feelings of frustration. Still, your sacrifices may be worth it if you're inspired by the service you provide. The Sun's entry into friendly Libra on the **22nd**—the Autumn Equinox—raises your profile and boosts your self-confidence. It's time to focus on your needs and act as the initiator in relationships. On the **29th**, Mercury enters psychologically astute Scorpio and your 2nd House of Values, showing you how to make the most of your resources and abilities.

> ### KEEP IN MIND THIS MONTH
>
> *Don't be distracted by trying to figure out what other people want. Focus on fully appreciating your own resourcefulness and acting in your own best interests.*

KEY DATES

SEPTEMBER 1–2 ★ *running down a dream*

Sentimentality can be very sweet on **September 1** with adorable Venus's sesquisquare to wistful Neptune. Yet those tender feelings may be misplaced when reality doesn't match your imagination. Enjoying yourself is fine as long as you don't try to build a lasting future on a passing cloud of pleasure. Pursuing illusions may also be an issue on the **2nd** when Mars misaligns with ephemeral Neptune. If you find yourself spinning in circles, it's time to reset your course in a more reliable direction.

SEPTEMBER 8-9 ★ *too clever by half*

You may be able to resolve a sticky issue at home or squeeze out what you want in a relationship with Venus's ingenious quintile to Pluto on **September 8**. But be careful; smartly extracting what you desire or saving some money can quickly bring serious consequences. A harsh square between prideful Mars in Leo and your 11th House of Groups and controlling Saturn in Scorpio and your 2nd House of Possessions on **September 9** can leave you with the burden of heavy obligations. Be patient and persistent, and you'll eventually earn respect and enhance your status.

SEPTEMBER 14 ★ *dancing in the dark*

Romantic moments, deep thoughts, and inspirational experiences make this a memorable day. A harmonious Venus-Neptune trine serves up love, compassion, and imagination, which are rooted in the profound perceptions of a Mercury-Pluto square. Yet if your mind gets stuck in a negative place, an experimental Mars-Uranus trine can connect you with playful pals to help you enjoy the present instead of being trapped in the past.

SUPER NOVA DAY
SEPTEMBER 18 ★ *cut to the chase*

You are unlikely to allow pleasantries to get in the way of the hard decisions you have to make today. When value-conscious Venus forms a sextile with penetrating Pluto, you're ready to push past politeness and get to the bottom line in financial and emotional matters. You can't escape from reality with Venus's conjunction to austere Saturn keeping you in line. It's time to take a stand by setting limits on what you're willing to give and clearly defining your needs and expectations of others. Yet the most demanding challenge is to find the discipline you'll need to maximize your abilities.

SEPTEMBER 26-28 ★ *marketing maven*

You discover an economical way to grow a business on **September 26** thanks to a lucrative Venus-Jupiter trine. Your promotional creativity or understanding of a target audience could lead to long-term success. However, conflicts with an ally are possible with a passionate but destabilizing Venus-Mars square on the **28th**.

OCTOBER

A BRAND-NEW DAY

The ever-fascinating subject of relationships is front and center in your life this month. If you have a partner, it's time for a refresh to keep this union interesting; if you're single, you may be ready to take a shot at getting back in the game. The Sun is in your sociable sign when October begins, casting you in a bright spotlight. However, the traditionally moderate Libra New Moon in your 1st House of Self on the **4th** is a wild one that has the potential to turn your life upside down. Maintaining your cool isn't easy with tense lunar aspects to demanding Pluto, rebellious Uranus, and pompous Jupiter. Sticking with the status quo is, perhaps, your least effective option with this transformative pattern. On the other hand, making radical changes in all aspects of your life can free you from boredom and introduce you to new worlds of power and excitement.

Stretch yourself even further beyond familiar and comfortable limits when your ruling planet, Venus, moves into exploratory Sagittarius on **October 7**. Just remember to set out a safety net before you take any big leaps on **October 15** as militant Mars moves into meticulous Virgo and your discreet 12th House. The impulsive Aries Full Moon Eclipse on the **18th** lights up your 7th House of Others, which can incite unexpected behavior from someone close to you. It can also provoke you to act more aggressively to initiate new connections and sell your ideas. Introspective Mercury's retrograde turn on the **21st** and the Sun's entry into skeptical Scorpio on the **23rd** could slow you down long enough to reconsider recent events and make any necessary corrective action.

KEEP IN MIND THIS MONTH

Be the change you want to see. Lead through innovation instead of planting yourself on shifting ground or trying to turn back the clock.

KEY DATES

SUPER NOVA DAYS
OCTOBER 1–3 ★ *zen warrior*

Brace yourself, because it's time to face your deepest desires and most hidden fears. Dark Pluto forms an intense aspect with the Sun on **October 1** and with innocent Venus on the **2nd**, possibly triggering power struggles, sowing seeds of mistrust, and undermining your sense of self-worth. Yet if you can honestly recognize what you need, you'll tap into a rich vein of resources that can transform loss into gain. Freedom is the reward for your courage when the Sun and Venus stress anarchistic Uranus on the **3rd**, yet chaos and alienation may be the price to pay if you continue to deny your feelings.

OCTOBER 10–12 ★ *precious illusions*
You long to escape reality on **October 10** as affectionate Venus and the willful Sun align with wayward Neptune. Creative endeavors, romantic pursuits, and spiritual activities can be sublime with these aspects, although you'll tend to ignore practical considerations. Venus and the Sun follow with dicey connections to inflated Jupiter on **October 11–12**, continuing your dreamy voyage through fantasyland. Enlightenment, imagination, and ecstatic visions are the inspiring gifts of these ungrounded days.

OCTOBER 16 ★ *fun and games*
You're open to unusual forms of play today as agreeable Venus in your 3rd House of Learning forms a constructive trine with unorthodox Uranus in your 7th House of Partners. Indeed, your uninhibited approach and easygoing attitude attract new people who find your playful personality appealing. Experiencing pleasure without commitment allows you to live comfortably in the moment and share your newfound sources of joy with equally open-minded individuals.

OCTOBER 19 ★ *magical mystery tour*
Intuition and instincts take over as you leave logic behind with Mars's opposition to mystical Neptune. Acting with compassion and following spiritual pursuits lift you beyond the bounds of ordinary life—but be careful not to wander off course. You might struggle to discern other people's motives when they mask anger or frustration behind a passive-aggressive smile. Put off a confrontation or a difficult task until you're ready to handle its consequences.

OCTOBER 26 ★ *wait it out*
Misjudging people or overestimating the value of objects and activities can be expected with a warm and fuzzy quincunx between Venus and Jupiter. This fun-seeking pair of planets coaxes you into viewing life through rose-colored glasses, and you could find yourself paying or giving more than you should. This is not an ideal time to make serious decisions, although an imaginative Venus-Neptune quintile could turn it into an enchanting day.

NOVEMBER

COUNT YOUR BLESSINGS

Yours isn't a particularly materialistic sign, Libra, but money is likely to weigh heavily on your mind this month. The Sun's presence in your 2nd House of Income until **November 21** reminds you to manage your resources carefully by avoiding frivolous expenses, being a patient bargain hunter, and seeking the most value for your expenditures of time and effort. An astute Scorpio New Moon Eclipse on **November 3** occurs in your 2nd House, where its conjunction with strict Saturn requires economic discipline. If finances are tight, counter fear by taking positive action however you can. You might return to using underexploited abilities or discover forgotten treasures that can be turned into marketable assets. You have a better chance of sustaining prosperity if you take a long-term view rather than looking for fast money from an immediate fix.

The lingering effects of the long-lasting Uranus-Pluto square on **November 1** can continue to destabilize relationships and drive you to accomplish more at work. However, your ruling planet Venus's shift into businesslike Capricorn and your 4th House of Inner Security on **November 5** returns your focus to the bottom line. Mercury's direct turn in your 2nd House on **November 10** can also help get money matters moving forward again. A breakthrough in awareness about personal and financial alliances is likely with the tangible Taurus Full Moon in your 8th House of Shared Resources on the **17th**. A reliable partner can provide a reassuring sense of solidity, but if your companion is greedy or lazy, you'll want to reassess the value of the relationship. On **November 21**, the Sun soars into forward-looking Sagittarius and your 3rd House of Information, stimulating your mind with fresh ideas, new connections, and a more optimistic attitude.

> **KEEP IN MIND THIS MONTH**
>
> *Gaining control of your cash flow may involve tightening your belt or taking on a second job, but the sense of safety you obtain can be worth the price.*

KEY DATES

NOVEMBER 4–5 ★ *labor of love*

Don't let others' opinions or your own doubts reduce your self-respect on **November 4**, when Venus's challenging semisquare to exacting Saturn leads you to underestimate your abilities. You may have to work harder now or wait longer to get the love and recognition that you deserve, but when you earn it the hard way it will be yours to keep. Venus's entry into ambitious Capricorn on the **5th** reinforces the message: Patience and persistence are your real keys to prosperity.

NOVEMBER 7–8 ★ *try a little tenderness*
Enjoy the free flow of affection on **November 7**, when amorous Venus's cuddly sextile to spiritual Neptune favors compassionate connections, self-forgiveness, and creative inspiration. Retrograde Mercury backs into a sextile with Venus on the **8th,** offering you a second chance to make peace with someone and to put artistic ideas in order. Use kindness and careful communication to heal wounded relationships and bring harmony and beauty into your home.

SUPER NOVA DAYS
NOVEMBER 14–15 ★ *embrace the unknown*
Relationships get weird when alluring Venus slams into an explosive square with wild and crazy Uranus on **November 14.** Your own moods include sudden desires and instant turnoffs, while those around you are also behaving erratically. Shaking up current alliances and your connections with people can be healthy if you let unexpressed needs and fears rise to the surface. Venus's conjunction with transformative Pluto on the **15th** intensifies the situation, although you're tempted to hide uncomfortable emotions instead of facing them. Honesty is your best policy; manipulation only creates suspicion. Just choose a safe situation where you can be truthful without embarrassing anyone.

NOVEMBER 22–23 ★ *trial and error*
You're hypersensitive to other people's opinions of you thanks to an uneasy Sun-Venus semisquare on **November 22.** If you feel that you're not receiving the love, pleasure, or approval you seek, you'll quickly discover what it takes to earn them. Venus's favorable sextile with responsible Saturn on the **23rd** offers clarity, discipline, and persistence so you're able to buckle down and work hard to fulfill your needs.

NOVEMBER 27–28 ★ *know your limits*
You can discuss delicate matters with skillful sensitivity on **November 27** due to a persuasive sextile between verbal Mercury and gracious Venus. Your economic acuity is high, too, making it easier to get the most out of limited resources. You're in a more effusive and free-spending mood on the **28th** when Venus opposes grandiose Jupiter, reducing restraint and tempting you to overvalue people and things.

DECEMBER

TIME IN A BOTTLE

Nostalgic feelings draw you back to the past this month. Your romantic ruling planet, Venus, slows down in your 4th House of Roots before turning retrograde on **December 21**. Holiday memories evoke both joy and regret, of course; this year, work to build on the best of them and finally let go of the worst. The call of the future is loud on **December 2** with the visionary Sagittarius New Moon in your 3rd House of Learning. Even if emotions linger behind, your mind can leap ahead with radical ideas and unusual perspectives as Uranus the Awakener trines this fiery conjunction of the Sun and Moon. Another motivating factor is superhero Mars's entry into peaceable Libra on the **7th**. The action planet's presence in your sign and 1st House of Self encourages you to be more physically active and take the initiative in personal and professional relationships.

On **December 12**, the second strategic trine between Jupiter in your 10th House of Career and Saturn in your 2nd House of Income tunes you in to a bigger picture of your professional future. But instead of making a hurried move, this is an excellent time to step back and evaluate your long-term goals—which you might ultimately set into place with the final Jupiter-Saturn trine on **May 24, 2014**. Although the inquisitive Gemini Full Moon on the **17th** in your 9th House of Faraway Places increases your interest in travel and education, it can make it harder to focus on what's right in front of you now. But then on the **21st**—the Winter Solstice—responsibilities on the home front take precedence with the Sun's entry into dutiful Capricorn in your domestic 4th House.

> **KEEP IN MIND THIS MONTH**
>
> *Old feelings may not fade away but you don't have to repeat the past. You can turn life in a totally different direction with original ideas and an attitude adjustment.*

KEY DATES

DECEMBER 7–9 ★ *take the wheel*

Attend to your own interests instead of trying to please everyone else on **December 7**, when Mars dances into your sign to energize your personable 1st House. Thankfully, you can be polite without losing sight of your own priorities. A brilliant Mars-Jupiter quintile in your 10th House of Career on **December 9** helps you sell a plan or promote a big idea without sounding pushy.

DECEMBER 13–14 ★ *one step at a time*

Your touch can be so tender and your words so sweet on **December 13** that your intentions may not be clear to others. A mushy Mercury-Venus semisquare and a slippery Mars-Neptune quincunx mean that this is a less-than-ideal moment for making a point or staying on track. But you won't get to wander too far without facing the consequences when taskmaster Saturn disciplines meandering Mars with a tough semisquare on the **14th**. If frustration follows, don't swallow your anger; let it motivate you to tackle a tough task. Slowing down and narrowing your focus reduce mistakes and increase your productivity.

DECEMBER 25 ★ *break the mold*

This might not be the mellowest Christmas of your life as circumstances can change suddenly and strong emotions may arise out of nowhere. Pushy Mars opposes rowdy Uranus, making it nearly impossible to remain cool and keep the peace. Your desire for harmony tempts you to dampen down dissent and gently keep everyone in line. Yet it's probably safer to allow a little chaos and unplanned activity to blow off steam rather than unsuccessfully adhering to a fixed schedule. In fact, this can be a uniquely different holiday experience if you put a twist into old traditions and spontaneously invent new ones. Instead of fighting the tides of change, use the electricity in the air to create an exciting and unforgettable day.

SUPER NOVA DAYS
DECEMBER 29–31 ★ *cuts like a knife*

Expect the unexpected when witty Mercury and the expressive Sun spark impulsive thoughts and actions as they square uncontainable Uranus on **December 29–30**. Your own mouth can move more quickly than your ability to contain bold statements and outrageous comments. What one person thinks is a clever remark may provoke a less-than-friendly response with Mars's forceful square to suspicious Pluto on the **30th**. Unresolved issues and long-standing resentments could surface with dangerous intensity. Mercury joins Pluto and squares Mars on the **31st**, which can deepen your perceptions and lead you to meaningful conversations—if you can tame your temper with reason.

SCORPIO

OCTOBER 23–NOVEMBER 21

SCORPIO

2012 SUMMARY

The variety of people, ideas, and experiences you encounter can reinvigorate your interest in a current alliance or excite curiosity about a new person or venture while simultaneously driving you crazy with distraction. Coming to terms with old partnerships by letting go of any remaining anger and resentment can clear the way to smoother sailing ahead. The process of untangling knots of mistrust and confusion requires patience and a willingness to focus on specific tasks instead of personality differences.

AUGUST—*ladder of success*
Setting your own standards of excellence along with a sustainable pace can get you to the top of almost any mountain.

SEPTEMBER—*riders on the storm*
Yes, you must behave politely in front of others, but don't let that keep you from acknowledging the truth you feel in your heart.

OCTOBER—*blue skies ahead*
Facts are only the starting point, not the end of a significant question. It's what you do with the information that dictates your future.

NOVEMBER—*turning the page*
Your truth doesn't have to be describable to have meaning for you. The best answers lie within and can't always be put into words.

DECEMBER—*labor of love*
The limits of your current circumstances only reflect what lies ahead if you don't set your financial imagination free.

2012 CALENDAR

AUGUST

THU 2 ★	Take what you hear with a grain of salt
TUE 7–THU 9 ★	Set aside some time for pleasure
WED 15–THU 16 ★	**SUPER NOVA DAYS** Secrets may surface that rock relationships
WED 22–THU 23 ★	Settling for less is not a viable option

SEPTEMBER

MON 3 ★	Heed the advice of an astute friend
WED 5–FRI 7 ★	Open your heart and mind, but don't go too far
THU 13 ★	Stretch your limits
THU 20–FRI 21 ★	Good humor keeps tension from getting out of hand
TUE 25–SAT 29 ★	**SUPER NOVA DAYS** Initiate an honest dialogue

OCTOBER

TUE 2–WED 3 ★	Don't lose touch with common sense
MON 8–WED 10 ★	Be very astute about people and money
TUE 16–WED 17 ★	A dose of reality is disappointing if you've gone too far
MON 22–THU 25 ★	**SUPER NOVA DAYS** Avoid making promises you can't keep
SUN 28–MON 29 ★	Your words are packed with more punch than you realize

NOVEMBER

THU 1–SUN 4 ★	Look before you leap
FRI 9 ★	Promise only what you can deliver
SAT 17–SUN 18 ★	Conversations reveal secrets that challenge relationships
WED 21–THU 22 ★	Desires can move beyond the bounds of reason
MON 26–THU 29 ★	**SUPER NOVA DAYS** Set relationship agendas with clarity

DECEMBER

SAT 1–SUN 2 ★	It's tempting to overdo just about everything
MON 10–WED 12 ★	**SUPER NOVA DAYS** Follow your heart bravely
SAT 15–SUN 16 ★	Be wary of impractical choices about love or money
FRI 21–SAT 22 ★	Find a healthy balance between hope and realism

SCORPIO OVERVIEW

The pressure is on you this year, Scorpio, as your past and future meet in an intense whirlwind of transformation that affects many areas of your life. You will get what you deserve as karmic Saturn spends the entire year in your formidable sign. The Taskmaster's shift into passionate Scorpio on October 5, 2012, sets into motion a period of significant endings and beginnings that change your life, bringing professional fulfillment along with personal difficulties. Saturn remains in Scorpio and your 1st House of Self until December 23, 2014, giving you plenty of time to redirect your life in a way that's more suitable to your long-term goals. You can now achieve deep satisfaction in areas where you have applied methodical efforts and persistence over the past few years. However, you will also be confronted with the realization that some things have not worked out in your best interest. **It's time to cut your losses and acknowledge that today's failures can become tomorrow's successes if you have the wisdom to let go without a struggle.** For example, you may receive a hard-earned promotion at work while facing difficult decisions in a floundering relationship. Fortunately, you Scorpios thrive in the transformational fires of the forge, emerging stronger and better than ever.

Although you typically prefer steady and gradual change as your method of growth, when shocking Uranus forms two dynamic squares to unstoppable Pluto this year, you'll experience unexpected changes that release previously suppressed emotions. You are in a long-term process of reevaluating and updating the assumptions on which you structure your thinking as your key planet, Pluto, slowly moves through your 3rd House of Learning. However, Uranus in your 6th House of Self-Improvement electrifies your life with lightning bolts of awareness as it squares powerful Pluto on May 20 and November 1. **Change occurs in sudden energetic bursts that can turn your life upside down, empowering you to break free from old habits, restrictive jobs, and boring routines.** These exciting and revolutionary aspects are part of a series that began on June 24, 2012, culminating on March 16, 2015.

Stern Saturn's current visit to mysterious Scorpio makes it harder to express your feelings as you build a wall between you and the outer world. Meanwhile, spiritual Neptune's long-term visit to compassionate Pisces helps to soften your heart. A harmonizing Saturn-Neptune trine on June 11 that recurs July 19 creates a magical balance between your ideals and dreams and your ability to make them real. On June 25, propitious Jupiter enters sensitive Cancer for a yearlong visit that enriches your emotional life and expands your intuitive faculties. **Even if you enjoy the idea of staying home and entertaining, you're still likely to venture out to visit friends and family** when Jupiter moves through your 9th House of Adventure. Additionally, Jupiter's Grand Water Trine with Saturn and Neptune on July 17–19 is an ideal time to initiate a new project, do a bit of traveling, or just kick back and enjoy the pleasures of life.

DREAM A LITTLE DREAM

It's challenging to keep your romantic fantasies separate from reality this year, especially when a parade of planets—beginning with spirited Mars on February 1—swims into poetic Pisces and your 5th House of Love. Thoughtful Mercury is next on February 5, followed by the Sun on February 18 and pleasure-seeking Venus on February 25. Your charm is irresistible, with up to seven planets congregating in this playful house through March 12, enabling you to captivate others with your creative energy. However, Mercury's retrograde turn on February 23–March 17 triggers misunderstandings that might impede the flow of intimacy. Fortunately, a long-lasting trine from realistic Saturn to surreal Neptune on June 11 and July 19 gives you a chance to turn an elusive fantasy into an enduring relationship.

ANYTHING CAN HAPPEN

You would like more stability on the job, but aspects to unpredictable Uranus in your 6th House of Work are bound to stir up unexpected changes throughout the year. Naturally, the dramatic Uranus-Pluto squares on May 20 and November 1 reflect the ongoing instability of your employment situation, but you'll find great opportunities for new experiences here, too. Something has to give in order to relieve the stress at work from unsettling aspects to Uranus on March 22–28, June 8–12, July 4, July 31, August 21, October 3, and December 25–30. Clinging to the status quo doesn't make sense, and initiating action is better than sitting back and waiting for something momentous to occur.

HIGH HOPES

Your expectations for making money this year may be overblown from the beginning, because lavish Venus is in risk-taking Sagittarius and your 2nd House of Income until January 8. Meanwhile, with roving Jupiter in restless Gemini and your 8th House of Investments and Shared Resources until June 25, you struggle to put in the hard work required to turn an opportunity into cash in hand. But an inflationary Sagittarius Full Moon Eclipse on May 25 rattles your 2nd House and can pop your dreams of a luxurious lifestyle. The Sun and Moon square deceptive Neptune in your speculative 5th House, reminding you to be realistic and save your money rather than count on a get-rich-quick scheme.

LET'S GET PHYSICAL

Enhance your well-being and revitalize your immune system this year by taking a new approach to your body as innovative Uranus continues its journey through your 6th House of Health. Stress can exhaust your nervous system with unrelenting Pluto's squares to Uranus, which are exact on May 20 and November 1. Fortunately, supportive aspects to Uranus from Mercury and the Sun on January 22–24 and from Venus on February 6 inspire you to make positive changes to your routine. Recommit to a regular exercise program when active Mars conjuncts electric Uranus on March 22. Raise the intensity of your workouts on August 6 when the fiery Leo New Moon harmoniously trines Uranus. Be careful not to overextend yourself around October 18, when the impulsive Aries Lunar Eclipse shakes your 6th House to the core.

HOME IS WHERE THE HEART IS

You're ready to shake things up at home this year with energetic Mars in Aquarius and your 4th House of Roots until February 1. Mercury, the Sun, and Venus visit your 4th House to keep your home fires burning brightly through February 25. Bountiful Jupiter's shift into nurturing Cancer and your 9th House of Adventure on June 25 enables you to feel at home anywhere. No matter where you go, increasing your involvement with your family can be an exciting journey encouraging you to grow in new ways.

HOMEWARD BOUND

Believe it or not, you can satisfy your need for excitement this year by going on a voyage of the mind. However, if you plan on traveling, you'll probably be taking your family with you, visiting relatives in another city, or exploring your ancestral roots, because journeying Jupiter enters familial Cancer and your 9th House of Travel and Education on June 25 for a yearlong visit. Wanderlust could kick in on May 31 when fleet-footed Mercury enters your 9th House, followed by Venus on June 2 and the Sun on June 21. Pay extra attention to details if you're on the road or involved in educational matters when trickster Mercury retrogrades in your 9th House on June 26–July 20. Mars's visit to your 9th House on July 13–August 27 encourages your impulsiveness and raises the odds that you'll escape on a quick getaway to fulfill your need for adventure.

 LIGHTEN UP

The road to spiritual awareness is paved with lightheartedness and humor now that otherworldly Neptune is drifting in your 5th House of Fun and Games. Learning how to laugh more often can be serious business and good for your emotional well-being—especially when Neptune trines sobering Saturn on June 11 and July 19. You yearn for deeper soul connections when beautiful Venus moves through your 12th House of Spiritual Mystery on August 16–September 11. Mental Mercury's visit to your 12th House on September 9–29 boosts your interest in studying metaphysics. Finally, Mars enters your 12th House on December 7, motivating you to step away from the noise of commercialism and family expectations to seek the real holiday spirit.

> **RICK & JEFF'S TIP FOR THE YEAR:**
> Be True to Yourself
>
> Stand up for those things and people that you consider to be most important in your life—what you do this year will have lasting consequences. However, don't exhaust yourself trying to force your will onto the world when circumstances indicate it's wiser to choose another direction. Be brave enough to start something new, but finish up old business and tie up loose ends first.

JANUARY

NOTHING BUT THE TRUTH

You have something important to say this month. But don't just spontaneously blurt out the truth; deliver your message at the right time with clarity on **January 3**, when verbose Mercury squares irrepressible Uranus. Fortunately, Mercury hooks up with your key planet, Pluto, in your 3rd House of Communication and forms a supportive sextile with somber Saturn on **January 6**, intensifying your words while focusing your thoughts on practical matters. The presence of the Sun, Pluto, and Mercury in your 3rd House enables you to discuss sensitive issues rationally by keeping your emotions in check. Although alluring Venus's entry into calculating Capricorn and your 3rd House of Immediate Environment on **January 8** tempts you to wander off in pursuit of pleasure, you would be better off tackling a difficult subject now. Nevertheless, a frustrating Mars-Saturn square on **January 7** reveals the gulf between what you're working toward and what you have to do to get there. The ambitious Capricorn New Moon on **January 11** lands in your data-rich 3rd House, turning today's ideas into successful strategies to reach tomorrow's goals.

Tension between your thoughts and your feelings grows as rational Mercury and the willful Sun shift into conceptual Aquarius and your 4th House of Foundations on **January 19**. A problem that troubled you around **January 7** at the Mars-Saturn square might return with a slightly different emphasis when Mercury and the Sun square serious Saturn on **January 25** and **January 30**, respectively. Meanwhile, the heart-centered Leo Full Moon on **January 26** illuminates your 10th House of Status, encouraging you to take a risk in order to become more involved in your community or to get ahead professionally.

> **KEEP IN MIND THIS MONTH**
>
> *Although it's important to communicate what you're feeling, the best way to earn trust is to match your words and your actions with your purest intentions.*

KEY DATES

JANUARY 4–7 ★ *uphill battle*

You can rely on the support of your close friends and family on **January 4** when benevolent Jupiter harmoniously trines insistent Mars in your 4th House of Domestic Conditions. However, your sound strategy doesn't easily translate into a smooth execution of your plans as other people's resistance to your efforts impedes your progress. Your willingness to stand up for what's right can make a big difference when communicator Mercury aligns with formidable Pluto and ethical Saturn on **January 6**. The restraining Mars-Saturn square on the **7th** indicates a possible setback, but your patience and persistence can bring success if you work diligently to achieve your goals.

JANUARY 10–12 ★ *reality check*
You're sure you can solve all your problems if you have the right information with value-conscious Venus in your 3rd House of Learning on **January 10**. But you may arrive at an incorrect conclusion as an imaginative Venus-Neptune sextile makes your fantasies tantalizingly real. Get your facts straight and consider the consequences of acting on your desires, or you might do something you'll later regret when Venus squares uncontainable Uranus on the **12th**. Thankfully, the cautious Capricorn New Moon on **January 11** reminds you that exercising self-restraint is a more intelligent choice at this time.

SUPER NOVA DAYS
JANUARY 16–17 ★ *the power of love*
Sometimes your feelings are so strong, you can't contain them. Normally, sultry Venus's happy hookup with relentless Pluto creates an emotional tidal wave that's beyond your control, causing you to heat up a romance to the boiling point. However, the Venus-Pluto conjunction on **January 16** occurs in conservative Capricorn and your 3rd House of Communication, allowing you to talk about your desires in a responsible manner rather than simply acting on them. Additionally, Venus creates a cooperative sextile with restrictive Saturn on the **17th**, further encouraging you to forgo immediate gratification to cultivate the kind of love that is more enduring.

JANUARY 24–26 ★ *actions speak louder than words*
It's difficult to say exactly what you mean now as the winged messenger Mercury squares constricting Saturn on **January 25**. Even if you find the words, they may fall upon deaf ears or overly critical minds. However, the Sun's harmonious aspects to surprising Uranus and auspicious Jupiter on **January 24–25** portend a fortunate outcome to action taken at this time. The expressive Leo Full Moon on **January 26** indicates that your current efforts will be appreciated as long as you keep your priorities straight.

FEBRUARY

DARE TO BELIEVE

The ease with which you share your feelings this month is facilitated by speedy Mars's sojourn through your 5th House of Love and Creativity on **February 1– March 12**. You're eager to express yourself when talkative Mercury enters emotional Pisces on **February 5** and stays in your 5th House until **April 13**. This desire for living in the moment is heightened on **February 18** when the Sun joins the party in your 5th House, followed by sweet Venus on **February 25**. However, you could exhaust yourself if you don't pay attention to sensible limits when Mercury and Mars square boisterous Jupiter on **February 9–10**. You may set aside your need for emotional safety when the cerebral Aquarius New Moon on the **10th** activates your 4th House of Security. Taking a risk sounds exciting because a stressful lunar aspect to electric Uranus stirs up your adrenaline, but a reserved Venus-Saturn square on **February 11** reminds you that a little caution could save the day.

The challenge is to give yourself permission to dream—without letting fantasies take over your life. Establishing and maintaining clear boundaries is difficult with up to six planets in starry-eyed Pisces this month. It's particularly tricky to discern what's real when Mars conjuncts mystical Neptune on **February 4**, followed by the Sun on **February 21** and Venus on **February 28**. However, cerebral Mercury retrogrades in your 5th House of Romance on **February 23– March 17**, turning your thoughts inward and requiring you to revisit recent conversations about love. The analytical Virgo Full Moon on **February 25** in your 11th House of Dreams and Wishes narrows your perspective so that you can focus your current efforts on achieving your long-term goals.

> **KEEP IN MIND THIS MONTH**
>
> *No matter how magical it feels to be appreciated by someone you love, don't become infatuated or lose yourself in the exhilaration of the moment.*

KEY DATES

FEBRUARY 1–4 ★ *fantasy island*

You're attracted to an unusual person as flirty Venus enters freethinking Aquarius on **February 1**; you might not act on these unconventional desires, though, while Venus visits your 4th House of Security. Meanwhile, physical Mars enters dreamy Pisces and your 5th House of Love, motivating you to bring romantic fantasies to life. Be cautious; you're increasingly deceived by your own imagination when Mars reaches a conjunction with illusory Neptune on **February 4**. Nevertheless, your creative vision can inspire you to believe in miracles, whether or not the potential is fully manifested.

FEBRUARY 8–12 ★ *a bridge too far*

Your words are emotionally charged by communicator Mercury's hookup with combative Mars in your 5th House of Self-Expression on **February 8**. You could inadvertently put someone off if you're too pushy when pompous Jupiter in your 8th House of Deep Sharing squares Mercury on **February 9** and Mars on **February 10**. The New Moon on the **10th** is in quirky Aquarius, along with enticing Venus, inviting you to step beyond normal constraints to get what you want, even if your goals don't align with others' expectations. Although you may be dissatisfied when Venus squares austere Saturn on the **11th**, harmonious Mercury's aspects to passionate Pluto and persistent Saturn on the **12th** indicate that your disappointment will be short-lived. Be patient, and you'll find your way back to pleasure.

SUPER NOVA DAYS
FEBRUARY 15–16 ★ *seize the day*

Heroic Mars and dynamic Pluto are your two key planets, and their cooperative sextile on **February 15** infuses you with enough energy to launch a creative endeavor. Courageous Mars in your 5th House of Fun and Games forms a harmonious trine to karmic Saturn in your sign on **February 16**, indicating that you're playing for keeps now. Thankfully, your leadership skills are extraordinary and your ability to organize a complex project is exceptionally good. Don't wait for a better time to begin a new project or grab an amazing opportunity.

FEBRUARY 25–26 ★ *stick to the plan*

Your friends come riding to your rescue on **February 25** when the trustworthy Virgo Full Moon lands in your 11th House of Social Networking, helping to keep your feet on the ground. Even so, you struggle to avoid outrageous behavior because the Sun and the Moon square opulent Jupiter. You may sound angrier than you actually feel when retrograde Mercury joins contentious Mars on **26th**. Unfortunately, deviations from your established agenda won't move you closer to your goals.

MARCH

PLAY IT FORWARD

The first part of March has a stabilizing quality that makes it an ideal time to solidify your plans before you set them into motion. Although several aspects to pragmatic Saturn in resourceful Scorpio focus your attention on serious matters, you're also feeling restless with six planets in your 5th House of Fun until **March 12,** when action-planet Mars leads the planetary parade into your 6th House of Work. You turn a creative idea into a real project when the Sun, valuable Venus, and clever Mercury trine Saturn and sextile Pluto on **March 1, 6,** and **7,** respectively. Heavyweight Saturn sextiles insightful Pluto in your 3rd House of Communication on **March 8,** deepening your convictions and providing you with the skills to get your ideas across in a simple and straightforward manner.

The fanciful Pisces New Moon on **March 11** falls in your 5th House of Self-Expression, unleashing your playful and romantic spirit, and planting a seed of joy in your heart. Even as you push into new territory, though, you continue to review recent experiences, rework your strategies, and reconsider your options. Thankfully, forward progress is just around the corner when messenger Mercury turns direct on

March 17, ending its three-week retrograde cycle that began **February 23.** The Sun's entry into impetuous Aries and your 6th House of Details on **March 20** marks the Spring Equinox, and is another reminder that this is a time for new beginnings. Nevertheless, you must temper your eagerness with reason as overconfident Jupiter forms crunchy quincunxes with Saturn and Pluto on **March 23 and March 29,** encouraging you to use extreme measures to get what you want.

> **KEEP IN MIND THIS MONTH**
>
> *Problems happen even when things are looking good. Don't get discouraged; just be prepared to handle issues as they surface with a healthy sense of humor.*

KEY DATES

MARCH 1 ★ *claim your power*

Others pay attention to what you do when impressive Pluto and ambitious Saturn form supportive aspects to the radiant Sun in your 5th House of Self-Expression. Fortunately, your creative imagination is grounded in common sense now, giving you the ability to dream up a solution to a current problem and then turn it into reality.

MARCH 6–8 ★ *speak your truth*

You reconnect with your deepest desires when magnetic Venus in your 5th House of Love and Creativity sextiles dark Pluto and unequivocal Saturn on **March 6**. Loquacious Mercury joins Venus later in the day, enabling you to turn on the charm so you can approach a difficult subject without putting someone off. On **March 7**, Mercury takes its turn to aspect Pluto and Saturn, giving you an irrefutable air of authority. Others are intently tuned in to what you might say because they believe that you know what you're talking about. Fortunately, a Saturn-Pluto sextile on the **8th** intensifies your perspective and sharpens your understanding of what's happening. Don't be afraid to speak your piece while people are listening.

MARCH 11–12 ★ *happy days*

You're the life of the party on **March 11** with a cluster of seven planets, including the fantasy-prone Pisces New Moon, in your 5th House of Love and Play. But try to keep your imagination in check; too much enthusiasm prompts you to waste energy. You're feeling confident when brave Mars enters spontaneous Aries on **March 12**, and his presence in your 6th House of Self-Improvement motivates you to make positive changes.

MARCH 22 ★ *hold on to your hat*

An explosive Mars-Uranus conjunction in your 6th House of Daily Routine indicates that the winds of change are shifting so quickly you won't have any time to develop a strategy. Instead, jump into the center of the storm and simply react on a visceral level to whatever happens. Following your instincts is a sensible tactic if you remember to remain flexible in your approach.

SUPER NOVA DAYS
MARCH 25–27 ★ *on the edge*

You may be very busy now, making it difficult to keep up with all of your obligations. An anxious aspect between expressive Mars and constrictive Saturn on **March 25** heightens your frustration—you don't know whether to push harder or quietly retreat. Intense emotions could burst into conflict when Mars squares domineering Pluto on **March 26**. Try a new strategy to restore balance at work on **March 27**, when the objective Libra Full Moon in your karmic 12th House opposes agreeable Venus and rebellious Uranus.

APRIL

WE CAN WORK IT OUT

You have a lot to do this month, and four planets in enterprising Aries and your 6th House of Self-Improvement prompt you to get started right away. On **April 1**, the Sun sextiles Jupiter in your 8th House of Shared Resources, setting the stage for a beneficial joint venture that you're currently fueling with your unrelenting drive and courage. The pioneering Aries New Moon on **April 10** lands in your 6th House of Employment, encouraging you to work even harder for what you want. Its conjunctions with enthusiastic Mars and charming Venus enhance your creativity and balance your sense of urgency with enough social grace to charm your co-workers. However, an irritating quincunx between unpredictable Uranus in reckless Aries and reliable Saturn in your inflexible sign on **April 12**—the second in a long-lasting series that began on **November 15, 2012**, and completes on **October 5**—can throw obstacles in your path if you push ahead too quickly without laying the proper groundwork.

You long to bond with others when affectionate Venus dances into sensual Taurus and your 7th House of Others on **April 15**, followed by the Sun on **April 19** and Mars on **April 20**. Yet your impatience may get the best of you on **April 17** when ardent Mars joins the Sun. Although a close relationship may cool on **April 22** when Venus opposes stoic Saturn, passion returns on **April 24** as a Venus-Pluto trine enables you to rekindle the intensity and move into new emotional territory. The penetrating Scorpio Lunar Eclipse on **April 25** highlights your relationship houses, showing you the unresolved issues that need your undivided attention.

> **KEEP IN MIND THIS MONTH**
>
> *You're eager to solve problems as they arise, but your solutions won't last unless you slow down and work closely with others in order to stabilize your gains.*

KEY DATES

APRIL 4–7 ★ *pursuit of happiness*

You begin a long-term process of deep psychological renewal as you reorganize your approach to learning. Maverick Chiron sextiles transformational Pluto on the 4th in your 3rd House of Data Collection in a series that began on **May 12, 2012**, and culminates on **February 25, 2014**. Chiron in your 5th House of Play indicates that it's time to reclaim your innocence and enhance your creativity by addressing communication issues with children or nurturing your inner child. Your imagination tells you what you must change when spiritual Neptune sextiles Venus and Mars in your 6th House of Daily Routines on **April 6**. The spicy Venus-Mars conjunction on the **7th** arouses your desires and stimulates your appetite for pleasure.

APRIL 10 ★ *baby steps*

You're ready to jump into a radical new health regime when the fearless Aries New Moon on **April 10** fires up your 6th House of Health and Habits. However, it's also wise to establish a work schedule that increases your efficiency. Instead of taking on too much too fast, remember that small improvements will last longer than major changes.

APRIL 19–22 ★ *live wire*

You hunger for harmony as the Sun and Mars shift into your 7th House of Relationships on **April 19–20**. Quicksilver Mercury joins brilliant Uranus on **April 20** to spark your creative genius and produce a stream of high-voltage ideas. If you can't act on them immediately, write the best ones down to use later. A tense Mercury-Pluto square on **April 21** can fuel an argument, with tensions continuing as unyielding Saturn staunchly opposes tactful Venus on **April 22**. Allow for differences of opinion without trying to resolve them at this time.

SUPER NOVA DAYS
APRIL 24–26 ★ *in the name of love*

Your talent for creating success through relationships is solidified by resolute Pluto's flowing trine to loving Venus in your interactive 7th House on **April 24**. The magnetic Scorpio Full Moon Eclipse on **April 25** shakes up your plans, prompting you to wonder if you'll be able to achieve your current objectives. An idealistic Mars-Neptune sextile on the **26th** stirs your soul, inspiring you to tap into the creative power of your imagination to make your dreams come true.

APRIL 28 ★ *tough as nails*

Is your determination an asset—or are you so obstinate that others don't want to work with you? You might learn the answer today when the stubborn Taurus Sun in your 7th House of Partners opposes Saturn the Taskmaster in fixed Scorpio. Instead of being critical and unforgiving, take a kinder and gentler approach to improve your personal and professional relationships.

MAY

SHIFTING SANDS

You're afraid there's nowhere secure to stand this month as circumstances create growing pressure for change. Normally, you can hold your position even in the face of intensity or adversity. However, you could be pleasantly surprised by what happens when you let go of an agenda that no longer serves your purpose. Your frustration is already palpable when forceful Mars and insistent Mercury in bullheaded Taurus oppose obstinate Saturn in your 1st House of Self on **May 1** and **May 5**, respectively. Don't admit defeat, even if it seems like others are unwilling to acknowledge your point of view. Instead, go ahead with the changes that will improve your life. Four planets in determined Taurus and your 7th House of Partners help you overcome the resistance that you're encountering from someone else. Fortunately, Venus shifts into adaptable Gemini on **May 9**, the same day as a Taurus New Moon Eclipse in your 7th House revitalizes a relationship by offering alternative ways to work together.

You can take your partnerships to the next level when mental Mercury enters friendly Gemini and your 8th House of Deep Sharing on **May 15**. The weight of responsibility continues to lift when the Sun enters airy Gemini on **May 20**, followed by Mars on **May 31**. Meanwhile, the long-lasting square between reactionary Uranus and evolutionary Pluto that began in 2012 and continues through 2015 is exact on **May 20**, raising the stakes in the current game of change. The adventurous Sagittarius Full Moon Eclipse on **May 25** fires up your 2nd House of Self-Worth, inspiring you to take decisive action in order to realign your life with your core values.

> **KEEP IN MIND THIS MONTH**
>
> *Maintaining the status quo because you're afraid of what's around the next corner takes more energy than it's worth—and could prevent you from fulfilling your dreams.*

KEY DATES

MAY 1–5 ★ *no surrender*

You don't like it when others are too insistent—especially if they're trying to coerce you to change your mind. Bossy Saturn in your sign opposes pushy Mars in your 7th House of Partners on **May 1**, prompting you to dig in your heels against the wishes of someone else. An argumentative Mercury-Saturn opposition on **May 5** brings out your fixed and unyielding nature for all to see. Meanwhile, your key planet, Pluto, harmoniously trines the Sun on the **1st** and Mars on the **5th**, strengthening your convictions and empowering you to defend your point of view at all costs.

MAY 9 ★ *winning isn't everything*

Someone's unwilling to meet you halfway today as a Solar Eclipse in purposeful Taurus polarizes your 7th House of Relationships. Venus's move into flighty Gemini loosens your attachment to your previous plans. You may see a compromise clearly, but you also recognize that it requires give-and-take from both parties. The New Moon Eclipse conjuncts interactive Mercury, signaling that dynamics can change if you remember that communication is a two-way street.

MAY 16–20 ★ *trust the process*

You continue to question your own assumptions and reevaluate how to work with the information at hand. Your daily routine is changing right before your eyes with revolutionary Uranus in your 6th House of Self-Improvement locked in a long-lasting square with uncompromising Pluto in your 3rd House of Information; this is exact on **May 20**. But the Sun's stressful aspects to Uranus and Pluto on **May 16** are as disquieting as fingernails on a chalkboard, pitting your straightforward agenda against someone else's more complex expectations. A mix of conflicting aspects from analytical Mercury and vulnerable Venus on **May 18** challenges you to find a clear path through an emotional minefield. There are many exciting routes to follow now, and the Sun's shift into fickle Gemini on the **20th** reminds you to keep your options open as circumstances surprise you.

SUPER NOVA DAYS
MAY 25–28 ★ *in it to win it*

Your cash flow is stretched to the max on **May 25** as the Sagittarius Lunar Eclipse intensifies your 2nd House of Resources, shaking up your finances. Militant Mars has you up in arms to defend your current lifestyle or aggressively seek more money when he harshly aspects Pluto and Uranus on **May 25–26**. However, an enriching triple conjunction of eloquent Mercury, skillful Venus, and auspicious Jupiter in your 8th House of Investments and Shared Resources on **May 27–28** bodes well for any project you undertake now, provided you don't expect too much in return for very little effort.

JUNE

MAGIC HAPPENS

You must be rooted in your feelings this month if you hope to express your vision creatively, especially with dreamy Neptune increasing the power of your imagination as it journeys through boundless Pisces and your 5th House of Love and Play. Fortunately, crystallizing Saturn in your sign forms a fluid trine to Neptune on **June 11**, grounding your fantasies in reality and enabling you to turn a passing fancy into an enduring expression of who you are. Saturn and Neptune move so slowly that you'll feel these beneficial effects almost the entire month, beginning on **June 3** when both planets trine Mercury. You think that you know what you want, and your concentrated effort can turn an idea into a sensible plan. The waxing Saturn-Neptune trine is stimulated by sensual Venus as it completes an emotionally balanced Grand Water Trine on **June 7**, bringing your desires into the mix.

Love may be in the air, but it's not all fun and games when the restless Gemini New Moon on **June 8** stirs up trouble in your 8th House of Intimacy. Your hopes for a happier future—one that offers the excitement of adventure and the security of love—grow stronger as the Sun enters evocative Cancer and your 9th House of Big Ideas on **June 21**, marking the Summer Solstice. The methodical Capricorn Full Moon on **June 23** illuminates your 3rd House of Immediate Environment, pulling your thoughts back to the serious matters at hand. However, the month finishes on an optimistic note as joyful Jupiter shifts into your 9th House on **June 25**, followed by the Sun's reactivation of the wonderful Grand Water Trine with practical Saturn and magical Neptune on the **26th**.

> **KEEP IN MIND THIS MONTH**
>
> *Don't worry that an awesome experience won't last; enjoy what you have in the moment. Paradoxically, letting go of control helps you sustain the good times.*

KEY DATES

JUNE 1–3 ★ *visualize success*

Call on your persistence and ingenuity when the Sun in your 8th House of Shared Resources forces you to compromise as it aspects unwavering Pluto and unruly Uranus on **June 1**. Fortunately, your intuition is on point with cerebral Mercury perched in instinctive Cancer and your 9th House of Future Vision. Imagination and common sense align as Mercury trines visionary Neptune and systematic Saturn on **June 3**. If you're willing to put in hard work to reach your goals, your unflappable determination will all but ensure success.

SUPER NOVA DAYS
JUNE 7–8 ★ *tread lightly*
A self-sufficient Grand Water Trine among delicious Venus, dreamy Neptune, and dependable Saturn on **June 7** convinces you that manifesting your visions is easy. But your plans are challenged as outspoken Mercury opposes ominous Pluto in your 3rd House of Communication. Being honest is important, but so is being kind, because your words could turn cruel if you don't manage your anger. An electric Mercury-Uranus square on **June 8** increases your chances of saying something you might later regret. Although the clever Gemini New Moon on the **8th** should help you start something fresh, difficult aspects from Mars to Neptune and Saturn on **June 7–8** make it tough to know what to do.

JUNE 11–12 ★ *dangerous liaisons*
Your intrinsic taste for the exotic and for adventuring is alive and kicking when Pluto, the planet of extremes, opposes provocative Venus in your 9th House of Faraway Places on **June 11**. Take time out to cool off or you might push the wrong buttons in a relationship, creating conflict with family members, neighbors, or a lover. You struggle to control your desires as a hyperactive Venus-Uranus square on the **12th** awakens an unconventional attraction. Step outside your comfort zone and take an emotional risk to reenergize a relationship or start a new one if you're single, but remember that this thrilling energy tends to produce short-lived results.

JUNE 23–26 ★ *an ounce of prevention*
The judgmental Capricorn Full Moon on **June 23** requires that you temper your emotions with a bit of practical reality. However, hopeful Jupiter's shift into your 9th House of Big Ideas on **June 25** inspires you to dream about the future. Thankfully, you can rely on your instincts as the Sun in self-protective Cancer trines solid Saturn and psychic Neptune on **June 26**. Just make sure that you don't skip over any important details because trickster Mercury's retrograde turn can unravel hastily made plans.

JULY

IN YOUR ELEMENT

Once you make up your mind, you can become so fiercely focused on your goal that your unwavering determination might seem obsessive to others. Fortunately, your intensity could pay off this month by giving you the drive to turn your idealistic dreams into reality. In return, you must be willing to patiently wait for your labor to bear fruit. Although your heightened sense of urgency leaves you frustrated, avoid risky behavior on **July 4** when the Sun squares thrill-seeking Uranus. Mischievous Mercury is retrograde in your 9th House of Big Ideas until **July 20**, thwarting forward movement, bringing unexpected delays, and revealing where your plans still need work. Saturn's direct turn on **July 8** eases the resistance to your progress, but it takes time for this slow-moving planet to gain momentum. The caring Cancer New Moon, also on the **8th**, falls in your 9th House of Higher Truth, urging you to water the seeds of your beliefs and gently nurture them as they grow. When restless Mars enters tenacious Cancer and your 9th House on **July 13**, you redouble your efforts toward realizing your goals.

An emotionally grounding Grand Water Trine on **July 17–19** magically blends the energies of promising Jupiter, strategic Saturn, and intuitive Neptune, enabling you to harness your creativity as you continue to pursue your dreams. The combination of brainy Mercury turning direct and Mars reactivating the grand trine on **July 20–22** rewards your persistence. When the Sun's shift into showy Leo and your 10th House of Career opposes the futuristic Aquarius Full Moon on the **22nd** in your 4th House of Home and Family, however, you must choose between your professional and personal lifes.

> **KEEP IN MIND THIS MONTH**
>
> *Although you might feel as if your efforts are not paying off, you're on your way to success. Don't stop now; observable results may take time to manifest.*

KEY DATES

JULY 1–5 ★ *embrace the unknown*

The month gets off to a difficult start as needy Venus in your 10th House of Career runs into a tough square to stingy Saturn on **July 1**; you may feel rejected if you think you're not being heard. Resentful Pluto's opposition to the Sun in your 9th House of Beliefs indicates additional friction, potentially sending you into a tailspin if you begin to doubt yourself. Additionally, a misleading Venus-Neptune alignment increases your current uncertainty. The Sun's dynamic square to spontaneous Uranus in your 6th House of Work on **July 4** provokes you to play your cards prematurely, reducing your chances of success. Challenging aspects from Venus to Mars and Pluto on **July 5** can tempt you to give up, believing that your efforts have been for naught. However, these stressful days can empower you to turn lead into gold if you process your intense feelings. Don't let your need for immediate gratification pull you off course and jeopardize your long-term goals.

JULY 12–13 ★ *what a day for a daydream*

You can get yourself into trouble now by believing that your fantasies are real. A surreal Sun-Neptune alignment on **July 12** can ramp up your creativity, and a self-indulgent Venus-Jupiter aspect on **July 13** makes it nearly impossible to know when to stop. Even Mars's shift into hesitant Cancer and your 9th House of Adventure on the **13th** encourages you to plan a getaway rather than actually going somewhere.

SUPER NOVA DAYS
JULY 17–22 ★ *ready, set, go!*

You'll feel the equilibrium generated on **July 17–19** by Jupiter, Saturn, and Neptune as they form mutual trines. Still, the big news is that mobile Mercury turns direct on **July 20**, releasing you from a three-week holding pattern and giving you the green light to go ahead on a big project. Although it may take a few days for you to feel the effects of Mercury's forward movement in your 9th House of Future Vision, fearless Mars gives you the courage to push ahead as he trines inspirational Neptune and steadfast Saturn. A Mars-Jupiter conjunction, along with the intelligent Aquarius Full Moon, on **July 22** amplifies your enthusiasm, making you feel as if you can accomplish anything now.

JULY 27–31 ★ *stand up for your rights*

A tug-of-war between macho Mars and tough-guy Pluto on **July 27** agitates a conflict between you and someone who is opposing your plan. The confining Sun-Saturn square makes it difficult to get your way. Fortunately, a cunning Venus-Pluto trine on **July 30** uncovers hidden resources, leading you to take radical action on **July 31** when Mars squares progressive Uranus.

AUGUST

THE GREAT ESCAPE

You're inspired to get ahead professionally this month and poised to seize the opportunity whenever it arrives. The charismatic Leo Sun visits your 10th House of Career until **August 22** and is followed there by expressive Mercury on **August 8-23**. The creative Leo New Moon on **August 6** harmoniously trines innovative Uranus in your 6th House of Work, provoking you to suddenly initiate action on your latest project. A final boost of ambition this month comes from go-getter Mars on **August 27** as he enters proud Leo and your professional 10th House. The possibilities ahead are very exciting, yet you also have some feelings of trepidation— you don't like advancing too fast without knowing exactly where you're going.

Your fears about the future may be exacerbated by giant Jupiter journeying through your 9th House of Big Ideas, turning even the smallest task into a grandiose plan for world domination. One part of you realizes that it's best to proceed with caution, but another part cannot resist the temptation to make your mark professionally. Jupiter's opposition to uncompromising Pluto on **August 7** drives you to reach for power and success, but also may unleash a backlash of resistance. The individualistic Aquarius Full Moon on **August 20** brightens your 4th House of Security, reminding you that building a healthy foundation at home is as important as worldly success. However, Jupiter's disruptive square to rebellious Uranus in your 6th House of Routine on **August 21** leads you to act impulsively in your pursuit of freedom. Cosmic lightning strikes to wake you up, rattle your life with unexpected change, and bring thrilling new opportunities.

> **KEEP IN MIND THIS MONTH**
>
> *Even if your plans are up in the air, the future is brighter than you think. Stay open to change and you'll go places you never dreamed of.*

KEY DATES

SUPER NOVA DAYS
AUGUST 4-7 ★ *reckless abandon*

The Sun's superconductive trine to electrifying Uranus on **August 4** lights up your mind with exciting ideas and original solutions to existing problems. This thrilling aspect is reactivated on **August 6** when the audacious Leo New Moon in your public 10th House acts like a lightning rod that attracts an unexpected event or encourages radical behavior at work. You may feel like a skilled surfer, riding an enormous wave of ambition as opportunistic Jupiter opposes powerful Pluto on **August 7**. Instead of seeking attention by showing off, control your ego and just do your job to the best of your ability. Success can be yours if you don't become arrogant or expect everything to just fall your way.

AUGUST 11–14 ★ *break on through to the other side*
You may have to hold your tongue on **August 11** when talkative Mercury in dramatic Leo runs into a tough square to authoritative Saturn. You might tell your boss about a plan you've been developing, only to learn what's wrong with your idea. But don't dig in your heels; this is an opportunity to improve what you've already started by incorporating the criticism you receive into your strategy. Nevertheless, an irritating Mercury-Pluto quincunx on **August 13** indicates that a power struggle could ensue if you exert too much control. Thankfully, Mercury smoothly trines ingenious Uranus on the **14th**, stimulating your nervous system, provoking witty repartee, and increasing the speed of change.

AUGUST 20–22 ★ *bundle of nerves*
You might long for the peace of quieter days if the intellectual Aquarius Full Moon's erratic energy on **August 20** has you running around like a hamster on a spinning wheel. The Moon's opposition to high-strung Mercury makes it difficult to stop your thoughts. Fortunately, you could receive an epiphany that opens up an entirely new approach to a current problem when philosophical Jupiter squares radical Uranus on **August 21**. But you still have details to iron out, and Mercury's challenging aspects to Jupiter and Uranus on the **22nd** act like several cups of coffee, speeding up your mental processing.

AUGUST 26–30 ★ *all's well that ends well*
You're feeling unusual desires that may temporarily turn your life upside down thanks to unstable sextiles from Venus in your 12th House of Destiny to wild Uranus on **August 26** and to indulgent Jupiter on the **27th**. Relationships are further confused by a fuzzy Sun-Neptune opposition on the **26th**. Thankfully, you'll find decisive action easier once assertive Mars enters bold Leo and your public 10th House on **August 27**. Life finally begins to settle down when Mercury and the Sun each form stabilizing sextiles to Saturn on **August 27–30**.

SEPTEMBER

BE TRUE TO YOURSELF

You're focusing on the future as this month begins, because the Sun and Mercury the Messenger are in your 11th House of Long-Term Goals. The meticulous Virgo New Moon on **September 5** lands in your 11th House, reinforcing your need to plan ahead, and its cooperative sextile to optimistic Jupiter in your 9th House of Big Ideas expands your horizons and opens your mind to a wide array of possibilities. Everything seems to fall into place when sweet Venus enters your passionate sign on **September 11**, increasing your charm and sociability. However, solemn Saturn joins the karmic North Node of the Moon as it moves through incisive Scorpio on **September 17**, challenging you to eliminate some aspect of your past to make room for what's next. Venus joins the North Node and Saturn on **September 18**, delaying gratification and indicating that working toward meaningful goals is more important now than feeling good in the moment.

The psychic Pisces Full Moon on **September 19** shines in your 5th House of Self-Expression, invigorating your dreams and gently reminding you that logic will only take you so far. You are driven by your ambitions and have a deep reserve of energy, so you can work diligently to reach your destination when steady Saturn and transformative Pluto align in a supportive sextile on **September 21**. The Autumn Equinox on **September 22** is marked by the Sun's shift into Libra and your 12th House of Soul Consciousness, prompting you to pursue a more metaphysical path. Use this time to balance the mundane circumstances of your life with your ongoing search for spiritual purpose and meaning.

KEEP IN MIND THIS MONTH

Delays may test your patience, but they don't spell failure. It's worth waiting for the things that matter most.

KEY DATES

SEPTEMBER 1–5 ★ *take one for the team*

You feel a deep sense of camaraderie on **September 1** when profound Pluto aligns with the Sun in your 11th House of Friends and Wishes. But your social life can undermine your work as contentious Mars in your 10th House of Career forms difficult aspects with cranky Mercury and spacey Neptune on the **2nd**. Asserting your individuality creates more problems on the **3rd**, when the Sun quincunxes irrepressible Uranus in your 6th House of Employment. Thankfully, you can get back on course by eliminating unnecessary activities and refocusing your intentions on **September 5**, when the exacting Virgo New Moon is supported by generous Jupiter.

SEPTEMBER 9–11 ★ *soldier of love*

Your path to success is blocked by a frustrating square from anxious Mars in your 10th House of Profession to repressive Saturn in your 1st House of Self on **September 9**. Fortunately, you gain clarity about what you want when Venus, the planet of desire, enters enigmatic Scorpio and your 1st House on **September 11**, increasing your magnetism, deepening your feelings, and complicating your love life. Nevertheless, you can be your own worst enemy when warrior Mars rubs unforgiving Pluto the wrong way. Instead of succumbing to fear by fighting for your survival, change the game by transforming competition into cooperation. Everyone wins when you're playing on the same team.

SUPER NOVA DAYS
SEPTEMBER 17–19 ★ *honorable intentions*

A triple conjunction of accountable Venus, responsible Saturn, and the soulful Lunar North Node in your passionate sign on **September 17–18** reinforces your self-discipline and empowers you to say no to anything that doesn't further your cause. What other people think isn't important when gossipy Mercury sextiles action-hero Mars on the **17th**, enabling you to authentically walk your talk. But don't get enamored with the sound of your own voice as chatty Mercury squares overblown Jupiter on **September 19**. This expansive aspect, encouraged by a nebulous Pisces Full Moon, prompts you to lose focus unless you keep reminding yourself that you're on a critical mission.

SEPTEMBER 26–29 ★ *count your blessings*

Lovely Venus trines lucky Jupiter on **September 26**, driving the dark clouds from your sky. Don't pass up this delightful opportunity to enjoy a bit of pleasure or daydream about the better days ahead. A high-spirited Venus-Mars square on the **28th** can spur a lovers' quarrel, but also offers a sweet resolution to the tension. Your bigger-than-life fantasies are fueled by an idealistic Jupiter-Neptune alignment. However, Mercury's shift into pointed Scorpio on the **29th** can return you to reality—just in time to handle an important personal matter.

OCTOBER

HIDE AND SEEK

You long to work behind the scenes and withdraw from social activities this month with the Sun in your 12th House of Privacy until **October 23**. The peace-seeking Libra New Moon on **October 4** reinforces your need to retreat by stimulating your reclusive 12th House. But you might not be able to don your invisibility cloak quite yet with energetic Mars remaining in your 10th House of Career until **October 15**. Nevertheless, you aren't necessarily happy about being in the public eye or having to defend your unpopular position when Mars forms uncomfortable aspects with secretive Pluto and unorthodox Uranus on **October 5–7**. In fact, you may be frustrated with the pace of your progress as methodical Saturn in your determined sign forms an anxious quincunx to erratic Uranus in your 6th House of Work on **October 5**. Your patience is running low, for this is the third and final recurrence of this aspect in a series that began on **November 15, 2012**, and returned on **April 12**. If you aren't seeing results, you may be tempted to try something risky or just throw up your hands and walk away.

Your desire for material comfort inspires you to seek ways to earn more money when luxury-loving Venus shifts into carefree Sagittarius and your 2nd House of Finances on **October 7**. Mars enters timid Virgo and your 11th House of Long-Term Goals on **October 15**, extending your longing further into the future. Sudden changes at work are prompted by the brash Aries Lunar Eclipse on **October 18** that rattles your 6th House of Daily Routines. Contemplative Mercury reinforces your need to journey inward when it retrogrades in shadowy Scorpio on **October 21–November 10**.

> **KEEP IN MIND THIS MONTH**
>
> *Spending time on spiritual pursuits allows you to reconnect with your inner world and is an excellent way to recharge your emotional batteries.*

KEY DATES

OCTOBER 1–4 ★ *question authority*

Your creative energies are running strong on **October 1** as verbal Mercury in your evocative sign forms a fluid trine with whimsical Neptune in your 5th House of Self-Expression. But the Sun's hard square to suspicious Pluto in your 3rd House of Information makes things uncomfortable when someone challenges your integrity or doubts the veracity of your facts. Proving yourself to others is tricky business if the Sun in your private 12th House prevents them from understanding your motives. However, the Sun's dynamic opposition to shocking Uranus on **October 3** can instantaneously change the game by suddenly bringing everything out into the open. Although the diplomatic Libra New Moon on the **4th** is tensely aspected to Venus, Pluto, and Uranus, your controlled and unique approach to resolving conflict enables you to handle the current pressure with grace.

OCTOBER 8–12 ★ *lost in space*

Don't let your serious thinking turn into self-doubt when rational Mercury joins critical Saturn in obsessive Scorpio on **October 8**. A misleading Venus-Neptune square prompts you to give in to escapist behavior on the **10th**, because it's easier to chase an unrealistic dream than to deal with your current situation. On **October 12**, the Sun's square to outrageous Jupiter in your 9th House of Big Ideas tempts you to reach so far that you lose your center of gravity. Nevertheless, recognizing your limits can prevent trouble before it happens.

OCTOBER 18–21 ★ *fools rush in*

You look for ways to eliminate a bad habit or add a healthy one when an enterprising Aries Full Moon Eclipse on **October 18** energizes your 6th House of Self-Improvement. But impulsive behavior won't have the positive effects you seek, because a confusing Mars-Neptune opposition on the **19th** may disconnect your actions from your intentions. Additionally, Mercury's backward turn on the **21st** is another indicator that hasty decisions can lead you astray.

SUPER NOVA DAYS
OCTOBER 29–31 ★ *learning curve*

If you didn't learn your lesson when curious Mercury connected with karmic Saturn on **October 8**, you have another chance as it retrogrades over the ringed planet on **October 29**. This time, however, you should be able to get to the core of the matter without much trouble. Take decisive action that moves you toward your goals on **October 31** as incorrigible Mars in your futuristic 11th House forms a powerful trine with masterful Pluto. Although you may feel invincible with your two key planets working together so harmoniously, an awkward Mars-Uranus quincunx makes it difficult to integrate your dreams into your daily life. Be patient; your lessons aren't quite complete yet.

NOVEMBER

A FORCE OF NATURE

You're the center of attention this month with the radiant Sun shining in your sign until **November 21**. Nevertheless, being in the spotlight may feel like a burden because stern Saturn's long-term visit to loyal Scorpio insists that you take your responsibilities seriously, especially if others are observing and even judging you. The fourth of seven powerful squares between unstable Uranus and relentless Pluto on **November 1** indicates a quickening of the changes that began to unfold last summer and continue to transform the daily rhythms of your life throughout the month. You're in a contemplative period with thoughtful Mercury retrograding in ruminating Scorpio and your 1st House of Personality until **November 10**, then remaining in your sign throughout the month.

Everyone is watching you as the Scorpio Solar Eclipse on **November 3** intensifies your feelings and tempts you to withdraw because it's difficult to maintain your composure. Although retreating might sound like a sensible strategy, there's no reason to step back from your power just to avoid making others uncomfortable. You may judge yourself harshly or doubt your worthiness to act with authority, but the Sun-Saturn conjunction on **November 6** and the Mercury-Saturn conjunction on **November 25** give you more impact on others than you realize. The steady Taurus Full Moon on **November 17** brightens your 7th House of Partnerships, yet its challenging alignments with vulnerable Venus and the unstable Uranus-Pluto square increase your desire for relationship security without necessarily bringing satisfaction. The Sun's shift into inspirational Sagittarius on **November 21** offers the hope of easier days ahead, and its trine to futuristic Uranus on **November 30** reaffirms your optimism.

> **KEEP IN MIND THIS MONTH**
>
> *Trust your intuition, even if the answers you receive are not what you expect. There's more going on than meets the eye.*

KEY DATES

SUPER NOVA DAYS
NOVEMBER 1–3 ★ *stranger than fiction*
Change crashes into your life with unexpected fits and starts as the Sun and retrograde Mercury create annoying quincunxes with quirky Uranus

on **November 1**, fueled by the volcanic Uranus-Pluto square that continues its disruptive ways. Fortunately, friends and co-workers offer you support when Mars in your 11th House of Social Networking picks up on harmonizing aspects from the Sun, Mercury, and Pluto, enabling you to integrate newly acquired information and flow with the shifting tides. The intensity of your willpower is like a high-powered laser on **November 3** when the concentrated Scorpio New Moon Eclipse cuts through the noise, unveiling a fresh perspective and resetting the rules of the game. Act on your truth, knowing that what you do now will have an enduring impact over the weeks ahead.

NOVEMBER 9-12 ★ *window of opportunity*
Although your life is full of complications, you're blessed with a harmonious sextile from competent Mars to taskmaster Saturn in your 1st House of Self on **November 9**. Don't panic over how much work you have to do; break down complex jobs into manageable tasks, prioritize them by importance, and then get busy. Mercury's direct turn in your sign on the **10th** restarts stalled conversations if misunderstandings have recently slowed your progress. The long hours you put in all but ensure success, but the power of positive thinking allows you to take each action a bit further. Visualize the ideal outcome, for the willful Sun's superconductive trine to exuberant Jupiter on **November 12** can help make your dreams come true.

NOVEMBER 14-17 ★ *double trouble*
Seductive Venus stirs up unusual desires on **November 14** by squaring unconventional Uranus and intensifies your penchant for brutal honesty by conjoining perceptive Pluto in your 3rd House of Communication on the **15th**. Additionally, the Sun aggravates the dynamic Uranus-Pluto square by creating stressful aspects to both planets on the **16th**, adding to your current frustration over how a touchy situation is unfolding in your immediate environment. Thankfully, the bucolic Taurus Full Moon on the **17th** reminds you to put your current worries into perspective by focusing on one thing at a time.

NOVEMBER 27-30 ★ *into the wild blue yonder*
On **November 27-28**, fleet-footed Mercury comes to your rescue with a plan to have fun as it harmonizes with the happy-go-lucky Venus-Jupiter opposition. Thankfully, the excitement continues as a risk-taking Sun-Uranus trine on **November 30** encourages you to stretch your wings and fly confidently into the future.

DECEMBER

TAKE THE HIGH ROAD

The decisions you make this month concerning your long-term goals will impact your future in ways you cannot yet imagine. The forward-looking Sagittarius New Moon on **December 2** highlights your 2nd House of Income, emphasizing your need for material security. However, the New Moon's trine to independent Uranus in your 6th House of Work urges you to escape from the restraints of a job that's not aligned with your inner purpose. Although logical Mercury's move into your financial 2nd House on **December 4** is good for money management, active Mars shifts into your 12th House of Soul Consciousness on **December 7** to remind you that your spiritual journey is just as important as mundane matters.

You can make steady progress toward your goals on **December 12**, when propitious Jupiter in your 9th House of Big Ideas forms a fluid trine with realistic Saturn in your sign. The inquisitive Gemini Full Moon on **December 17** illuminates your 8th House of Shared Resources, potentially giving rise to a disagreement over joint property. But an expansive Jupiter-Neptune alignment the same day shows you the conflict from a larger perspective so you can sidestep an avoidable confrontation. The Winter Solstice on **December 21**, and the Sun's shift into ambitious Capricorn, indicate that you still have plenty of work to do to reach your goals. Expect to be busy right up until the end of the year because the Sun, Mercury, and Mars form challenging aspects with Uranus and Pluto on **December 29–31**. Although the holidays may not be as restful as you wish, at least you can still accomplish a lot if you are flexible enough to adapt to a few surprises along the way.

> **KEEP IN MIND THIS MONTH**
>
> *Sure, you need enough money to cover your basic requirements. But there's more to life than worldly success. Balance your professional ambitions with a spiritual practice that resonates with your soul.*

KEY DATES

DECEMBER 2–3 ★ *the importance of being earnest*

You're ready to expand your financial horizons when the opinionated Sagittarius New Moon on **December 2** occurs in your 2nd House of Self-Worth. But making money isn't the only thing that's important now, so consider setting aside your previous plans in order to stay true to your personal values. An easy Mercury-Mars sextile on the **3rd** empowers you to say what's on your mind and then practice what you preach.

DECEMBER 10–14 ★ *nothing ventured, nothing gained*

Your judgment may be off on **December 10** as the cavalier Sagittarius Sun creates a crunchy quincunx with pompous Jupiter in your 9th House of Future Vision. It can be frustrating when your goals are further away than they appear, but an ingenious Mercury-Uranus trine graces you with brilliant solutions to your current problems. Thankfully, a harmonious trine from Jupiter to reliable Saturn in resourceful Scorpio on **December 12** indicates that your hard work will pay off. However, achieving success may take more time than you realize, because this stabilizing aspect is the second in a series of three that began on **July 17** and doesn't finish until **May 24, 2014**.

DECEMBER 21 ★ *listen to your heart*

The Sun slips into traditional Capricorn and your 3rd House of Immediate Environment to take your attention off the future and bring it back to the here and now. However, romantic Venus turns retrograde today in your 3rd House, turning your desires inward and prompting you to review events of the recent past as you search for stability in love.

DECEMBER 24–27 ★ *simple twist of fate*

You want to discuss practical issues on **December 24** when communicative Mercury enters no-nonsense Capricorn. But visions of sugarplum fairies pull you into a delicious dreamland as the Sun sextiles imaginative Neptune. The tug-of-war between fantasy and reality reaches a crescendo when reckless Mars in your 12th House of Escapism opposes irreverent Uranus in your 6th House of Details on **December 25**.

SUPER NOVA DAYS
DECEMBER 29–31 ★ *give peace a chance*

Forget about figuring out what's going to happen next when thrilling Uranus in your 6th House of Daily Routine squares trickster Mercury and the Sun on **December 29–30**. Your interactions with others can get very tense when angry Mars squares ruthless Pluto on the **30th**. Mercury hooks up with Pluto on **December 31**, charging your words with excessive emotion. If you're locked in a power struggle with someone, retreat in the name of love. It's better to be flexible than to win the battle and lose your happiness.

SAGITTARIUS

NOVEMBER 22–DECEMBER 21

SAGITTARIUS

2012 SUMMARY

This is a year of progress, and what you accomplish during the first half can prepare you for the important people who enter your life during the second. It's crucial to recognize what's holding you back, manage your frustration, and keep your eyes on the distant prize, rather than allowing yourself to become discouraged if success takes longer than expected. Instead of pretending that you have all the answers, allow your openness to learning attract someone who shows you how to go beyond whatever limitations you previously accepted.

AUGUST—*big picture show*
Be patient with yourself. Coming up with new ways to add fun and excitement to your life is easier than turning them into reality.

SEPTEMBER—*no easy escape*
Change is inevitable—but it doesn't have to happen right away. Explore ways to reinvent yourself over time.

OCTOBER—*in the zone*
Even if others think they know what you're doing, you have more going on than they realize. There's nothing wrong with keeping some of your plans to yourself.

NOVEMBER—*good things come to those who wait*
Although you picture yourself as the overconfident hare, you'll be much more successful in the long run if you act like the slow-moving but obstinate tortoise.

DECEMBER—*home for the holidays*
As important as others are to you, if you don't take care of your own needs first then you won't have much to give anyone else.

2012 CALENDAR

AUGUST

__WED 1–SAT 4__ ★ Stick to the facts and choose your words carefully

__TUE 14–FRI 17__ ★ **SUPER NOVA DAYS** You receive mixed messages from friends

__MON 20–FRI 24__ ★ Avoid the distractions of idle fantasies

__WED 29–FRI 31__ ★ Be quiet and listen to your inner voice

SEPTEMBER

__MON 3–WED 5__ ★ Watch your temper while making your case

__FRI 7–MON 10__ ★ You can reach your goals if you practice self-discipline

__THU 13–SUN 16__ ★ Let everyone know what you want

__THU 20–SAT 22__ ★ Seek more balance in your life

__TUE 25–SAT 29__ ★ **SUPER NOVA DAYS** Avoid reckless behavior

OCTOBER

__WED 3–FRI 5__ ★ The spotlight of recognition shines brightly on you

__TUE 9–WED 10__ ★ Your intuition won't lead you astray now

__MON 15–TUE 16__ ★ **SUPER NOVA DAYS** You're all fired up

__THU 25__ ★ Confront the truth

__SUN 28–MON 29__ ★ You could exhaust yourself if you don't pay attention

NOVEMBER

__THU 1–SUN 4__ ★ Obligations require you to work more than you wish

__TUE 6–FRI 9__ ★ Your optimism about a current relationship is contagious

__TUE 13–THU 15__ ★ Feed your soul and not just your need for adventure

__FRI 23–SAT 24__ ★ A bit of patience pays off

__TUE 27–THU 29__ ★ **SUPER NOVA DAYS** Transform fear into love

DECEMBER

__SAT 1–SUN 2__ ★ You're restless without knowing why

__MON 10–FRI 14__ ★ **SUPER NOVA DAYS** Put your enthusiasm and joy into words

__TUE 25–WED 26__ ★ Place your long-term goals into proper perspective

__FRI 28–MON 31__ ★ Make a bold statement of your individuality

SAGITTARIUS OVERVIEW

You'll enjoy many opportunities to go public with your plans and make connections this year. Your optimistic ruling planet, Jupiter, is in versatile Gemini and your 7th House of Partners until June 25, empowering you to enhance your image, launch new projects, and seek out advantageous business contacts. **Your willingness to adapt to a wide variety of situations opens doors that are closed to less flexible individuals.** However, it's tempting to accept others too quickly when hopeful Jupiter in sometimes superficial Gemini inhibits you from seeing past the surface to recognize their subtle strengths and weaknesses. People may find you attractive for less-than-substantial reasons as well, reminding you that confidence easily gained can be lost just as readily. While clever ideas and instant chemistry can point the way to meaningful alliances, a deeper analysis of your needs and others' assets is a key to turning these potentially beneficial unions into reality.

It's time to take your relationships to the next level or admit failure on June 25, when Jupiter enters nurturing Cancer and your 8th House of Intimacy. This yearlong transit opens emotional channels that are comforting when you trust the one you're with, but can feel suffocating when your partner is too needy. Nevertheless, if abstractions and big ideas don't drown out your emotional instincts, the benefits from your relationships may be greater than ever. **Exploring feelings that you might not be able to explain can make the difference between your fulfillment and endless frustration.** Saturn, the planet of hard reality, is in watery Scorpio, where it's trawling for buried desires and doubts in your 12th House of Soul Consciousness. This demanding planet is telling you to look into your dark closet of fear. Facing your limits directly can release their grip on your psyche, which has kept you from reaching your full potential.

On July 17, visionary Jupiter forms harmonious aspects with practical Saturn and imaginative Neptune. This Grand Water Trine marks a magical moment when you can reach a perfect balance between the ideal and the real, placing you on track to finding more inspiration in your public life. **Success is more likely if you contribute to organizations that serve others or pursue a career aligned with your highest hopes.** The Jupiter-Saturn trine repeats on December 12, but you may not reach the top of the mountain until the final occurrence on May 24, 2014. Nevertheless, your good judgment and strong strategic sense are pointing you in the right direction. There's no need to advertise your plans prematurely, as the life-changing alchemy of this Grand Water Trine is better nourished by your own inner voice than by the input of others. Trusting your instincts is essential, even if they betray you at times, because learning to listen to yourself is the most valuable lesson of the year.

PLAYING THE FIELD

Relationships rock with boisterous Jupiter starting the year in your 7th House of Partners and finishing it in your 8th House of Deep Sharing. It's nearly impossible to avoid flirtations with a potential lover or business associate even if you're already in a committed partnership. Promises can be made without conviction with irreverent Uranus in your 5th House of Romance, stirring restless feelings and increasing your taste for extreme experiences. You grow more cautious with Jupiter's shift into protective Cancer and your intimate 8th House on June 25. However, the Sun's smooth trines to realistic Saturn and dreamy Neptune on June 26 draw you out of your shell and enable you to successfully pursue a fantasy that might elude you at other times. The impulsive Aries Full Moon Eclipse on October 18 can pull the rug out from under a love affair. Your partner may suddenly not be available, or your own boredom might put an end to a playful but short-lived adventure. Knowing the difference between a fast fling and a lasting thing brings gain instead of pain.

CUT TO THE CHASE

Be discriminating about where you invest your time, money, and energy this year. Opportunities to change jobs, reach new customers, or make a public splash tempt you to scatter your resources. The pragmatic Virgo Full Moon shines in your 10th House of Career on February 25, exposing problems if you're spread too thin. Working with more conservative colleagues who are reliable—even if they're less than passionate—provides a healthy balance to your natural enthusiasm. On September 5, the efficient Virgo New Moon in your professional 10th House is favorably aligned with Jupiter, allowing you to recognize how perfecting your skills in one specific area is more lucrative than trying to be a Jack (or Jane) of all trades.

WHEELER-DEALER

You gain a fresh perspective on finances with the ambitious Capricorn New Moon in your 2nd House of Resources on January 11. Valuable Venus's conjunction with Pluto and square to innovative Uranus during this lunation can open your eyes to unconventional ways to increase your income. Learning the art of the deal, when to gamble, or how to get the most money for your work is an ongoing story with profitable Pluto in your 2nd House of Self-Worth. You should seek good economic advice and, perhaps, forge a business partnership after opportunistic Jupiter enters your 8th House of Shared Resources on June 25. Leveraging your relationships by recognizing the needs of others and making connections among people who can help one another will earn you more than you'd get operating independently or working for an hourly wage. Just be cautious and double-check every detail when trickster Mercury is retrograde in your 8th House on June 26–July 20.

 RUN YOUR OWN RACE

Speedy Mars enters steady Taurus and your 6th House of Health on April 20, helping you settle into a regular routine of physical activity that won't wear you out. Avoid excessive workouts or burning the candle at both ends, especially with a pair of eclipses in May. A Solar Eclipse in Taurus on May 9 joins Mars in your 6th House, tempting you to push too hard. The Sagittarius Full Moon Eclipse on May 25 is square to squishy Neptune; this tense aspect with the planet of dissolution represents a lack of boundaries or self-control that can lead to fatigue and vulnerability. Staying within your limits instead of trying to keep up with others is key to your physical well-being this year.

 OUT WITH THE OLD

You continue to focus this year on acting with sensitivity to both your own needs and the needs of those with whom you live with compassionate Neptune in your 4th House of Home and Family. You may pick up mixed signals as Mercury's retrograde in your 4th House on February 23–March 17 dredges up old emotional issues while the psychic Pisces New Moon on March 11 prompts fresh ideas and spiritual interests. Artistic Venus and passionate Mars join with this lunation, inspiring more love and beauty in your household. However, it's best to clean up unfinished business before you start redecorating the place or invite someone to move in with you.

DUTY-FREE ZONE

Your hunger for travel and learning continues this year, but don't let someone talk you into taking a trip when the Leo Full Moon illuminates your 9th House of Faraway Places on January 26. Spontaneous Uranus's trine to the Moon can spur an exciting opportunity, yet a lunar square with constraining Saturn indicates difficulties that exceed your expectations. A better time to hit the road arrives on August 6, when thrill-seeking Uranus zaps the gallant Leo New Moon unencumbered by the restrictions of heavy-duty Saturn.

BURIED TREASURE

Your spiritual journeys take you down complex paths, because Saturn in emotionally intense Scorpio occupies your 12th House of Divinity all year. Facing fears can be a painful but productive way to remove obstacles from your life. The Scorpio New Moon Eclipse on November 3 could drive you to the depths of your soul, but a supportive sextile from Mars in skillful Virgo will show you the methods you can use to rebuild your faith from the ground up.

RICK & JEFF'S TIP FOR THE YEAR:
Follow Your Instincts

Your most important challenge this year is making the best choices in relationships. Many people may find you desirable, providing additional chances to socialize personally and professionally. Yet good might not be good enough if it keeps you from connecting with the person who can offer you so much more. Take the time to listen to your heart instead of allowing impulsive thinking to dictate your decisions.

JANUARY

UPHILL CLIMB

You're naturally a person of big ideas and adventurous experiences who is typically more into doing things than having things. But material concerns may weigh heavily on your mind this month with five planets passing through goal-oriented Capricorn and your 2nd House of Income. January begins with the willful Sun, brainy Mercury, and obsessive Pluto in this economically oriented part of your chart. Resourceful Venus joins them on **January 8** to reward your persistence, patience, and careful execution of a plan. On **January 11**, the orderly Capricorn New Moon supplies practical energy that you can apply with a clear sense of purpose. If you can shift from a strategic big-picture view to a perspective from down in the trenches where you're able to efficiently take care of business, you will overcome almost any obstacle. But if you're stuck in a dead-end job without an exciting vision of your future, spending time and money to learn the tools of another trade can turn your career in a desirable new direction.

It's time to take a break from your hard work when Mercury and the Sun fly into unconventional Aquarius and your 3rd House of Communication on **January 19**. New connections and original ideas bring more variety and excitement to your daily life. Interesting individuals are more likely to cross your path and inspire you with sparkling conversations. The travel bug may bite with the outgoing Leo Full Moon in your 9th House of Faraway Places on the **26th**, but Saturn's restrictive square might delay your takeoff. However, your ruling planet Jupiter's forward turn on the **30th** in your 7th House of Relationships attracts helpful allies and raises your public profile.

> ### KEEP IN MIND THIS MONTH
>
> *Establishing a steady pace of productivity and sticking to it may lack the excitement you crave, but the tangible results this produces are worth the sacrifice.*

KEY DATES

JANUARY 4–5 ★ *shifting into overdrive*

A high-octane trine between hyperactive Mars and exuberant Jupiter gets you moving physically and mentally on **January 4**. Your over-the-top enthusiasm, though, may motivate you to oversell or overreach. A tight-fisted Venus-Saturn semisquare is a reminder that limited resources or lack of support from others may constrain your efforts. Still, it's nearly impossible to narrow your focus as mental Mercury misaligns with a quincunx to Jupiter on the **5th**. You might try to skirt reality with flippant statements that are unlikely to accurately assess your situation. While stretching your mind reveals untapped potential, it's wise to do some serious research before you make any promises.

JANUARY 11 ★ *unnecessary distractions*

Your attention is scattered in several different directions when the commitment of today's earthy Capricorn New Moon is diffused by an awkward sesquisquare between the creative Sun and boundless Jupiter in breezy Gemini. While you find it useful to consider alternative paths to your goals, choose one and stick to it. If you find yourself entangled in exhausting explanations to people who don't understand what you're doing, it might be best to save your breath unless they're critical to your plan.

JANUARY 14 ★ *separation of work and play*

Good intentions aren't enough today when friendly Mercury and lovable Venus form difficult aspects with promising Jupiter. Minor matters grow out of proportion with your needs. Trying to charm someone (or being charmed by them) is more about entertainment and flattery than getting work done. Keep the value of your resources firmly in mind to avoid spending too much on discussions that lead nowhere. Having fun is fine as long as it doesn't get in the way of your higher priorities.

JANUARY 22 ★ *lucky charms*

You can think and speak with considerable skill today, contributing brilliantly to conversations. Quicksilver Mercury's favorable aspects to inventive Uranus and philosophical Jupiter make you an energetic and effective spokesperson for your beliefs. Keep all channels of communication open, since your positive perspective receives an additional boost if long-awaited news finally comes through.

SUPER NOVA DAYS
JANUARY 25–26 ★ *delusions of grandeur*

Your powers of persuasion are strong with an inspirational Sun-Jupiter trine on **January 25**. However, you must have all your facts in order since a demanding Mercury-Saturn square will reveal any flaws in your argument. The **26th** is complicated by the contrast between a playful Venus-Jupiter sesquisquare and a take-no-prisoners Mars-Pluto semisquare. Your mood could sour if your unrealistic expectations set you up for disappointment, yet delight will be yours when you can more carefully measure your desire.

FEBRUARY

Domestic matters take precedence this month with a parade of planets floating through your 4th House of Home and Family. On **February 1**, energetic Mars swims into sensitive Pisces and this part of your chart to stir up the emotional waters in your household. Long-lingering issues may surface to provoke conflict, yet this transit can also provide you the drive to turn your living space into a launching pad for long-term ambitions. Sweet Venus's entry into airy Aquarius on the **1st** provides a dash of objectivity and spurs collaboration in conversations with creative people. Communicative Mercury moves into mystical Pisces on **February 5**, enhancing your psychic powers. However, your hypersensitivity also gives you an extra layer of vulnerability. Mercury's retrograde turn in your introspective 4th House on the **23rd** brings up issues from the past to inspire your imagination or confuse you with uncertainty.

You're blessed with original thinking on **February 10**—a gift of the conceptual Aquarius New Moon in your 3rd House of Information. However, your unconventional visions of the future might discomfit others as a Venus-Saturn square on the **11th** evokes resistance from conservative individuals. The Sun's passage into Pisces on the **18th** supplies courage and compassion to deal with complicated emotions, but forgiveness is your key to applying them effectively. Obligations at work can reach a critical point on the **25th** when the perfectionist Virgo Full Moon lights up your 10th House of Career. A lunar square to limitless Jupiter in jittery Gemini could overwhelm you with millions of tiny tasks. Fortunately, the Moon's perceptive trine with purging Pluto requires you to eliminate unnecessary obligations to clarify your professional priorities.

> **KEEP IN MIND THIS MONTH**
>
> *The key to the happiness you seek is a sense of security. You can create this by attending to personal issues and working toward a more nurturing environment at home.*

KEY DATES

FEBRUARY 4 ★ *chasing unicorns*

You might feel like you're spinning in circles without getting much done as action-planet Mars joins mysterious Neptune. Pursuing illusions or playing the martyr is exhausting, so rein yourself in before you run out of gas. Still, this sensitive transit also helps you make a little magic at home by engaging in creative activities and showing tenderness to those you love.

SUPER NOVA DAYS

FEBRUARY 6–10 ★ *fasten your seat belt*

You enjoy new forms of pleasure on **February 6** with an adventurous Venus-Uranus sextile. An intuitive Mercury-Neptune conjunction helps you read between the lines, yet you risk being sloppy with facts or falling for someone's misleading story. A delicious Venus-Jupiter trine on the **7th** amplifies your social charms, attracts generous people, and brightens your day. This delightful mood may be shaken with a verbally aggressive Mercury-Mars conjunction on **February 8**. While this planetary pair can sharpen thinking and empower words, you might go to extremes when eloquent Mercury squares opinionated Jupiter on the **9th** and excitable Mars makes the same aspect on the **10th**. The Aquarius New Moon contributes to these powerful patterns by urging you to promote yourself with enthusiasm. Managing your energy effectively can enable you to be very productive, but letting it run freely could trigger conflicts.

FEBRUARY 15–16 ★ *efficiency expert*

You get a tight grip on your passion and apply it very effectively thanks to two favorable connections of dynamic Mars. A supportive sextile with surgical Pluto on **February 15** cuts through clutter, cleans up messes, and connects you with the core of an issue. A responsible Mars-Saturn on the **16th** is equally focused and highly productive. Anger can be converted into positive action and problems solved by behaving with patience and maturity.

FEBRUARY 21 ★ *sentimental journey*

You may be wistful about the past as the Sun joins Neptune in your 4th House of Roots. Idealizing your childhood or someone close to you lifts your spirits and inspires new aspirations even though this also can be an easy way to escape the reality of the here and now. Take some time off from your obligations to bask in the light of possibilities that, for the moment, might seem out of reach.

FEBRUARY 25–26 ★ *stick to the point*

You incline toward excess and overstating your beliefs at the best of times, Sagittarius—a tendency that's stoked on **February 25** by an overblown Sun-Jupiter square. However, even if you're off somewhere on cloud nine, a sharp-eyed Mercury-Mars conjunction on the **26th** motivates you to turn clever ideas into constructive action. Don't waste time getting caught up in petty arguments; they distract you from the real tasks at hand.

MARCH

HOME IS WHERE THE HEART IS

The fires of passion and creativity burn brightly in you this month. You can set the stage for the excitement by beautifying your residence or resolving family squabbles with the compassionate Pisces New Moon on **March 11**. This lunation in your 4th House of Roots conjuncts gracious Venus, inviting harmony into your home, healing old wounds, nourishing faith in yourself, and stimulating your imagination. It won't take you long to put your dreams into action, because irrepressible Mars rams into impatient Aries and your 5th House of Romance on the **12th**, provoking impulsive and sometimes reckless behavior. However, it's better to carefully test the waters than immediately plunge into a love affair or make a sudden business move. Logical Mercury's forward turn in your foundational 4th House on **March 17** gives you the information and healthy perspective you need to guide your actions more skillfully.

On **March 20** the Sun enters ardent Aries, marking the Spring Equinox, and adds fuel to your 5th House of Self-Expression. Amorous Venus follows the next day, further enhancing your ability to attract attention, entertain others, and display your creative gifts. Your desire for immediate satisfaction can provoke foolhardy actions in matters of the heart. This is a terrific time to enjoy yourself by reigniting the flame of love to revive a fading relationship or to pursue a new one. Just be careful about assuming that one night of bliss guarantees a lifetime of happiness. Downsizing your expectations ensures that the pleasure you receive won't be too costly. The partnership-oriented Libra Full Moon on the **27th** shines in your 11th House of Community, balancing your desire for pleasure with a willingness to honor what others need.

> **KEEP IN MIND THIS MONTH**
>
> *Making yourself more comfortable at home doesn't mean that you're lazy; instead, it gives you the confidence you need to be even more expressive and outgoing than ever.*

KEY DATES

MARCH 4 ★ *less is more*

Today you risk seeing people, experiences, and objects as more valuable than they are thanks to evaluative Venus's stressful square with excessive Jupiter. You may also be so optimistic that you overindulge in pleasurable activities. While it's good to stretch your social boundaries and broaden your tastes, be sure you also maintain your moral compass.

MARCH 7-9 ★ *step by step*
You're thinking solidly on **March 7**, when cerebral Mercury's favorable aspects with Saturn and Pluto deepen your perceptions, but you may not get the results you want if an unruly Mars-Saturn sesquisquare slows your progress. Incremental gains won't satisfy your need for speed, but will eventually take you where you want to go. You may throw patience out the window on the **9th** when a verbose Mercury-Jupiter square undercuts your capacity to focus on one subject at a time. It's tempting to overstate if you're enthusiastic about something, but careless speech could create expectations you cannot meet. More modest claims allow you to make your point and maintain credibility.

MARCH 16 ★ *buried treasure*
The Sun's sesquisquare with strict Saturn can evoke painful memories. You're not one to live in the past, yet self-doubt or delays caused by others could lead you to question your competence. However, if you step around your emotions, you can find answers in unexpected places. A creative quintile between artful Venus and insightful Pluto garners support from others and reveals assets that could save a wounded relationship or provide the resources needed to take care of business.

MARCH 22-23 ★ *lightning strikes*
An explosive Mars-Uranus conjunction in your 5th House of Fun and Games brings out your wild side on **March 22**. Innovation and spontaneity are strong, yet your need for freedom can trigger rebellious behavior. Going too far in what you say or do leads to disapproval as clumsy Jupiter forms an awkward quincunx with cynical Saturn on the **23rd**.

SUPER NOVA DAYS
MARCH 28-31 ★ *crazy love*
New pleasures and sudden eruptions of desire put you in strange situations on **March 28**, when sexy Venus, the heartfelt Sun, and reactive Uranus meet in your romantic 5th House. Although you're wise to experiment with your attitude and appearance, you might go to extreme measures with an overbearing Jupiter-Pluto quincunx on the **29th**. Venus's tense square with suspicious Pluto on the **31st** increases your sensitivity to manipulation and may force you to let go of a radical idea. Happily, Venus's favorable sextile with bountiful Jupiter should compensate you with other rewards.

APRIL

HIT THE GROUND RUNNING

You can practically count on finding new forms of fun and experiencing breakthroughs in creativity this month. The pioneering Aries New Moon falls in your 5th House of Self-Expression on **April 10**, offering fresh opportunities to demonstrate your talents and showcase your desirability. This Sun-Moon conjunction is joined by spicy Mars and sultry Venus, stimulating romantic impulses and flirtatious behavior. You're ready to take the lead in your personal life and in any professional situation that calls for putting on a good show. Fleet-footed Mercury blasts into uncontainable Aries and your 5th House of Spontaneity on the **13th**, sparking even more bright ideas and brash statements. The fun quotient in your life is definitely on the upswing, but making it last long enough to produce enduring results could be a major challenge for you. Living in the moment comes easily to your adventurous sign, but when excitement cools you struggle to maintain your interest.

The pace starts to change when sensual Venus enters stable Taurus and your 6th House of Employment on **April 15**. Slowing down to enjoy your work, instead of rushing to get things done, can improve your skills and earn you additional approval for your efforts. The Sun and Mars enter Taurus on the **19th** and **20th**, placing more emphasis on your job and increasing your commitment to excellence. Your persistent efforts at self-improvement are admirable, but a stubborn streak could make you less flexible about changing your methods. The emotional Scorpio Lunar Eclipse on **April 25** rattles your 12th House of Secrets, where it could expose an inconvenient truth. Saturn's conjunction to this Full Moon reminds you to redouble your efforts to work through your fears and self-limitations instead of taking the easy way out and settling for less.

> **KEEP IN MIND THIS MONTH**
>
> *Investing more of yourself in the activities that you enjoy ensures that they will continue to be significant sources of pleasure for many years to come.*

KEY DATES

APRIL 1 ★ *window of opportunity*

You can impress others easily today when the confident Aries Sun in your 5th House of Self-Expression forms a supportive sextile with lucky Jupiter in your 7th House of Others. It's an excellent time to make a sales pitch or initiate a professional relationship. Enrolling people in your plan works especially well if you can match your enthusiasm with your command of the facts.

APRIL 6–8 ★ *smoke and mirrors*
Your taste for fantasy could provide you with a magical day on **April 6**, when squishy semisquares from dreamy Neptune to the cosmic lovers, Venus and Mars, turn your imagination's volume up high. Still, you can roam so far from reality that you may have a hard time finding your way back. The urge to connect emotionally and physically intensifies when Venus joins Mars in your playful 5th House on the **7th**. It's all too easy to overlook someone's flaws and see him or her through rose-colored glasses. A Sun-Neptune semisquare on the **8th** underscores the likelihood that what you're seeing is not what you'll get.

APRIL 14–15 ★ *blessing in disguise*
A careless Venus-Jupiter semisquare on **April 14** lures you into believing a story that's either incomplete or not on the level. If this doesn't concern a serious issue, it could be more bothersome than problematic. However, you can quickly adjust to bad judgment when a brilliant Mercury-Jupiter quintile on the **15th** shows you how to fix mistakes and correct misunderstandings.

SUPER NOVA DAYS
APRIL 20–21 ★ *curb your enthusiasm*
The smartest way to use a bright idea is to test it before fully committing to it. An optimistic Sun-Jupiter semisquare and ingenious Mercury-Uranus conjunction on **April 20** lights up your mind with brainstorms of originality. But a tendency to act too quickly or say too much too soon can undermine your plan before it gets off the ground. You might feel like you can do anything on the **21st** when zealous Jupiter stresses superhero Mars. Fighting for your beliefs may seem like a noble endeavor, but passion alone doesn't prove that you're right. When the truth is on your side, you can present it in a calm, self-confident manner.

APRIL 28 ★ *no second chances*
You have little room for error today thanks to the Sun's opposition to demanding Saturn. Take your time with a difficult task and get it done correctly the first time. If you lack the skill to handle a particular job, let an expert show you how it's done.

MAY

GONE WITH THE WIND

Evaluating your contentment, or lack thereof, with personal and professional partners challenges you to step back from your daily distractions to take a longer range view of your relationships this month. The most significant astrological event is the Sagittarius Full Moon Eclipse on **May 25**, which falls in your 1st House of Personality. Every major decision is fraught with uncertainty, which is why adaptability is essential now. You try to lock into a steadier routine at work when the dependable Taurus New Moon on **May 9** activates your 6th House of Habits. Your desires for constancy and security are strong, yet this lunation is a Solar Eclipse that's more about altering patterns than holding on to them. Fortunately, your capacity to skillfully shift gears is supported by a slew of planets entering adaptable Gemini and your 7th House of Others. Sociable Venus starts the parade on **May 9**, followed by verbal Mercury on the **15th**, the willful Sun on the **20th**, and mobile Mars on the **31st**.

Making connections should come easily now, but being discriminating about who you share your time and energy with is critical. The long-lasting Uranus-Pluto square that began on **June 24, 2012**, and repeats on **May 20** emphasizes your 5th House of Play and can act like a lightning rod that attracts exciting people into your life. Fascinating individuals can be like shiny objects that grab your attention but have little real value. A career-shaping Jupiter-Saturn sesquisquare, also on the **20th**, reminds you to think strategically instead of overreacting to immediate events.

KEEP IN MIND THIS MONTH

You must prioritize your long-term goals to avoid those fleeting temptations that look good in the moment . . . but don't have the substance to fulfill your dreams.

KEY DATES

MAY 2 ★ *talk is cheap*

You're popping with bright ideas and enjoying lively conversations today while chatty Mercury forms an energetic semisquare with buoyant Jupiter. However, you run the risk of turning one small factoid into a bigger story than is necessary. Making mountains out of molehills isn't productive and could become rather costly. It's great to open your mind to new ideas as long as you don't compromise your ability to critically evaluate them.

MAY 7 ★ *no more drama*

A conjunction of argumentative Mercury and combative Mars triggers intense conversations. This contentious union occurs in resistant Taurus and your 6th House of Work and Service, which is likely to add more pressure on the job. Dealing with a stubborn person can be frustrating, especially when you're trying to learn something new or establish a different system. Try to focus on the task at hand instead of getting sidetracked by personal issues; it's a good way to reap the benefits of your shrewd competence without creating unnecessary conflict.

MAY 13–15 ★ *just say no*

An escapist Venus-Neptune square on **May 13** blurs your judgment, especially when you're projecting your fantasies onto someone else. This delicious feeling may not be rooted in reality—so enjoy the experience, but don't make any serious commitments. Besides, you may change your mind quickly as Mercury shifts from a tense aspect with jumpy Uranus on the **13th** to one with inscrutable Pluto on the **14th**. Flirtatious Venus in your 7th House of Relationships encounters delays and possible rejection with a quincunx to Saturn on the **15th**. Being choosier about your companions will eliminate individuals who wouldn't be desirable allies.

MAY 24 ★ *cocktail party chit-chat*

A sociable Mercury-Venus conjunction is likely to make you more captivating to others, enabling you to attract a charming person into your life. It's not difficult to find interesting things to talk about just avoid serious subjects. Luckily, you can enjoy some lighthearted play without worrying about long-term expectations.

SUPER NOVA DAYS
MAY 27–28 ★ *sweet as sugar*

Mercury's conjunction with magnanimous Jupiter gives greater impact to your words on **May 27**. You seem to have plenty of information to share without coming across as a know-it-all. Lovely Venus's conjunction with propitious Jupiter on the **28th** continues a positive people trend because you're able to gain appreciation from others and draw interesting individuals into your life. Be wary, though, of someone who chatters all the time and isn't very good at listening. The compliments you hear are flattering, yet they may be lacking in sincerity. Flirting and teasing are sweet pastimes now, but only have the staying power of cotton candy.

JUNE

RAISING THE STAKES

It's time to take relationships to the next level—or recognize that it may be best to let some go. June begins with the Sun in friendly Gemini and your 7th House of Partners, which enlivens personal and professional unions. However, complications could start to arise when amenable Venus shifts into sensitive Cancer and your 8th House of Deep Sharing on **June 2**. Financial and emotional rewards may grow, but you might need to compromise your independence and pay more attention to the needs of others. On **June 8**, the inquisitive Gemini New Moon in your 7th House invites entertaining people into your life. Bright ideas are sparked by flames of interest that can burn out as quickly as they begin, so don't make serious commitments without further investigation.

Relationships deepen when the Sun enters Cancer and your 8th House of Transformation on **June 21**, marking the Summer Solstice. Navigating murky emotional waters isn't your favorite activity, yet the vulnerability it can trigger opens hearts and strengthens alliances. Money matters may come to a head when the responsible Capricorn Full Moon shines in your 2nd House of Resources on **June 23**. Commit yourself to righting your economic ship and patiently cultivate your talents to set yourself on a firmer financial foundation. Saturn's stabilizing sextile to the Full Moon can help you uncover hidden assets and tame your spending habits. Joyful Jupiter's entry into caring Cancer on the **25th** is the beginning of a one-year journey through your 8th House that's likely to bring you the assistance of generous individuals who appreciate your abilities. You'll reconnect with potential supporters when Mercury the Messenger turns retrograde in your 8th House of Deep Sharing on **June 26**.

> ### KEEP IN MIND THIS MONTH
>
> *You're usually more comfortable giving than receiving, yet learning how to receive the love and approval of others is a more valuable lesson now.*

KEY DATES

JUNE 1 ★ *dancing in the dark*

Expect strange encounters when the Sun in your interactive 7th House forms an awkward quincunx with Pluto and a clever sextile with Uranus. The former evokes suspicion, secrecy, and power struggles, but its higher purpose is to purge unrealistic expectations in partnerships and to focus you on the essential work you have to do together. The latter is a free-and-easy aspect that lets bygones be bygones as you open yourself to new and unconventional ways to connect with inventive individuals.

JUNE 7-8 ★ *off the beaten track*

Macho Mars in your 7th House of Others attracts impatient individuals into your world. But don't rush into agreements with them on **June 7**, when a stressful square between unstoppable Mars and nebulous Neptune takes you on a wild goose chase that costs you time, energy, and credibility. Go ahead and enjoy an escape from reality with a playful partner, but beware spreading yourself too thin on the **8th** as the diverse distractions of the flighty Gemini New Moon pull you in several directions at once. Stern Saturn, though, forms a corrective quincunx with impetuous Mars that can impose harsh penalties for careless behavior.

SUPER NOVA DAYS
JUNE 17-19 ★ *learning to fly*

You're at your innovative best on **June 17** when you hook up with an open-minded individual to solve sticky problems or initiate creative activities. Mars forms a smart sextile with quirky Uranus in your 5th House of Self-Expression that can combine play and productivity. An instant attraction might be so exciting that you toss caution to the wind. The buoyancy you're feeling increases when the radiant Sun joins cheerful Jupiter in your 7th House of Partners on the **19th**. Your high hopes are probably justified, so go public with an idea, make a professional pitch, or pursue a personal relationship. Just remember that promises come easily—yet turning them into reality requires a concrete plan and consistent follow through.

JUNE 27-28 ★ *no rest for the weary*

You're dreaming of faraway places and distant lovers on **June 27**, when vivacious Venus strides into dramatic Leo and your 9th House of Travel. Paying attention to immediate obligations takes priority on the **28th** as reckless Mars is slowed by a stressful sesquisquare from authoritative Saturn. You may be held accountable for tasks that you've either ignored or not completed well enough. Don't let resentment waste your time and keep you from buckling down to meet your responsibilities.

JULY

THE JOURNEY WITHIN

This is a very significant month—but it's more about what's going on inside you than external events. On **July 17**, your philosophical ruling planet, Jupiter, forms a Grand Water Trine with serious Saturn and spiritual Neptune. This uncommon pattern touches the depths of your soul to provide insights into the most intimate areas of your life. Jupiter in your 8th House of Deep Sharing illuminates the heart of relationships and connects that awareness with your 12th House of Secrets and your 4th House of Home and Family. You may not be able to put what you're learning into words, but a profound sense of inner knowing can guide you to make wise decisions about your long-term goals. The moody Cancer New Moon in your 8th House on **July 8** squares surprising Uranus, spurring a sudden shift of feelings or circumstances in close emotional and professional partnerships. You must be more sensitive on the **13th**, when proactive Mars shifts into protective Cancer, if you hope to keep alliances on track.

You slowly begin to think more about collaborating with others with rational Mercury's forward turn in your 8th House on **July 20**, but the unconventional Aquarius Full Moon on the **22nd** is loaded with mixed messages. This lunation in your 3rd House of Information encourages you to be receptive to fresh ideas and new channels of communication. However, its square to restrictive Saturn provokes resistance that may complicate exchanges of information. Delays and inner doubts demand that you study the situation carefully and organize your thoughts before expressing them openly. Yet the Sun's entry into theatrical Leo and your 9th House of Big Ideas later in the day tempts you to jump the gun, which should be avoided at all costs.

> **KEEP IN MIND THIS MONTH**
>
> *Tuning in with your feelings may not produce immediate answers, but they will provide more valuable insights than counting on your rational mind alone.*

KEY DATES

JULY 1-4 ★ *look but don't leap*

It's easy to be grumpy on **July 1** with an opposition from possessive Pluto darkening the Sun with control issues while ominous Saturn inhibits pleasure with a square to needy Venus. Patiently weigh the costs and benefits of any partnership, and you'll make more responsible decisions. An electrifying Sun-Uranus square on the **4th**, though, provokes spontaneous reactions or attracts unreliable people. You may be tempted to radically alter the course of a relationship, but it's smarter to wait until things settle down before making your move.

JULY 9 ★ *listen up!*
Retrograde Mercury backs over the Sun in your 8th House of Intimacy and Transformation, providing a second chance to discuss delicate partnership issues. Although you may have very strong feelings, it's helpful to listen carefully to others instead of simply pushing your point of view. A real exchange can be difficult when intense emotions are involved, but avoid dramatic language if your intention is to resolve issues without inciting a meltdown.

JULY 13 ★ *the high cost of love*
You may play too hard, pay too much, or expect more from someone than he or she can deliver today when pleasure-seeking Venus in your 9th House of Adventure forms an overamped semisquare with indulgent Jupiter that can mar your judgment. Although you love to stretch your boundaries in search of big experiences, use a bit of self-restraint to avoid spending more love, money, or goodwill than you can afford.

SUPER NOVA DAYS
JULY 19–22 ★ *soft launch*
Your dreams seem more real when concrete Saturn trines illusory Neptune on **July 19**. The next day, dynamic Mars forms an emotional Grand Water Trine with Saturn and Neptune, motivating you to take decisive action. The enthusiastic Mars-Jupiter conjunction on **July 22** in defensive Cancer and your 8th House of Intimacy suggests that gaining the cooperation of a key partner could be challenging, but gently expressing your feelings should lead to success. The Sun enters brassy Leo and Venus slips into demure Virgo on the same day, mixing enthusiasm with caution. Starting a new project or planning a vacation with a loved one requires a mutual understanding if it's going to work.

JULY 27–28 ★ *labor of love*
You'll need hard work and dedication on **July 27** as a Mars-Pluto opposition and a Sun-Saturn square seem to offer limited return for maximum effort. If you can slow down to focus, though, you could see a sweet outcome when resourceful Venus forms a supportive sextile with benevolent Jupiter on the **28th**.

AUGUST

SEEDS OF CHANGE

The deep rumbling you may be feeling now is the beginning of a process that could radically alter your life by next spring. Visionary Jupiter in your 8th House of Deep Sharing makes the first in a series of three oppositions with transformational Pluto on **August 7** and the first of three squares with revolutionary Uranus on **August 21**. Pluto can provoke a power struggle or financial squeeze, while Uranus incites a desire to get away from it all. On the positive side, the intensity of these aspects motivates you to maximize your abilities and seek new sources of inspiration through creative activities with children or, perhaps, an unconventional love affair. The impact of these urges climaxes on **April 20, 2014**, when these transits are complete. The Leo New Moon on **August 6** falls in your 9th House of Higher Truth, opening your mind to a new direction in life with its harmonious trine to progressive Uranus. Temper an impulse to act too quickly; unexpected moves may not be well received by others, who need more time to understand your change of plans.

Intellectual Mercury's shift into proud Leo and your educational 9th House increases your thirst for learning and ramps up your powers of persuasion on **August 8**. Cooperative Venus moves into gracious Libra and your 11th House of Social Networking on the **16th** to stimulate your interest in community service and attract new friends. Practical issues take center stage when the Sun and Mercury enter hardworking Virgo and your 10th House of Career on **August 22** and **23**. Concentrating on immediate tasks and refining your skills could raise your status on the job, but a lack of focus reduces your effectiveness.

> **KEEP IN MIND THIS MONTH**
>
> *If you aspire to turn your life in a radical new direction, lay down a solid foundation with discipline and competence to create positive change.*

KEY DATES

AUGUST 4 ★ *the amazing race*

A fiery trine between the Sun in lively Leo and Uranus in audacious Aries stimulates your hunger for new experiences. You find yourself taking chances in pursuit of a good time and expressing your feelings in a more dramatic way thanks to this alignment of high-energy planets in your 9th House of Getaways and your 5th House of Fun and Games. Romantic feelings may be aroused when you push past personal limits and explore unfamiliar territory.

AUGUST 7–9 ★ *heroic efforts*

Your high hopes, unreasonable fears, and strong opinions are out of proportion with reality on **August 7**, when giant Jupiter opposes potent Pluto. Yet going too far could stir up the passion you need to overcome obstacles. Fortunately, a highly creative Venus-Jupiter quintile on the **9th** sharpens your imagination and can show you how to produce amazing results with limited resources. This quasi-magical aspect is also helpful for reestablishing your faith in the future of a relationship.

SUPER NOVA DAYS
AUGUST 19–22 ★ *embrace the unknown*

Your patience runs out, along with your willingness to follow rules, on **August 19** when the Sun makes stressful aspects with Jupiter and Uranus. Rebellious feelings are not favorable for cooperation, but a breakthrough conversation, propelled by the futuristic Aquarius Full Moon in your 3rd House of Communication on the **20th** could aim you in an exciting new direction. The high energy of the Jupiter-Uranus square on the **21st** intensifies when Mercury forms hard aspects to this planetary pair on the **22nd**. Brilliant insights pop out of thin air while your nerves are pulled taut by unexpected news. An overflow of information and last-minute deadlines creates tension and provokes verbal conflict. Adopting a flexible attitude allows you to learn something new without unraveling from the pressure.

AUGUST 26–27 ★ *guilty pleasures*

Friends and colleagues may shock you when sweet Venus in your 11th House of Groups opposes disruptive Uranus on **August 26**. Switching up your plans, though, could make life more interesting than sticking to the old schedule. A greedy Venus-Jupiter square on the **27th** amplifies appetites and raises expectations, challenging you to live up to your promises. Recognizing your true priorities helps you make the right choice instead of feeling like you have to satisfy everyone's needs.

AUGUST 30 ★ *partners in success*

You are quick to spot great opportunities and notice talented people, enabling you to build efficient new alliances or successfully patch up old ones. A slick sextile between clever Mercury in your 10th House of Career with propitious Jupiter creates a perfect environment for making sound business decisions.

SEPTEMBER

TRUST IN THE PROCESS

It's the little things that count this month, especially when it comes to your career. September starts with the Sun and Mercury in detail-oriented Virgo and your professional 10th House, while the industrious Virgo New Moon on **September 5** encourages you to initiate training that can elevate your skills. Concentrating on a limited range of tasks may not be your idea of excitement, but narrowing your perspective now can broaden your opportunities for success and recognition later. Advantageous Jupiter and powerful Pluto align favorably with this Sun-Moon conjunction, attracting enthusiastic supporters and offering a strategic viewpoint that enables you to maximize your resources and make useful contacts. Collaborative conversations with friends and colleagues are likely when interactive Mercury moves into sociable Libra and your 11th House of Groups on **September 9**. However, promised cooperation may be slow to arrive once amicable Venus disappears into the shadows of Scorpio and your obscure 12th House on **September 11**.

You might be flooded with feelings when the supersensitive Pisces Full Moon illuminates your 4th House of Roots on **September 19**. Issues at home can distract you from your work, but this is also a gentle reminder that you need a refuge from your public responsibilities to find inner inspiration. The last of three subtle Saturn-Pluto sextiles on the **21st** can empower your dreams while also asking you to manage your resources more carefully. On the **22nd**, a little help from your friends arrives with the Sun's entry into congenial Libra and your 11th House of Groups, which marks the Autumn Equinox. But an imaginative Jupiter-Neptune sesquisquare on the **28th** that repeats on **December 17** and **June 11, 2014**, inflates your hopes with unrealistic fantasies.

> **KEEP IN MIND THIS MONTH**
>
> *Approach your work like an apprentice, even if you have plenty of experience. You'll learn how to do a better job with less time and effort.*

KEY DATES

SEPTEMBER 7 ★ *joy to the world*

Your enthusiasm rises to a whole new level when resilient Jupiter forms a heartwarming sextile to the Sun, increasing your confidence and allowing your generosity to shine. Having fun with friends or volunteering for a cause can fill you with deep satisfaction. Additionally, a creative Mercury-Jupiter quintile stimulates your curiosity and helps you find the information you need to solve a tricky problem.

SEPTEMBER 9–11 ★ *addition by subtraction*

The harder you push, the more resistance you meet on **September 9**, when aggressive Mars in your 9th House of Big Ideas squares controlling Saturn. Travel delays and educational setbacks are possible—try to avoid them by planning in advance and creating a less ambitious schedule. Doing one thing well is better than overloading your days with too many activities. Failing to focus your efforts produces additional pressures and power struggles on the **11th**, when punishing Pluto quincunxes Mars. Productivity falters and frustration follows unless you're able to set aside distractions and deal with one tough task at a time.

SUPER NOVA DAYS
SEPTEMBER 14–17 ★ *agent of change*

A lack of support from peers dampens your mood on **September 14**, when Mercury forms a tense square with manipulative Pluto. Yet if you dig more deeply into the situation, you may recognize that you're not heading in the right direction. Happily, experimenting with innovative methods can produce surprisingly positive results as courageous Mars trines avant-garde Uranus in your 5th House of Creativity. You might persuade others to accept your unusual ideas—or be convinced that someone else is mentally off track—with an intellectually charged Mercury-Uranus opposition on the **16th**. If you can stay cool and remain on point, a smart Mercury-Mars sextile on the **17th** clears the air, enhancing cooperation and increasing productivity.

SEPTEMBER 19 ★ *too many cooks*

A gregarious Mercury-Jupiter square offers you too much input today, and you may shut off your mind from any more noise. Conversely, overexplaining yourself can be equally dissuasive to others. More information doesn't help you garner the understanding you seek, so try to boil your position down to a few key points that are easier to digest. A diversity of perspectives is certainly stimulating, yet you can't make wise decisions if you take everyone's opinions into account.

SEPTEMBER 26 ★ *pleasant surprise*

A juicy trine between loving Venus and ebullient Jupiter offers delight in even the dreariest circumstances. Your willingness to seek value in everyone you meet can uncover assets that are usually invisible to you. Asking for what you need in a non-demanding manner produces positive reactions when you might least expect them.

OCTOBER

ELEMENT OF SURPRISE

Your interactions with others are off the wall this month with the ambiguous Libra New Moon falling in your 11th House of Groups on **October 4**. The harmony associated with Libra can be unsettled by mistrust and manipulation as it runs into some rough waters choppy with surprises. Unpredictable Uranus's opposition to this Sun-Moon conjunction and stressful squares from secretive Pluto and judgmental Jupiter can complicate almost any gathering. Graciously adjusting to changes in alliances and breakdowns in cooperation reduces risks, while adapting to shifts in collective goals could create unexpected opportunities. Your eagerness to take risks catches the attention of others when Venus enters adventurous Sagittarius on the **7th**. But don't let vanity and personal matters push work completely out of the picture, because enterprising Mars enters conscientious Virgo and your 10th House of Career on **October 15**. Initiating projects and dedicating yourself to do the best job possible can garner you recognition—or at least avoid weakening your position.

The impetuous Aries Full Moon Lunar Eclipse on **October 18** in your 5th House of Romance, Children, and Creativity tempts you to leap without looking. Engaging in new forms of fun and self-expression is fine if you don't upset friends and colleagues by ignoring their concerns. Mercury begins a three-week retrograde cycle in enigmatic Scorpio and your 12th House of Privacy on the **21st**, a move that slows down the flow of information and may even cause you to misplace messages. However, this is also a great time to explore the mysteries of metaphysics or the depths of your psyche if you are so inclined. The Sun's entry into Scorpio on the **23rd** underscores how important it is that you work quietly behind the scenes until it's your time to shine.

> **KEEP IN MIND THIS MONTH**
>
> *If frustration makes it too difficult for you to get along with others, working independently until the dust settles may be your best move.*

KEY DATES

OCTOBER 1–3 ★ *be the change*

The Sun's move from a complex square with Pluto on **October 1** to an explosive opposition to Uranus on the **3rd** could push you to a breaking point. If you're dealing with unrelenting pressure from an unreasonable individual, you could be tempted to suddenly end the relationship. A more desirable story is one where you gain more power in an organization, which you then use to radically alter the structure of the group.

OCTOBER 7 ★ *honest to a fault*
You're ready to play and might even create some mischief with an itchy Mars-Uranus sesquisquare and tantalizing Venus entering your 1st House of Personality. It's all too easy to lower your guard and express yourself with disturbing honesty. Of course, you might just be teasing, but that's not necessarily obvious to everyone else. Make sure your signals are clear so that people know whether you're just having fun or are finally getting something off your chest by speaking the truth.

SUPER NOVA DAYS
OCTOBER 11–12 ★ *pushing the envelope*
Your lust for life knows few bounds as fun-loving Venus in Sagittarius forms an unbalanced sesquisquare with expansive Jupiter on **October 11**. You may be ready to take a chance on love, but your evaluation of its costs may be off base. Seeking unusual ways to enjoy yourself makes sense as long as you avoid overestimating someone and underestimating the consequences of risky behavior. Your unbridled enthusiasm, though, is likely to continue on the **12th** with an unwieldy Sun-Jupiter square, yet your careless remarks and brash behavior could alienate a person close to you. It's fine to express your opinions as long as they're tempered by a healthy dose of sensitivity to the beliefs of others.

OCTOBER 16 ★ *anything goes*
A sassy trine from Venus in your 1st House of Personality to Uranus in your 5th House of Creativity encourages you to experiment with your appearance. Switching up your style makes your day more fun and attracts a good deal of attention. Of course, your provocative behavior will make you even more intriguing to others. Luckily, you should be able to have a blast breaking a few social rules without getting into too much trouble.

OCTOBER 24 ★ *proceed with caution*
A tendency to go into hard-sell mode doesn't necessarily help your cause on **October 24**. It's not easy for you to keep your enthusiasm in check with a hyperactive Mars-Jupiter semisquare, but taking your foot off the gas once in a while will make everyone feel safer.

NOVEMBER

OUT OF THE SHADOWS

This is a transitional month when spending time completing unfinished business will free you to start on your next big adventure. The recurring Uranus-Pluto square on **November 1** can leave you questioning a previous financial decision, but looking back with regret is not your style. Nevertheless, an intense Scorpio Solar Eclipse on **November 3** may force you to confront issues you don't want to face. This eclipse occurs in your 12th House of Endings and joins sobering Saturn to push you up against uncomfortable realities. However, if you're willing to do the hard work of honestly addressing your doubts and tackling your obligations, you can build an inner strength that carries you far into the future. Managing your resources carefully is the message of value-conscious Venus's entry into stingy Capricorn and your 2nd House of Self-Worth on the **5th**. Exercising financial discipline, investing in the right tools, and developing your talents pays dividends if you're patient and persistent. Your visionary ruling planet, Jupiter, turns retrograde on **November 7**, requiring reflection and, perhaps, readjustment of long-range plans. While the big picture may be fuzzy, communicative Mercury's forward shift on the **10th** is great for catching up on details during the days ahead.

Spiritual Neptune's direct shift in your 4th House of Roots on **November 13** revives old dreams and brings more imagination into your household. However, you still must handle mundane matters and deal with boring routines with the steadfast Taurus Full Moon illuminating your 6th House of Work on the **17th**. On **November 21**, the Sun emerges from the shadows of your 12th House and enters your enthusiastic sign. A boost of energy and optimism comes with this solar shift into your 1st House of Personality, where your effervescent charisma and confidence cast you in the spotlight for everyone to admire.

> **KEEP IN MIND THIS MONTH**
>
> *It's not easy to let go of unrealizable fantasies and move on from regret, but this emotional process creates fertile soil in which you can grow new dreams.*

KEY DATES

NOVEMBER 6 ★ *attitude adjustment*

You may feel constrained, frustrated, or ignored with the Sun's conjunction to repressive Saturn in your 12th House of Obscurity. Avoid getting bogged down in regret or resentment; focus on possible constructive actions instead. Taking responsibility for your situation helps empower yourself with faith and discipline, which is vastly preferable to undermining reactions of guilt, shame, or blame.

NOVEMBER 12 ★ *sunshine on your shoulders*
You receive the nurturing support of a caring ally today—and, with it, a rising tide of hope. The Sun harmoniously trines generous Jupiter in your 8th House of Deep Sharing, bringing light into the darker parts of your mind. A partner, colleague, or friend provides encouragement by recognizing abilities or accomplishments that are usually underappreciated. It may take time to ride this wave all the way to the shores of success, but at least you can feel that you're on your way to a better place.

NOVEMBER 19–20 ★ *get smart*
A sextile from dynamic Mars in your 10th House of Career to jovial Jupiter in your 8th House of Joint Ventures supplies the impetus for tackling team projects on **November 19**. Planning ahead, though, takes you further than simply working diligently. Mercury's messy quincunx with unruly Uranus on the **20th** can distract you with irrelevant ideas and quirky conversations. Fortunately, your focus returns later in the day when Mercury sextiles laserlike Pluto, putting your mind back on track.

SUPER NOVA DAYS
NOVEMBER 24–25 ★ *lost and found*
Your spirit soars when the Sagittarius Sun squares phantasmagoric Neptune on **November 24**. While your heart may open with compassion and images of a better tomorrow, your chronic tendency to overlook details can lead to costly decisions. With a romantically foolish Venus-Neptune semisquare on the **25th**, you continue losing sight of practical considerations in a fog of fantasies. Enjoying delicious moments of escapism is delightful as long as you don't build your entire future on them. Mercury's conjunction to no-nonsense Saturn will quickly tear away the veils of illusion and demand that you face the simple facts.

NOVEMBER 28 ★ *sweet spot*
Applying a bit of common sense helps you seize today's opportunities for more money, love, and pleasure and bring them within reach. The caution of Venus in conservative Capricorn encounters temptations that are hard to resist when it opposes jocular Jupiter. However, the practical wisdom of a Mercury-Jupiter trine allows you to recognize any errors of judgment and quickly correct them.

DECEMBER

COUNT YOUR BLESSINGS

Reevaluating major plans and projects adds a useful dose of pragmatism to this joyous holiday season. Farsighted Jupiter's favorable trine with strategic Saturn on **December 12** gives you a chance to review decisions you've made since their first trine on **July 17** and adjust them as needed to reach your goals before their final alignment on **May 24, 2014**. You could, however, act impulsively with the flamboyant Sagittarius New Moon in your 1st House of Personality on **December 2**. Breaking free of old habits to discover new approaches to creativity, play, and romance comes naturally with unorthodox Uranus's trine to this lunation. Ideas start flowing more readily, encouraging you to become more outspoken and willing to discuss your aspirations openly when talkative Mercury enters Sagittarius on the **4th**. You're likely to find the Winged Messenger's visit to your sign delightful, but sensitive individuals may respond better to more discreet discussions.

Nerves run rampant when the frisky Gemini Full Moon brightens your 7th House of Partners on **December 17**. Uranus the Awakener turns direct on the same day, attracting unconventional and sometimes unstable people. Yet this lunation also enables you to see relationships in a different light and increases your ways to connect with others. The Winter Solstice arrives on **December 21** with the Sun's entry into traditional Capricorn and your 2nd House of Income—it would be wise to take your economic situation more seriously. Venus turns retrograde in your resourceful 2nd House, also on the **21st**, reminding you that reorganizing finances and questioning your values can help your cash flow.

> **KEEP IN MIND THIS MONTH**
>
> *Setting aside time for serious thought about your future may be the best present you can give to yourself and those you love.*

KEY DATES

DECEMBER 6–7 ★ *wearing rose-colored glasses*

A fuzzy Mercury-Neptune square on **December 6** encourages idealization that can make you see and hear what you want to believe rather than experiencing things as they really are. This hopeful illusion feeds your imagination but can lead to confusing conversations and misstatements of facts. An unbalanced Mercury-Jupiter sesquisquare continues this pattern on the **7th**, amplifying your tendency toward exaggeration. Happily, assertive Mars's entry into accommodating Libra provides the diplomatic skills necessary to alleviate awkward situations.

DECEMBER 9–10 ★ *smooth operator*

Thanks to a brilliant Mars-Jupiter quintile on **December 9**, you seem like a magician for getting incompatible people to work well together. But a wayward Sun-Jupiter quincunx on the **10th** tempts you to press your luck and expect everyone to go along with your plans. If you take on unreliable partners or stretch your credibility by promising too much, an ingenious Mercury-Uranus trine reveals innovative ways to get you out of a jam.

DECEMBER 16 ★ *consider your audience*

It's fun to be funny and people love to laugh, but your sense of humor could rub some people the wrong way today. Mischievous Mercury in carefree Sagittarius is entangled in a clunky quincunx with Jupiter in touchy Cancer and your 8th House of Intimacy. Even if there's truth in what you say, tailor your message to those around you to avoid embarrassment and make your point in a less controversial way.

DECEMBER 25 ★ *chaotic christmas*

You might be eager to have an exciting holiday—but this one is unlikely to unfold as planned. Impatient Mars in your 11th House of Groups opposes shocking Uranus in your 5th House of Self-Expression, which can spring surprises and trigger explosive reactions from uncooperative individuals. You may be unabashedly bored by the predictable family rituals that you've done so many times before. Celebrating in new and unusual ways puts an unexpected spin on the day's activities and calms your restless feelings.

SUPER NOVA DAYS
DECEMBER 29–31 ★ *mind games*

Your patience for compromise is limited as mental Mercury and the Sun in your 2nd House of Income slam into a square with erratic Uranus on **December 29–30**. Conversations about your finances may suddenly veer off in odd directions, breaking down ordinary patterns of perception and leaving you uncertain about your future. An intense Mars-Pluto square on the **30th** incites fear and mistrust, which may be amplified when analytical Mercury aspects both planets on the **31st**. Nevertheless, if you can articulate your concerns clearly, you might just be on your way to resolving a financial problem.

CAPRICORN
DECEMBER 22–JANUARY 19

CAPRICORN

2012 SUMMARY

This year sees you uproot unhealthy habits and uncover underexploited resources. Take time to explore the swirling seas of unfamiliar ideas and emotions that are altering your perception of yourself before you abandon any major commitments or make any new ones. The weight you've been carrying on your shoulders since Saturn entered your dutiful 10th House on October 29, 2009, may earn you respect and advance your professional ambitions. Innocent play and childlike self-indulgence remind you of the sweetness of life, which makes all your hard work worthwhile.

AUGUST—*team spirit*
Instead of seeking someone who always agrees with you, find a trustworthy partner who cares enough to tell you the truth—even if it makes you mad—for the sake of success.

SEPTEMBER—*a change is gonna come*
Uncertainty can be your friend when you give your mind permission to wander. Your imagination can lead you to treasures you wouldn't otherwise find.

OCTOBER—*pace yourself*
When you feel the heat of desire rising, slow down and make sure you're on the path to take you where it can be fulfilled.

NOVEMBER—*agent of change*
Sometimes too much of a good thing is more than even you can handle. Fewer options can make your life easier.

DECEMBER—*bend like a willow*
The greatest strength you have now is the ability to adjust your approach to shifting situations instead of trying to resist the winds of change.

2012 CALENDAR

AUGUST

FRI 3 ★ Transform a vague idea into a constructive one

TUE 7–WED 8 ★ Listen carefully to someone's concerns

WED 15–FRI 17 ★ **SUPER NOVA DAYS** Inconsistency can rattle relationships

WED 22 ★ Map out the details of a complex journey

TUE 28–WED 29 ★ Don't panic if surprising news knocks you off stride

SEPTEMBER

MON 3–WED 5 ★ You may feel underappreciated by a partner

SAT 8–MON 10 ★ Too much information can be more dangerous than not enough

SUN 16–MON 17 ★ Keep an open mind and smooth over misunderstandings

THU 20 ★ Watch out for anger, irritability, and mistrust

SAT 29 ★ **SUPER NOVA DAY** Your feelings swell to extremes

OCTOBER

FRI 5 ★ Ask questions if you need more information today

TUE 9–WED 10 ★ **SUPER NOVA DAYS** Opportunity knocks

MON 15–WED 17 ★ Aim for long-term gains

WED 24 ★ Saying no is probably your best option

TUE 30 ★ You can motivate your peers effortlessly

NOVEMBER

THU 1 ★ Pay careful attention to where you're going

FRI 9 ★ Avoid committing to tasks until you have all the details

FRI 16–SAT 17 ★ **SUPER NOVA DAYS** Planning and persistence bring success

THU 22–SAT 24 ★ Find fresh approaches to resolving issues

MON 26–TUE 27 ★ You have the passion to go for exactly what you want

DECEMBER

FRI 7 ★ You may be anxious to try something new

WED 12–FRI 14 ★ Be ready to handle whatever happens

FRI 21–SAT 22 ★ **SUPER NOVA DAYS** Surprises may be just around the corner

TUE 25 ★ Tradition goes out the window

SUN 30 ★ Shed the negative baggage of the past

CAPRICORN OVERVIEW

The waves of change that began in 2008 when transformational Pluto entered your sign grow stronger this year, continuing to reshape your sense of identity while leaving few areas of your life untouched. **Although sudden shifts on the home front last year may have already forced you to reconsider old assumptions, it's time to create new strategies to carry you through the current turbulence and into the future.** Unpredictable Uranus began a series of seven revolutionary squares with formidable Pluto on June 24 and September 19, 2012, initiating a roller-coaster ride of self-discovery, full of surprising twists and turns that can alter the direction of your life. Uranus in your 4th House of Foundations dynamically squares Pluto for the third and fourth times on May 20 and November 1, keeping the pressure for change aimed directly at you. It may seem as if the very ground upon which you have built your world is shaking beneath you. Keep in mind as you make any plans that this profound Uranus-Pluto square will recur three more times through March 16, 2015. Instead of worrying that the current instability is permanent, recognize that you are in a period of unprecedented growth that won't begin to settle down for a few years. Trying to resist the inevitable or force events to a finish will only bring frustration and unhappiness.

Fortunately, you can rely on the support of others as trustworthy Saturn moves through your 11th House of Social Networking. Saturn entered into Scorpio and your 11th House on October 5, 2012, shifting your responsibility away from proving yourself in your job toward working with others for the good of all involved. Hardworking Saturn remains in your social 11th House until December 23, 2014, giving you time to consolidate your successes through cooperation and collaboration. Saturn's smooth trines with imaginative Neptune on June 11 and July 19 enable you to turn your fantasies into reality by combining a realistic assessment of current conditions with your most idealistic dreams.

You may not make much progress toward your long-term goals during the first half of the year with Jupiter in your 6th House of Service. Still, you can find a sense of purpose by fulfilling your day-to-day responsibilities and doing your job as best you can. Expansive Jupiter moves from your 6th House of Self-Improvement into your 7th House of Partnerships and Public Life on June 25, bringing opportunities to you through your interactions with others. This is one more signal that **you're less likely to reach professional heights as a solo performer than as part of a team.** In fact, your personal growth may be tied to someone who acts as an encouraging teacher while also being a good partner.

TWIST OF FATE

Relationship stability is usually a top priority for you, but this year your practical Capricorn nature continues to be rocked by external forces as you seek to balance other people's changing needs with your own. The underlying question of who is in control may be exacerbated when Mars and Venus, the cosmic lovers, conjunct surprising Uranus and square domineering Pluto on March 22–March 31. Although beautiful Venus moves through your 5th House of Love and Romance on April 15–May 9, her tense opposition to restrictive Saturn on April 22 can cool the heat of passion or challenge your commitment to your partner. Make peace with your partner when Venus visits your 7th House of Companions on June 2–27. Reach for your romantic dreams on June 7 as Venus completes a magical Grand Water Trine with idealistic Neptune and pragmatic Saturn. Luckily, Jupiter's presence in your 7th House from June 25 to July 16, 2014, tends to bring magnanimous people into your life.

CONSOLIDATE YOUR GAINS

Step back from your immediate job responsibilities this year and make plans for the future while ambitious Saturn is in your 11th House of Long-Term Goals. Take stock of where you are and how to strengthen your current position so you can withstand the oncoming changes. Although you may face a setback as the intense Scorpio Lunar Eclipse on April 25 conjuncts taskmaster Saturn, its favorable trine to poetic Neptune empowers your words with idealism that can inspire your associates to support your efforts. Value-conscious Venus visits your 10th House of Career on August 16–September 11, bringing recognition and financial rewards for a job well done.

DOUBLE OR NOTHING

Focus on solidifying work relationships and laying the groundwork for increasing your earnings this year as reliable Saturn, the planetary ruler of your financial 2nd House, passes through the 11th House of Teams. Although you're known for your ambitious nature, you're even more intent on making money through February 25 as Mercury and Venus emphasize your 2nd House of Possessions. Jupiter in your 6th House of Daily Routine until June 25 suggests that you might prefer working alone, yet other people become more involved in your success since this planet spends the rest of the year in your 7th House of Partners. Additionally, enriching Venus visits your 8th House of Shared Resources on June 27–July 22, increasing your chances to earn more while collaborating with someone else.

BASIC TRAINING

It's more important than ever to take good care of yourself this year with unforgiving Pluto's long-term visit to your 1st House of Physicality. Don't procrastinate when it comes to handling issues related to your well-being, since opportunistic Jupiter travels through your 6th House of Health and Habits until June 25. Consider an accelerated program of physical activity to improve your vitality when energetic Mars is in your 6th House on May 31–July 13. Make sure to get enough sleep, good food, and exercise when Mars forms challenging aspects to your ruling planet, Saturn, on May 1, June 8, and September 9.

SWEEP OUT THE COBWEBS

Unpredictable Uranus is shaking up the status quo around your home and shocking your 4th House of Domestic Conditions. Initiating new projects is healthier than battling those around you when hyperactive Mars revs up the atmosphere in your 4th House on March 12–April 20. It's smart to complete small, manageable projects throughout the year instead of letting them pile up. Putting off regular maintenance can lead to a crisis that requires significant work on April 12 and October 5, when Saturn the Tester creates disquieting quincunxes to wayward Uranus.

EARLY-BIRD SPECIAL

Although you may have plans for several trips when journeying Jupiter is in scattered Gemini through June 25, you aren't as motivated to travel during the latter half of the year when Jupiter moves through security-conscious Cancer. Nevertheless, sweet Venus visits your 9th House of Travel on July 22–August 16, and her harmonious aspects to strategic Saturn, optimistic Jupiter, and mysterious Pluto on July 26–30 make this a great time for a getaway. Mars energizes your 9th House on October 15–December 7, marking a second window of opportunity for taking a vacation. However, reserve time for extra planning if you travel during Mercury's retrograde on October 21–November 10 to allow for possible snafus or delays along the way.

HIGHER EDUCATION

Visionary Neptune continues its long-term visit to your 3rd House of Communication, inspiring you to gather more information about metaphysical subjects. A philosophical Sagittarius Lunar Eclipse that rattles your 12th House of Soul Consciousness on May 25 can shake your previous beliefs as it squares otherworldly Neptune. Fortunately, you have a chance to put a new set of spiritual teachings to practical use when disciplined Saturn trines Neptune on June 11 and July 19. You're more receptive to theories that elude proof when broad-minded Jupiter and impetuous Mars enter the picture to trine Neptune and Saturn on July 17–20.

> ### RICK & JEFF'S TIP FOR THE YEAR:
> Go with the Flow
>
> When you're riding a bicycle, it's easier to stay balanced if you're moving than if you're sitting still. Likewise, as the speed of change in your life picks up, it's a mistake to hold tightly to the present moment thinking it offers you more security than the unknown future. Once you accept that resistance is futile, you can find comfort by keeping pace with the accelerating currents and surprisingly could discover that it's not as difficult to maintain your equilibrium when you are in motion.

CAPRICORN

JANUARY

UP AGAINST THE WALL

You're ready for nearly anything as the New Year begins, but your optimism can quickly fade as obstacles pile up to impede your progress. Fortunately, with the willful Sun, logical Mercury, and potent Pluto all in your hardworking sign, you're prepared to meet the challenges. Mercury's powerful alignments with Pluto and Saturn on **January 6** strengthen your mental fortitude; however, red-hot Mars's conflictive square to cold Saturn on **January 7** stops you in your tracks as you face a seemingly insurmountable wall of resistance. Your core beliefs may clash with those of your peers as Mars in your 2nd House of Values crosses your ruling planet, Saturn, in your 11th House of Friends and Associates. The hard edges of your life are softened when gentle Venus enters Capricorn and your 1st House of Self on **January 8**. The persistent Capricorn New Moon on **January 11** can be considered your true astrological New Year's Day. Its alignment with buoyant Jupiter restores your lost confidence and starts you on a new path to success.

Your thoughts turn to money matters and issues of self-worth on **January 19**, when Mercury and the Sun enter conceptual Aquarius and your financial 2nd House. You become more certain of your ideas on **January 22–25** as Mercury and the Sun form supportive aspects with ingenious Uranus and beneficial Jupiter, but this expansive period transforms into a serious one when Mercury squares solemn Saturn on the **25th**, followed by the Sun-Saturn square on the **30th**. Meanwhile, the melodramatic Leo Full Moon on **January 26** illuminates your 8th House of Shared Resources, indicating the complexity of your current fiscal condition. Its square to hard-nosed Saturn is another not-so-gentle reminder that shortcuts aren't an option.

> **KEEP IN MIND THIS MONTH**
>
> *Instead of trying to accomplish too much too fast, establish a methodical work style at the beginning of the year to improve your chances for success.*

KEY DATES

JANUARY 3–4 ★ *flexibility counts*

Your brain lights up with original ideas on **January 3**, when trickster Mercury in your 1st House of Self squares brilliant Uranus. However, your brusque manner of communication can provoke an argument, and it's easy to waste time and energy trying to prove that you're right. Luckily, you experience a positive outcome when assertive Mars blends with auspicious Jupiter in your 6th House of Employment on **January 4**. This high-energy combination could bring you earning opportunities and a healthier self-esteem.

SUPER NOVA DAYS

JANUARY 6-7 ★ *true confessions*

Be careful with your words on **January 6**; once they're spoken, you cannot take them back. Perceptive Mercury hooks up with penetrating Pluto that day, which facilitates peering through the veils of illusion or simply intensifies your relentless inner chatter. Truth is palpable and secrets can be exposed. If you go too far, you could run into trouble on **January 7** when combative Mars conflicts with authoritative Saturn. Unfortunately, you won't gain much by pushing harder, except maybe increasing your frustration and raising your blood pressure. Cultivate patience, and take this time to refine your craft instead of trying to swim upstream.

JANUARY 16-19 ★ *dark side of the moon*

You exude magnetism when sensual Venus joins passionate Pluto in your 1st House of Personality on **January 16**. Your newfound lust for life can revitalize a relationship, but also can create control issues or problems stemming from possessiveness or jealousy. Thankfully, your sense of social responsibility could rescue you from your intense personal desires as Venus cooperatively sextiles conscientious Saturn in your 11th House of Teamwork on **January 17**. The Sun and Mercury enter futuristic Aquarius and your 2nd House of Personal Resources on **January 19**, clearing your mind and enabling you to focus on business for the next few weeks.

JANUARY 22-25 ★ *face your fears*

Your thinking is hyperactive and new ideas pop into awareness so quickly that you can't keep track of them when brainy Mercury connects with electrifying Uranus and giant Jupiter on **January 22**. Although you're buzzing, you can approach a serious issue with good judgment and an appropriate sense of humor. Nevertheless, your confidence may be shaken on **January 25** when Mercury squares naysaying Saturn, requiring you to confront your inner saboteur and the fear that it arouses. Thankfully, you should be able to overcome your concerns now. An exuberant Sun-Jupiter trine indicates that a lucrative opportunity at work could bring you the monetary gains you are seeking.

FEBRUARY

DAZED AND CONFUSED

This month brings you an overabundance of incoming data, much of which doesn't help you achieve your goals. You grow busier day by day, yet have little to show for your efforts as macho Mars enters meandering Pisces and your 3rd House of Immediate Environment on **February 1**. Then, on **February 4**, Mars hooks up with indefinite Neptune—already in the 3rd House for a long-term visit—which prompts you to inadvertently mislead others with your confusing actions and unclear motives. Messenger Mercury adds to the uncertainty when it enters your 3rd House on **February 5** and conjuncts Neptune on the **6th**. Your life shifts into high gear when Mercury and Mars square boisterous Jupiter on **February 9–10**. The intellectual Aquarius New Moon on the **10th** occurs in your 2nd House of Values, encouraging you to look at what's most important to you personally and to set priorities based on your individual needs.

You're ready to bring your visions down to earth and make your dreams come true with fluid trines to industrious Saturn from Mercury on **February 12** and Mars on the **16th**. The Sun's shift into Pisces and your information-rich 3rd House on **February 18** repeats a now-familiar theme as the tempo picks up another notch. But when your key planet, Saturn, turns retrograde also on the **18th**, followed by rational Mercury on the **23rd**, it creates an undertow in the currents that begins to pull you backward. Review your plans and reconsider recent decisions. The selective Virgo Full Moon on **February 25** brightens your 9th House of Big Ideas, challenging you to narrow your field of vision by ignoring interesting yet distracting messages that don't further your development.

> **KEEP IN MIND THIS MONTH**
>
> *You like having good information at your disposal in order to get where you're going, but collecting too many unrelated facts could just leave you stranded.*

KEY DATES

FEBRUARY 4–7 ★ *surprise ending*

Your energy level may be low and you could feel discouraged on **February 4**, when high-powered Mars runs into diffusive Neptune in your 3rd House of Communication. Although this aspect bodes well for artistic endeavors or flights of fancy, it may be frustrating if you're trying to accomplish something practical. Mercury's shift into dreamy Pisces on the **5th** and its conjunction with

Neptune on the **6th** blurs the lines between creativity and delusion; you could inadvertently mislead others even if you think you're being perfectly clear. However, positive aspects from lovely Venus to thrilling Uranus and generous Jupiter on **February 6–7** could mean that unexpected pleasures leave you smiling or that an unexpected windfall puts a bit of cash into your pocket.

SUPER NOVA DAYS
FEBRUARY 10–12 ★ *saving for a rainy day*
You're overconfident about your income-earning potential when the brilliant Aquarius New Moon on **February 10** activates your 2nd House of Finances and an inflationary Mars-Jupiter square blows your optimism out of proportion. However, self-doubt and discouragement can set in on the **11th** as fears of scarcity overtake your initial enthusiasm, triggered by a frugal Venus-Saturn square. Your chances for success are greater if you pay attention to the obstacles you now face and respond to this reality check by reining in your expectations and acting with self-discipline. Thankfully, realistic thinking returns on the **12th** when a pragmatic Mercury-Saturn trine enables you to make a concrete plan and stick to it.

FEBRUARY 21–23 ★ *lost in space*
Even if you're certain of your current direction, the Sun's conjunction to nebulous Neptune on **February 21** could take the wind out of your sails, leaving you to drift aimlessly through the day without knowing where you're going. Although this feeling can be disorienting, it is a great time to reconnect with your dreams. Mercury's retrograde turn in your 3rd House of Learning on **February 23** is yet another sign that it's time to stop pushing ahead until you regroup and realign your ambitions to more closely match your spiritual journey.

FEBRUARY 25–28 ★ *know your limits*
You're lost in fantasy and illusion when loving Venus enters compassionate Pisces on **February 25** and conjuncts spiritual Neptune on the **28th**. The Sun's square to extravagant Jupiter on the **25th** encourages blind faith and can make anything seem possible. However, these expansive transits are countered by the narrowing Virgo Full Moon that squares indulgent Jupiter to remind you of the value of just saying no.

MARCH

DRESS FOR SUCCESS

You're poised to make great progress this month as you strive to establish yourself professionally. Your ruling planet, Saturn—now moving through your 11th House of Long-Term Goals—forms a series of beneficial aspects throughout the month, supplying you with a deep reserve of energy, the willingness to work hard, and the patience to wait for what you want. On **March 8**, Saturn's supportive sextile to unrelenting Pluto in your 1st House of Personality puts everyone on notice that you are on the move; they should either lend their support or get out of your way. This long-lasting Saturn-Pluto alignment first occurred on **December 26, 2012**, and returns on **September 21**, giving you ample time to develop current projects so you can bring them to their next stage of implementation later this year. However, you don't need to wait to make the most of exciting opportunities because the intuitive Pisces Sun in your 3rd House of Communication harmoniously aspects Pluto and Saturn on **March 1**. Charming Venus follows suit on **March 6**, enabling you to convince others that collaborating with you will be beneficial for all involved.

Unfortunately, things may not unfold as fast as you wish, because interactive Mercury is retrograde until **March 17**. But even the backward-moving messenger planet can contribute to your prosperity as it, too, positively aligns with Saturn and Pluto on **March 7**. You can improve your productivity by reviewing your plans and making necessary corrections. If a discouraging Jupiter-Saturn quincunx on **March 23** blocks your progress, be flexible. This quickly sets you back on track so you can take advantage of Mercury's positive aspects with stabilizing Saturn on **March 28** and perceptive Pluto on **March 29**.

> **KEEP IN MIND THIS MONTH**
>
> *The climb to the top of the mountain is long, yet the best way to ensure that you reach your destination is by initiating strategic action right now.*

KEY DATES

MARCH 1–4 ★ *in the zone*

The Sun's smooth connections with powerful Pluto and dependable Saturn on **March 1** galvanize your desire to achieve more by showcasing your organizational abilities and productivity. When you persevere with prudence and consistency, you'll be recognized for your hard work. Your determination to succeed is fueled by courageous Mars's creative quintile to Pluto in your 1st House of Personality on **March 3**. However, voracious Venus squares opulent Jupiter on **March 4**, accentuating wasteful behavior and encouraging pleasurable activities. Be extra mindful of overindulgent behavior, especially in matters of the heart.

MARCH 9–12 ★ *follow your instincts*
It's challenging for you to stick to one idea on **March 9** when mental Mercury squares roving Jupiter. Although rational thinking is difficult with seven planets swimming in irrational Pisces and your 3rd House of Information, the Pisces New Moon on **March 11** is a turning point that can reveal the futility of logical analysis while coaxing you to trust your feelings. Although your intentions may not be obvious to others, you're eager to cautiously push your agenda forward when enterprising Mars shifts into initiating Aries and your 4th House of Security on **March 12**.

MARCH 17–21 ★ *off you go*
Obstacles seem to disappear soon after Mercury turns direct on **March 17** in your 3rd House of Communication, making this the right time to hit the restart button, armed with all the new information you've gathered since this retrograde phase began on **February 23**. The Sun's shift into spontaneous Aries and your 4th House of Home and Family on **March 20** is the Spring Equinox. You must learn to trust your intuition to build a stronger personal foundation. You might want to spruce up your residence when stylish Venus follows the Sun into your 4th House on **March 21**.

SUPER NOVA DAYS
MARCH 25–30 ★ *trial and error*
Stop and regroup on **March 25**, when an unpleasant Mars-Saturn quincunx tests the validity of your newly revised goals. Although your confidence isn't likely to fade as enthusiastic Mars sextiles cheerful Jupiter on the **26th**, quincunxes to unyielding Saturn from Venus and the Sun on the **30th** have you reconsidering your decisions. Domestic issues can interfere with your work, especially as Mars in your 4th House of Family squares controlling Pluto on the **26th**. The people-pleasing Libra Full Moon on **March 27** illuminates your 10th House of Career, exacerbating the tension between home and work. This is a highly volatile time, so consciously choose love over fear and avoid unnecessary ego battles.

APRIL

The earth shifts beneath your feet this month, causing you to question the life path you've chosen. April begins with four planets, including volatile Uranus, moving through restless Aries and your 4th House of Foundations, stirring up excitement on the home front. The ardent Aries New Moon on **April 10** energizes your domestic 4th House and shifts your concerns away from work so you can spend more time with your family. An anxious Uranus-Saturn quincunx highlights your 11th House of Community on **April 12**, pitting your need for freedom against the restrictions of social and professional obligations. This destabilizing aspect is the second in a series of three that began on **November 15, 2012**, and will recur on **October 5**. Instead of waiting for Uranus the Awakener to reveal a problem you've been avoiding, consider what adjustments you can make now to ease unexpressed tension before it reaches a breaking point.

You can recover your sense of control by letting others know what you want when three planets move into unambiguous Taurus and your 5th House of Self-Expression; affectionate Venus leads the shift on **April 15**, followed by the Sun on the **19th** and insistent Mars on the **20th**. Instead of withdrawing into the privacy of your inner world, seek creative and playful ways to show others what's really in your heart. But it's not all fun and games when the inflexible Scorpio Full Moon Eclipse on **April 25** conjuncts somber Saturn in your futuristic 11th House, testing your commitment to going the distance in pursuit of your goals. Paradoxically, recognizing your limitations gives you the freedom to accomplish even more than you expect.

> **KEEP IN MIND THIS MONTH**
>
> *Although your anxiety grows in proportion with your uncertainty, you're wiser to choose a radical approach now rather than always following the most reliable path.*

KEY DATES

APRIL 1 ★ *fearless leader*

Your self-confidence soars as the Sun in bold Aries sextiles effervescent Jupiter in your 6th House of Self-Improvement. You should be able to skillfully handle all the necessary details today as long as you don't let your enthusiasm run wild. A new approach or attitude helps you to enjoy increased productivity along with the abundance it brings.

APRIL 7–10 ★ *fools rush in*

You're riding a creative wave on **April 7** when flirty Venus in impulsive Aries hooks up with sexy Mars. This passionate combo may trigger romantic urges, but might be a bit overwhelming for your naturally reserved personality. Being overly aggressive, insensitive, or even inappropriate could damage your reputation. The impetuous Aries New Moon lands in your 4th House of Home and Family on **April 10**, freeing you to make a fresh start. But cerebral Mercury crosses paths with resistant Saturn, so think about the consequences before you begin a project around the house or at work. Proper planning could prevent headaches down the road.

SUPER NOVA DAYS
APRIL 12–15 ★ *call of the wild*

If your goals have become rigid, you may see them shattered by the disruptive Saturn-Uranus quincunx on **April 12**. You're ready for action on the **13th** when inquisitive Mercury fires into fearless Aries to blast you out of your cautious mental grooves. But just as you talk yourself into doing something significant, delectable Venus enters bucolic Taurus and your 5th House of Love and Play on **April 15**, enticing you to slow down and enjoy yourself instead of pushing forward. Slip into something more comfortable, settle into a delicious meal, or turn on the charm in the pursuit of sensual pleasures.

APRIL 20–22 ★ *stormy weather*

Expect insights on **April 20**—but erratic ones, because quicksilver Mercury is joining sporadic Uranus in headstrong Aries. Nevertheless, you may find your communication blocked on the **21st** when Mercury squares manipulative Pluto. You've nothing to gain by obsessing about something beyond your control. Romantic difficulties may arise on the **22nd** when austere Saturn opposes needy Venus in your 5th House of Love. Avoid being overly defensive or taking someone's coolness too personally.

APRIL 24–28 ★ *listen to your heart*

You're more willing to share intense feelings on **April 24** when a spicy Venus-Pluto trine highlights your 5th House of Self-Expression, renewing a current relationship or stimulating a new one. But social complications require your unwavering attention on the **25th** as the Scorpio Full Moon Eclipse activates your 11th House of Friends. Even if your vitality is low when the Sun opposes bossy Saturn on the **28th**, you're smarter to rely on your self-sufficiency than to count on others.

MAY

If your determination meets dogged resistance early in the month, it's a signal telling you to get busy rather than falling victim to discouragement or self-doubt. Your creativity feels blocked when constrictive Saturn opposes energetic Mars on **May 1** and expressive Mercury on **May 5**; step back so you can solidify your thoughts and strengthen your plan of attack. Thankfully, Pluto in your ambitious sign trines the Sun on the **1st**, Mars on the **5th**, and Mercury on the **7th**, empowering you to overcome whatever obstacles you face. A Taurus Solar Eclipse on **May 9** can push your creativity to the limit, yet its conjunction with Mercury in your 5th House of Self-Expression reminds you that logical analysis doesn't always lead to the best solution.

Your naturally methodical approach to your daily routine at home and on the job becomes scattered when resourceful Venus enters flighty Gemini and your 6th House of Habits on **May 9**, followed by chatty Mercury on the **15th** and the Sun on the **20th**. Your desire to widen your vistas reaches a turning point when optimistic Jupiter in your detail-oriented 6th House runs into an anxious sesquisquare with pessimistic Saturn. Meanwhile, the life-changing Uranus-Pluto square that drives deep changes in your personal life from June 24, 2012, through **March 16, 2015**, is exact on **May 20**, agitating unrest on the home front and triggering your need for freedom. The Sagittarius Lunar Eclipse on **May 25** illuminates your 12th House of Escapism and squares dreamy Neptune, luring you to retreat into fantasies, rather than dealing with the serious issues of your life.

KEEP IN MIND THIS MONTH

Give your inner child permission to play without fear or guilt. The emotional breakthrough you experience could change your life.

KEY DATES

MAY 1 ★ *against all odds*

Don't give in to frustration on **May 1** when cranky Mars opposes stingy Saturn in your 11th House of Long-Term Goals. Even if your worries about scarcity are over the top, a radiant Sun-Pluto trine tells you that acting with unwavering persistence is the answer. Although Mercury's shift into steady Taurus cultivates patience, working smarter accomplishes more than just working harder.

MAY 4–7 ★ *claim your power*

Your imagination play tricks on you as mischievous Mercury in your 5th House of Play sextiles surreal Neptune on **May 4**. Enjoy the daydreams while you can, because a Mercury-Saturn opposition on **May 5** snaps you back to reality. A formidable Mars-Pluto trine the same day makes you feel invincible, and a Mercury-Pluto trine on the **7th** adds weight to your words. You may need to bite your tongue, however, because an excitable Mercury-Mars conjunction can incite an unnecessary argument.

MAY 9 ★ *lighten up*

The sensual Taurus New Moon Eclipse supplies your 5th House of Love and Creativity with fresh sources of delight. Your workplace seems to be friendlier when pretty Venus prances into breezy Gemini and your 6th House of Employment. Making small talk with colleagues and being adaptable in business negotiations allow you to appear more approachable and get the appreciation and respect that you deem so valuable.

SUPER NOVA DAYS
MAY 16–20 ★ *agent of change*

The steadfast Taurus Sun forms stressful aspects to unstable Uranus and transformational Pluto on **May 16**, pitting your desire to maintain the status quo against the urgent pressure to shake things up. A thrilling Venus-Uranus sextile makes change seem irresistible on the **18th**, but an uncomfortable Venus-Pluto quincunx triggers fear if you must relinquish control. However, your underlying motivation for change comes from the reactionary Uranus-Pluto square on the **20th** that stimulates conflict between your 1st House of Self and your 4th House of Family. Your current willingness to risk stability can bring you what you want, but at the potential cost of upsetting others.

MAY 25–28 ★ *work in progress*

Seek solace from within on **May 25**, when a philosophical Sagittarius Full Moon Eclipse brings awareness to your 12th House of Soul Consciousness. Avoid making important decisions because a square to mystical Neptune can be confusing. A Sun-Saturn quincunx may require you to make adjustments at work on the **27th**, but everything seems to improve when curious Mercury and congenial Venus join jovial Jupiter in your 6th House of Employment on **May 27–28**. It's easy to overdo or overindulge, so establish priorities and set limits instead of wasting time on the job.

JUNE

BRIDGE OVER TROUBLED WATERS

Significant changes continue to rock your world, yet this month offers you a chance to integrate your feelings with your rapidly evolving perspective. Existing conflicts between domestic responsibilities and your drive to succeed are exacerbated by harsh aspects to power-hungry Pluto and rebellious Uranus from the Sun on **June 1**, Mercury on **June 7-8**, Venus on **June 11-12**, and Mars on **June 15-17**. However, a stabilizing Saturn-Neptune trine on **June 11** empowers you to counterbalance the uncertainties by visualizing your ideal future, regardless of the demanding circumstances you currently face. This long-lasting aspect is the second in a series that began on **October 10, 2012**, and recurs on **July 19**, indicating that the seeds of dreams that you sowed last fall may be ripe for harvesting.

On **June 3** rational Mercury forms a magical Grand Water Trine with Saturn and Neptune, steadying your emotions so you can make plans to transition from the world you're leaving behind to the one that awaits you in the future. On **June 7**, delicious Venus completes the grand trine, sweetening the picture with friends who support your goals. Personal and business partnerships grow more important throughout the month after Venus shifts into nurturing Cancer and your 7th House of Others on **June 2**. The Sun follows suit—marking the Summer Solstice—on **June 21**, to shine additional light onto your relationships. Global Jupiter joins the 7th House party on **June 25**, heralding its yearlong visit to emotional Cancer and inviting you to balance worldly ambitions with meaningful one-on-one interactions. Fortunately, the Sun's trines to Saturn and Neptune on **June 26** bring your perspective back to a personal level.

> **KEEP IN MIND THIS MONTH**
>
> *Don't rely on facts and logic alone as you make your decisions; add magic to your life by also factoring in your dreams and emotions.*

KEY DATES

JUNE 1-3 ★ *genius at work*

Focus on building your skills and refining your craft with the Sun in your 6th House of Daily Routines. However, on **June 1** its awkward quincunx to emphatic Pluto in your ambitious sign pressures you to organize your work and apply what you've learned. Although you may be unsure of the best way to let go of old habits and develop new ones, an open-minded Sun-Uranus sextile urges you to try new approaches to existing problems. You receive additional support and useful ideas from your friends and co-workers on **June 3** when smart Mercury trines both constructive Saturn and intuitive Neptune.

SUPER NOVA DAYS
JUNE 8–11 ★ *running against the wind*
The interactive Gemini New Moon on **June 8** buzzes in your 6th House of Employment, prompting you to juggle your work schedule so you can increase your efficiency. Remember, however, that this lunation's uncomfortable aspect to critical Saturn—along with a frustrating Mars-Saturn quincunx—can delay your progress with complications that require time and effort to manage. Fortunately, on **June 11** a fluid trine from solid Saturn in your 11th House of Goals to idealistic Neptune in your 3rd House of Communication gives structure to your vague dreams and empowers you to talk about them in an inspiring manner. Nevertheless, you may be too quick to speak when loquacious Mercury squares irrepressible Uranus on the **8th**. Innocent Venus opposes passionate Pluto on the **11th**, revealing a more compulsive need to express yourself, so be vigilant about being too opinionated, intense, or stubborn.

JUNE 19–23 ★ *tug of war*
You're ready to take on the world on **June 19** when the confident Sun-Jupiter conjunction in your 6th House of Self-Improvement tantalizes you with exciting opportunities. However, the Sun slips into self-protective Cancer and your 7th House of Partnerships and Public Life on the **21st**, highlighting the conflict between your naturally ambitious nature and your current need for privacy. The challenge of harmonizing your inner and outer worlds reaches a peak when the determined Capricorn Full Moon opposes the reserved Cancer Sun on **June 23**. Give equal importance to your family matters and your career objectives.

JUNE 25–26 ★ *no more drama*
Mixed messages can be confusing on **June 26** as troublesome Mercury begins its three-week retrograde phase in your 7th House of Relationships. The potential for stress or irritation temporarily counteracts your optimism from jolly Jupiter's move into this interactive house on the **25th**. Thankfully, the Sun forms a happy Grand Water Trine with loyal Saturn and compassionate Neptune on the **26th**, enabling you to balance your personal interests within the context of your partnerships.

JULY

GREAT EXPECTATIONS

Your month gets off to a rough start, but things improve considerably as the days go by. Your ruling planet, Saturn, turns direct on **July 8**, freeing you from obligations that have recently prevented you from reaching your goals. The dreams you dreamed when strategic Saturn in your 11th House of Friends and Wishes trined prophetic Neptune on **October 10, 2012**, came back into focus on **June 11**. Now the third and final Saturn-Neptune trine on **July 19** enables you to grab hold of an elusive pursuit and make it real. Luckily, limitless Jupiter and physical Mars both form synergetic trines with Saturn on the **17th** and Neptune on the **20th**, boosting your confidence and enthusiasm. This emotionally expansive Grand Water Trine—activating your 7th House of Companions—is a good omen for personal relationships and business partnerships. Keep your mind and heart open and prepare to take advantage of what others may offer.

Nevertheless, your ambitions might conflict with the plans of someone close to you, and success will probably take longer than you prefer. The cautious Cancer New Moon on **July 8** highlights your interactive 7th House, yet you could withhold sharing your feelings if you think they will impede your progress. But undelivered messages, misplaced emails, and misunderstood conversations can create unnecessary delays while trickster Mercury retrogrades in your 7th House until **July 20**; at that point its direct turn slowly releases you from these communication complications. The intelligent Aquarius Full Moon on **July 22** brightens your 2nd House of Finances. Its uncomfortable quincunx with valuable Venus raises questions about money management and urges you to tighten the reins on unnecessary spending.

> **KEEP IN MIND THIS MONTH**
>
> *Don't get sidetracked by petty disagreements or anything that distracts you from manifesting your dreams. Your long-term happiness depends on your unwavering commitment to your future.*

KEY DATES

JULY 1-4 ★ *living on the edge*

You're highly sensitive to rejection on **July 1**, when vulnerable Venus in your 8th House of Intimacy and Transformation squares aloof Saturn. You can gain a new perspective by softening your resistance to sharing resources as Venus anxiously aspects ethereal Neptune. Still, relationships are strained as foreboding Pluto opposes the Sun in your

7th House of Partnerships. Unexpected upsets or sudden twists of fate may derail your plans when the Sun squares capricious Uranus on **July 4**. Your best strategy is to cultivate flexibility and shake off the need to be in control.

JULY 7-8 ★ *share the love*
You may surprise yourself by overcoming your inhibitions and expressing what you really want when pleasure-seeking Venus in playful Leo trines thrill-seeking Uranus on **July 7**. Fortunately, you have an excellent chance of getting your needs met once you reveal your true feelings. The tender Cancer New Moon on **July 8** joins retrograde Mercury in your 7th House of Partners, mellowing your approach to relationships and coaxing you to show your vulnerability. Being patient works in your favor, especially if you're beginning a new partnership or redefining an old one.

SUPER NOVA DAYS
JULY 17-20 ★ *now or never*
Success seems within reach as confident Jupiter forms a Grand Water Trine with industrious Saturn and inspirational Neptune on **July 17–19**. Your breadth of vision, combined with the keen awareness of realistic limitations, creates an easy equilibrium between the spiritual and material realms. Jupiter's presence in your 7th House of Others enables you to integrate someone else's idealism into your strategy for achieving your goals. You won't likely take no for an answer as headstrong Mars, also in your 7th House, enters the picture to trine Neptune and Saturn on the **20th**. Progress in partnerships becomes apparent, especially when messenger Mercury's direct turn allows you to resolve differences with business or romantic partners.

JULY 26-31 ★ *rebel with a cause*
You may spend money unwisely or feel disillusioned by people on **July 26**, when receptive Venus opposes deceptive Neptune. Fortunately, a realistic Venus-Saturn sextile enables you to remove the rose-colored glasses and adopt a more practical outlook on life. But an oppressive Sun-Saturn square on the **27th** reveals tension between your goals and your social obligations. Meanwhile, a combative Mars-Pluto opposition, also on the **27th**, and a hot-tempered Mars-Uranus square on the **31st** leave you impatient with an ongoing power struggle. If you must act rebelliously, at least be kind to those you love.

AUGUST

TRUE GRIT

The same challenges that stop others in their tracks motivate you to work harder to reach your lofty goals. You may long for calmer days, but the obstacles in your path reveal what you must do to reach the top of the mountain. You have little margin for error now; unless you have a concrete plan and an unwavering commitment, you could exhaust yourself by scattering energy without much to show for your efforts. The expressive Leo New Moon on **August 6** stimulates your 8th House of Shared Resources, making this an excellent time to shore up strategic alliances. This lunation trines unconventional Uranus, so don't limit your choice of partners to the same familiar people that you've collaborated with in the past.

You feel as if relationships are taking over your life with Mercury, Mars, and Jupiter congregating in your 7th House of Partnerships and Public Life. However, working with others can bring a whole new set of problems when overbearing Jupiter opposes demanding Pluto on **August 7** and squares unruly Uranus on **August 21**. You're so driven to succeed that your ambitions can become obsessive. Your intensity may inadvertently create unseen resistance or attract manipulative behavior from a formidable opponent. This is the first of Jupiter's three stressful alignments with the long-lasting Uranus-Pluto square that finishes on **April 20, 2014**, giving you time to turn a no-win conflict into a win–win situation based on cooperation rather than competition. The emotionally detached Aquarius Full Moon on **August 20** illuminates your 2nd House of Finances. Conflicting aspects with Pluto, Jupiter, and Uranus indicate that careless spending or underestimating the size of a job can drain your resources, leaving you overspent in more ways than one.

> **KEEP IN MIND THIS MONTH**
>
> *You aren't in this alone,*
> *so be sure your ambitions*
> *consider the overall good—not*
> *just your individual success.*

KEY DATES

AUGUST 1-4 ★ *the hero in you*

It's not easy to adjust your personality, yet the Sun's crunchy quincunx to powerful Pluto in your 1st House of Self on **August 1** requires you to change your ways. The need for immediate action to manage your finances is brought to a head by another quincunx, this one from luxurious Venus to Uranus the Awakener. If you're spending excessively or living beyond your means, it's time to act responsibly. Fortunately, you can take advantage of a sweet Venus-Mars sextile on the **2nd** that enables you to share your dilemma and benefit by collaborating with others. Don't wait for someone to come to your rescue; the dramatic Leo Sun's trine to radical Uranus on the **4th** calls for bold action that will bring both emotional and financial rewards.

AUGUST 11–14 ★ *flight or fight*

You may doubt yourself following a harsh exchange of words on **August 11**, when Mercury the Messenger squares judgmental Saturn. Mercury's visit to your 8th House of Transformation challenges you to rethink your strategy and respond to valid criticism, although you might want to withdraw from conflict. Your mind is working overtime and it's difficult to control your thoughts as Mercury quincunxes compulsive Pluto on the **13th**. Others may be unwilling to negotiate, so don't sign on the dotted line immediately. Wait until the communication planet trines Uranus on the **14th**; at that point your intuition is strong, and your insights reveal surprisingly simple ways to resolve existing issues.

SUPER NOVA DAYS
AUGUST 20–23 ★ *bite your tongue*

You may discover difficulties with joint finances when the independent Aquarius Full Moon on **August 20** opposes the charismatic Leo Sun. But keep your reaction in check; overblown Jupiter's square to spontaneous Uranus on the **21st** can trick you into believing you've discovered a quick fix. On **August 22**, clever Mercury's tough aspects to the Jupiter-Uranus square further tempt you to substitute wit for wisdom. Fortunately, the Sun shifts into analytical Virgo and your 9th House of Future Vision on the **22nd**, followed by Mercury on the **23rd**, facilitating a more practical approach to creating positive change.

AUGUST 26–30 ★ *hold your ground*

The attraction you're feeling to unusual people or ideas may be an overreaction to instability at work when desirable Venus in your 10th House of Career opposes wild Uranus and squares exuberant Jupiter on **August 26–27**. Thankfully, a sensible Mercury-Saturn sextile on the **27th** followed by a reassuring Sun-Saturn sextile on the **30th** help you find and follow the voice of reason amid the noise of turbulent change.

SEPTEMBER

DOMINO EFFECT

You have significant choices to make this month as changing circumstances require you to reconsider your plans and adjust them as needed. It's tempting to seek security in what you know, rather than facing the unknown, especially on the days preceding the focused Virgo New Moon on **September 5** that lands in your 9th House of Big Ideas. Frustration may set in as you try to balance your need to gather reliable information with your relentless drive to distinguish yourself professionally when messenger Mercury shifts into your 10th House of Career on **September 9**. However, pushy Mars in heroic Leo runs into a confining square with your ruling planet, Saturn, the same day, forcing you to slow down even if you're ready to forge ahead.

Karmic Saturn—moving through Scorpio and your 11th House of Friends and Wishes—can reveal a widening gulf between your personal goals and the commitments you've made to others as it forms an uneasy semisquare to the Sun on **September 16**. Saturn joins the soulful North Node of the Moon on the **17th**, confirming the importance of your current decisions that could drastically alter your path in life. Sexy Venus stimulates intense feelings when entering Scorpio on **September 11**, yet her conjunctions with the North Node and sobering Saturn on the **18th** demand that you must take responsibility for your long-term goals, rather than seek immediate gratification. The imaginative Pisces Full Moon on the **19th** illuminates your 3rd House of Learning, reminding you to hold on to your dreams. Thankfully, a profound but subtle transformative Saturn-Pluto sextile on **September 21** blesses you with the resources you need for the metamorphosis you've already begun.

> **KEEP IN MIND THIS MONTH**
>
> *You won't reach your goals overnight; however, you're making more progress than you realize. Slow down long enough to appreciate how much you've already accomplished.*

KEY DATES

SEPTEMBER 1–5 ★ *dare to believe*

You may feel invincible on **September 1** when the Sun in your 9th House of Adventure trines indefatigable Pluto. But uncertainty creeps into the picture on the **2nd** when action-hero Mars forms an ill-adjusted quincunx with vague Neptune. You're tempted to overreact to your uncertainty by taking an unnecessary risk on the **3rd** when the Sun quincunxes explosive Uranus. But intelligent Mercury semisquares unforgiving Saturn on **September 4**, sending you back to the drawing board to fix what's wrong with your current plans. Thankfully, the exacting Virgo New Moon on **September 5** sextiles bountiful Jupiter, planting seeds that encourage learning and inspire you to seek more meaning by broadening your horizons.

SEPTEMBER 9 ★ *reality check*

Change is in the air as thoughtful Mercury shifts into fair-minded Libra and your 10th House of Career on **September 9**. But you grow frustrated as reckless Mars squares no-nonsense Saturn and your enthusiasm meets resistance from colleagues or friends. Balance your buoyancy with realism rather than resorting to aggressive behavior or blaming others for your difficulties.

SEPTEMBER 14 ★ *tunnel of love*

You're emboldened to act immediately today when an idealistic Venus-Neptune trine enchants you with romantic dreams while expressive Mars in your 8th House of Intimacy harmonizes with edgy Uranus. At the same time, contemplative Mercury's square to insatiable Pluto can trick you into obsessing about a fantasy. If you give others emotional breathing room, you'll improve your chances for success.

SUPER NOVA DAYS
SEPTEMBER 19–22 ★ *the power of now*

Nervous Mercury's square to excessive Jupiter could bring information overload on **September 19**; meanwhile, the mystical Pisces Full Moon distracts you further from the workings of everyday life. However, the subtle direct turn of evolutionary Pluto on the **20th** is strengthened by its cooperative sextile to orderly Saturn on the **21st**, helping you eliminate anything that has become obsolete in your life. The Sun's shift into Libra and your professional 10th House on **September 22** is the Autumn Equinox and a reminder to balance pursuing your career ambitions with relaxation.

SEPTEMBER 26–28 ★ *sweet surrender*

Sultry Venus in magnetic Scorpio trines joyous Jupiter in your 7th House of Partners on **September 26**, blessing you with the delight of pleasurable relationships. A romantic interlude is possible and the exciting Venus-Mars square on **September 28** can incite passion for some or a power struggle for others. Meanwhile, a metaphysical Jupiter-Neptune sesquisquare coaxes you to sail past your usual boundaries to explore the magic of spiritual love.

OCTOBER

A FORK IN THE ROAD

Your drive to succeed professionally is in high gear this month with the strategic Libra Sun moving through your 10th House of Career until **October 23**. However, instability on the home front is likely to distract you from your work because of noisy aspects to uncontainable Uranus as it journeys through your 4th House of Foundations. The Sun's opposition to untamable Uranus on the **3rd** increases your restlessness, tempting you to walk away from a domestic conflict or surprising you with radical behavior from a family member. Although the Uranus-Pluto square—the fourth in a series that started in 2012 and lasts through 2015—occurs on **November 1**, you can feel the pressure between your inner and outer worlds intensify throughout October. The shocking Uranus-Pluto square is reactivated on **October 4** by the Libra New Moon in your 10th House, forcing you to choose between your public responsibilities and personal issues that require your undivided attention.

On the one hand, you recognize that the direction of your life has already begun to shift in profound ways. On the other, conservative Saturn's uneasy quincunx to progressive Uranus on the **5th** heightens your resistance to change. Venus shifts into inspirational Sagittarius on the **7th** and Mars moves into your 9th House of Adventure on **October 15**, encouraging you to look ahead rather than hold on to the past. The speedy Aries Lunar Eclipse on the **18th** fires up your 4th House of Family, leading you to believe that you can quickly patch up a wounded relationship, but Mercury's retrograde turn on the **21st** indicates that it will take longer to solve the current crisis.

KEEP IN MIND THIS MONTH

It's important to consider the long-term ramifications of your current choices as tension between home and career rises, rather than limiting your analysis to the immediate situation.

KEY DATES

SUPER NOVA DAYS

OCTOBER 1–5 ★ *phoenix rising*

You may have to prove that you're able to meet tough challenges on **October 1** when the punishing Sun-Pluto square stacks the odds against you. However, a psychic Mercury-Neptune trine advises you to trust your intuition when making decisions. Still, a rebellious Sun-Uranus opposition on the **3rd** provokes you to overreact if you believe that someone's working against you. The Libra New Moon on **October 4** in your professional 10th House forms stressful aspects to Pluto, Uranus, Venus, and Jupiter; this is a cosmic wake-up call that reminds you what great potential you have for growth and transformation—if you're willing to reinvent yourself. But don't move too quickly: An awkward Saturn-Uranus quincunx on the **5th** reminds you to temper your strong sense of urgency with a more traditional approach to change.

OCTOBER 8 ★ *bundle of nerves*
Your ideas are challenged by friends as contentious Mercury connects with obstinate Saturn in your 11th House of Social Networking. Seriously consider your next move; Mercury's anxious quincunx to independent Uranus jangles your nervous system and tempts you to speak prematurely. Listen to others, even if the advice seems harsh; self-restraint is more effective now than doing damage control later.

OCTOBER 14-18 ★ *reckless abandon*
A creative quintile between restless Mars and restrictive Saturn on **October 14** reveals whether it's wiser to hold your cards or fold them. You may grow more opinionated when Mars enters your 9th House of Big Ideas on the **15th**, enticing you to gamble with your money or your heart. Anything is possible in love when vivacious Venus trines outrageous Uranus on the **16th**. However, selfish motives can interfere with your success as the uncooperative Aries Full Moon Eclipse on **October 18** emphasizes the differences between your needs and those of your family or friends.

OCTOBER 29-31 ★ *creative genius*
Your ability to concentrate your intentions and focus your thoughts is strengthened on **October 29** when retrograde Mercury backs into disciplined Saturn in your 11th House of Dreams and Wishes. However, rather than working with new ideas, you may find yourself reconsidering old ones from earlier in the month. On **October 31**, fearless Mars trines unwavering Pluto, convincing you that you're on the right track. But Mars also quincunxes erratic Uranus, throwing curveballs your way. You may act decisively one moment, only to be uncertain the next. Nevertheless, the situation calls for your special talents. By demonstrating consistency and commitment, you are able to reach unexpected heights.

NOVEMBER

LOVE IS IN THE AIR

This month begins on an intense note; you must confront unresolved psychological issues that prevent you from reaching your full potential as eye-opening Uranus squares regenerating Pluto on **November 1**. The transformative Scorpio Solar Eclipse on **November 3** shakes up your 11th House of Social Networking, indicating sudden shifts in your personal life that can break your connections with people who no longer support your goals. Sobering aspects from Venus and the Sun to austere Saturn on **November 4–6** infuse your life with a somber tone. However, beautiful Venus sashays into your earthy sign on the **5th**, setting the stage for sweet romance and more pleasurable times through the end of the year. Venus sextiles enchanting Neptune and persuasive Mercury on **November 7–8**, casting a magical spell over you and mesmerizing others with your charms. On **November 10**, Mercury ends its three-week retrograde period in your communal 11th House, prompting you to participate in more group activities.

Your desires may be difficult to manage, complicating current relationships or attracting a dangerous new love interest on **November 14–15** when Venus squares irrepressible Uranus and hooks up with enigmatic Pluto. The sensual Taurus Full Moon on **November 17** lands in your 5th House of Romance and Self-Expression, motivating you to ask for exactly what you want. However, stressful lunar aspects to Uranus and Pluto could bring a surprise that creates a sudden change of heart. Thankfully, positive Saturn aspects establish healthy limits on **November 23–25**, but they don't stop the fun. Mercury and Venus are harbingers of good cheer as they align with joyful Jupiter on the **28th**. An exciting Sun-Uranus trine on the **30th** awakens you to the amazing possibilities ahead if you're willing to embrace the future.

> **KEEP IN MIND THIS MONTH**
>
> *You're not one to throw caution to the wind, but taking a calculated risk for love just might bring you the happiness you deserve.*

KEY DATES

SUPER NOVA DAYS
NOVEMBER 1–3 ★ *embrace the unknown*
Long-term changes that began with the first occurrence of the repeating Uranus-Pluto square on **June 24, 2012**, come back into sharp focus on

November 1. Thankfully, supportive sextiles from the Sun and Mercury in your 11th House of Goals to incisive Pluto provide you with sufficient mental clarity to understand the far-reaching implications of your current choices. But don't move too quickly, because unmanageable quincunxes from the Sun and Mercury to Uranus make it difficult for you to gauge how much support you'll receive from friends and family. You might feel as if you're completely on your own when the New Moon Eclipse stresses your 11th House of Teamwork on **November 3**. Strengthen your body and cultivate your beliefs, since this eclipse sextiles physical Mars in your 9th House of Higher Truth.

NOVEMBER 9-12 ★ *forward march*
You have more strength, will, and endurance when persistent Saturn sextiles energetic Mars on **November 9**. Mental Mercury in perceptive Scorpio turns direct on the **10th**, reinforcing how important it is that you clean up any confusion, communication glitches, or unfinished business. Working in partnership with someone who can inspire you is an excellent way to move into the future with confidence as the Sun trines benevolent Jupiter in your 7th House of Companions on **November 12**.

NOVEMBER 14-17 ★ *tangled up in blue*
Your charms attract plenty of attention with captivating Venus in your sign, but its square to high-strung Uranus on **November 14** may have you feeling nervous about your appearance. While the seductive Venus-Pluto conjunction on the **15th** deepens your emotions, try not to suppress them; it can build pressure that might suddenly erupt. Your natural resourcefulness is highlighted by the practical Taurus Full Moon on **November 17**. Relationship intimacy can lead to jealousy or a melodramatic power struggle as difficult aspects from this lunation to extreme Uranus, possessive Pluto, and needy Venus intensify your feelings. Instead of making mountains out of molehills, focus on the gifts that simple pleasures bring.

NOVEMBER 23-25 ★ *keep it real*
You're the master of your emotions on **November 23**, able to delay gratification thanks to a reserved Venus-Saturn sextile. But deviating from the facts can prove problematic when a whimsical Sun-Neptune square warps your sense of proportion on the **24th**. Thankfully, a meeting of reflective Mercury and earnest Saturn on the **25th** in your 11th House of Dreams and Wishes banishes the clouds of illusion from the sky, enabling you to refocus on what's most important.

DECEMBER

GIVE PEACE A CHANCE

It's nearly impossible to imagine that this year of dramatic twists and turns still holds a few surprises, but the winds of change continue to blow strongly through the end of the month. You're ready for the next phase of your journey as the adventurous Sagittarius New Moon on **December 2** accentuates your 12th House of Endings. Its accommodating trine to Uranus the Awakener opens your eyes to what you can accomplish if you don't let your fear of the unknown get in the way. Fortunately, you're able to rely on the encouragement and support of others as magnanimous Jupiter in your 7th House of Partners trines trustworthy Saturn in your 11th House of Long-Term Goals on **December 12**. This benevolent aspect revives realistic dreams that you felt stirring during the first stabilizing Jupiter-Saturn trine on **July 17**. Nevertheless, don't be lulled into complacency; there's still plenty of work to do before the third and final recurrence of this trine on **May 24, 2014**.

The versatile Gemini Full Moon on **December 17** lights up your 6th House of Work. Although you want to make improvements to your daily routine, a diffusive Jupiter-Neptune alignment tempts you to spread yourself too thin. The Sun's shift into your sign on the **21st** marks the Winter Solstice, inspiring you to shine your inner light. Simultaneously, Venus turns retrograde in calculating Capricorn, possibly postponing the personal or professional satisfaction you thought was so close. Aggressive Mars adds stress to the holidays by opposing disruptive Uranus on the **25th** and squaring suspicious Pluto on the **30th**. Fortunately, you're able to minimize domestic squabbles by concentrating on sharing love rather than closing down with fear.

KEEP IN MIND THIS MONTH

You are at a nexus of powerful cosmic currents. Only through extra effort can you balance your goals with the stresses and joys of the holidays.

KEY DATES

DECEMBER 4–7 ★ *dream catcher*

Your thoughts grow less practical and more visionary as pensive Mercury slips into farsighted Sagittarius and your 12th House of Soul Consciousness on **December 4**. Even if you're not usually interested in spiritual matters, someone may awaken you to the creative power of your dreams on the **5th** when boundless Jupiter in your 7th House of Others aspects the Sun. A foggy Mercury-Neptune square on the

6th continues to emphasize imagination over reality, while an overblown Mercury-Jupiter sesquisquare on the **7th** further encourages you to ignore details if they conflict with your aspirations. But Mars's shift into accommodating Libra and your 10th House of Public Responsibility refocuses your efforts on a more pragmatic approach to professional success.

DECEMBER 14-17 ★ *out of bounds*

You may be so obsessed with reaching your goals when forceful Mars in your 10th House of Status semisquares ambitious Saturn on **December 14** that you temporarily forget about social graces. But persistence alone won't let you overcome the resistance of others. You have to adjust your attitude when outspoken Mercury forms an argumentative quincunx with pompous Jupiter on the **16th**. It's difficult to gauge how flexible you need to be on the **17th**, when the fickle Gemini Full Moon tempts you to change your position too quickly. Don't count on others for sound advice now, because Jupiter in your interactive 7th House forms an undependable sesquisquare to deceptive Neptune the same day.

SUPER NOVA DAYS
DECEMBER 24-27 ★ *take the high road*

You can grasp and apply metaphysical or psychological concepts on **December 24**, allowing you to get along with others—even amid chaos and mayhem—thanks to an intuitive Sun-Neptune sextile. Focus on compassion when a cantankerous opposition between hotheaded Mars and incorrigible Uranus on the **25th** incites conflict and tempts you to give in to irritability. Controlling your temper prevents tensions from escalating, but hard aspects from the Sun and Mercury to authoritative Saturn on **December 26-27** test your resolve. Exercising objectivity and double-checking your facts should eliminate or minimize the potential damage.

DECEMBER 29-31 ★ *independent streak*

Mercury and the Sun square unorthodox Uranus on **December 29-30**, triggering you to recklessly break out of your routine in your search for freedom. Impatient Mars squares intense Pluto and messenger Mercury on **December 30-31**, motivating you to say and do whatever's necessary to make your case. It's useless to pretend that you're willing to submit to someone else's point of view; the most peaceful way to handle this potentially volatile situation is to just smile and walk away.

AQUARIUS

JANUARY 20–FEBRUARY 18

AQUARIUS

2012 SUMMARY

You've been stewing in a mix of symbols that flow into your imagination from the hidden realms of your dreams. An overhaul of your finances and a reevaluation of how you produce income will be gradual, but you'll get what you deserve—and if you've defined your goals and worked hard to achieve them, this can be the payoff. Just remember that during these hectic times, flexibility is your friend.

AUGUST—*do what you love, love what you do*

Hard work is child's play when you do it for a cause or project you fully believe in.

SEPTEMBER—*complicated connections*

Minor adjustments may save a relationship, even if you think that drastic changes are the only way to keep it from falling apart.

OCTOBER—*balancing act*

You can balance utopian dreams with earthbound necessities if you develop the flexibility to adjust your behavior.

NOVEMBER—*listen to your heart*

Persistence is only useful if it's moving you toward a better place. Don't just hold on out of habit or fear.

DECEMBER—*buried treasure*

Looking into your heart of darkness is not a ticket to despair, but rather a passport to a brighter future where you can put your talents to use.

2012 CALENDAR

AUGUST

WED 1–THU 2 ★	**SUPER NOVA DAYS** The spotlight is on you
THU 9 ★	Bring an extra dose of creativity and commitment to your job
WED 15–SAT 18 ★	There's no room for nonsense now
MON 20–WED 22 ★	Finding the right pace may be difficult
TUE 28 ★	Your ideas might be too far ahead of their time

SEPTEMBER

THU 6–FRI 7 ★	Watch out for a tendency to overindulge
THU 13 ★	A light touch helps you to work around resistance
THU 20 ★	Supercharged conversations put everyone on edge
MON 24–TUE 25 ★	**SUPER NOVA DAYS** You're reluctant to follow the rules
SAT 29 ★	Make a quick getaway before anyone notices you're gone

OCTOBER

FRI 5–SUN 7 ★	Mastery of information is critical
TUE 9–WED 10 ★	**SUPER NOVA DAYS** Look beyond short-term issues
MON 15 ★	Consolidate gains before you push ahead
SAT 20–SUN 21 ★	Step back and try a simpler approach
SUN 28–MON 29 ★	Stay calm and narrow your focus

NOVEMBER

THU 1–SAT 3 ★	An unexpected event shakes up your life
FRI 9–SUN 11 ★	Embrace intimate feelings in spite of any differences
THU 15 ★	Earn your freedom one small step at a time
THU 22–FRI 23 ★	**SUPER NOVA DAYS** Hopes and dreams override reality
MON 26 ★	Express your originality

DECEMBER

SAT 1–SUN 2 ★	Your enthusiasm could be contagious
FRI 7 ★	Attraction to an unusual individual or activity can be risky
FRI 14–SUN 16 ★	Experiment with new techniques to get things done
WED 19 ★	You can have your cake and eat it, too
TUE 25–WED 26 ★	**SUPER NOVA DAYS** Start new traditions

AQUARIUS OVERVIEW

This year is complex for you, because revolutionary Uranus awakens your mind to fresh ideas and new ways to communicate as it continues to occupy your 3rd House of Information and Education. At the same time, however, a powerful series of squares between your ruling planet Uranus and potent Pluto that began last year pressures you to avoid risks and unfamiliarity. These contradictory aspects occur on May 20 and November 1 and complete this cycle of alignments on March 16, 2015. **Fortunately, if you're willing to face your fears, you could discover that some aren't real and that you can finally let them go.** Self-awareness is essential to recognizing the beliefs that stand between you and success, empowering you to eliminate unproductive attitudes from your life. You'll be ready to take action and break free from the past with the arrival of spring, for Uranus is joined by energetic Mars on March 22, by the Sun and Venus on March 28, and by perceptive Mercury on April 20. Even if you're unable to make a radical move during these chaotic times, you can catch glimpses of a more exciting future that's worth pursuing later.

Opportunities for personal growth abound as Jupiter visits your 5th House of Self-Expression, bringing out the playful kid in you. On June 25, visionary Jupiter enters your 6th House of Employment to increase opportunities for professional growth and add meaning to your work. **A strategic perspective allows you to step back and reassess your skills to determine how to apply them more effectively.** Greater efficiency in your current workplace is likely, but this new awareness of your abilities can also inspire you to seek additional training and aim for a more rewarding position. Wise Jupiter's presence in emotional Cancer awakens strong feelings about how you serve others. If you're stuck in a dull and lifeless situation, this transit triggers a desire to change your career trajectory. Security comes from following your instincts instead of holding on to a job that pays your salary but robs your soul.

Heavy-handed Saturn in scrutinizing Scorpio occupies your 10th House of Career and Public Life, weighing you down with extra responsibilities. Therefore, **a more discriminating sense of judgment helps you to avoid taking on obligations that aren't worth the time and effort required to fulfill them.** This comes in very handy when optimistic Jupiter squares impulsive Uranus on August 21 and you're tempted to take a giant leap without fully considering where you will land. Fortunately, you're given a more strategic perspective when well-balanced Jupiter-Saturn trines activate your work-related 6th and 10th Houses on July 17 and December 12, repeating on May 24, 2014, motivating you to make a serious career decision. Your assessment of where it's appropriate to expand and seek opportunities and what you must do to strengthen your skills to support these ambitions should be right on target.

FUN AND GAMES

Romantic Venus enters unconventional Aquarius and your 1st House of Self to enrich your personal life on February 1. Update your appearance and experiment in relationships; you'll garner plenty of attention and affection. Outgoing Jupiter occupies your 5th House of Love until June 25, which is bound to raise your social profile. Your capacity to have fun in a wide variety of circumstances might lead some people to take you less seriously. On August 6, the New Moon in bighearted Leo in your 7th House of Others forms a harmonious trine with eye-opening Uranus. Unexpected events and unusual people can lead to breakthroughs in your current alliance or spawn opportunities for exciting new connections.

WORK IN PROGRESS

Responsible Saturn in passionate Scorpio and your 10th House of Career indicates the importance of being emotionally engaged in your job this year. But stress can squash the creativity that will help you professionally. Happily, buoyant Jupiter's entry into caring Cancer and your 6th House of Employment on June 25 should lift your spirits. Learning new skills or finally gaining recognition for the ones you already have should make your work more rewarding. Jupiter's transit encourages you to start or expand your own business as well, but don't spread yourself too thin or grow too fast. A Solar Eclipse in your 10th House on November 3 is conjunct to constraining Saturn, which can slam the brakes on a major project, push you past your limits, or even wear you down mentally or physically. Taking a long-term view of your aspirations enables you to cut your losses now so you can gain more later.

DREAMING FOR DOLLARS

Inspiration is key to maintaining your income this year as imaginative Neptune continues its long-term presence in your 2nd House of Money. Still, there's a risk of letting idealism go too far when introspective Mercury in intuitive Pisces is retrograde in your 2nd House on February 23–March 17. Pay careful attention to economic matters to avoid making any expensive mistakes. Jupiter and Neptune, the traditional and modern rulers of your 2nd House, form an opportunistic trine on July 17, which fills you with newfound faith in yourself and awakens a vision of future prosperity. Managing expectations and providing a solid foundation to bring them down to earth could be critical when Jupiter and Neptune form fuzzy sesquisquares that can blur your judgment on September 28, December 17, and June 11, 2014.

SHOCK TO THE SYSTEM

It's tempting to ignore physical concerns while oppressive Pluto continues its long-lasting series of squares with irrepressible Uranus. Yet denying your body's needs could lead to an unpleasant surprise when overblown Jupiter squares Uranus on August 21. This is the first of three tense aspects that are meant to alert you to health concerns you might prefer to ignore. A radical shift in diet or exercise may be appealing, but it's better to make less dramatic modifications that you can stick with. Jupiter and Uranus will meet again on February 26 and April 20, 2014, indicating the importance of being flexible enough to respond quickly as you learn new ways to strengthen your immune system and improve your overall physical well-being.

REBUILD FROM THE GROUND UP

A Taurus Solar Eclipse in your 4th House of Domestic Conditions on May 9 shakes family traditions, destabilizes your home life, and forces you to reexamine your relationship to the past—potentially influencing your life for the next six months. Four planets in stubborn Taurus make change difficult as either you or someone close to you resists it. If you're willing to step out of outmoded emotional patterns and surrender old ways of thinking, the certainty that's lost will be richly compensated by the sense of freedom you gain.

PLEASURE PRINCIPLE

It's a perfect time to embark on a trip when sensuous Venus, the ruler of your 9th House of Faraway Places, joins adventurous Jupiter on May 28. This cosmic union in your 5th House of Love and Play can inspire you to journey to an exotic locale. The artistic Libra New Moon on October 4 occurs in your 9th House, which may also spur you to dream of travel and enjoyable educational experiences. However, exigent Pluto's tense square to this Sun-Moon conjunction suggests that you should consider the hidden costs and personal risks before investing in a pricey excursion.

DIVINE INSPIRATION

Spiritual studies are interesting but won't affect your life as much as regular devotional practices. The Sun's presence in orderly Capricorn and your 12th House of Soul Consciousness when the year begins nourishes your soul with a regular routine of prayer, meditation, or communing with nature. Alluring Venus's union with transformational Pluto in your 12th House on January 16 may test your faith, yet rededicating yourself to a higher purpose empowers you to create positive change. Astonishing Uranus opens your eyes to a whole new universe of possibilities on May 20 and November 1, when it squares evolutionary Pluto.

> ### RICK & JEFF'S TIP FOR THE YEAR:
> #### Agility Creates Options
>
> Your incessant need to be right can get in the way of learning, growing, and discovering more effective ways to run your life. Recognizing that there are many different roads to happiness frees you from hanging on to impossible goals and unrealistic expectations. Adaptability, innovation, and exploration are more rewarding allies than persistence in the face of unyielding obstacles.

JANUARY

WAITING IN THE WINGS

You start the year on an energetic note with dynamic Mars in Aquarius and your 1st House of Physicality, yet obtaining results and recognition for your efforts may not be easy at first. The Sun lurking in the shadows of your 12th House of Secrets until **January 19** makes it hard to get noticed. But you might like the privacy, as it may be more comfortable to work outside the glare of the spotlight. In fact, on **January 8** resourceful Venus shifts into well-organized Capricorn and your 12th House, suggesting that your most significant personal and professional encounters occur behind closed doors. Discretion in relationships is a must, since exposing intimate issues could be especially embarrassing now. The ambitious Capricorn New Moon on **January 11** can spur interest in big projects, but you have a great deal of preparation to do before you can go public with your plans. Completing unfinished business and increasing your efficiency must come first.

Your personal New Year begins on **January 19** when brainy Mercury and the confidence-building Sun enter Aquarius. A fresh wave of enthusiasm encourages you to get your body in shape and to start reaching out to more people. Your capacity to engage others in what you're doing expands with the growing force of your personality. The melodramatic Leo Full Moon in your 7th House of Partners on **January 26** forms a tense square with resistant Saturn. However, you can overcome delays, doubts, and denial from others with originality as farsighted Jupiter and progressive Uranus align favorably with this lunation to show you new solutions to old problems.

> **KEEP IN MIND THIS MONTH**
>
> *Even your most brilliant ideas will fail if they're not rooted in an orderly life that gives you the freedom to take chances without losing your solid footing.*

KEY DATES

SUPER NOVA DAYS
JANUARY 3–7 ★ *color between the lines*

Expect surprising information to arrive—as well as a sudden change of mind—with a brilliant but volatile Mercury-Uranus square on **January 3**. Don't overreact or respond recklessly if your instinct to move quickly is fired up by a high-energy trine between impatient Mars and boundless Jupiter on the **4th**. This supercharged alignment helps you push your body and sell your ideas with entrepreneurial fervor. But pesky Mercury fakes you out on the **5th** with an awkward quincunx to Jupiter that spawns misstatements or prompts you to misconstrue facts. The hammer of reality starts to fall when Mercury joins incisive Pluto on **January 6**, demanding concentration, exposing flaws, and intensifying communication. The final shot comes with a stern Mars-Saturn square on the **7th** that allows no room for errors. Accountability is high, especially at work, but you can garner some hard-earned respect if you demonstrate discipline and patience.

JANUARY 12 ★ *love interrupted*
Affable Venus's square with strange Uranus can upset a relationship with a sudden change of moods, tastes, or plans. It's helpful to leave yourself an exit strategy if you're not sure that you want to stick to a social engagement. Taking time to be alone or exploring unconventional forms of fun are appropriate ways to express this aspect.

JANUARY 19-20 ★ *velvet revolution*
Your excitement rises when friendly Mercury and the radiant Sun enter your sign on **January 19**. You act impulsively with an explosive Mars-Uranus semisquare on the **20th** that can find you in a less-than-cooperative mood. Inventing your own rules and acting independently could upset others unless you temper your behavior with a spoonful of sweetness.

JANUARY 24-25 ★ *back to the books*
You may be cooking up some new ideas with an ingenious Sun-Uranus sextile on **January 24**, allowing you to present an odd concept in ways that others can understand. Maintaining support, though, is challenging on the **25th** when Mercury forms a square with skeptical Saturn, leading people to doubt you or to demand proof that what you're saying is actually true. Don't force an issue; you may need to exercise self-restraint and do some further research to build a solid case.

JANUARY 30 ★ *work now play later*
Joyful Jupiter's forward turn in your 5th House of Play on **January 30** is ready to unlock some chances for fun that have been on hold for too long. But you may have to wait patiently to cash in your golden ticket since a somber Sun-Saturn square dominates the day. Work responsibilities come first and require a level of commitment that doesn't allow much room for distraction.

AQUARIUS

FEBRUARY

FOLLOW YOUR BLISS

Money matters are on your mind as four planets move into quixotic Pisces and your 2nd House of Income this month. Action-planet Mars leads the way on **February 1**, followed by messenger Mercury on the **5th**, the Sun on the **18th**, and lucrative Venus on the **25th**. Economic issues are closely connected to your ideals; if your work aligns with your beliefs, the cash will flow more readily. But if you're stuck in an uninspiring job, being well paid will not be enough to keep you happy and healthy. Finding a higher purpose and putting more passion into what you do are well worth the effort; if that's impossible in your current situation, looking elsewhere is a good idea. You might find it easier to change directions now, because amicable Venus enters Aquarius and your 1st House of Self on **February 1** to make you more appealing to others. An image makeover gives you confidence that infuses your professional and personal lifes, adding to your charisma.

The intelligent Aquarius New Moon on **February 10** empowers you to tackle unfamiliar tasks and take the initiative in relationships. Quicksilver Mercury slips into reverse gear on the **23rd**, turning retrograde in your 2nd House of Resources, where it backpedals until **March 17**. Reviewing financial records could save you from some costly errors, and reminiscing about the past can revive interest in long-ignored talents. If you have been overpaying with money, commitment, love, or energy, the bill may come due with the exacting Virgo Full Moon that highlights your 8th House of Deep Sharing on **February 25**. It's time to closely examine what you're receiving from others and to restate your expectations as precisely as you can.

> **KEEP IN MIND THIS MONTH**
>
> *The most practical moves for others won't necessarily benefit you. Trust your instincts before following someone else's advice.*

KEY DATES

SUPER NOVA DAYS
FEBRUARY 6–7 ★ *irresistible you*
Brains and personality are a tough combination to beat—and you have both working in your favor now. Charming Venus's slick sextile to innovative Uranus on **February 6** enables you to lead people where you want them to go and make them think it's their idea. The imaginative power of cerebral Mercury's

conjunction with Neptune, the fantasy planet, inspires you to paint beautiful verbal pictures that help you iron out conflicts with others. Smooth talking, however, is only a temporary bridge to overcome differences, so remember that you must fill in many details before you can turn this dream into reality. Still, a beautiful Venus-Jupiter trine on the **7th** is astrology's most favorable aspect between its two traditional "benefics." It's bound to lift your spirits and show off your captivating personality; people will have a hard time refusing your requests. Don't spend all this goodwill on trivial matters when you can gain acceptance and even support that grows into love and professional admiration.

FEBRUARY 9–11 ★ *patience is a virtue*
Use your common sense on **February 9**, when a rebellious Sun-Uranus semisquare can trigger you to act impulsively. You may have a brilliant new idea, but you tend to go too far too fast with an overheated Mars-Jupiter square on **January 10**. Being right isn't an asset when your opinions are so strong that they push others away or provoke you into careless behavior. The quirky Aquarius New Moon, also on the **10th,** marks the beginning of a personal cycle of development. A serious Venus-Saturn square on the **11th** can take some air out of your social balloon, but it's meant to encourage you to make careful calculations before investing too much of yourself. Don't try to race past your doubts; you're more likely to find fulfillment when you diligently work for it.

FEBRUARY 15–16 ★ *eye of the tiger*
You feel physically strong and tremendously productive with two days of friction-free aspects involving muscular Mars. A sextile with powerful Pluto on **February 15** and trine with hardworking Saturn on the **16th** ensure concentration that permits you to operate at a very high level of efficiency.

FEBRUARY 19–22 ★ *change of heart*
Relationships could go askew with flirty Venus's edgy semisquare to unruly Uranus on **February 19**. Your tastes may suddenly shift as the potential for boredom rises. It's best, though, to avoid playing games with those you love, because provocative Pluto's semisquare to Venus on the **22nd** can lure you across a line that permanently alters a partnership.

MARCH

THINK DIFFERENT

If you're a lover of new ideas—which most Aquarians are—you're in for an amazing month. Valiant Mars leads the way on **March 12** when he enters pioneering Aries and your 3rd House of Information and Education to fire up your brain with intellectual challenges. The Sun shifts into bold Aries on the **20th**, marking the Spring Equinox, to add confidence in your search for answers and inspire courage in your drive to express yourself. Sassy Venus makes the same transition on the **21st**, spicing up your conversations and learning experiences with flirtatious intrigue. Yet before you start indulging in pleasure, it pays to take another look at money matters, because the spacey Pisces New Moon falls in your 2nd House of Income on **March 11**. Conjunctions with aesthetic Venus and ardent Mars give you a boost of creativity to increase your cash flow, enhance your self-worth, and put more delight in your personal life.

It's time to leave financial fantasies behind and address current economic issues in a realistic manner when Mercury's direct turn in your 2nd House of Finances on **March 17** occurs very close to dreamy Neptune. If you've had a moneymaking plan on hold, however, the messenger planet picks up speed in the weeks ahead, which could get your deal moving again. On **March 27**, the usually languorous Libra Full Moon in your 9th House of Faraway Places is agitated by hard aspects to Uranus, Pluto, Venus, and Mars that could shake up travel plans. A sudden impulse to change your itinerary or take off for an exotic locale can inspire your mind, but may be overly ambitious for your budget.

> **KEEP IN MIND THIS MONTH**
>
> *If you can't apply an exciting insight in your life right now, let it go. Many more bright ideas will be coming your way.*

KEY DATES

MARCH 4 ★ *money can't buy you love*

An old financial scheme could reappear with retrograde Mercury rejoining the Sun in your 2nd House of Assets. However, it's likely to look a lot better than it really is with an overly optimistic square between value-conscious Venus and opulent Jupiter. A small expenditure of energy, hope, or money is an inexpensive way to add more pleasure to your life without locking yourself into a long-term commitment that can prove very costly.

MARCH 7–9 ★ *cut to the chase*

If you're in a jam on **March 7**, it makes sense that you try to force a resolution to get out of it, because pushy Mars is tangling with stubborn Saturn. However, a brilliant Mars-Jupiter quintile suggests that there are more inventive ways to address the issue. Brains definitely work better than brawn today. The second of three profound but subtle sextiles between constructive Saturn and productive Pluto on the **8th** reminds you to narrow your focus and concentrate on one task at a time. Hard work now can pay off later with their third and final sextile on **September 21**. Maintaining the discipline needed to follow through, though, may not be easy when Mercury's square to Jupiter on **March 9** scatters your attention in several directions.

SUPER NOVA DAY
MARCH 22 ★ *rebel without a cause*

Electricity is in the air with fire-starter Mars joining high-frequency Uranus in combustible Aries. This bolt of energy rattles your 3rd House of Communication, awakening intuition and sparking instantaneous reactions. You could release this energy through misdirected anger, rebellious refusal to follow the rules—or sudden enlightenment. Warrior Mars hooking up with radical Uranus is a fight for freedom, but you're not the only one feeling it, which can cause conflict on all fronts. Trying your hand at new experiences puts you in sync with this aspect, but a dash of detachment is needed to avoid an emotional meltdown.

MARCH 26 ★ *no guts, no glory*

Go-getter Mars's ambitious sextile with gigantic Jupiter encourages you to express yourself more energetically, which is fabulous for making your point. Yet Mars's square with unforgiving Pluto punishes imprecision, so don't promise more than you can deliver.

MARCH 28 ★ *chemical attraction*

You find wondrous things around every corner when delectable Venus joins the heartfelt Sun and extraterrestrial Uranus to delight your senses in unexpected ways. Your tastes are turned upside down as delicious new flavors of people and experiences offer surprising forms of joy. Love at first sight, touch, or smell can excite you in an instant . . . but could be so fleeting that it does not last the day.

APRIL

STOP, LOOK, AND LISTEN

You can charm the birds right out of the trees this month with several planets rolling through enthusiastic Aries and your 3rd House of Communication. And even if you don't get what you want, you'll have a lot of fun trying. The pioneering Aries New Moon lands in this chatty part of your chart on **April 10**, hooking up with creative lovers Venus and Mars to put a twinkle in your eye and a sparkle in your speech, making this a great time to jump into an artistic project. Your capacity for pleasure grows, and lively connections with others should come easily. However, a more sobering moment arrives when strict Saturn forms a corrective quincunx to independent Uranus on the **12th**. This aspect first occurred on **November 15, 2012**, possibly derailing an original plan or a break for freedom. It's time to adjust your course so that you can keep the essence of a revolutionary idea instead of having it completely fall apart with the final Saturn-Uranus quincunx on **October 5**.

Your thinking speeds up when quick-witted Mercury zips into fast-moving Aries on **April 13**, but lovable Venus ambles into leisurely Taurus and your domestic 4th House on the **15th** to slow things down at home. Taking time to explore sensual delights and beautify your environment enriches your life. While you continue to sizzle with hot new ideas, the shifts of the Sun and Mars into Taurus on the **19th** and **20th** are not-so-subtle reminders to pace yourself. Caution is also called for on **April 25** when the emotionally intense Scorpio Full Moon Eclipse joins ethical Saturn in your 10th House of Career, challenging you to face the music and make a major decision in your professional life.

> **KEEP IN MIND THIS MONTH**
>
> *No matter how quickly your brain races, slow down to consider your options. Besides, taking the scenic route provides delight you won't find in the fast lane.*

KEY DATES

APRIL 1 ★ *courage of your convictions*

There's no fooling you today as wise Jupiter aligns in a smart sextile with the Sun. Your voice will be heard, and your high ideals can inspire others. Creativity also pops with this harmonious aspect since the bold Sun is illuminating your 3rd House of Communication and Jupiter is expanding your 5th House of Self-Expression.

APRIL 6–7 ★ *tunnel of love*

Believing in illusions is tempting as insistent Mars and enchanting Venus form anxious semisquares with surreal Neptune on **April 6**. Romantic fantasies and artistic flights of fancy are wonderful, but don't bet your heart or spend your money on anything less than a sure thing. The urgency to jump into someone's arms or into an irresistible project intensifies with a Venus-Mars conjunction on the **7th**. The heat of your enthusiasm is palpable and encourages you to take risks both personally and professionally. Just consider this a test drive instead of a long-term commitment.

APRIL 14 ★ *know your limits*

You're enchanted with what others have to offer today—but it may sound better than it really is. Appreciative Venus in excitable Aries makes an errant semisquare with generous Jupiter, which often leads to overestimating people or inflating the worth of an experience. The Moon joins Jupiter in your 5th House of Fun and Games in fast-talking Gemini and can entice you into a playful activity before you consider the consequences. Pushing the limits of pleasure and creativity is a good idea as long as you don't go to extremes.

APRIL 17 ★ *hit the ground running*

The Sun joins contentious Mars in your conversational 3rd House, where it can easily provoke arguments. Uncontainable impatience and excessive certainty about one's ideas are the likely triggers of verbal sparring. If you have a point, make it and move on instead of getting bogged down in a petty dispute. However, if you can apply the passion you're feeling to create a meaningful connection with someone you admire or begin a fascinating new course of study, the powerful fire of this conjunction propels you in an exciting new direction.

SUPER NOVA DAYS
APRIL 20–22 ★ *genius at work*

Your ability to think outside the box can lead to breakthroughs in awareness on **April 20**, thanks to the intellectual electricity of an incandescent but nervous Mercury-Uranus conjunction. Still, you must remain patient and pragmatic with Mercury's square to exacting Pluto on the **21st**. Purging unessential information reveals what's most important, which can earn you trust from others when Venus opposes stern Saturn on the **22nd**.

MAY

THE CHOICE IS YOURS

A pair of powerful eclipses leads you to reconsider long-term goals this month. On **May 9**, a conventional Taurus Solar Eclipse in your 4th House of Roots may cause you to take a step back from a home-based project or address a family matter that you thought was already settled. It's crucial that you firm up your foundation with a visionary Sagittarius Full Moon Lunar Eclipse in your 11th House of Dreams and Wishes on **May 25**. Illusory Neptune's stressful square to the eclipse might attract you to an unrealizable goal or inspire you to invest more in a project that's already draining your resources. It's best to unburden yourself of unnecessary obligations, especially with the earthshaking Uranus-Pluto square on the **20th**. Save your strength to deal with unexpected emergencies or sudden opportunities that require your attention.

Your thoughts about the future may be nourished with new information this month—or overstuffed with choices that complicate decision making. Vivacious Venus, curious Mercury, the willful Sun, and hyperactive Mars enter diverse Gemini and your 9th House of Higher Thought and Faraway Places on **May 9, 15, 20**, and **31**, respectively, presenting you with more options than you have time to explore. Your attraction to a variety of belief systems and distant cultures is enormously entertaining and educational but is likely to distract you from the real work of your daily life. It's time for you to choose one direction on **May 20**, with dispersive Jupiter's third and final sesquisquare to steadfast Saturn. Commit yourself to one major goal by gathering your attention and pointing it in a singular direction. Doing so will advance your ambitions; failing to can keep you stuck where you are.

> **KEEP IN MIND THIS MONTH**
>
> *Recognizing the difference between a passing interest and an enduring passion will help you to stop flirting with plans that have little likelihood of fulfillment.*

KEY DATES

MAY 1 ★ *no pain, no gain*

Conflicting obligations at home and work can put you in a pressure-packed situation. An opposition between active Mars in your 4th House of Domestic Conditions and exigent Saturn in your 10th House of Profession can leave you feeling hemmed in and, perhaps, frustrated by all that's demanded of you. The good news is that all this stress could cause you to clarify your priorities and establish a more disciplined approach or a better system, becoming more effective in both places.

MAY 5–6 ★ *agent of change*
Expect surprises in your personal life on **May 5** when loving Venus misaligns with unsettling Uranus. Irrational behavior and irresponsible people can rattle your relationships. You may be exhilarated to discover newfound freedom and forms of fun, but you're more likely to feel uncomfortable. If you go out on a limb, primal Pluto's connection with Venus on the **6th** will either break it off or pull you back down to the ground. You could meet the consequences of carelessness, yet you might also realize that altering the nature of your partnerships is worth whatever price you have to pay.

MAY 16–18 ★ *call of the wild*
An anti-authoritarian Sun-Uranus semisquare on **May 16** could put you in a less than cooperative mood. Dealing with bosses and bossy people more than you like stirs you up enough to rebel against them. Still, following your own path might spur you to create innovative methods that put your individuality in a favorable light. Happily, even if you go too far, an open-minded Venus-Uranus sextile on the **18th** earns acceptance for your unconventional ways. You'll find it easier to let go of the past and live more freely in the present.

MAY 20 ★ *stroke of genius*
If you're faced with a difficult problem today, thinking it through can pay off with an illuminating breakthrough when Uranus squares Pluto. Thoughtful Mercury's quincunx with compelling Pluto runs you into a wall of doubt or a frustrating conversation. However, Mercury's subsequent sextile to liberating Uranus awakens you with an epiphany that helps you discover an unexpected solution to this impasse.

SUPER NOVA DAYS
MAY 26–28 ★ *give peace a chance*
An uncompromising Mars-Uranus semisquare on **May 26** can spark a surprising conflict. Your unwillingness to meet others halfway could be genius or folly, but might alienate people either way. Philosophical Jupiter's conjunctions with mental Mercury on the **27th** and diplomatic Venus on the **28th** arm you with insights and information that can resolve a sticky situation. Your willingness to see all sides of an issue restores intellectual and emotional connections.

JUNE

LIVING IN THE MATERIAL WORLD

Strong feelings about your job tempt you to push logic aside this month and get in touch with your deeper needs regarding your professional life. Vulnerable Venus shifts into security-seeking Cancer and your 6th House of Employment on **June 2** to bring personal matters into the workplace. Overly sensitive colleagues and customers could seem more demanding, but it's your inner needs that have to be addressed first. Still, the New Moon in friendly but noncommittal Gemini occurs in your 5th House of Romance on **June 8th**, offering numerous distractions from serious issues. On the plus side, you could be crackling with creativity and flirting with everyone you meet. Nevertheless, don't allow superficial interests to tempt you to take your eye off the ball.

On **June 11**, your attention turns to your highest economic dreams with the harmonious trine between constructive Saturn in your 10th House of Career and idealistic Neptune in your 2nd House of Resources. Focusing on your strategy for reaching these goals now will put you in a stronger position to make this happen when this trine recurs on **July 19**. Your vocational aspirations are illuminated by the Sun's shift into Cancer and your 6th House of Employment on **June 21**, marking the Summer Solstice. The well-organized Capricorn Full Moon on the **23rd** forms a supportive sextile with Saturn, making this an excellent time to complete unfinished tasks. It brightens your 12th House of Inner Peace, inviting you to commit to a regular spiritual practice. Although Jupiter begins a yearlong visit to your 6th House on the **25th**, helping you integrate your metaphysical interests into your daily routine, Mercury's retrograde turn on the **26th** buys you time to reflect on the past before moving forward.

> **KEEP IN MIND THIS MONTH**
>
> *Don't set aside emotions just because they're uncomfortable or irrational. You can only find satisfaction if you acknowledge the deeper meaning behind your feelings.*

KEY DATES

JUNE 1 ★ *leader of the pack*

You get off to an awkward start today, seeing any outside influence as undue pressure thanks to the tunnel vision of a Sun-Pluto quincunx. But the stress is relieved with a solar sextile to surprising Uranus that allows you to leap over earlier resistance with a radically new perspective. Your sparkling ideas and magnetic personality enable you to enlighten others about the need for personal freedom and the possibility of finding alternative ways to get along.

JUNE 7–8 ★ *embrace the unknown*

Amorous Venus's harmonious hook-ups with compassionate Neptune and practical Saturn bring balance to public and private relationships on **June 7**. But restraint is recommended as impetuous Mars squares delusional Neptune, enticing you to chase illusions instead of acting rationally. Although the Gemini New Moon on the **8th** scatters your energy, Mars skids into a quincunx with Saturn, bringing down the hammer of reality. Instead of being caught between a rock and a hard place, an inventive Mercury-Uranus square shatters your operating paradigm and opens up new worlds of possibilities.

JUNE 12 ★ *occupational hazard*

Be flexible on the job today when sociable Venus in your 6th House of Service crashes into a volatile square with unpredictable Uranus. You may be confronted by unexpected events and unusual individuals, or find that you're easily bored by routine tasks. Yet adapting quickly to situations could produce excitement that elevates your interest in others and in your work.

SUPER NOVA DAYS
JUNE 17–19 ★ *consider your audience*

Two powerful planetary aspects fuel you with energy and enthusiasm. Initiating Mars's smart sextile to irrepressible Uranus on **June 17** excites you with creativity that ignites fresh opportunities and outflanks old obstacles. The beat goes on when the Sun joins limitless Jupiter in your 5th House of Love and Play on the **19th**. You're still effervescent with excitement, which makes you a powerful presenter of whatever you want to sell. Just don't overwhelm your listener with every last bit of information because it's easier to get what you want when you don't clutter the conversation with extraneous details.

JUNE 27–28 ★ *star of the show*

You're in the spotlight on **June 27** as Venus prances into bold and brassy Leo and your 7th House of Relationships. Expressing yourself openly is a risk worth taking. Still, don't rush or bite off more than you can chew on the **28th**, when conservative Saturn's constraining aspect to incorrigible Mars rewards patience and punishes haste.

JULY

ROOM AT THE TOP

In a life overflowing with fascinating ideas, you're not always able to find a viable one and stick to it, Aquarius—but that's exactly what you can do this month. Crystallizing Saturn turns direct in your 10th House of Profession on **July 8**, which prompts you to clarify current issues and career objectives. On the **17th**, enthusiastic Jupiter in your 6th House of Employment creates a Grand Water Trine with strategic Saturn and imaginative Neptune that helps you formalize a successful plan for advancing your interests. However, these ambitions may fail unless they're aligned with your highest ideals as Neptune occupies your 12th House of Spirituality. The nurturing Cancer New Moon lands in your 6th House on **July 8**, indicating changes at the workplace since challenging aspects to this lunation from evolutionary Pluto and shocking Uranus are bound to shake up the status quo. Consider a radical shift in your professional trajectory. You have the drive to learn new skills when physical Mars enters tenacious Cancer on the **13th** to put more passion into your daily activities.

The Winged Messenger makes a forward shift in your 6th House of Daily Routines on **July 20**, easing the communication that was stalled during Mercury's retrograde period beginning on **June 26**. Take a more rational approach to personal and professional partnerships when valuable Venus enters analytical Virgo and your 8th House of Deep Sharing on **July 22**. You may be dealing with picky people or find yourself becoming more critical of others. The need to balance your desires in a relationship is underscored on the **22nd** by the Aquarius Full Moon's opposition to the dramatic Leo Sun in your 7th House of Partners.

> ### KEEP IN MIND THIS MONTH
>
> *Innumerable little issues require your attention this month, but save the majority of your time for thinking about major long-term goals.*

KEY DATES

JULY 1 ★ *hard to please*

You're less than satisfied with how people are treating you today. It's due to Venus in prideful Leo moving from a restricting square with Saturn to a confusing quincunx with Neptune. You might feel underappreciated or choose to avoid an unpleasant individual. However, this is also a chance to redefine your expectations of others and then make compromises when necessary.

JULY 4–7 ★ *flags of freedom*

These are exciting days that are kicked off by a cage-rattling Sun-Uranus square on **July 4** that provokes you to rebel against rules and break with tradition. Sweet Venus is jostled by sexy Mars and stressed by suspicious Pluto on the **5th**, which can undermine trust but can also intensify your desires. Happily, you can resolve whatever conflicts arise with help from a supportive Venus-Uranus trine on the **7th**. Taking a different approach to a complicated relationship feels like a fresh start, allowing you to let go of the past to create a more harmonious yet stimulating future.

JULY 17–20 ★ *dare to believe*

Your workplace abounds with opportunities when giant Jupiter forms a Grand Water Trine with Saturn and Neptune on **July 17**. The strategic Saturn-Neptune trine on the **19th** puts your dreams within reach. However, partnerships continue to challenge you as innocent Venus tangles with manipulative Pluto on **July 18** and unstable Uranus on the **20th**. You risk extreme reactions as your natural resistance to being controlled is activated. But there are benefits to these disruptive patterns: You might drop people from your life who can't meet your needs, as well as discovering surprising new sources of joy.

SUPER NOVA DAY

JULY 22 ★ *mixed messages*

Caution is stressed when modest Venus minces into meticulous Virgo, but the Sun boldly strides into flamboyant Leo and your 7th House of Partners, encouraging you to take chances with others. Meanwhile, the nonconformist Aquarius Full Moon suggests that breaking into unfamiliar territory requires a greater degree of self-mastery. Serious Saturn's square to this lunation picks up Venus's current theme of being reasonable and responsible, which is what it takes to be assertive without losing credibility or self-control.

JULY 31 ★ *mad genius*

If your life feels like a delicate balancing act between responding logically and following your impulses, your wilder side is likely to tilt the scales today. An explosive Mars-Uranus square can trigger instantaneous reactions that are less than reasonable. Blowing up at someone or steaming with silent anger is not the best way to apply this energetic firestorm. Inventing original ways to manage tasks, though, can produce brilliant results.

AUGUST

DIPLOMATIC MEASURES

Relationships are front and center this month with the New and Full Moons activating your socially oriented 1st and 7th Houses. On **August 6**, the self-confident Leo New Moon lands in your 7th House of Partners, which widens the field for finding creative personal and professional alliances. Uncontainable Uranus's favorable trine to this lunation spurs breakthroughs in current unions and shows you unusual ways to make new friends. Expect strong emotions and increased sensitivity on **August 20** when the brilliant Aquarius Full Moon illuminates your 1st House of Self. You can easily enchant others, since mystical Neptune conjuncts this lunation. You may wander off into fantasyland and fail to see individuals you meet as they really are, but being more forgiving and sympathetic is a healthier expression of this pattern.

Battles over beliefs could break out with the first of three oppositions between opinionated Jupiter and propagandist Pluto on **August 7**. Don't lock yourself into a fixed position; Jupiter's square with unexpected Uranus on the **21st** can suddenly shift your point of view. The issues triggered by these transits won't settle until their final aspects on **April 20, 2014**. You'll enjoy better relations with intellectual adversaries, though, with Venus's entry into diplomatic Libra and your 9th House of Higher Mind on **August 16**. However, principles give way to pragmatism as the Sun and Mercury enter earthy Virgo and your 8th House of Intimacy on the **22nd** and **23rd**. Picking through the details of relationships can seem tedious and petty, but this planetary shift suggests that the future success of important partnerships requires careful analysis of your mutual needs and expectations.

> **KEEP IN MIND THIS MONTH**
>
> *Being flexible enough to adjust from making plans for the future to addressing the nuts and bolts of the present is essential for creating more effective alliances.*

KEY DATES

SUPER NOVA DAYS
AUGUST 1–4 ★ *reversal of fortune*
On **August 1**, a pair of persnickety quincunxes could put you on edge. Power struggles are stirred by the Sun's irritating misalignment with Pluto, and social unease accompanies Venus's uncomfortable connection with Uranus. But better news follows on the **2nd**, when graceful Venus's smooth sextile to bold Mars provides the charm and social skills you need to transform awkward

moments into playful or romantic ones. The thrilling Sun-Uranus trine on the **4th** offers you the chance to maintain your freedom of expression while collaborating with a brilliant partner.

AUGUST 11–14 ★ *jumbled wires*
Think clearly, speak slowly, and remain patient on **August 11** in order to stay calm and get your message across. That's because communications grow complicated when verbal Mercury is delayed by a square with dense and demanding Saturn. A similar struggle is possible on the **13th** when Mercury quincunxes enigmatic Pluto, which could darken conversations with mistrust and mystery. Fortunately, an ingenious Mercury-Uranus trine on the **14th** helps you leap over these obstacles and enliven dialogues with wildly unconventional thoughts.

AUGUST 19–20 ★ *reconcilable differences*
The Sun's hard aspects to Jupiter in sentimental Cancer and Uranus in pioneering Aries on **August 19** pull you between two very different views of reality. Unsettled feelings and uncertainty suggest that this is not an ideal time to make a major decision. The Aquarius Full Moon on the **20th** could result in an illumination that shows you how to reconcile the seemingly contradictory needs for stimulation and safety.

AUGUST 22 ★ *free your mind*
Nervous energy and intellectual restlessness could be high as cerebral Mercury forms stressful angles with electrifying Uranus and judgmental Jupiter. Concentration is difficult when the flow of information is constantly interrupted. Yet if you can relax enough to remain flexible and open-minded, exciting discoveries offer unexpected answers and create surprising new connections.

AUGUST 27 ★ *fools rush in*
You could be in the mood to party like it's Saturday night, but opportunities at work challenge you to find the time for it. Nevertheless, sensual Venus's over-the-top square with bountiful Jupiter in your 6th House of Employment encourages you to seek pleasure and approval that might cost more than you anticipate. You're likely to overpay for desirable objects and experiences or overestimate the value of other people. Macho Mars moves into theatrical Leo and your 7th House of Partners, motivating you to fall madly in love or attempt to dazzle potential business allies. This dynamic planet will continue to embolden your actions until **October 15**, so it's better to pace yourself rather than trying to force something to happen too soon.

SEPTEMBER

COLLABORATIVE EFFORTS

Taking care of unsettled relationship business is your top priority this month. Avoid the temptation to assume that personal and professional partners are on the same page as you—because there's a good chance they're not. The discerning Virgo New Moon falls in your 8th House of Deep Sharing on **September 5** to bring your attention to the effectiveness of your alliances. Visionary Jupiter's smart sextile to this lunation shows you how your long-term goals resonate with the methods and routines you currently have in place. You may feel picky being more specific about what you need from others, but you must weave a tighter web of cooperation to achieve your highest potential. Perceptive Mercury's move into objective Libra and your 9th House of Higher Truth on the **9th** opens your eyes to opposing points of view, which should facilitate negotiations of all kinds.

You learn to extract more value from your working relationships on **September 11**, when Venus enters shrewd Scorpio and your 10th House of Career. Money matters are on your radar with the psychic Pisces Full Moon brightening your 2nd House of Finances on the **19th**. The presence of this lunation in your imaginative sign is a reminder that faith, idealism, and creativity are among your major economic assets. Your professional productivity rises with dutiful Saturn's third and final sextile with Pluto on the 21st. What you did during their first two aspects on **December 26, 2012**, and **March 8** will likely determine how successful you are now. The Autumn Equinox occurs when the Sun shifts into lovely Libra and your 9th House of Travel and Education on the **22nd**, giving you an itch for adventure and learning.

> **KEEP IN MIND THIS MONTH**
>
> *Criticism is helpful when it's constructive; share your comments with kindness and listen carefully when others have advice for you.*

KEY DATES

SEPTEMBER 2–4 ★ *stay on track*

Small differences provoke arguments when mouthy Mercury semisquares cranky Mars on **September 2**. Stick to the subject if you want results, because a slippery Mars-Neptune quincunx prompts you to fire verbal arrows in the wrong direction. You'll want to focus on real issues in a more rational manner when Mercury semisquares responsible Saturn on the **4th**. Patiently handling one specific problem at a time is more likely to produce a useful outcome than turning this into a philosophical debate.

SEPTEMBER 9–11 ★ *reality check*

You may have to slam on the brakes to stop someone from pushing you too hard or demanding too much as forceful Mars is stifled by a square to restrictive Saturn on **September 9**. You could see a setback at work—or simply a lack of progress — although narrowing your focus to address one tough task can earn you some respect. Be prepared to pare back or completely drop a project, especially when purging Pluto quincunxes Mars on the **11th**.

SUPER NOVA DAYS

SEPTEMBER 14–16 ★ *ahead of the curve*

An inspirational Venus-Neptune trine on **September 14** tempts you with sweet visions of romance. A Mercury-Pluto square could bring criticism that undermines your dreams, but an inventive Mars-Uranus trine prompts creative actions that allow you to leap over doubts with a radically different way of getting things done. A Mercury-Uranus opposition on the **16th** stimulates unconventional thinking that shakes previous connections. Your ideas may be too far ahead of the times, requiring you to simplify them or keep them to yourself to avoid causing confusion.

SEPTEMBER 19 ★ *deluge of details*

More is not necessarily merrier when it comes to ideas, information, and input from others. An overload of data accompanies the watery Pisces Full Moon and long-winded Mercury's tense square to bombastic Jupiter. Watch out for exaggerating your motives and making a mountain out of a molehill. On the other hand, if you can stretch your mind to include both intellectual and emotional truths, your awareness will grow and your capacity to educate and influence people will increase.

SEPTEMBER 26–28 ★ *luck of the draw*

You earn recognition for your work on **September 26** with a favorable trine between admirable Venus in your 10th House of Career and auspicious Jupiter in your 6th House of Service. Jupiter's sesquisquare to serene Neptune on the **28th** enables you to use your imagination to convince others that you're on the right track. Enjoying the company of colleagues, material rewards, and emotional satisfaction in your job are all high on your agenda. But Venus's challenging square with reckless Mars intensifies relationships in ways that may be sexy, but might also create conflict.

OCTOBER

PUSH THE ENVELOPE

Your keen intelligence normally gives you a higher-than-average degree of certainty about what you know. A couple of key events this month, however, may raise questions for which you don't have the answers. The Libra New Moon in your 9th House of Big Ideas on **October 4** is bent by stressful squares to Pluto and Jupiter and shocked by an incendiary opposition to Uranus. While the upside could be the sudden revelation of the meaning of life—or at least of your life—you're more likely to see your perspective on the future shaken and stirred. If you're able to let go of old concepts, you could receive a heavy download of useful insights. Adaptability is also a must with the last of three Saturn-Uranus quincunxes happening on the **5th**. This oil-and-water mix of duty and freedom occurred on **November 15, 2012**, and **April 12**, throwing you curveballs that you can finally hit out of the park.

The impulsive Aries Lunar Eclipse on **October 18** falls in your 3rd House of Information, interrupting patterns of communication and learning. If you've rushed into a class or a relationship too quickly, you may need to go back and fill in some critical details before you can get back in gear. Trickster Mercury's switch from forward to reverse on **October 21** takes this theme of tying up loose ends to the next level. The messenger planet is retrograde in your 10th House of Career until **November 10**, possibly hindering professional activities with delays and miscommunications. This is your chance to do some serious research, reconnect with people from the past, and prepare for a new project at work.

> **KEEP IN MIND THIS MONTH**
>
> *Your natural curiosity and genuine desire to learn make it easy for you to move on from outmoded ideas and discover new ones that work.*

KEY DATES

SUPER NOVA DAYS
OCTOBER 1–3 ★ *sink or swim*

Expect disagreements over matters of principle on **October 1** with the willful Sun in your 9th House of Higher Truth, creating a harsh square to controlling Pluto. This struggle could become more personal on the **2nd** when needy Venus semisquares Pluto, encouraging you to examine your values and assess your resources more carefully. On the **3rd**, Venus and the Sun run into trouble with maverick Uranus, rattling personal relationships and professional alliances. Your chances of making brilliant discoveries and avoiding chaos improve when you and those around you are open and willing to change.

OCTOBER 7–8 ★ *ready to rumble*
There's an intense buzz in the air on **October 7** as combative Mars in your 7th House of Partners clashes with wayward Uranus, provoking rebellious and impetuous behavior. Cooperation eludes you as the desire to do things your own way or the challenge of dealing with an unreliable individual keeps you on edge. Intellectual Mercury's quincunx with Uranus on the **8th** adds more static, confusion, and crankiness. However, the messenger planet joins strict Saturn to set some requirements for logic, order, and accountability in your life.

OCTOBER 16 ★ *fearless leader*
You may gain the enthusiastic support of others with enticing Venus in your 11th House of Groups creating a thrilling trine with trendsetting Uranus. You respond eagerly to unconventional sources of fun and are willing to try an irreverent approach to overcome obstacles in personal and professional relationships. Experimenting with alternative ways of working with others could produce surprisingly positive results.

OCTOBER 24–25 ★ *the audacity of hope*
Mars in fussy Virgo forms an expansive semisquare with Jupiter on **October 24** that can entangle you in a never-ending task. Before you embark on a new project or a complex negotiation, set parameters about how much time, energy, and money you're willing to invest. Frustration may trigger criticism that weakens an important relationship. Forgiving, forgetting, and letting go come easily on the **25th,** when the Sun forms a generous trine with ethereal Neptune. Faith, creativity, and camaraderie flow freely, especially with those who share your altruistic ideals.

OCTOBER 31 ★ *the edge of glory*
Unexpected circumstances are likely to shift even the most carefully crafted agenda. A potent and purposeful Mars-Pluto trine would normally make this a very productive time. Eliminating unnecessary people, things, and activities is meant to make you more efficient and not to hurt anyone's feelings. However, Mars's quincunx with quirky Uranus tosses a monkey wrench in your plans. Be prepared to adjust your approach to resolve an issue by using unconventional means or surprising tactics.

AQUARIUS

NOVEMBER

You could be facing heavy issues in your professional life this month, with significant activity in your 10th House of Career. The action starts with a jolt of energy on **November 1** from the transformational Uranus-Pluto square. If you're dissatisfied with your job, it's smarter to look in other directions than to just quit and walk away. The potent Scorpio New Moon Solar Eclipse in your 10th House on **November 3** could have a profound effect on your future. A karmic Saturn conjunct to this eclipse indicates an overload of responsibilities, growing frustrations, or hard-earned accomplishments. Supportive aspects from unstoppable Mars and formidable Pluto add the punch you need to ride out the storm or, better yet, fuel your desire to move in a more fulfilling direction. There's little advantage to playing your hand openly now as pleasure-seeking Venus rewards discretion when it slips into the shadows of your 12th House of Privacy on the **5th**.

Opportunistic Jupiter's retrograde shift in your 6th House of Work on **November 7** points you toward the past for inspiration about your vocational choices. Data-driven Mercury's forward turn in your 10th House on **November 10** sets information flowing more freely. Domestic issues are in the spotlight when the steady Taurus Full Moon on the **17th** illuminates your 4th House of Roots. This is a signal to stop and smell the roses at home regardless of how demanding your job might be now. Making your environment more comfortable and spending time with those closest to you solidifies your emotional and physical foundations. The Sun shoots into adventurous Sagittarius and lights up your 11th House of Teamwork on **November 21**, encouraging you to connect more with friends, groups, and organizations.

> **KEEP IN MIND THIS MONTH**
>
> *Take your time with a key career-related matter because the quickest solution may not be the most beneficial one in the long run.*

KEY DATES
NOVEMBER 6 ★ *trust your instincts*
Constrictive Saturn joins the expressive Sun in your 10th House of Profession, presenting a challenge that requires patience and leadership skills. Avoid making any hasty moves; the impact of your actions may be greater than you think. Difficulties with a boss or your own leadership style are possible. Delays and self-doubt could cause you to question your performance. But don't rely on intellect alone—this conjunction in watery Scorpio demands emotional awareness to manage stress.

412 ★ YOUR ASTROLOGY GUIDE 2013

NOVEMBER 12 ★ *lucky streak*

Your capacity for recognizing others' needs and abilities allows you to sell ideas today and inspire people to follow your lead. Fortuitous Jupiter's supportive trine to the Sun in your 10th House of Public Responsibility increases on-the-job optimism, broadens your vision, and expands your professional base. Once again, the answers you seek are not just in your head, but need to correspond with your instincts. It's good strategy to take calculated risks on this propitious day.

SUPER NOVA DAYS
NOVEMBER 14–16 ★ *rocking the free world*

Feelings that you've been keeping to yourself may pop out unexpectedly on **November 14**. Social Venus's kinetic square with volatile Uranus may provoke you to reveal a secret or wake up to a hidden truth about your own desires. But your liberated feelings may not last long, because Venus is squeezed by a hookup with mysterious Pluto on the **15th** that reveals deeper layers of meaning. You could be going on a relationship roller-coaster ride, especially with the Sun forming challenging aspects with both Uranus and Pluto on the **16th**. The benefits of these potentially upsetting alignments include discovering unique sources of pleasure, uncovering unexpressed talents, and breaking free of unrewarding alliances and responsibilities.

NOVEMBER 25 ★ *singular focus*

Analytical Mercury's conjunction with unyielding Saturn might stifle or impede communication. Yet the real message is to concentrate your attention on the single most important issue of the day. While operating within these narrow confines isn't your idea of fun, the extra attention you give to a critical matter could enable you to solve a vexing problem once and for all.

NOVEMBER 30 ★ *free at last*

You could be nervous enough to interrupt conversations today with a sketchy Mercury-Uranus sesquisquare. Yet you should be able to turn the strange perceptions this triggers into useful information. The Sun's creative trine to wild Uranus frees you to express yourself more openly. Collaborating with forward-thinking individuals makes new social experiences more exciting and also ignites brilliant ideas that serve a cause or group.

DECEMBER

KEEP THE FAITH

Your role in the community is especially important this month with a good deal of planetary activity happening in your 11th House of Social Networking, starting with the high-spirited Sagittarius New Moon on **December 2**. This inspirational lunation cultivates friendships, initiates group activities, and encourages you to be a more enthusiastic teammate. Unorthodox Uranus's favorable trine to this Sun-Moon conjunction can reinvigorate your interest in an organization. Verbose Mercury blasts into Sagittarius on the **4th**, bringing bigger ideas and more contacts to the table—but possibly carrying you away with impractical beliefs. Warrior Mars turns peaceful in cooperative Libra on **December 7** as it enters your 9th House of Faraway Places. Advocating for the truth often creates conflict, yet now you may be able to do it graciously enough to maintain civil conversations with those who don't agree with you.

You have a solid grasp of your professional ambitions on **December 12** with the second of three strategically sound Jupiter-Saturn trines. You might reassess goals that came with their first trine on **July 17** and make adjustments to them that could bear fruit with their final recurrence on **May 24, 2014**. A flirtatious Gemini Full Moon on **December 17** charges your 5th House of Self-Expression, prompting playful, creative, and even romantic impulses. The metaphysical Jupiter-Neptune sesquisquare amplifies your holiday spirit, while retrograde Uranus turns forward the same day, releasing energy that increases your taste for freedom. The Sun's shift into traditional Capricorn on **December 21** marks the Winter Solstice while heart-centered Venus turns retrograde in your 12th House of Divinity, reviving old questions about the purpose of life. Thankfully, clever Mercury's move into Capricorn on the **24th** just might give you some of the answers you seek.

> **KEEP IN MIND THIS MONTH**
>
> *Instead of following familiar traditions throughout the holiday season, shake things up. Dynamic times call for you to embrace change.*

KEY DATES

DECEMBER 6–7 ★ *lost in space*

Your mind can float off to some interesting places with a surreal Mercury-Neptune square on **December 6**. Your creativity is off the charts, but so is the potential for confusion, cloudy thinking, and miscommunication. Yet pushing your point or trying to get the clarity you need from others may not be easy when Mercury forms an overstated sesquisquare with outlandish Jupiter on the **7th**. Facts remain fuzzy, so take what you hear with a grain of salt.

DECEMBER 10 ★ *in the zone*
You're working with your full arsenal of intelligence and ingenuity today when a brilliant Mercury-Uranus trine enhances your intuition, emboldening you to contribute original ideas that can be immediately useful. Your keen sense of people and economic acuity are also heightened and brightened with value-setting Venus's creative quintile with Uranus. You can be smart and socially skillful at the same time.

DECEMBER 14–16 ★ *face the music*
If you hit a wall of resistance from others, you will be tempted to jump over it or ignore its presence. Mars in extra-polite Libra aligns with Saturn in stubborn Scorpio, presenting a barrier that impedes your progress on **December 14**. However, an escapist Mercury-Jupiter quincunx on the **16th** prompts you to refuse to face facts. But denial is only a delaying tactic, so it's wiser to buckle down and address a difficult task or unpleasant person right away. Honestly dealing with the issues enables you to build trust and create the time and space for thinking about more interesting subjects.

DECEMBER 25 ★ *break from the past*
A reactive Mars-Uranus opposition doesn't advise following rules, executing plans, or taking orders. This high-tension alignment may elicit accidents or outbursts of anger. Overcome your boredom with old traditions by inventing new ones. Just don't spring them on anyone without warning. If you tell others that this is an experiment, the pressure to succeed is reduced and acceptance of alternatives can grow.

SUPER NOVA DAYS
DECEMBER 29–31 ★ *no turning back*
Mercury joins the Sun on **December 29**, which usually clarifies thinking and empowers speech; however, their squares to erratic Uranus on **December 29–30** can overload your nervous system and galvanize your desire for independence. The revolution that counts, though, is the one within. Be certain of what the real battle entails, because a relentless Mars-Pluto square on the **30th** means you're playing for keeps. Mercury's conjunction with Pluto and square to Mars on the **31st** underscore the importance of any changes you make.

PISCES

FEBRUARY 19–MARCH 20

PISCES
2012 SUMMARY

Simply just getting by isn't enough for you, Pisces; you need a more meaningful life. For the first part of this year the gap between the real and the ideal may shrink as you find ways to infuse your daily routine with faith and imagination that restore your belief in humanity and in your own higher potential. But this isn't just about satisfying your own desires; your personal success is a contribution to the collective well-being of the universe.

AUGUST—*oscar-winning performance*
The purpose of dreaming is to take what floats to the surface of your subconscious mind and creatively integrate it into your everyday life.

SEPTEMBER—*talk it out*
You don't need brilliant partners to be successful, but you do require individuals ready to work hard to make the most of your relationships.

OCTOBER—*honesty is the best policy*
Confidence in the value of what you have to say will give you the authority to broach difficult subjects without arousing resistance.

NOVEMBER—*professional reorientation*
Look into the bottom of your heart, where your deepest desires lie, for that's where you can find the passion and power to achieve success.

DECEMBER—*adjust and advance*
It's hard to trust your progress when unexpected obstacles arise, but keep plugging. You'll find your way around before you know it.

2012 CALENDAR

AUGUST

FRI 3–SAT 4 ★	Examine every idea with skepticism
WED 15 ★	Draw a line when it comes to relationships
MON 20–WED 22 ★	Advance your agenda but don't come on too strong
FRI 24–SUN 26 ★	Look beyond the limits of reality
FRI 31 ★	**SUPER NOVA DAY** Forgive yourself for past mistakes

SEPTEMBER

SUN 2 ★	Double-check your assumptions
WED 5–SAT 8 ★	**SUPER NOVA DAYS** Push the intellectual envelope
SUN 16–MON 17 ★	Adjust your approach and consider the best response
THU 20 ★	Your support can mean the world to someone in need
TUE 25–THU 27 ★	Don't rush to meet others' unrealistic expectations

OCTOBER

WED 3–FRI 5 ★	A magical connection stirs romantic feelings
TUE 9–WED 10 ★	**SUPER NOVA DAYS** Believe in your work
MON 15–TUE 16 ★	Look out for financial partners or soul mates
TUE 23 ★	Let the goodies come to you for a change
SUN 28–MON 29 ★	Move forward with your plans

NOVEMBER

TUE 6 ★	Finish what's already on your plate before adding more to it
FRI 9 ★	You feel like a winner today
TUE 13–WED 14 ★	**SUPER NOVA DAYS** Letting go is the way to grow
WED 21–THU 22 ★	You favor fantasy over reality now
MON 26–TUE 27 ★	Don't let stingy people determine your value

DECEMBER

SUN 2 ★	Overlook immediate problems and see future possibilities
MON 10–WED 12 ★	Connect with a passionate partner in pursuit of knowledge
SUN 16–TUE 18 ★	**SUPER NOVA DAYS** Your faith inspires others
SAT 22 ★	Love without limits
FRI 28 ★	You can create calm in the middle of a storm

PISCES OVERVIEW

The worlds of imagination and spirituality continue to play a vital role in your life now. Your modern ruling planet Neptune settled into compassionate Pisces on February 3, 2012, and continues to expand your consciousness with its presence in your sign until March 30, 2025. Certainly other trends will shape your experiences this year, but opportunities to lift yourself above materialism and the practical considerations of your daily routine beckon when fast-moving planets join supernatural Neptune early in 2013. Its conjunction with assertive Mars on February 4 spurs creativity and increases your willingness to set aside your own needs to serve others. Quicksilver Mercury's hookup with poetic Neptune on February 6 puts imagery in your words that can inspire, heal, or confuse others. Your heart opens to dreams of divine love when the Sun and Venus join Neptune on February 21 and February 28. **A key to your success throughout the year is learning the difference between pipe dreams and true inspirations that you can realistically apply in ways to enhance your life.**

Your traditional ruling planet Jupiter starts out in flexible Gemini, where it occupies your 4th House of Roots until June 25, bringing a more objective perspective on your personal history. **Moving beyond the limits of unconscious emotional reactions allows you to make more intelligent choices for yourself and your loved ones.** On June 25, jolly Jupiter enters cuddly Cancer and your 5th House of Self-Expression to encourage creativity, romance, and childlike innocence. The planet's harmonious trines with responsible Saturn on July 17, December 12, and May 24, 2014, frame your ambitions in a perfect combination of optimism and reality. These strategically savvy aspects also activate metaphysical Neptune in a Grand Water Trine on July 17–19, showing you how to merge your personal ideals with your professional goals. This grand trine is also the culmination of a series of Saturn-Neptune trines that began on October 10, 2012, and recur on June 11 and July 19, further enabling you to balance your real-world ambitions with your secret dreams.

Saturn, the planet of order and discipline, spends the entire year in emotionally intense Scorpio and your 9th House of Higher Mind; you may find yourself preoccupied with the meaning of life this year—perhaps altering your belief systems or questioning your personal philosophies. Saturn in succinct Scorpio works best when you eliminate intellectual clutter and focus on the core of what you're studying. The ringed planet is especially useful for identifying limits so that you can see when you're off track. Saturn's favorable sextiles with evolutionary Pluto on March 8 and September 21 provide more incentive to **clean up careless thinking and discard outmoded expectations.** This aspect first occurred on December 26, 2012, and its last two transits this year empower you to be a more effective teacher and a powerful advocate for causes close to your heart.

LISTEN TO YOUR HEART

Relationship matters take a positive turn in the second half of the year. Lucky Jupiter's entry into your 5th House of Romance on June 25 increases your opportunities for happiness in a current alliance or your chances of connecting with someone new. It's important to know how to please yourself so that you don't wind up spending all your time making another person happy while minimizing your own desires. You may have to double back to untangle misunderstandings while mischievous Mercury is retrograde in your 5th House on June 26–July 20. Sticking to your commitments is generally the honorable thing to do, yet during this period reconsidering your promises—spoken or implied—is an act of necessity, not a sign of disloyalty. Love helps to fulfill practical as well as emotional needs, so don't give up one for the other. The Grand Water Trine of Jupiter, Saturn, and Neptune on July 17–19 reveals how passion and practicality can work together to satisfy your needs.

RISKY BUSINESS

If you approach your career cautiously this year, you're less likely to find the fulfillment and safety you seek than if you simply follow your heart. A visionary Sagittarius Lunar Eclipse on May 25 lands in your 10th House of Profession, where it can significantly alter your long-range plans throughout the year. If your expectations are not being met, this powerful event signals you to look for a more rewarding career. Sacrificial Neptune's stressful squares to the Sun and Moon tempt you to overlook major problems and put off a serious analysis of your employment situation. However, opening yourself up to unusual concepts could lead the way to an unexpectedly exciting job.

BE THE CHANGE

You struggle to maintain a consistent cash flow this year, due to the ongoing presence of surprising Uranus in your 2nd House of Finances. Dynamic squares between unpredictable Uranus and transformational Pluto on May 20 and November 1 highlight your fiscal instability and indicate a possible change of fortune. Magnanimous Jupiter's square to Uranus on August 21 could suddenly fill your coffers. Yet without assurance of a steady income stream to back it up, it's wise to bank what you can instead of spending like a drunken sailor. A pioneering Aries Lunar Eclipse on October 18 occurs in your resourceful 2nd House, which can provoke a financial crisis but is, fortunately, just as likely to motivate you into making a bold move to earn money in a different way. Being proactive in pursuing new sources of income is wiser than passively accepting your economic fate.

MOVE IT OR LOSE IT

Health-related issues could arise with mental Mercury's retrograde turn in your 1st House of Physicality on February 23. Unhooking from old habits may come more easily now—at least until the messenger planet turns forward again on March 17. The wistful Pisces New Moon on March 11 is conjunct to sweet Venus, which can lead you into self-indulgence; a better goal is to find enjoyable ways to stay in shape, like dancing or practicing yoga. For optimum well-being, improve your exercise regimen when energetic Mars moves through courageous Leo and your 6th House of Health on August 27–October 15. Establishing regularity in your workouts during this phase has a long-lasting positive impact on your life.

WINDOW OF OPPORTUNITY

Messages are mixed on the home front with enthusiastic Jupiter in your 4th House of Family until June 25. Generally, the presence of this fortunate planet represents opportunities for growth. Digging into your personal history and discovering how your past affects your present can provide the awareness you need to let go of old wounds. However, broad-minded Jupiter in diversity-seeking Gemini could produce more words than meaning and an overemphasis on minor matters. The airy Gemini Full Moon in your 4th House on December 17 enlivens family gatherings with spirited conversations to spice up your holidays.

LEARN AS YOU GO

Travel should be well planned and purposeful with dutiful Saturn camping out in your 9th House of Journeys. This could require some faraway business trips or family visits that are more about obligation than fun. Passion and patience, though, will produce educational opportunities. Trickster Mercury is retrograde in your 9th House on October 21–November 10, which can complicate communications and muddle messages that make leaving town and learning new subjects challenging. Double-check details and review paperwork to minimize the little errors that can make travel troublesome.

WAKE UP!

You're swept up by a wave of spiritual awakening with the electrifying Aquarius New Moon on February 10. This energizing event occurs in your 12th House of Divinity to stimulate fresh insights about your soul's journey. A dynamic square from philosophical Jupiter to intellectual Uranus on August 21 is another opportunity for you to glimpse a deeper meaning in life. Surprises, though, could shake your existing model of metaphysical truth. These brilliant aspects recur on February 26 and April 20, 2014, triggering additional twists and turns of consciousness to further your spiritual development.

RICK & JEFF'S TIP FOR THE YEAR:
Integrate Instinct and Intellect

Yes, innumerable little events and experiences seem to require rapid responses. Nevertheless, taking a big-picture view of your life will offer you the best results. Make sure to contemplate your actions and their possible ramifications in advance. This process, though, is more than just intellectual; your emotions are a valuable source of information and inspiration. When both feeling and thinking are equal partners in your decisions, success and fulfillment are much more likely to follow.

JANUARY

IT TAKES A VILLAGE

Cultivating your relationships with friends and colleagues is especially important this month while the Sun is in orderly Capricorn and your 11th House of Groups. Hard work, patience, and commitment also prove more rewarding with loving Venus's entry into Capricorn on **January 8**. The disciplined Capricorn New Moon on **January 11** lands in your 11th House. The patterns you set now with allies will either make your relationships more productive or reduce trust if you can't get past self-interest. You'll find it easier to stick to a well-designed plan when it's part of a team effort; more gets done when you know that others are relying on you and also watching your back. Competition can kill cooperation if it gets out of hand, so make sure to help others keep pace when you push yourself.

You may long for solitude when thoughtful Mercury and the Sun enter quirky Aquarius and your 12th House of Privacy on **January 19**. Give yourself plenty of time to think without the pressure of explaining yourself to others. This is a period for inner reflection, meditation, and spiritual experiences that needn't be translated into words. If you feel like you're being overlooked, don't mourn the lack of attention; revel in the peace that lets your imagination run free. In fact, your reverie is likely to be interrupted when the theatrical Leo Full Moon on the **26th** brightens your 6th House of Work, casting you in the spotlight thanks to your leadership and creative abilities. Plans that have been put on hold start to move forward again and your natural optimism returns when your traditional ruling planet, Jupiter, turns direct on **January 30**.

> **KEEP IN MIND THIS MONTH**
>
> *Successful collaboration requires mutual trust that everyone is working to achieve the same goal. Feeling sorry for others or covering for their mistakes doesn't help anyone.*

KEY DATES

JANUARY 4–7 ★ *work smarter not harder*

Hopeful ideas put wind in your sails with an energizing Mars-Jupiter trine in intellectual air signs on **January 4**. This enthusiastic planetary pair could reveal shortcuts or innovative methods that allow you to go further faster. However, an overly optimistic Mercury-Jupiter quincunx on the **5th** may lead you astray with unreliable information. Reality lands with a thud due to a scrutinizing Mercury-Pluto conjunction in your 11th House of Goals on **January 6** and a brake-slamming Mars-Saturn square on the **7th**. Avoid stubbornly sticking to a position that's too difficult to maintain. Recognizing limits reduces frustration and adds efficiency to ensure that your best efforts are not wasted.

JANUARY 10–12 ★ *the trouble with love*
You may experience relationship breakthroughs and discover new sources of pleasure during these few days, yet unplanned experiences can be upsetting. A sympathetic sextile between Venus and Neptune takes the hard edge off relationships on **January 10**. Unfortunately, wishful thinking could be costly and confusing with a Mercury-Neptune semisquare. You're apt to see life as you want it to be with the blind optimism of the ambitious Capricorn New Moon that is sesquisquare to outlandish Jupiter on the **11th**. Misinterpretations of reality might even lead to financial or social surprises when indulgent Venus crashes into an explosive square with erratic Uranus on **January 12**.

JANUARY 14 ★ *know your limits*
Too much of a good thing complicates your life when gregarious Mercury and lavish Venus form difficult aspects with excessive Jupiter. Stretching your mind and social boundaries is healthy as long as you recognize when expectations become unreasonable and you start to rein them in. Exercising a little self-restraint today will keep you out of trouble in the long run.

JANUARY 22 ★ *reason versus romance*
A kind and gentle Venus-Neptune semisquare may inspire you to squander money foolishly or love without limits. Yet a brilliant trine between rational Mercury and opinionated Jupiter quickly shows you the error of your ways, empowering you to effectively analyze the situation and speak with greater authority.

SUPER NOVA DAYS
JANUARY 25–26 ★ *incurable optimist*
A lucky Sun-Jupiter trine on **January 25** raises your confidence so high, you don't have to shout to make yourself heard. A big-picture perspective shows you how to get from where you are to where you want to be. Faith in yourself is well founded and earns you more trust from others. Still, an unbalanced Venus-Jupiter sesquisquare on the **26th** may prompt a premature celebration. Spending too much money or overestimating the value of others may seem generous, but might not be the wisest move.

FEBRUARY

YOU'RE THE BOSS

This very special month may set the tone for the rest of the year, starting with a push from muscular Mars entering your 1st House of Self on **February 1**. Take charge of your life by being more physically active and willing to act on your own initiative. You're unlikely to come on too strong with value-conscious Venus's shift into cool Aquarius and your subtle 12th House on the **1st**. Your desire to please people recedes as you become more independent and require less approval from others. Perceptive Mercury moves into psychic Pisces on **February 5** to stimulate your mind and loosen your tongue. However, finding the right words to express your thoughts might not be easy; metaphors, symbols, and forms of expression such as art, poetry, music, and dance are all wonderful ways to tell your story. Don't overload your schedule with too many tasks since fleet-footed Mercury slows down in the second half of the month before turning retrograde on **February 23**, complicating communications, muddling details, and messing with travel plans until it turns direct on **March 17**.

You gain spiritual insights when the conceptual Aquarius New Moon on **February 10** occurs in your 12th House of Divinity. The Sun's entry into Pisces on the **18th** boosts confidence and raises your profile. Relationships take the spotlight with the pragmatic Virgo Full Moon shining in your 7th House of Partners on the **25th**. You're wise to fix current alliances by attending to specific issues—unless the limitations imposed by a personal or professional union become unbearable and you consider leaving it. If you keep your heart open, you can feel the love wherever you go when adoring Venus visits your dreamy sign on **February 25–March 21**.

> **KEEP IN MIND THIS MONTH**
>
> *You learn more and achieve better results by tuning into your feelings and following your own instincts rather than by letting other people tell you what to do.*

KEY DATES

FEBRUARY 4–6 ★ *heaven sent*

Your imagination and compassion can melt obstacles in your path on **February 4**, when a Mars-Neptune conjunction heats up your 1st House of Personality. But faith won't work unless you're committed to following through on your intentions. Communicative Mercury's conjunction with elusive Neptune on the **6th** could keep you on an idealistic track, yet reality may slip through the cracks and lose you in a cloud of illusion. Your compelling stories can convince others to buy into your dreams; just make sure that they're rooted in something solid to avoid wasting everyone's time and energy.

FEBRUARY 9–10 ★ *spread your wings*
Stressful squares to boundless Jupiter from Mercury and Mars on **February 9–10** motivate you to push past the usual limits of what you say and do. You may expose an inconvenient truth, challenge yourself to try something new, or vent your repressed anger. Yet you can say too much or go too far if you don't temper your enthusiasm with a dash of self-restraint. Stirring conflict or promising more than you can handle might be more foolish than brave unless you stop to consider the consequences of your behavior.

SUPER NOVA DAY
FEBRUARY 21 ★ *dream weaver*
The willful Sun's conjunction with spiritual Neptune expands your consciousness and strengthens your intuition. You can enchant people with the power of your faith and your ability to appear as others want to see you. Yet it's easy to lose yourself in the midst of a fantasy if you're not careful. Stepping into this magical world of creativity may be intoxicating while it lasts, but turning your visions into reality requires the clarity, consistency, and commitment that stem from planting your feet firmly on the ground.

FEBRUARY 25–26 ★ *go big or go home*
The picky Virgo Full Moon squares pompous Jupiter in chatty Gemini, tempting you to express strong opinions on the **25th**. However, your beliefs may not be as solid as they seem and you might be embarrassed if you can't back them up with facts. Retrograde Mercury's conjunction with Mars on the **26th** puts people in a combative mood, yet the battle may be frustrating if your point isn't crystal clear.

FEBRUARY 28 ★ *beautiful dreamer*
Graceful Venus's conjunction with imaginative Neptune in your sign today arouses artistic and social sensibilities. If you feel vulnerable and uncertain of your worth, forgive yourself for your faults and let your heart lead the way. It's better to love foolishly than to never love at all.

MARCH

STRIKE IT RICH

Taking fleeting moments of inspiration and building something lasting from them is a key trend this month. Your authority with friends and colleagues is strengthened on **March 8** when serious Saturn in your 9th House of Higher Truth favorably sextiles powerful Pluto in your 11th House of Groups—the second in a series of three that first occurred on **December 26, 2012**, and will finish on **September 21**. The watery Pisces New Moon on the **11th** enhances the sensitivity of this dynamic planetary pair, bringing a fresh wave of social awareness that enables you to get to the core of the matter without upsetting anyone. Gracious Venus joins this alluring lunation to highlight your endearing charm and compassionate nature. But don't spend all that goodwill on self-aggrandizement; Saturn and Pluto empower you to apply it professionally and within the community.

Your pace quickens as you create new ways to earn money and augment your resources when impetuous Mars rushes into his spontaneous home sign, Aries, on **March 12** to initiate activity in your 2nd House of Self-Worth. Mercury's forward turn on the **17th** frees your mind before the Spring Equinox, when the Sun enters Aries on the **20th**, followed by Venus on the **21st**, adding more fuel to your financial fire. Be ready to adjust your course of action instead of stubbornly sticking to a long-term strategy when strategic Saturn forms an anxious quincunx with sporadic Uranus on **March 23**. The peace-seeking Libra Full Moon on **March 27** is hot-wired with oppositions to Uranus, Mars, and Venus, as well as a square to Pluto. Allies can be unreliable and circumstances weird in a general atmosphere of unpredictability. Happily, open-minded Jupiter in clever Gemini saves the day and offers you a variety of exciting opportunities.

> **KEEP IN MIND THIS MONTH**
>
> *Take chances and explore different ways to increase your worth. The rewards are much greater than anything you'd receive by playing it safe and sticking to what you know.*

KEY DATES

SUPER NOVA DAY
MARCH 1 ★ *master of ceremonies*
You have a firm sense of conviction and a willingness to do what's necessary to meet your goals today. The Pisces Sun's favorable aspects with penetrating

Pluto and strong-willed Saturn provide the resolve to cut through social clutter, establish your priorities, and take care of business. Developing a clear plan and eliminating distractions empower your sense of authority and can earn you the admiration of others.

MARCH 6 ★ *state of grace*
You grow sentimental with retrograde Mercury joining affectionate Venus in your 1st House of Self. You can share sweet words and artistic ideas with sensitivity that calms the seas of stormy relationships. Yet your desire to smooth over rough waters could blur the truth in a haze of unfounded hope. It's tempting to allow pleasant memories to blind you to the significance of the present moment. Seeing beauty in every situation is a gift, yet it can be a costly and confusing one if your vision becomes too fuzzy.

MARCH 16–18 ★ *honorable intentions*
The Sun's stressful sesquisquare with hard-nosed Saturn could put you in a bind on **March 16**. Your generous spirit wants to treat everyone with kindness, yet it's vital that you establish your expectations of others. You need the discipline to focus on fulfilling your obligations and living up to your word. The Sun's creative quintile with bubbly Jupiter in your 4th House of Family on the **18th** lightens the atmosphere at home and allows you to relax. Recognizing that there may be more than one reasonable answer to any question calms your need to be right.

MARCH 25–26 ★ *trust in the process*
You may feel like you're constantly being shunted aside with a crunchy quincunx between impatient Mars in your 2nd House of Self-Worth and no-nonsense Saturn on **March 25**. Your ideas could be rejected or your actions diverted by unimaginative individuals. Even if you hurry to complete an unpleasant task, trying to go faster winds up costing you more time. Your energy flows more freely on the **26th**, when a supportive Mars-Jupiter sextile enables you to get a moneymaking project off the ground.

MARCH 31 ★ *turn the other cheek*
Your emotions are raw and you experience conflicts over jealousy or money as the Sun and Venus in your 2nd House of Values create tense squares with possessive Pluto. Thankfully, this intense day is brightened by a sociable sextile between playful Venus and cheerful Jupiter, expanding your capacity to appreciate your current blessings in your pursuit of happiness.

APRIL

PLANTING SEEDS OF INSPIRATION

Fresh ideas keep popping up this month and concepts start to consolidate in the later part of April. The fun starts with the lively Aries New Moon in your 2nd House of Resources on **April 10** and its conjunctions with attractive Venus and ardent Mars turn on your creativity and your social skills. Generating more income may be a desirable goal, but having fun is more likely to get you there than taking life too seriously. Your willingness to take risks and adopt a more straightforward approach may rub some people the wrong way; nevertheless, you need adventurous allies who know how to play so you can feel free to blaze new personal and professional paths. Your head will definitely be in the game when brainy Mercury fires into fearless Aries on the **13th** to accelerate thinking and communication.

You impress people with your common sense on **April 15**, when sensual Venus enters practical Taurus and your 3rd House of Communication, adding a healthy dose of reason to your conversations. The Sun enters earthy Taurus on the **19th**, lending another degree of solidity to your thoughts. Being well informed strengthens your confidence and makes your proposals sound more substantive to others. You might crank up the pressure when pushy Mars enters Taurus and your chatty 3rd House on **April 20**, but don't let your desires lead to stubbornness that can undercut your influence. Cultivate patience with restrictive Saturn's conjunction to the resolute Scorpio Lunar Eclipse on the **25th**. Travel and educational plans may be postponed as this powerful Full Moon activates your 9th House of Higher Learning and Faraway Places, giving you time to reconsider whether your current endeavors are worthwhile.

> **KEEP IN MIND THIS MONTH**
>
> *You're most convincing when you calmly address one subject at a time instead of letting your mind wander and overloading others with information.*

KEY DATES

APRIL 1 ★ *panoramic view*

The Sun's smart sextile with judicious Jupiter in your 4th House of Roots broadens your understanding of family matters and places your personal history into a more meaningful perspective. This greater level of awareness helps you get along better with those closest to you while you distance yourself from the burdens of the past. Eliminating negative self-judgment frees you to express your aspirations more openly and explore a future rich with intriguing possibilities.

SUPER NOVA DAYS
APRIL 6–8 ★ *addicted to love*
Romantic foolishness is in the air as erotic Mars and Venus hook up on **April 7** after creating semisquares with squishy Neptune on **April 6**. These quixotic aspects inspire compassion and leave you ready for self-sacrifice, but the cause may not be worthy of your idealism. Your imagination runs rampant, yet it isn't easy to recognize the difference between an impossible dream and an achievable goal. Taking time to fantasize is healthy as long you don't try to build something permanent from these fleeting visions. The confusing role of Neptune continues on the **8th** with its semisquare to the Sun. Misreading authority figures or relying on poorly constructed plans will disappoint you. However, your ability to forgive bad behavior could smooth over a rough situation.

APRIL 17–18 ★ *extreme measures*
You have plenty of passion and punch, along with a bit of sweet tenderness to cover a full spectrum of behavior. An overheated Sun-Mars conjunction in your 2nd House of Income on **April 17** intensifies your efforts to earn more money. Pushing yourself is fine as long as you've thought through your plan and aren't just blowing off steam. Yet if anger does escape, a delicious Venus-Neptune sextile on the **18th** can soothe jangled nerves. A little kindness goes a long way to soften hearts and restore peaceful relations.

APRIL 23 ★ *smart as a whip*
Your mind is sharpened to a perceptive point with a slick sextile between data-driven Mercury and big-picture Jupiter. Communicating is a breeze, especially if you have to come up with some quick answers. Knowing your subject and understanding your audience enable you to influence others without seeming to apply any pressure.

APRIL 25–28 ★ *lost and found*
The provocative Scorpio Lunar Eclipse on **April 25** joins constrictive Saturn, forcing you to focus your feelings, but a slippery Mercury-Neptune semisquare adds confusion on the **26th**. Fortunately, a harmonious Mars-Neptune sextile allows you to correct your course with a subtle shift of direction. If careless speech or cloudy thinking has complicated a situation, the Sun-Saturn opposition on the **28th** sets you back on track.

MAY

LET GO TO GROW

Expect the unexpected during this transitional month that's intensified with two powerful eclipses and a pair of significant outer planet transits that motivate you to reassess major plans. On **May 9**, talkative Mercury and aggressive Mars join a Taurus Solar Eclipse that falls in your 3rd House of Communication, prompting animated conversations that could lead you into conflict. Stubborn Taurus, though, tends to hold on to ideas even when they don't fit current circumstances and future aspirations. Simplifying concepts by concentrating on one or two that are solid and letting the others go should make your life much easier. Expansive Jupiter makes its third and final sesquisquare with contractive Saturn on **May 20**, a pattern that occurred on **July 20** and **October 15, 2012**. This awkward alignment of outer planets requires you to narrow your focus and adjust your professional or educational expectations.

Your home life warms up on **May 20** as the Sun skips into blithe Gemini and your 4th House of Domestic Conditions. But the third of seven transformational squares between Uranus and Pluto happens nearly simultaneously, which may set off financial issues or power struggles. This aspect recurs on **November 1** and culminates on **March 16, 2015**, giving you plenty of time to enhance your moneymaking abilities and become a better friend and co-worker. Professional issues are likely to be up for review with a Sagittarius Lunar Eclipse that highlights your 10th House of Career on **May 25**. Starry-eyed Neptune's squares to the Sun and Moon could have you chasing unicorns, falling for a sob story, or spreading yourself too thin. Let go of romantic illusions now; it's wiser than holding on to unrealizable dreams until you're exhausted or driven to despair.

> **KEEP IN MIND THIS MONTH**
>
> *Opportunities arise when you free yourself from outmoded hopes and fruitless struggles. Clearing your mind now helps you to find a deeper fulfillment later.*

KEY DATES

MAY 1–4 ★ *midcourse correction*

Take your time and speak carefully on **May 1** when naysaying Saturn opposes impulsive Mars in your 3rd House of Communication. If you receive negative responses from others, only research and patience will allow you to prove your point. However, you may skip over key details or scatter your attention when busy Mercury forms a sketchy semisquare with bountiful Jupiter on the **2nd**. If you've said more than you should or allowed your attention to wander, an intuitive Mercury-Neptune sextile on the **4th** can gently guide you back in the right direction.

MAY 9 ★ *paradigm shift*

Today's Taurus Solar Eclipse may instigate a dispute and force you to defend your ideas. Yet if you're open-minded, what you learn will be worth the struggle. Sure, you might feel silly having to let go of a comfortable position, but an inquisitive Mercury-Neptune quintile reveals information that never crossed your radar before now. Look beyond the manner in which the issues are being presented and you can find creative answers to your problem.

MAY 13 ★ *testing the waters*

This could be one of those magical days when you're inspired by romantic dreams and shiny objects. Desirous Venus's square to glamorous Neptune stimulates your imagination but weakens your sense of practicality. Your current attachments to people and things may be ill advised, but you may feel too vulnerable to stand up for yourself, leading to unnecessary sacrifice and unwarranted expense. Nevertheless, this is a great time to window-shop as long as you wait awhile before you buy.

MAY 18 ★ *alice in wonderland*

The good news and the bad news is that there are no limits to where your mind can go today thanks to a fanciful Mercury-Neptune square. The benefits include imaginative thinking and captivating conversations. Yet the stories being told may be too far from the truth to apply them in real-world situations. Perhaps you're misunderstanding others or allowing vital details to slip through the cracks. It's best to avoid making commitments until you have facts that you can rely on.

SUPER NOVA DAYS
MAY 25–28 ★ *dare to believe*

Dreamy Neptune's square to the adventurous Sagittarius Full Moon Eclipse on **May 25** fills your head with illusions, and it's worthwhile to let your imagination run wild. Daydreaming is likely to produce positive results even if your facts are wrong, because cerebral Mercury and valuable Venus hook up with auspicious Jupiter on **May 27–28**. Create your own fantasies instead of falling for someone else's, since good fortune rewards following your instincts.

JUNE

SOMEWHERE OVER THE RAINBOW

The gap between your dreams and reality is shrinking this month. Productive Saturn's harmonious trine with inspirational Neptune on **June 11** crystallizes plans that can give structure to your aspirations. This is the second in a series of three supportive alignments that began on **October 10, 2012**, and will finish on **July 19**. Patience, planning, and discipline help you perform wonders that can positively impact the rest of your life. Personal matters get a boost when Venus enters Cancer and your 5th House of Romance on **June 2**. This joyously expressive transit only lasts a month, but generous Jupiter enters caring Cancer and your 5th House on **June 25** to provide a year's worth of additional opportunities for cultivating love, expressing creativity, and enjoying children. The multifaceted Gemini New Moon in your 4th House of Domestic Conditions emphasizes family matters on the **8th**. Opening fresh channels of communication with loved ones and redecorating your home are positive ways to ride this bubbly wave of energy.

Warm feelings keep coming with the Sun's move into Cancer and your 5th House of Fun and Games on **June 21**, marking the Summer Solstice. You'll get a self-esteem boost, yet it's equally important that you recognize the needs of others with the responsible Capricorn Full Moon lighting up your 11th House of Groups on the **23rd**. This could spur a crisis that requires you to compromise. Fortunately, Saturn's stabilizing sextile to this lunation provides the maturity and commitment needed to achieve a common goal. However, even the clearest communications may become muddied during Mercury's retrograde from **June 26–July 20**.

> **KEEP IN MIND THIS MONTH**
>
> *Pleasure is not an enemy of productivity. Having a good time and putting your heart into a project highlights your creativity and makes you the ultimate team player.*

KEY DATES

JUNE 3 ★ *in the zone*

You intuitively understand the magic formula for blending inspiration and execution as smart Mercury forms a Grand Water Trine with mystical Neptune and competent Saturn today. Your ability to see what you want, recognize what it takes to get there, and communicate effectively to gain the support you need are all operating at optimum levels. Don't let a lack of experience or concern about initiating a new project hinder your efforts because even if you have butterflies in your tummy, you look and sound confident to others.

JUNE 7–8 ★ *off the charts*
You can sweet-talk the birds out of the trees on **June 7** as charming Venus trines enchanting Neptune. A purposeful Venus-Saturn trine strengthens the cool charisma of this irresistible cosmic couple. Staying calm, though, comes in handy later as conversations become heated with a verbally intense Mercury-Pluto opposition and a misfiring Mars-Neptune square that could find you fighting with phantoms. The flighty Gemini New Moon on the **8th** makes it tough to focus your energy. Frustration builds when active Mars is sidelined by a quincunx with controlling Saturn and nerves grow taut with a high-frequency Mercury-Uranus square.

JUNE 12 ★ *live wire*
There's electricity in the air as magnetic Venus squares shocking Uranus, triggering unconventional social interests and strange spending habits. Your insatiable appetite for new people and experiences is exciting, yet attractions may be fleeting and relationships uncertain under these volatile circumstances.

JUNE 19–20 ★ *flights of fancy*
You can't help but smile with a buoyant Sun-Jupiter conjunction in your 4th House of Roots on **June 19**. Your ambitions grow, yet you must be careful not to let your optimism get out of hand. The expansive qualities of Jupiter can raise your hopes beyond reason, especially when followed by a dreamy Venus-Neptune sesquisquare. Romantic, artistic, and financial pursuits are unbound by reality as your fantasies overcome facts. Mercury's conjunction with flirtatious Venus on the **20th** is ideal for sweet conversations, yet also favors self-indulgence over seriousness.

JUNE 26–27 ★ *ladder of success*
The Sun's trines with Saturn and Neptune on **June 26** allow you to plant your feet solidly on the ground while your heart and mind soar to the stars. You have the good sense to step back from your emotions to gain a strategic perspective, but also instinctively understand when to let go and trust the flow. Your leadership skills work because of your quiet sense of purpose and faith in your actions. Investing your heart in your work makes sense with resourceful Venus entering risk-taking Leo and your 6th House of Employment on the **27th**.

JULY

HARMONIC CONVERGENCE

This is a very special month: A Grand Water Trine connects idealistic Neptune in Pisces, optimistic Jupiter in Cancer, and realistic Saturn in Scorpio on **July 17–19**. This harmonious alignment puts your highest hopes in a practical framework that shows you how to best fulfill them. An almost perfect balance between aspiration and application illuminates your vision of the future with a blueprint for building it. Saturn's forward turn on the **8th** starts to bring discipline into the picture, reinforcing your resolve and commitment to long-term change. Creativity is emphasized with the nurturing Cancer New Moon on **July 8th** occurring in your 5th House of Self-Expression. Yet the cautious nature of this protective sign is shattered by electrifying Uranus's square to this lunation, encouraging you to act independently, prompting impulsive behavior, and inspiring romantic risk taking. Passionate Mars's entry into your 5th House on **July 13** adds more fuel to the fires of desire.

Your ability to express your feelings and your artistic ideas grows after chatty Mercury turns direct in your 5th House of Play on **July 20**. Messages are mixed, though, on the **22nd** when friendly Venus moves into analytical Virgo and your 7th House of Partners, cooling your romantic ardor, bringing greater clarity, and raising concerns about practical relationship matters. On the other hand, the Sun's entry into loud Leo pumps up the volume in your 6th House of Employment, increasing your hunger for recognition at work. The emotionally detached Aquarius Full Moon on the same day squares sobering Saturn, suggesting you might need to calm down and act with greater self-restraint.

> **KEEP IN MIND THIS MONTH**
>
> *Passion expressed with patience is an unbeatable combination. Know what you want and pursue it at your own pace.*

KEY DATES

JULY 1 ★ *hold your ground*

Colleagues oppose your ideas today, and cooperation eludes you with the willful Sun's opposition to unyielding Pluto. Don't fold under the pressure, though; it's better to find your inner strength and push harder for what you believe. Tense aspects from evaluative Venus to doubtful Saturn and wistful Neptune might undermine your confidence. But if you can overcome hurt feelings and adjust your expectations to make them more realistic, the outcome can still be favorable.

JULY 9 ★ *personal retrospective*

Retrograde Mercury hooks up with the Sun in your dramatic 5th House to provide an insightful second look at love, play, and children. Recent decisions made in these areas are up for review. You may not want to share your thoughts right now; it's more important to clarify your thinking than to explain yourself to others. Recognizing when you need to make modifications helps you know where to backtrack and try again.

JULY 12–13 ★ *curb your enthusiasm*

Knowing your limits and noticing when others are overstepping theirs is advantageous now. The Sun's inelegant sesquisquare with Neptune on **July 12** can weaken wills and invite illusions. Faith and inspiration may be present but need to be grounded with well-planned action. Lovely Venus's semisquare with extravagant Jupiter on the **13th** continues this overly enthusiastic theme. Make promises with caution, and take them with a grain of salt. Stretching social boundaries and exploring new forms of pleasure are fine as long as the cost isn't too high.

SUPER NOVA DAYS

JULY 20–22 ★ *a force of nature*

You can be both tough and tender to advance your agenda on **July 20**, when macho Mars's friction-free trines with Neptune and Saturn put some muscle into your pursuit of your goals. A slow and cautious start can lead you to a big finish at the brilliant Aquarius Full Moon on the **22nd** when go-getter Mars joins jaunty Jupiter. This energizing and enterprising conjunction in your expressive 5th House creates an excellent moment for selling an idea and being an inspiring leader of vision and strength. You can have a good time without damaging your productivity since your passion is fed by fun and maybe even a bit of romance.

JULY 26–27 ★ *fair trade*

A partner may lack credibility when vulnerable Venus in your 7th House of Associates opposes sometimes-deceptive Neptune on **July 26**. Compassion is admirable yet difficult to maintain if it's not reciprocated. Knowing what you want and holding people accountable for their actions are essential pieces of the puzzle with a relentless Mars-Pluto opposition on the **27th**. You can't afford to have weak or untrustworthy allies when you're putting forth so much effort.

AUGUST

EMBRACE THE UNKNOWN

You're tempted to go to extremes this month as your traditional ruling planet, Jupiter, triggers the ongoing squares of Uranus and Pluto. The flames of change are fanned with intense rhetoric when Jupiter opposes formidable Pluto on **August 7**. If your belief systems are challenged, your opinions grow stronger in a pattern that recurs on **January 31** and **April 20, 2014**. Intellectual agitation rises with Jupiter's square to rebellious Uranus on **August 21**, generating bright ideas and unorthodox concepts that return on **February 26** and **April 20, 2014**. You might make incredible discoveries about your future and the meaning of your life, but avoid committing to radical changes of course without thinking through the steps that will bring you success. Innovation comes to your workplace with the lively Leo New Moon falling in your 6th House of Employment on **August 6**. This energizing lunation forms a creative trine with inventive Uranus to galvanize you to learn new skills so you can be more proficient at your job.

Your lifelong pursuit of higher meaning receives an inspirational message when the intellectual Aquarius Full Moon on **August 20** joins ethereal Neptune in your 12th House of Spirituality. Yet what you discover may not be in a clear enough form to explain to others. You might be tempted to run away from the responsibilities of your daily tasks—and taking a break from them is a good short-term plan, but escaping is not a viable long-term solution. Fortunately, the Sun's entry into ethical Virgo and your 7th House of Relationships on the **22nd**, followed by interactive Mercury on the **23rd**, emphasizes partnerships in general while encouraging you to work through specific unresolved issues with others.

> **KEEP IN MIND THIS MONTH**
>
> *Discovering a new truth is a powerful source of inspiration, but testing it diligently will reveal whether it's actually useful or just a passing fancy.*

KEY DATES

AUGUST 2 ★ *lucky charms*

You're feeling very sociable with a sassy sextile between flirty Venus in your 7th House of Partners and sexy Mars in your 5th House of Romance. This yummy cosmic combination magnifies your desirability, making you more successful at getting what you want from others. Your playful mood and creative approach make you a skillful collaborator in an artistic or altruistic project.

AUGUST 10–11 ★ *cleanup on aisle one*
You might be a little wobbly on your feet on **August 10–11** when thoughtful Mercury and physical Mars slide into stressful aspects with slippery Neptune. Forcing an issue when you're uncertain is like hitting the brakes during a skid. Don't do it. If you clear your head and control your fear, you can avoid trouble and even get a glimpse of inspiration. Mastering the mind is your next assignment as Mercury squares strict Saturn. Knowing exactly what you want to say empowers your message, but confusion and frustration linger if you don't rehearse your lines.

AUGUST 19 ★ *stormy weather*
No one wants to be told what to do today, yet everyone wants to be the boss when the Sun forms electrifying aspects with Jupiter and Uranus. Strong wills grow restless, and pride could spark a conflict at work. Opinions explode with judgment and unreasonable resistance to opposition. Luckily, if you can express a more playful side of yourself, a world of wonder could transform your visions of your job and the purpose of your life.

SUPER NOVA DAYS
AUGUST 25–27 ★ *stranger than fiction*
You could easily be taken in by other people's weaknesses on **August 25,** when the sharp analytical lens of Mercury in Virgo is diffused by its opposition to surreal Neptune. This conversationally confusing yet potentially imaginative aspect is amplified on the **26th** when the Sun faces off with Neptune. Make sure the needs you're seeing are real, or you may sacrifice yourself for something that's not what you think it is. Get a fresh take on relationships with Venus's opposition to Uranus—but be careful not to run off and do anything too crazy, because your appetite for pleasure may be hard to control with an indulgent Venus-Jupiter square on the **27th.**

AUGUST 30 ★ *smooth operator*
Mercury, master of the lower mind of details, meets Jupiter, master of the higher mind of meaning, in a friendly sextile that eases the flow of conversation. Your capacity to sincerely express your feelings while paying close attention to what others say makes you an excellent student as well as a persuasive spokesperson for your ideas.

SEPTEMBER

BUILDING BRIDGES

You have wonderful opportunities to improve the quality of your relationships this month, beginning with the discerning Virgo New Moon in your 7th House of Partners on **September 5**, bringing logic and clarity to your alliances. This lunation's favorable aspects to philosophical Jupiter and insightful Pluto expand your capacity to present your point of view with eloquence and power. You can negotiate more successfully, too, when verbal Mercury enters diplomatic Libra and your 8th House of Deep Sharing on the **9th**. On **September 11**, insatiable Venus enters passionate Scorpio and your 9th House of Future Vision, where your appetite for truth, travel, and adventure drives you to dig up the resources you need to fulfill these desires.

You can't hide strong emotions on **September 19** when the supersensitive Pisces Full Moon illuminates your 1st House of Personality. However, maintaining balance makes you more fascinating to others. Yet if you're flooded with feelings of self-doubt, others may wonder if you're unreliable or distracted. Finding healthy outlets where you can express yourself openly—even a little dramatically—will provide you some much-needed emotional release. Saturn's third and final sextile with Pluto on the **21st** stabilizes your position within a group, especially if you've prepared the way during their first two alignments on **December 26, 2012**, and **March 8**. The Sun's entry into cooperative Libra and your 8th House of Intimacy on **September 22** heralds the Autumn Equinox, a seasonal shift that can change the course of significant connections. A flexible attitude is the key to enjoying the kind of meaningful dialogue that improves partnerships.

KEEP IN MIND THIS MONTH

Honestly discussing your expectations, concerns, and objectives with an open mind and heart makes working and living with others more enjoyable for everyone involved.

KEY DATES

SEPTEMBER 1–2 ★ *spirit of generosity*

A confident trine from the reflective Sun in your 7th House of Others to intuitive Pluto in your 11th House of Groups on **September 1** empowers you to be a more effective leader. However, sympathy and sentimentality weaken your judgment with a Venus-Neptune alignment if you give people too much slack. While your compassion is admirable, you risk wasting time and resources. The bewildering Mars-Neptune quincunx on the **2nd** could divert your efforts into endless tasks unless you keep a firm grip on your goals.

SUPER NOVA DAY
SEPTEMBER 7 ★ *nothing ventured, nothing gained*
You have a chance to see far into the future and learn how to get there with propitious Jupiter's prophetic aspects with the Sun and Mercury today. A solar sextile to Jupiter allows you to look beyond short-term problems and spot the amazing opportunities that lie ahead. Mercury's creative quintile to this giant planet feeds your gift of gab and activates your analytical abilities. If you have something to sell, this is a good day to pitch it; if you're searching for answers to life's biggest questions, you just might find them now.

SEPTEMBER 14 ★ *heaven on earth*
On this delicious day, romance, pleasure, and approval are all accessible to you. Seductive Venus in Scorpio creates a harmonious trine with magical Neptune. This dreamy connection between the planets of personal and spiritual love reveals beauty almost everywhere you look. The adoring cosmic couple brightens even the darkest corners of your reality. Imagination, faith, and artistic sensibility lift your spirits, along with those of the people fortunate enough to be around you.

SEPTEMBER 19–20 ★ *stick to the facts*
More words and information are not merrier on **September 19,** when data-driven Mercury's stressful square to overblown Jupiter turns a minor fact into a major ordeal. Too many details and too much flowery language actually hide meaning and divert your attention from essential issues. Careless speech and costly exaggeration are also provoked by a fanciful Mercury-Neptune sesquisquare on the **20th.** Nipping inaccurate information in the bud helps you avoid foolish social or financial behavior when Venus quincunxes Uranus.

SEPTEMBER 26–28 ★ *some like it hot*
Relationships roll along smoothly for you on **September 26** when a sparkling trine from sensuous Venus to joyous Jupiter in your 5th House of Love and Romance invites generosity and creative self-expression. Let progressive thinking help you iron out the wrinkles of conflicting beliefs. Your fantasies know no bounds when Jupiter sesquisquares Neptune on the **28th.** Meanwhile, a saucy Venus-Mars square is a fighting, flirting, and falling-in-love aspect that enhances your sex appeal and spices up your personal life.

OCTOBER

RESISTANCE IS FUTILE

Relationships remain front and center this month; brace yourself for power struggles, breakthroughs, and significant discoveries in both personal and professional alliances. The action begins when the ambivalent Libra New Moon on **October 4** falls in your 8th House of Deep Sharing, provoking partnership problems. This Sun-Moon conjunction opposes independent Uranus while it squares manipulative Pluto and opinionated Jupiter, turning minor differences into major events. Buttons are pushed that could blow up an existing union or, hopefully, blast away obstacles that have kept it from reaching its highest potential. Your professional work receives a boost from your skills of artful persuasion when vibrant Venus moves into outgoing Sagittarius and your 10th House of Career on the **7th**. Efficiency is essential with Mars's shift into competent Virgo and your 7th House of Others on **October 15**. It's a day that could see you striving for perfection or working with overcritical colleagues. Your best chance for success is to be perfectly clear about your intentions and conscientious in your actions.

Money matters could come to a head with the impulsive Aries Full Moon Lunar Eclipse shining in your 2nd House of Income on **October 18**. If you recently rushed into a financial commitment, it may be cheaper to back out of it now than to push your luck. Economic independence is an admirable goal, yet this lunation suggests that you shouldn't try to go it alone. In fact, trickster Mercury's retrograde turn on the **21st** is another sign that you'll need to reassess recent decisions during the next three weeks. The Sun's shift into incisive Scorpio and your 9th House of Adventure on the **23rd** means you must eliminate ideas and activities before you can head in an inspiring new direction.

> **KEEP IN MIND THIS MONTH**
>
> *Complications arise in every relationship. Don't give up on working with or loving someone who's willing to make changes and grow with you.*

KEY DATES

OCTOBER 1–3 ★ *call of the wild*

A poetic Mercury-Neptune trine infuses your mind with inspiration and your words with artistry on **October 1**. Yet even the sweetest phrases may not avert the battle for control that often comes with a Sun-Pluto square. Profound dissatisfaction may be bubbling below the surface of your relationships, eroding trust and self-confidence. It could all erupt with a volcanic Sun-Uranus opposition on the **3rd**. Yet this transit might also bring you a sudden epiphany that frees you from the past with insights about an exciting future.

SUPER NOVA DAYS
OCTOBER 10–12 ★ *clouds of illusion*
You're blinded by your high hopes on **October 10** if they aren't supported by reality. A Venus-Neptune square blurs your common sense and prompts you to overrate the worth of an object, experience, or person. You may be vulnerable to deception, which is underscored by the Sun's confusing sesquisquare with illusory Neptune, so temper your inspiration with reason. Venus forms a difficult aspect with exuberant Jupiter on the **11th**, as does the Sun on the **12th**, exaggerating your expectations. Allowing yourself to imagine more love, money, or joy in your life is fine as long as you don't expect it to manifest overnight.

OCTOBER 19 ★ *soldier of love*
You could exhaust yourself battling for a losing cause today with militant Mars's opposition to sacrificial Neptune. Your best defense is a clear plan of attack. Nevertheless, this is a great time to be a spiritual warrior by acting with compassion and supporting those in need.

OCTOBER 24–26 ★ *dancing in the dark*
Conflict can grow due to overheated opinions when contentious Mars semisquares judgmental Jupiter on **October 24**. Your emotions may entice you to take on tasks that require more effort than you expected. You'll get a respite on the **25th** with a sensitive Sun-Neptune trine. However, the support you receive can inadvertently encourage you to continue on a trajectory that turns you in circles. Venus aspects Jupiter and Neptune on the **26th**, tempting you to dodge details and deny unpleasant facts, although addressing them plants your feet back on solid ground.

OCTOBER 29 ★ *better late than never*
Retrograde Mercury in skeptical Scorpio rejoins Saturn in your 9th House of Big Ideas, forcing you to reevaluate long-term plans that you thought about on **October 8**. Communication with people in faraway places may break down due to simple misunderstandings or missing information. Nevertheless, serious thinking pays off with the sometimes painful clarity of dealing with unpleasant truths.

NOVEMBER

TAKE THE HIGH ROAD

You must face the big questions about your future and the meaning of life head-on this month, because you could be making choices that will affect you for years to come. The fourth of seven world-shaking Uranus-Pluto squares on **November 1** creates an undertow of uncertainty and, perhaps, a desire to take risks. Yet November's key event is a Scorpio New Moon Solar Eclipse on the **3rd** that falls in your 9th House of Beliefs, requiring you to reconsider your view of reality. Its conjunction with stern Saturn puts a damper on idealism as you are forced to make practical issues your priority. Fortunately, Mars in reputable Virgo sextiles the eclipse, connecting you with competent allies—a trend that's reinforced when Venus enters productive Capricorn and your 11th House of Social Networking on **November 5**.

You gain traction in pursuit of your goals when communicative Mercury turns direct on **November 10**. There may even be a resurgence of faith and imagination when Neptune's retrograde period ends on the **13th**. Still, finding balance between your pursuit of impossible dreams and the need to attend to the concrete matters of everyday life is brought into focus on **November 17**, when the sensible Taurus Full Moon brightens your 3rd House of Immediate Environment. Although you might see yourself pulled apart by these contrasting paths, the Moon's opposition to the enigmatic Scorpio Sun in your 9th House of Philosophy can help you realize that taking care of routine tasks gives a solid base to your search for a higher purpose. The Sun's entry into inspirational Sagittarius and your 10th House of Career on the **21st** fuels your ambitions with visionary ideas.

> **KEEP IN MIND THIS MONTH**
>
> *It's smarter to seek a way out of obligations that aren't up to your ethical standards than to keep commitments that don't nourish your soul.*

KEY DATES
NOVEMBER 7–12 ★ *star of the show*
A sweet Venus-Neptune sextile takes the rough edges off relationships on **November 7**. You can maintain your integrity and still be compassionate with lovers, friends, and colleagues. Psychic connections and imaginative conversations flow easily with an empathic Mercury-Neptune trine on the **9th**. Mental magic continues when the messenger planet goes forward on the **10th** and trines spiritual Neptune again on the **11th**. The rising tide of hope empowers you with the radiant Sun's harmonious trine to visionary Jupiter on **November 12**. The Pisces Moon joins in to

create a Grand Water Trine with the Sun and Jupiter, casting a halo around you and inspiring others with your unwavering faith. With all your enthusiasm, it's a great time for promoting your talents, a product you believe in, or a cause dear to your heart.

NOVEMBER 15 ★ *face the music*

Pals and co-workers can create problems when Venus runs into cynical Pluto in your 11th House of Groups. Mistrust may arise among you due to secrecy or a severe difference in values. Although it's uncomfortable to deal with an unpleasant subject, bringing difficult issues to the surface is better than ignoring them or simply trying to wish them away.

NOVEMBER 19 ★ *courage of your convictions*

The encouragement you receive today from a supportive person or an accepting public boosts your morale and helps you express your beliefs more aggressively. Action-hero Mars in your 7th House of Others forms a cooperative sextile with boisterous Jupiter, amplifying your energy and adding punch to your performance. A burst of creativity enriches your work and opens a new dimension of pleasure in matters of the heart.

SUPER NOVA DAYS
NOVEMBER 24–26 ★ *daydream believer*

You could get lost in fantasyland or lose your sense of authority on **November 24** when the Sun squares spacey Neptune. If you're tired, don't try to overcompensate by misleading others about how you feel or by making impractical promises. Self-sacrifice is not desirable, especially with needy Venus's soft semisquare with Neptune on the **25th**. While these aspects might inspire dreams, Mercury's conjunction with demanding Saturn attracts doubters who won't respect your ideas unless you back them up with solid facts. If you're feeling negative, commit to doing the hard work and research needed to bolster your plan. Still, you're tempted to brush reason aside with a blissful Sun-Jupiter sesquisquare on **November 26**.

NOVEMBER 28 ★ *too clever by half*

Hope springs eternal as an upbeat Mercury-Jupiter trine convinces you that even the saddest stories can have happy endings. Your skill at convincing others to share in your optimism is impressive, yet an expansive Venus-Jupiter opposition presents visions that may require more resources than you currently possess.

DECEMBER

UP IN THE AIR

You're filled with optimism about your professional life this month, since the forward-looking Sagittarius New Moon on **December 2** falls in your 10th House of Career. Shocking Uranus's fluid trine to this lunation shatters the status quo by bringing original ideas to your current line of work or pointing you in a radically different direction. Intellectual Mercury's shift into fiery Sagittarius on the **4th** is another uplifting influence that not only broadens your thinking, but also helps you put your best ideas into action. The second of three harmonious trines between effervescent Jupiter and industrious Saturn occurs on the **12th**, giving shape to your aspirations. This productive pattern first occurred on **July 17** and recurs on **May 24, 2014**, allowing you to reap the rewards of bold thinking rooted in careful preparation.

The jittery Gemini Full Moon shines in your 4th House of Domestic Conditions on the **17th**, stirring up personal and family issues. Distractions at home can make it difficult to maintain focus at work, yet this lunation also reminds you that lighthearted pleasures in your private life provide relief from the pressure of your public obligations. You could become a team leader with the Sun's entry into ambitious Capricorn and your 11th House of Groups, marking the Winter Solstice. However, sociable Venus is retrograde on **December 21–January 31, 2014**, requiring you to put extra effort into cooperative relationships. A series of tumultuous aspects from the Sun, Mercury, and intense Pluto in your community-minded 11th House to unstable Uranus and combative Mars on **December 29–31** could bring unexpressed anger out in the open, creating conflict. However, all this 11th House activity emphasizes the value of cultivating supportive co-workers and friends.

KEEP IN MIND THIS MONTH

Speaking the truth is not always appreciated in the workplace, but being honest with yourself about your professional dreams might help them come true.

KEY DATES

DECEMBER 6–7 ★ *singing in the rain*

Avoid saying yes to an ill-defined project at work or making proposals that are based on hope but lack factual foundations on **December 6**, when Mercury in sunny Sagittarius squares cloudy Neptune to inspire sloppy thinking. Mercury's awkward alignment with blustery Jupiter on the **7th** continues the trend of big ideas that might be useful in the distant future, but aren't yet ready for the light of day.

Grandiose theories are fine as long as you patiently take the time to develop them before sharing them openly with others.

DECEMBER 10 ★ *push the envelope*
If you overstep your bounds today with an impractical Sun-Jupiter quincunx, you're ready to charm your way out of the situation. A socially astute Venus-Uranus quintile enables you to smooth ruffled feathers while an ingenious Mercury-Uranus trine provides intuitive answers that seem to come out of nowhere. It might be fun to stretch the limits just so you can explore unfamiliar territory.

DECEMBER 13–14 ★ *fasten your seat belt*
Have you ever skidded into a turn and almost lost control of your car—then gently touched the brakes to get back on track? That's what these days feel like. Active Mars travels from a queasy quincunx with drifty Neptune that could lead you astray on the **13th** to a semisquare with unforgiving Saturn on the **14th,** when carelessness causes disapproval or disappointment. Fortunately, you can regain traction and avoid a crash by staying cool and not committing to more than you can deliver.

DECEMBER 17–18 ★ *field of dreams*
You're uncomfortable and confused by Jupiter's second sesquisquare to Neptune on **December 17**—a repetition of an aspect that occurred on **September 28** and finishes on **June 11, 2014.** Your expectations rise to unrealistic levels with this alignment, but its upside is that it might awaken your spirituality and activate your intuition, especially since the versatile Gemini Full Moon stimulates your curiosity. Happily, a creative quintile between brainy Mercury and musical Neptune on **December 18** helps you overcome mistakes by using your imaginative powers.

SUPER NOVA DAYS
DECEMBER 24–26 ★ *burden of proof*
Mars in your 8th House of Deep Sharing opposes volatile Uranus on the **25th,** provoking conflict if you have been burying your feelings for too long. Fortunately, a slick Sun-Neptune sextile on **December 24** helps you smooth out bumps in even the most difficult situations, while a poetic Mercury-Neptune sextile on the **26th** provides the words to convey your inspiring concepts. Nevertheless, a stifling Sun-Saturn semisquare attracts skeptics who demand you provide concrete evidence that you're on the right track.